Studies of the Niagara Frontier

Frank H. Severance

HERITAGE BOOKS
2007

HERITAGE BOOKS
AN IMPRINT OF HERITAGE BOOKS, INC.

Books, CDs, and more—Worldwide

For our listing of thousands of titles see our website
at
www.HeritageBooks.com

A Facsimile Reprint
Published 2007 by
HERITAGE BOOKS, INC.
Publishing Division
65 East Main Street
Westminster, Maryland 21157-5026

Originally published by the
Buffalo Historical Society
Buffalo, New York
1911

— Publisher's Notice —
In reprints such as this, it is often not possible to remove blemishes from the original. We feel the contents of this book warrant its reissue despite these blemishes and hope you will agree and read it with pleasure.

International Standard Book Number: 978-0-7884-0845-8

CONTENTS

	PAGE
A FAMILIAR FOREWORD	1
EARLY LITERATURE OF THE NIAGARA REGION	9
NINETEENTH CENTURY VISITORS WHO WROTE BOOKS	25
THE NIAGARA REGION IN FICTION	77
A DREAMER AT NIAGARA: CHATEAUBRIAND IN AMERICA	97
THE NIAGARA IN ART	113
JOHN VANDERLYN'S VISIT TO NIAGARA IN 1802	159
THE NIAGARA IN SCIENCE	175
TWO EARLY VISITORS	217
HISTORICAL ASSOCIATIONS OF BUFFALO	237
FROM INDIAN RUNNER TO TELEPHONE	253
SOME THANKSGIVING CONTRASTS	261
ON THE NIAGARA FRONTIER WITH HARRIET MARTINEAU	277
HISTORY THAT ISN'T SO	291
NARRATIVES OF EIGHTEENTH CENTURY VISITORS TO NIAGARA	313
FROM THE "FOUR KINGS OF CANADA," 1710	316
THE "BORASSAW" NARRATION OF 1721	318
PIERRE F. X. DE CHARLEVOIX, S. J., 1721	319
FATHER BONNECAMPS' DESCRIPTION, 1749	323
PETER KALM'S ACCOUNT, 1750	324
THE ABBE PIQUET IN 1751	334
ADVENTURES OF M. BONNEFONS, 1753	334
DIARY OF RALPH IZARD, 1765	339
JONATHAN CARVER, 1766	346
ST. JOHN DE CREVECOEUR, 1785	346
CAPT. ENYS' VISIT IN 1787	363
JAMES SHARAN IN 1787	378
ANDREW ELLICOTT, 1789	384

CONTENTS.

	PAGE
PATRICK CAMPBELL, 1791	386
DUNCAN INGRAHAM, 1792	387
BENJAMIN SMITH BARTON, 1798	393
CHARLES WILLIAMSON, 1799	399

APPENDIX

OFFICERS OF THE SOCIETY	403
LIST OF PRESIDENTS OF THE SOCIETY	404
PROCEEDINGS, FORTY-NINTH ANNUAL MEETING	405
IN MEMORIAM, WILLIAM PRYOR LETCHWORTH	423
INDEX	425

MAPS AND DIAGRAMS

DIAGRAM OF NINETEENTH CENTURY TRAVEL	70
CRÈVECOEUR'S MAP OF THE NIAGARA	360
CAPT. ENYS' SKETCH OF THE FALLS	365

A FAMILIAR FOREWORD

IT is now a good many years since I sat, one summer day, on the river bank at Niagara-on-the-Lake, and looked across at Fort Niagara on the opposite shore. I had never been there, and knew nothing about it.

"It's worth seeing," said a friend at my side. "Queer old place. They say Louis the Fourteenth built it."

I was skeptical. It struck me as absurd that the French monarch should be concerned with anything away in the interior of America. I had everything to learn. But that chance remark of an idle hour gave spur to my curiosity. I soon found my way to Parkman, and his pages opened the door to many other sources of light. He gave me the general story of the French in America, and I was no longer skeptical as to the building of Fort Niagara by Louis XIV. But neither Parkman nor any other printed source afforded the details I sought to know regarding the early history of our Niagara region. Indeed, Parkman was always an aggravation with his innumerable footnote references to manuscript authorities and sources. I wanted to read the documents he cited; and soon learned, as any student of our history learns, that if one seeks to know what has happened hereabouts—seeks to know who have been the moving spirits on the Niagara since its discovery, to know what they did and when, and what their influence has been—one must go to the manuscript sources.

Old manuscripts are not infallible, but they afford the nearest approach to a true record that we can have. Although they present many difficulties to the student, they also offer him many pleasures impossible to the printed page. It is with somewhat the feeling of an explorer that one opens, let us say, a bundle of old documents that have lain hidden away and forgotten for many years. He soon learns to detect the grain of worth in a mass of the worthless. If the student has gained access to Government archives, he can pursue his especial theme as a hunter pursues his game, through mazes of correspondence, memoirs and official reports. Presently he finds that by putting this and that isolated fact together, with regard to other data of time, place and men, the little page of history which he seeks to know is somewhat brightened, the always dim past is made by his research a little clearer.

Thus it comes about that in trying to ascertain the facts of the early history of the Niagara region, I was led from books to documents, to Government depositories and archives. Fort Niagara continued to be the inspiration of my quest; for it is soon apparent to any student of the region, that the somnolent, half-forgotten old fort at the mouth of the Niagara is, historically, the one paramount spot in this part of the world. So it came to pass that on occasion I found myself in Paris, hunting for the early history of Fort Niagara. Official letters of introduction had opened the way; and I was cordially received at a certain office in the old *Pavillon du Flores,* on the Seine side of the Louvre. It was with uncommon satisfaction that here, one morning, as I turned over the contents of a *carton* of old papers, I came upon an ancient, well-preserved map of the mouth of the Niagara river, "at the foot of Lake Ontario, on which is shown the machicolated house and the proposed fort (Niagara)," drawn at Niagara by Chaussegros de Lery, June 21, 1726. Of even greater interest were De Lery's own drawings, the original elevations and floor plans of the fort, signed by him and dated at Quebec, January 19, 1727. The fort was being built then, and here were the plans, by the man who built it. These ought at least to settle some questions, to clear away some misinformation long current regarding the age and original appearance of Fort Niagara. That these old drawings and reports, made by a French military engineer in America almost two hundred years ago, should have escaped the vicissitudes of Paris—the Revolution, the Commune, the destruction of palaces and all they contained, the rage of mobs and the perpetual obliteration of old things, is matter for marvel. But here they were; and since the originals could not be carried off to the banks of the Niagara, the securing of copies was a simple detail in the work of collecting our regional records, for the Buffalo Historical Society.

I may as well confess that I have long been a book-hunter, and have pursued my obscure game, as opportunity offered, in divers queer corners of the world. I have tasted the pleasure of loitering, in quest of Niagarana, on the Quai Voltaire and among the stalls of St. Paul's Churchyard. As for the Paris quais I agree with the expert—I forget which one—who long ago declared that nothing was to be found in their boxes but Voltaire's *"Charles Douze."* Something else, of course, even less to be desired than Voltaire; but as for Americana, the collector wastes his time on the Paris quais. I suspect that they are regularly gleaned in the interests of dealers, whose shops in the near-by Quarter are apt to have all the rarities there are except a few—offered for all the money there is!

The always dreamed-of achievement, a book of great

value for an inconsiderable price, is of course never possible when the said book is in the hands of a very wise dealer. Only once or twice has it fallen to me to be able to make the usual book-hunter's boast. Years ago I did find, in Bristol, England, a perfect, clean copy of Hennepin's *"Louisiane,"* with the original map, but with no covers. It was a curious discovery. I know not what power hypnotized the dealer into letting me carry it off for two pounds! A suitable binding added by a London expert made an altogether desirable treasure of it, such as a dealer would offer today for perhaps $150. All of which is related with due apology, merely by way of assuring the student and would-be collector that although the booksellers have of late grown discouragingly wise as to values, bargains in Americana may still be found. Even without them, there is pleasure in the pursuit.

For the source books relating to the Niagara region London is, I think, the best hunting-ground, though the continental dealers are sometimes eccentric in their valuation, and occasionally offer rare works at lower prices than the leading dealers of London would consider just. The New York market is at times good, but never cheap; and always the book-auction is the collector's opportunity.

Several of the earliest authors who mention the Niagara, such as Champlain, Sagard, Le Clercq, Lescarbot and Hennepin in his first work, are among the great rarities in the field of Americana. In twenty years I have had but one opportunity to buy an original Le Clercq. Champlain's *"Des Sauvages,"* which is really the beginning book of a collection of Niagara literature, is one of the rarest of books, but five perfect copies being known. The only copy that has come to sale in recent years, so far as I am aware, was in the Robert Hoe library, sold at auction in New

A FAMILIAR FOREWORD.

York in April, 1911; on which historic occasion it brought the considerable figure of $3825. The collector of Niagara literature need not grieve, however, either at its rarity or its costliness. Although it is the first book in the literature of the Niagara, it tells us very little; and the price of it, judiciously expended, would buy nearly all that has been published since Champlain's day, of essential value relating to the Niagara. I am discoursing on these things because they are aspects of our regional—our home—history worthy of some record; and I am minded to discourse at some length in pages following, on what may be called the literary aspects of our local history, regarding which from time to time, numerous inquiries reach me. A recent visitor at the Historical Building, a school-teacher from Boston, after making many intelligent inquiries about the Niagara region, observed reflectively: "But you're so new here, you can't have much history!" I might have replied that white man's history on the Niagara runs back as far as it does on the Massachusetts coast; but she had gone back to Boston before I thought of it. It is just as well—she might have challenged the statement; some of these New Englanders take their Norumbega very seriously; though if it be a mere matter of conjecture and plausible theory, there is on our side Etienne Brûlè, forerunner of Champlain, and not unlikely the white discoverer of Niagara Falls and Chautauqua Lake and many other places between Lake Huron and the Susquehanna river. But leaving that shadowy figure out of consideration, there remains a century of history hereabouts, under the French, still waiting to be written, from the documents; followed by a third of a century of British domination on both sides of the Niagara; also as yet for the most part unwritten; and finally, for the American side, considerably more than a century of events

—of war and peace and progress. Surely all this does not leave us of the present generation exactly impoverished as to local history.

In two or three papers following, I shall try to make some review of the literature of the Niagara region, and especially of what has been said of it by travelers, the forgotten pages of whose books, if brought together, would afford us glimpses of our region and our city of Buffalo, year by year from the days of the beginnings hereabouts. Something may be said of the Niagara region in Fiction, in Science, even in Art; by way of demonstration, possibly, that there is something in our local history (I am now replying to another critic) besides the Burning of Buffalo and the Hanging of the Three Thayers.

I should like to include, too, in this volume, along with miscellaneous papers of local bearing, a few of the many addresses which have been given of late years before the Historical Society or other organizations, especially at the four o'clock Sunday afternoon "Talks" which for a time were a feature of the Society's activities. These talks, when given by the Secretary, were usually on historical subjects, often suggested by a passing anniversary or local event. Many speakers, including the most talented men and women of Buffalo, and an occasional celebrity from abroad, addressed these meetings. As a rule these addresses were not written, and are not preserved; but two or three of the papers which I propose to include in the present volume have been elaborated from notes made for these Talks, it being deemed well to preserve in the Society's Publications some record of this feature of its work.

As this volume is destined primarily for members of the Buffalo Historical Society, and for other students and institutions with which I have been brought into some measure of pleasant acquaintance, I venture upon a certain familiarity of discourse, which it is hoped will not lessen the value of what is offered. I feel that I am addressing my friends.

EARLY LITERATURE OF THE NIAGARA REGION

SOME time ago I was asked to point out, to a club engaged in literary study, what was the essential literature of the Niagara region. Possibly my notes, made in response to that request, may here be of service.

By "Niagara region" we mean not merely the immediate vicinity of the Falls, or of the river, but the whole mid-lake region, through which the Niagara runs. It is an exceptionally important region, in several ways.

The great cataract has made it a point of pilgrimage for nature lovers and travelers of all the earth, for more than two and a half centuries.

It has been the scene of important events, of trade, of strategy and of war, in the history of three nations.

And it has been, now for more than a century, a frontier, a boundary between two great powers, not always at peace.

These, and other aspects of it that might be named—especially the modern industrial—give it exceptional interest to the student. By way of reminder, of showing how rich our regional history is, I propose here something of a review of it, in some aspects that may prove helpful to the student. And first, as to its written records.

If by "literature of the Niagara region" we mean what has been written about it, we are confronted by a vast mass of material; for remember that from the era of discovery to the present day this frontier has played an important part in history; and that for 150 years at least it has been a Mecca of travelers who have thronged, pencil in hand, to gaze and to record their emotions. All of this descriptive writing—both objective and subjective—is undoubtedly literature of the Niagara region; but happily much of it need not detain us.

At the outset of our survey, we must consider the narratives of mission work, of exploration, and those wilderness campaigns inspired by the ministers of Louis XIV., the record of which is perhaps the most romantic page in American history. I find it difficult, as I study this early period, to dissociate the history of our region from the literature of that history. All we know of what took place here, say prior to the middle of the Eighteenth century, we glean from very few books. Much more is still to be gleaned from manuscript records, which abound; but the printed sources are few. It is not so with recent history, where we have all the corroborative evidence of many witnesses, participants in events described—a vast array of contemporary chronicle. But the student of the early Franciscan and Jesuit missions in this field; of the exploratory expeditions of La Salle, and of de Celoron; even of the early military campaigns hereabouts, can draw his information from but a very few printed sources.

Our Niagara literature begins with Champlain. In his very rare book, *"Des Sauvages"* (1604), there are allusions to the Great Lakes and a cataract—statements based on reports made by the Indians to him in 1603. These statements are virtually repeated in Lescarbot's *"Histoire de la Nouvelle France,"* published in 1609.

The next references to our region are in the narratives of the Franciscan missionaries among the Hurons. In 1626 one of these missionaries, Joseph de la Roche Dallion,

THE NIAGARA REGION. 11

appears to have reached the Niagara, though that name does not occur in the narrative. The record of that visit is to be found in Sagard's *"Histoire du Canada"* (1636) and Le Clercq's *"Premier Établissement de la Foy"* (1690).

Next in chronological order are the visits of the Jesuit missionaries Brébeuf and Chaumonot, in the winter of 1640-41. These are reported in the very rare "Relations" of the order, now made readily accessible in a well-edited reprint. The Jesuit Relations as a whole offer surprisingly little regarding our region. Le Jeune's narrative of 1635 relates to the Neutrals; and Father Jerome Lalemant's relation of 1641 has the first mention of our river by name. Writing from the mission at St. Mary's in the Huron country, May 19, 1641, to the Rev. Father Jacques Dinet, Provincial of the Society of Jesus in France, he gives the following account:

"From the first village of the Neutral Nation which one finds on arriving there from this place, and continuing to travel to the south or southeast, it is about four days' journey to the mouth of the celebrated river of that nation into the Ontario or lake of St. Louys. On this side of that river, and not beyond it, as a certain map shows—are the greater part of the villages of the Neuter Nation. There are three or four beyond, ranging from east to west, towards the Nation of the Cat, or Erieehronons.

"This river or stream is that by which our great Lake of the Hurons, or fresh-water sea, discharges itself; it flows first into the lake of Erie, or of the nation of the Cat; and there it enters into the lands of the Neuter Nation, and takes the name of Onguiaahra, until it discharges itself into the Ontario or lake of Saint Louys, from which finally flows the river that passes before Quebec, called the St. Lawrence. So that, if once we were master of the seacoast nearest to the dwelling of the Iroquois, we could ascend by the river St. Lawrence without danger, as far as the Neuter nation, and a good deal beyond that, with much saving of trouble and time."

There is no known earlier reference to the Niagara, by name. Half a dozen years later another Jesuit makes an interesting allusion to the cataract, without using the name. This is Father Paul Ragueneau, who writes in the "Relation" of 1647-48:

"Almost due south from the country of the same Neutral Nation, we find a great lake nearly two hundred leagues in circumference, called Erie; it is formed by the discharge of the fresh-water sea, and throws itself over a waterfall of frightful height, into a third lake, named Ontario, which we call Lake Saint Louys."

The next reference to Niagara that I am able to note is contained in Galinée's narrative.

Three famous men came to the Niagara in September, 1669: the Sulpitian missionaries, René de Bréhant de Galinée and Dollier de Casson; and with them, La Salle—but this was not the latter's great adventure; that awaited him nine years later. The narrative of this visit of 1669 is Galinée's. Here is what he says regarding our river:

"We discovered a river one eighth of a league wide and extremely rapid, which is the outlet or communication from Lake Erie to Lake Ontario. The depth of this stream (for it is properly the River St. Lawrence) is prodigious at this spot; for at the very shore there are fifteen or sixteen fathoms of water, which fact we proved by dropping our line. This outlet may be forty leagues in length, and contains, at a distance of ten or twelve leagues from its mouth in Lake Ontario, one of the finest cataracts or waterfalls in the world; for all the Indians to whom I have spoken about it said the river fell in that place from a rock higher than the tallest pine trees; that is, about two hundred feet. In fact, we heard it from where we were. But this fall gives such an impulse to the water that, although we were ten or twelve leagues away, the water is so rapid that one can with great difficulty row up against it. At a quarter of a league from the mouth, where we were, it begins to contract and to continue its channel between two steep and very high rocks, which makes me think it would be navigable with difficulty as far as the neighborhood of the falls. As to the part above the falls, the water draws from a considerable distance into that precipice, and very often stags and hinds, elks and roebucks, suffer themselves to be drawn along so far in crossing this river that they find themselves compelled to take the leap and to see themselves swallowed up in that horrible gulf.

"Our desire to go on to our little village called Ganastogué Sonontoua Outinaouatoua prevented our going to see that wonder, which I regarded as so much the greater, as the River St. Lawrence is one of the largest in the world. I leave you to imagine if it is not a beautiful cascade, to see all the water in this great river, which at its mouth is three leagues in width, precipitate itself from a height of two hundred feet with a roar that is heard not only from the place where we were, ten or twelve leagues distant, but actually from the other side of Lake Ontario, opposite this mouth, from which M. Trouvé told me he had heard it. We passed this river, accordingly, and at last, after five days' voyage, arrived at the end of Lake Ontario."

Incurious man, to have come within sound of the Falls, and not go to see them! Were the conditions of wilderness travel so exacting and peremptory, that one might not turn aside to behold the greatest wonder in the world? Was it eagerness to be on his missionary way, or fear of the Iroquois, that kept Galinée from being the discoverer of our cataract? His hearsay account is good. Although his distances on the river are wrong, his report of the height of the fall is much nearer right than that of Hennepin, who came nine years later.

Galinée's narrative, by the way, has only recently had its first complete publication in English (with French text, map and notes), thanks to the scholarship of Mr. James H. Coyne, and the enterprise of the Ontario Historical Society, in whose "Papers and Records" for 1903 it is to be found.

From the date of this visit to the coming of Hennepin there is no literature of the Niagara region. With the exception of the passing of Galinée there was none for more than forty years. This was due in part to the interruption of missionary work, for reasons which need not be entered upon here; but it may be noted that the work of the French missionary priests among the Indians in what is now New York State covers only the years 1655 to 1658, and a second brief period, 1667 to 1685—in all, about twenty years. There were a few visits outside of those dates, but by 1690 there was no missionary in this State save Father Milet, and he had just been carried captive to Oneida from Fort Frontenac. The early knowledge of our region was given to the world, not by missionaries who pushed their way westward through Western New York, for they did not do that, but by those who came south and east from the Huron missions. When those missions ceased, literary darkness resumed its sway over the Niagara. In 1664 the Jesuit historian, Father Francisco Creuxio, published his ponderous Latin *"Historiae Canadensis."* The map in this work is dated 1660, and indicates the Niagara Falls as *"Ongiara catarractes."* The author was never in America, and got his data from the missionary relations and from Champlain. It added nothing to the world's knowledge of our region; nor was anything added, that I know of, until one day in the year 1683, when there was issued from the printing-shop of the Widow Huré, in Paris, the first and most valuable of Father Hennepin's books, entitled *"Description de la*

Louisiane," etc. This contained an account of La Salle's expedition of 1678, and the first detailed description of the Niagara in literature.

In the years that followed we have other works by Hennepin, more or less trustworthy—there is reason to believe that he had little or nothing to do with the latest work bearing his name, entitled *'Nouveau Voyage,"* etc. But of his *"Louisiane"* and a second book, the *"Nouvelle Découverte,"* there were many editions in many languages. The narrative of the building of La Salle's vessel, the Griffon, above the Falls, and of the voyage up the Lakes and down the Mississippi, was probably more widely read— if we may judge from the many editions of Hennepin— than anything else relating to America that had appeared up to that time.

Next to Hennepin, chronologically, is I think the Baron La Hontan, an officer in the expedition of Denonville, that came to the Niagara in 1687. A very unpriestly man was the Baron; evidently a devil-may-care sort of fellow; an adventurous soldier, an easy and voluminous writer, whose pages, even thus long after, provoke many a smile for their satire and cleverness. He was the first visitor, not a priest, to write of the Niagara, and he did it with a degree of license which might well make him the patron saint of a certain sort of modern newspaper reporter. La Hontan had an eye to a "good story." As was usually the case with the early visitors, a good many years elapsed between La Hontan's visit to the Niagara, in 1687, and the publication of his *"Voyages dans l'Amerique Septentrionale,"* etc., the first edition of which bears date 1703, and is followed by well nigh as many others, as is the case with Hennepin.

Belonging to the great La Salle episode are the narratives of Tonty, and Joutel, and the documents of La Salle himself, which as published by Margry are source material, although modern in date of printing. There is much else of this class—material relating to the early days, but of recent issuance. This is not the literature that I seek now especially to designate, but rather the little list of books, the first issues of the first narratives relating to our region. To the Jesuit "Relations," and to the narratives of La Salle, Hennepin, Tonty and Joutel, we might add the earliest Canadian histories—Champlain, Lescarbot, Sagard, and of a later period, La Potherie and Charlevoix. Something of all these the student should know, who would claim familiarity with the literature of our region say prior to the middle of the eighteenth century.

It is a great pleasure, to one who would know the historic background of his home region, to read these old books. I confess a fondness for the original editions; the same information, in modern printing and fresh binding, does not make the same appeal to the mind, to the imagination. I like the tough, hand-made paper of the ancient books, I like their leather and parchment bindings; and I like to pore over their quaint old French. These things bring one nearer to the old days; and presently, out of the yellow pages, there step forth a procession of worthies—brave men and holy men; priests with their portable altars on their backs, strange-clad soldiers, explorers, *voyageurs* and *coureurs-de-bois,* even the red Indian himself. They play their varied parts, in this early Niagara drama, and pass each to his place, along the horizon of the imagination. They and their deeds are our early history, and we come to know them only through these rare and ancient volumes.

A well-defined period in the history of our region is that of the Old French War, which ended in 1760, or on our frontier, with the surrender of Fort Niagara in 1759. There is an abundance of contemporary and of modern literature relating thereto, but usually a lack of local detail. Parkman, who is easily first among historians of that subject, reviews it in due proportion to his general narrative. His ken is continental, whereas we are particularly concerned with events on or relating to the Niagara. Two or three of the earlier books, by participants in the conflict, the student should know. For the British side, there is the history of the war published in 1772 by Thomas Mante; there is Knox's "Journal"; and there is the journal of Sir William Johnson, who conducted the siege and achieved the capture of Fort Niagara. For the French side, we have the *"Mémoires sur la dernière guerre de l'Amerique septentrionale entre La France et l'Angleterre,"* by François Pouchot, who fortified and defended Fort Niagara, and finally handed it over to Sir William Johnson. He was the last official representative of French dominion on the Niagara. His narrative, published in 1781 at Yverdon in Switzerland, is one of our most precious "sources." The original edition, like most of the books I am mentioning, is hard to find, and costly to buy when found. An excellent translation was published in this country in 1866, but even that is not easy to procure.

Unique as a record of travel for mere sight-seeing, in the early years of British occupancy of this region, and a vivid narrative of genuine adventure in the Niagara gorge, is a rare old journal, printed in New York sixty-five years ago, entitled "An Account of a Journey to Niagara, Montreal and Quebec, in 1765; or, 'tis eighty years since." This is said to be the diary of Ralph Izard of South Carolina, Representative and later United States Senator, 1789-1795. The journal was published anonymously by his grand-daughter, Anna Izard Deal.

The literature of the Revolutionary War, so far as it relates to the Niagara, is largely incidental and fragmentary. One of the books which ought to be written and no doubt will be, some day, will give the history of the Niagara region, or of the Lower Lakes, under the British, say from 1760 to 1796, when the frontier posts were relinquished to the Americans. Much has been written of this time. Much more remains, in documents, in Government archives, waiting the coming of some student with taste and leisure to construct a narrative for the general reader. As Sir William Johnson was in a sense the most important personage hereabouts, or exercising authority here, from 1759 till his death in 1774, so everything relating to his official conduct and especially William L. Stone's "Life" of him, belongs to our literature of that period, as, for later periods, do Stone's books about Brant and Red Jacket.

The many works relating to the Indians of Western New York need not detain us for specification. Most of them are of general scope; others are narratives of Government embassies, or of missionary ministrations. Especially good, in the historic sense, are the several narratives of early philanthropic visits by members of the Society of Friends.

The reader has no doubt observed, in his own thought, that every phase of life in the region since its discovery, may have its literature. This is true. It is also true that events so overlap and run together; causes are so far-reaching in effect, that it is quite impossible to differentiate the literature of one region, however well defined. To illustrate: the student of the Revolutionary period on the Niagara soon finds his interest drawn to the migration of Loyalists from the United States into Canada. Much of the Niagara district of what is now Ontario, was settled by this class. Canada may well be proud of them, as they, today, are proud of their ancestors. The "First Families of Virginia" are not a truer aristocracy. The books that record their history, and the whole Loyalist or "United Empire" movement, may well have a place in our review, yet this subject in many of its relations takes us far afield from the Niagara. So again, if we consider the Civil War period, we find one of its most important antecedent phases to have been in connection with the "Underground Railroad" and the helping of runaway slaves into Canada. An ample and romantic literature on that subject awaits the inquirer.

The literature of the War of 1812, even of that part of it which belongs to the Niagara, runs into hundreds of volumes. So too of the Canadian political outbreak of 1837-38 known as Mackenzie's Rebellion, or better, as the "Patriot War." The catalogue of the library of the Buffalo Historical Society—an unpretentious collection—contains nearly four hundred titles of books or parts of books and other references relating to this particular subject. Even of the little comic opera war known as the Fenian Raid of 1866, there is a considerable literature, including some fiction, and some history so belligerently serious that it is vastly amusing.

So I might go on, specifying every phase of life, be it military, political or economic, and finding a considerable literature for every phase. The development of commerce on the lakes, the evolution of the canals and railroads, the very recent industrial development based on the utilization of Niagara power—all of these and other subjects have each a literature. Especially the last-mentioned subject has a large and constantly-growing literature, but it is chiefly to be found in the reports of scientific societies and in the pages of electrical, chemical, railway and other trade or technical journals.

The earlier years of the eighteenth century brought few professional writers to the banks of the Niagara. The earlier descriptions are to be found in the reports or letters of French officers who came to Fort Niagara, or passed through the Lakes in the course of duty. Of this sort was the visit of the Baron de Longueuil and other officers in 1721. Two of his companions, the Marquis de la Cavagnal and Captain de Senneville "had undertaken that voyage only out of curiosity of seeing the fall of the water at Niagara," according to the report of Chaplain Durant. The tourist procession began with them. The Rev. Father Bonnecamps, of De Celoron's expedition of 1749, has left a short description; and Peter Kalm, a Swedish botanist who reached the Niagara in 1750, has left a long one. After Kalm, I know of no visitor to our region who recorded his impressions until 1753, when there came to Niagara a soldier serving under Pouchot who had the enterprise to keep a journal. This was J. C. Bonnefons. Many years after the campaign in which he served had passed into history, his journal came to light and was published in Paris. It contains details of value. He records incidents of his sojourn at Fort Niagara in April of the year named, and gives a picturesque account of his adventures at the Falls, describing at length how, alone, he descended by means of roots and trees to the bottom of the chasm and after hours of fatigue climbed out again. So far as I am aware, Bonnefons' account of Niagara has never been published in English.

During the years of British control of this region and through the Revolutionary war, there was a growing literature of our region, but it was almost wholly embodied in the narratives of soldiers who shared in the campaigns or in the journals or official reports of men who, like Sir

William Johnson, bore a large part in the history of the region at that period. A notable exception is the journal of General Izard. To this period belongs the narrative of Jean Hector St. John de Crévecoeur, French consul at New York, 1783-93. In his *"Voyage dans la Haute Pensylvanie"* he gives a pleasant narrative of a visit to Niagara. It is without dates but the visit, as we learn from a letter to his son, was in July 1, 1785.

Toward the close of the century we find numerous works offering to the reading public better information regarding the Niagara than had hitherto been available. Not only in English, but in other European languages appear general compilations of travel in which the Niagara region received more and more attention. A notable work of this character, was a three-volume account of America, both descriptive and historical, by Christof Daniel Ebelings, professor of history and Greek in the gymnasium of Hamburg. This work, prepared with characteristic German thoroughness, appeared in 1793, antedating by a year or so the far more valuable accounts of enterprising travellers who are of real importance in the annals of our region.

Before noting them, however, mention should be made of a rare little book, entitled "Tour through Upper and Lower Canada by a Citizen of the United States." This was the Rev. John Cosens Ogden, who came in 1794 by schooner across Lake Ontario to Fort Niagara. He makes a good report of what he saw, paying especial attention to the transportation of merchandise over the Niagara portage. In a list of books which includes many rarities, his is one of the rarest. The author was a son-in-law of General David Wooster of Colonial and Revolutionary fame; he resided in New Haven, 1771-1785, and was afterwards an Episcopal minister at Portsmouth, N. Y. His long account of Upper Canada shows rather marked Loyalist sympathies.

Nearly a year after Ogden, in June, 1795, came the Duc de la Rochefoucault Liancourt. His elaborate "Travels through the United States of North America, the Country of the Iroquois and Upper Canada," is probably one of the best known books relating to the close of the eighteenth century. In spite of many errors, some of which, no doubt, in the English editions, are attributable to the translator, this work is one of the most valuable that we have for details of conditions hereabouts as they were at the close of the eighteenth century.

A year later, September, 1796, came Isaac Weld, Jr., a British writer and artist, whose handsome quarto volume is prized not merely for its record of early American conditions, but for its engravings from Weld's own drawings. He is, I think, the first writer of books who sojourned at Fort Niagara after it passed into the control of the Americans. He writes at some length of the conditions of the garrison and of all that he saw and experienced in a leisurely visit on the Niagara. Subsequent visitors found some things to criticise and to correct in Weld's pages, but on the whole he has given us a picture of conditions which is not surpassed in value in all our records of that period.

In this same year we have the visit to Niagara of a French *savant,* Charles F. Volney, member of the National Institute of France and of many learned societies. In the days of our grandfathers Volney's work was still read. Although looked upon in his day as an eminent scientist, I doubt if his work could be rated to-day as worthy of study. He came to America in 1795 and in October of the following year visited the Niagara. He travelled indeed for a time with Weld, but they do not appear to have been together in our region. His work, *"Tableau du Climat et du sol des Etats-Unis d'Amerique,"* is chiefly concerned with the geological or rather physical aspects of the lower lake region. Of popular description, his pages contain little. It is worth noting that Volney's memory is still cherished in his own country. Dying in Paris, in 1820, he left an endowment, so that there still is an annual Volney prize given by the French Institute for proficiency in camparative philology.

Alexander Henry in 1764, Jonathan Carver in 1766, James Sharan in 1787, and P. Campbell in 1793, visited the Niagara and wrote of it in their books; all now rare, especially so in the case of Campbell's "Travels in the Interior inhabited parts of North America," one of the scarcest of books relating to the Niagara. "The Adventures of James Sharan, compiled from the Journal written during his Voyages and Travels," etc., was published in Baltimore in 1808, and contains an account of his visit to Niagara Falls in 1787.

In the last year of the 18th century, came an English artist, John Maude, whose visit to the Falls of Niagara in 1800, published in London in 1826, is a book of undoubted value. Its illustrations from the artist's drawings are among the most interesting of our early views of Niagara. His journal records many matters of local interest relating to Buffalo and the Niagara frontier. It is from such pages as his that we come to know in some measure the conditions of our region at that remote time.

19TH CENTURY VISITORS WHO WROTE BOOKS

THE 19th century opened appropriately with the visit to the Niagara region of a British official, George Heriot, Deputy Postmaster-General of British North America. His quarto volume, "Travels through the Canadas," etc., published in London six years later, is a matter-of-fact, sensible account of conditions at the opening of the century. Statistician though he was, in contemplation of Niagara he became a sentimentalist: "The Falls of Niagara surpass in sublimity every description which the powers of language can afford of that celebrated scene, the most wonderful and awful which the habitable world presents." So unqualified a statement to-day would provoke challenge, but we know the world and its wonders now better than they did in Heriot's time. His exuberant description of Niagara was first published in the London *Sun* in 1801; translated and published in *Le Moniteur* of Paris, it had a wide currency throughout Europe. Few writers have contributed more to the spread of information regarding Niagara than this British official.

Three years after him came Tom Moore, whose letters to his mother from Niagara, and whose poems written there have been much copied. As I have written elsewhere of the poets, in relation to Niagara, I am ignoring them in the present review. Of more value to the student of local conditions are the grave, precise observations of Dr. Timothy

Dwight, President of Yale College, whose "Travels in New England and New York," published in four volumes, record what he saw on the Niagara in October, 1804. Dwight must rate among the best of our early authorities. Here is a portion of his account of Buffalo as he saw it in 1804:

"Buffaloe Creek, otherwise called New-Amsterdam, is built on the north-eastern border of a considerable millstream, which bears the same name. A bar, at the mouth, prevents all vessels larger than boats, from ascending its waters. For boats it is navigable about eight miles. Its appearance is more sprightly than that of some others in this region. The south-western bank is, here, a peninsula, covered with a handsome grove. Through it several vistas might be cut with advantage; as they would open fine views of the lake; a beautiful object. The prospect, which they would furnish towards the west and south-west, would be boundless.

"The village is built half a mile from the mouth of the creek; and consists of about twenty indifferent houses. The Holland company owns the soil. Hitherto they have declined to sell it; and, until very lately, to lease it. Most of the settlers have, therefore, taken up their ground without any title. The terms, on which it is leased, are, that the lessee shall within nine months build a house, thirty feet in front, and two stories in height; and shall pay, if I mistake not, two dollars, annually, for each lot of half an acre. The streets are straight, and cross each other at right angles, but are only forty feet wide. What could have induced this wretched limitation in a mere wilderness I am unable to conceive. The spot is unhealthy, though of sufficient elevation, and, so far as I have been informed, free from the vicinity of any stagnant waters. The diseases prevailing here, are those, which are common to all this country. The inhabitants are a casual collection of adventurers; and have the usual character of such adventurers, thus collected, when remote from regular society; retaining but little sense of Government, or Religion. We saw about as many Indians in this village as white people The superintendent of Indian affairs for the Six Nations resides here."

The next year came Timothy Bigelow, whose "Journal," privately printed many years afterward, is hard to find nowadays. In 1805 also came Robert Sutcliff, the first of several members of the Society of Friends who, visiting this region on missions of philanthropy and devotion to the Indian, have left exceedingly interesting narratives of what they saw and experienced hereabouts. Sutcliff's book, "Travels in Some Parts of North America," was not published until 1812, but it was in November, 1805, that he reached Buffalo on horseback and put up at Crow's tavern. Later he was a guest of Joseph Ellicott and his valuable narrative records many names of settlers, taverns, etc., which, perhaps, would be sought for without finding in other records.

The first decade of the century brought hither at least one other book-writing traveller, Christian Schultz, Jr., whose "Travels," etc., in the years 1807-8, record American wanderings of some six thousand miles. He came to Fort Niagara in August, 1807, by boat on Lake Ontario. He writes at length of the cataract and of all that he saw throughout the length of the Niagara. Coming to the little town at the foot of Lake Erie, he rested here for a time and recorded his impressions as follows:

"Buffaloe is a small village situated on Buffaloe Creek about three miles after you pass the outlet of Lake Erie, on your left hand side. I was present at the annual distribution of the presents to the six nations of Indians, most of whom now live within the British territories. There were about five hundred assembled together on this occasion, some of whom were painted and feathered off fine enough. They had likewise a council meeting, for the purpose of receiving and considering certain overtures that had been made to them by some hostile Indians, 'to take up the tomahawk against the United States'; but they wisely determined to remain neuter in case of hostilities between America and England.

"After their business was settled, they formed themselves into parties at ball-playing, and running races for prizes given by the State. Their manner of ball-playing is very similar to what you have seen by the name of hurley; but, instead of the curved hickory used on that occasion, they have a long curved racket, strung with deer sinews, with which they can strike the ball to an astonishing distance. Whenever the ball lodged among the crowd of players, you would have supposed there was a bloody battle going on, as every one struck pell-mell together with their rackets not in the least heeding whom he knocked on the head; but, whenever a lucky stroke drove the ball near to the goal, you would have thought hell itself had broke loose, for such a hideous yell and screaming was instantly set up as baffles all my attempts at a description.

"I was much amused by the pride and gallantry displayed by one of the victors on receiving, as a prize, a light calico shirt. As soon as he received it he put it on, and, after viewing himself for a moment, strutted through the crowd to display his finery. In a few minutes he returned to a circle of women, when he pulled off his prize and put it upon one of the lady squaws, who soon experienced the value of this mark of distinction, by attracting the admiration of some, and exciting the envy of more, among the crowd of females around her."

The succeeding decade, 1811-'20, brought into our region thrice as many book-writing travelers as had the first ten years. They included British tourists, missionaries, one French artist, one or two wandering Americans, and the President of the United States.

In 1811 our literary visitor was John Melish, whose portly volume of "Travels through the United States of

VISITORS WHO WROTE BOOKS.   29

America," published in London in 1818, was for many years a standard and authoritative work. He reached Buffalo in October of the year named and reported that the village was "now computed at 500." His pages are very good for miscellaneous data, especially in regard to the Indians and conditions up and down the river.

We now come to the period of warfare, during which there were practically no tourist visitors to the region. One devoted missionary, the Rev. Charles Giles, came in 1812, although it was not until 1844 that the record of his visit was published. By no means should the narrative of Levi Beardsley's visit—visits, rather—be overlooked. He was a man of note in New York State in his day, a member of the Senate for eight years, and its President in 1838. His first visit to Buffalo and Niagara was in 1815. Buffalo "had scarcely begun to build up; . . . in fact it was nothing." On Chippewa battle-field he was sickened by the stench from mounds where the dead had been deposited. He wrote well of the Falls, but with particular interest of Grand Island where in 1825 he made large purchase of lands. His "Reminiscences," published in New York in 1852 contain much of history, description and anecdote relating to our region.

Omitting the war literature I discover no other traveler who wrote books until 1816, in which year Lieutenant Francis Hall of the 14th Light Dragoons, visited Niagara Falls and Buffalo. I find him an agreeable, sensible writer. He notes that "the name of the Horseshoe, hitherto given to the larger fall, is no longer applicable: it has become an acute angle." It undoubtedly had been angular for many years before Hall, though long after him many visitors were unable to see it that way. Buffalo he found "not merely a flourishing village, but a considerable town, with shops and hotels which might anywhere be called handsome, and in this part of the country, astonishing." This, it will be remarked, was but three years after the destruction of the town.

A visiting author of 1817 was Joseph Sanson, a distinguished member of the American Philosophical Society who toured through the region and wrote his "Sketches of Lower Canada," etc., dedicated to DeWitt Clinton.

A more notable visitor in that year was President Monroe, who arrived at Fort Niagara early in August and proceeded up the river to Buffalo in the course of an extended tour through the country, the record of which was written by S. Putnam Waldo, his secretary. There is nothing in the record of President Monroe's visit to the Niagara region that need detain us. He was received in Buffalo by a deputation of citizens, to whom he made a speech; but that speech is not preserved in Waldo's pages.

This same year, too, brought hither a wandering Frenchman, Monsieur E. Montule, whose narrative in English was published in 1821, under the title of "Journey to North America and the West Indies." It contains a letter, dated "Buffaloe 31st July, 1817," in which the author sets forth his experiences in visiting the nearby Indians with a resident Frenchman named "Despares." This I take it was John Despard, whose name is usually recorded as that of Buffalo's pioneer baker; he was by no means an unknown character in the early years of Buffalo. Montule adds a graphic account of his adventures at Niagara Falls.

A far more valuable work is the "Sketches of Upper Canada," etc., by John Howison, a British subject resident for some years in Canada. His visit was in 1818. Traces of warfare were still fresh on the banks of the Niagara and he naturally devotes a portion of his pages to them. Note should be made of the "Journal" of Sarah Howland, who with her husband drove to the Niagara from New York and back in a carriage in the summer of this year, the tour occupying some two months. Mrs. Howland's journal records little regarding our region which is of consequence.

A singular book is the "Pedestrious Tour of 4000 Miles," etc., by Estwick Evans. This eccentric but enterprising New Englander walked from Concord, N. H., to Niagara and so on over a long route. His narrative is clumsily written, with some evidence of conceit and occasional display of ignorance; but he was a fair observer and saw many things especially among the Indians which could not be seen later, and is entitled to a place among the authors of 1818.

In marked contrast with the unlettered Evans is William Darby, an accomplished member of the New York Historical Society, who, in this same year of 1818, journeyed from New York to Detroit, making a considerable sojourn on the Niagara. His "Tour," etc., is one of the best accounts we have of Buffalo and vicinity at that time. At Niagara he notes that a "marked annual increase in visitors is to be observed"; the tourist procession had fairly begun in 1818. Still another author of this same year was John M. Duncan, a Scotchman, author of "Travels through part of the United States and Canada in 1818-19." His two-volume work published in Glasgow in 1823 is still good reading. He seems to have made at least two visits to Buffalo, which he reports as a "busy little town of 600 inhabitants." His pages on Niagara, the Indians and the mission work among them are very full and valuable.

The year 1819 brought to the banks of our river two authors of considerable note in their day. One, Miss Frances Wright, is well known even now by students of social reform for her devotion to what she regarded as human betterment in her day. Her book, "Views of Society and Manners in America," was long the subject of heated criticism and discussion on both sides of the Atlantic. She was one of the earliest of many distinguished travelers who were entertained at the hospitable home of the Wadsworth family in the Genesee Valley. She has left us a graphic picture of Niagara and vicinity. The other literary visitor of this year was a member of the Society of Friends, E. Howitt, who toured into the region to visit the Indians and to report on the work which was being done among them by the Quakers. In a letter dated "Buffalo, 8th month, 9th, 1819," he records many things now of interest to the student of history regarding our region. In May, 1819, came also William Tell Harris, author of a "Tour" published in 1821. In 1820, came Adam Hodgson, author of "Letters from North America," published in two volumes, 1824. He was a good, sensible observer; and in a chapter, dated Niagara, 2d August, 1820, he has given us one of the best early accounts of conditions at the great cataract. William Dalton's "Travels," and James Flint's "Letters from America," both record visits to the Niagara in 1820. Flint came to Buffalo from the West on the pioneer steamboat, "Walk-in-the-Water."

Still more literary visitors came in the decade ending 1830, but most of them fortunately need not detain us. In 1821 P. Stansbury, in the course of a walk of 2300 miles, reached Niagara Falls. He was, perhaps, willing to rest; at any rate, he lingered in the vicinity long enough to make minute record of many things now of interest. His little book, "A Pedestrian Tour of 2300 Miles in North America," devotes fifty pages to the Niagara region, not the least feature of it being the crude woodcuts, one of Niagara fort by A. Anderson, said to be the first American wood engraver—

a claim also made for Peter Maverick, among whose pictures, on wood, is a Niagara Falls.

Catherine M. Sedgwick, who made the "grand tour" in 1821, wrote graphically from Buffalo, June 29th, on what she discerned as the homesickness of settlers from New England. In a long Niagara letter she reports her interview with a Yorkshireman, a Niagara settler, who had a real complaint:

"When he laid in his bed he could never tell when it rained nor when it thundered, for there was always a dripping from the dampness, and the deafening roar of the fall; and then his poor cattle, in winter, were always covered with icicles. It was a mighty fine thing to come and see, but we should be sick enough of it if we had as much of it as he had. *Il n'y a rien de beau que l'utile.*"

An anonymous work, "A Summer Month, or Recollections of a visit to the Falls of Niagara and the Lakes in 1822," is understood to have been written by a Mr. Matthews. He had scholarly accomplishments and a poetic temperament; adorns his account of Niagara with quotations in Greek and from the Scriptures; and on the whole has given us a fine and useful picture of what he saw. Another anonymous work, "Excursion through the United States and Canada," by "An English Gentleman," also records a visit to Buffalo and Niagara in this same year. Its author was Captain William Newnham Blaney. The "Memoirs of William Forster," published in two volumes in London in 1865, contain the narrative of this Quaker's visit to Niagara in 1823. Edward Allen Talbot's "Five Years' Residence in the Canadas," etc., has a long Niagara chapter, of date 1823.

An English naturalist and traveler whose works were esteemed, was Charles Waterton. His name would hardly be associated with the Niagara to judge from the title of his book, "Wanderings in South America," etc., yet his wanderings brought him here in 1824. Perhaps because of his wide experience as a traveler, he did not take his scenery very seriously. He was much more interested in people. "Words," he says, "can hardly do justice to the unaffected ease and elegance of the American ladies who visit the Falls of Niagara," and he laments with some humor the fact that a sore toe prevented him from dancing with them.

I must be content with merely mentioning an attractive little volume published in Aarau, entitled *"Mein Besuch Amerika's in Sommer 1824 . . . ein Flug . . . zum Niagarafall,"* in which the practically anonymous author, "Von C. v. R.," tells of his visit to the Niagara in 1824. Another German tourist, by no means anonymous, came the next year. This was Bernhard, Duke of Saxe-Weimar Eisenach. The original German edition of his book of American travels appeared at Weimar in 1828; there are several editions in German and English. The author came by canal to Black Rock in 1825, and proceeded thence by stage to Buffalo. At the Falls, of which he gives elaborate description, he took special note of the phenomenon of the burning spring. He was entertained with his suite by Sir Perigrine Maitland at his once famous country seat at Stamford, near the Whirlpool.

We now come to an important year in the chronology of our region—1825. Throughout the years of the construction of the Erie Canal public attention had been more and more directed towards Western New York, its attractions and opportunities. It was natural that with the opening of this new highway of travel visitors should flock to see Niagara, Buffalo, and the West, much no doubt as visitors will flock to the Panama Canal to take note of that new and extraordinary highway of travel.

The most distinguished visitor to our region in this year of travel was Lafayette. The record of his visit was made by his secretary, A. Lavasseur, in whose volumes, entitled *"Lafayette en Amerique,"* is to be found one of the best chapters we have for intimate detail of conditions in Buffalo at the time. During his sojourn at Niagara, Lafayette was the guest of General Porter, and received hereabouts, as everywhere on his tour, many testimonials of the great affection which America had for him. At least two editions of Lavasseur's narrative have been published: the original one in Paris, in 1829, with an English translation published in Philadelphia in the same year. I note one other distinguished visitor in 1825. This was Joseph Story, Associate Justice of the Supreme Court of the United States, Professor of Law at Harvard, etc. Story came to the Niagara in July of 1825. He was entertained by General Porter, who escorted him to Fort Erie and to other battlefields of the vicinity. In the excellent "Life and Letters of Joseph Story," edited by his son, published in London in 1851, the student will find many graphic pages setting forth this early visit to our region.

The year 1826 gives us the visit of an officer of the Royal British Navy, the Honorable Fitzgerald de Roos, whose "Personal Narrative of Travels in the United States and Canada in 1826," was dedicated to the Duke of Clarence and ran through several editions. Like most other visitors, this author felt called upon to analyze his emotions when contemplating the cataract. He records that he experienced a depression of spirits by the magic influence of this stupendous fall. Others, it will be noted, experienced exhilaration. Indeed, these book-writing visitors have run the gamut of emotional experience. De Roos was also a guest of Sir Perigrine Maitland. Another visitor of 1826 was

Carl August Gosselman, in whose two-volume work, *"Resa i Norra Amerika,"* published at Nyköping in 1835, the reader of Scandinavian will rejoice to find a long Niagara chapter.

Comparatively few of our British visitors have taken the trouble to preserve their anonymity, but in 1827 there came to us a vigorous writer content to style himself merely "A British Subject," whose book, "Tour through United States and Canada," published in London, in 1828, is well worth reading today. As other British writers have done, he found many opportunities to ridicule the Americans, and professed to be shocked at finding an hotel at Niagara conducted by a General. Frontier conditions of travel displeased him: "The 23 miles from thence to Buffalo is a long and truly infamous road, made of trunks of trees and not in sight of the river, but through a thick wilderness in which black bears, wolves and rattlesnakes are not infrequent." Of Buffalo, however, as he saw it in 1827, he had a good word, predicting that the place "will certainly become one of the most important towns in America." At Niagara, too, he struck the right reflection when he perceived that the "grandeur of the scene before me becomes more perceptible to my senses the longer I am acquainted with it." A better known writer visiting us in the same year, was Captain Basil Hall of the Royal Navy, author of "Travels in North America," in three volumes. Captain Hall, though in his day subject to much criticism, was a thoroughly good writer, frank, full, honest in statement, clear-sighted, a good observer, and, I should judge from a careful reading of his pages, a thoroughly sensible and honest man. I count his book one of the most valuable as a record of that time.

In 1828, James Stuart, a conscientious, scrupulous Scotchman, came to Buffalo in the course of a three-years' sojourn in North America. His three-volume work, published in Edinburgh in 1833, was one of the most full and trustworthy reports of American conditions in the early years of the century.

The year 1830 sent to us at least three English authors, each of whom published a more or less readable account of his American wanderings. One of these was C. Colton, who wrote a long Niagara chapter and a most remarkable one on the Whirlpool. Another was S. A. Farrall, author of "A Ramble of 6000 Miles through the United States and Canada," and a third was John Fowler, a specialist on agriculture, whose "Journal of a Tour in the State of New York" in 1830, brought him to Buffalo, where he says:

"I was diverted in passing along Main-street at observing the extreme singularity of the names over the shop doors, &c.; a circumstance, indeed, I have often noticed elsewhere; and, in addition, you will mostly see portrayed upon a sign suspended over, or at the side of the door, some touch of the profession practised within; for instance, at a doctor's, I saw a mortar and pestle; at a bookseller's, two large folio volumes; at a Miss Jeremiah's, a most exquisitely trimmed bonnet; and at a fancy dyer's, a board, upon which was announced the character of their establishment, had every letter painted with different coloured paint;—so much for customs."

A thought must be given to Nathaniel Hawthorne, who was one of the earliest Americans of genius to write sedately and with insight of the Falls. His visit was in the early 30's, when the tourist approach was by stage via Lewiston. "Never," he says, "did a pilgrim approach Niagara with deeper enthusiasm than mine.

"I had lingered away from it, and wandered to other scenes, because my treasury of anticipated enjoyments, comprising all the wonders of the world, had nothing else so magnificent, and I was loth to exchange the pleasures of hope for those of memory so soon. At length the day came. The stage-coach, with a Frenchman and myself on the back seat, had already left Lewiston, and in less than an hour would set us down in Manchester [Niagara Falls village]. I began to listen for the roar of the cataract, and trembled with a sensation like dread, as the moment drew nigh when its voice of ages must roll, for the first time, on my ear. The French gentleman stretched himself from the window, and expressed loud admiration, while, by a sudden impulse, I threw myself back and closed my eyes."

He tells at length how he arrived at the hotel, dined, smoked, loitered over this and that inconsequential thing, illogically postponing the moment of actually beholding the scene. Finally he strolls about Goat Island, comes upon the great spectacle, views it from different points, and then, asking himself, "Were my long desires fulfilled?" analyzes his emotions as follows:

"Oh, that I had never heard of Niagara till I beheld it! Blessed were the wanderers of old, who heard its deep roar sounding through the woods, as the summons to an unknown wonder, and approached its awful brink, in all the freshness of native feeling. Had its own mysterious voice been the first to warn me of its existence then indeed I might have knelt down and worshiped. But I had come thither, haunted with a vision of foam and fury, and dizzy cliffs, and an ocean tumbling down out of the sky—a scene, in short, which Nature had too much good taste and calm simplicity to realize. My mind had struggled to adapt these false conceptions to the reality, and finding the effort vain, a wretched sense of disappointment weighed me down. I climbed the precipice, and threw myself on the earth, feeling that I was unworthy to look at the Great Falls, and careless about beholding them again."

He did, however, behold them again and studied them to good purpose. Besides his essay, "My Visit to Niagara," he weaves Niagara episodes into the "Journal of a Solitary Man," and perhaps into other sketches, to be found in his collected works.

One of the earliest Spanish tourists to visit our region was Don Lorenzo de Zavala, whose *"Viage a los Estados-Unidos del Norte de America,"* published in Paris in 1834, records the author's impressions of Buffalo—he was here in July, 1830—Black Rock, Waterloo (Fort Erie), Chippewa, Niagara Falls, etc., down to Fort Niagara.

We now come to the decade which produced more books about Niagara than any other of the century. From 1831 to 1840 I note forty-three works of American travel, touching our region, thirty-one of which were first published in London. Could anything more forcibly illustrate, by contrast, the paucity of American literary production—at any rate of the descriptive sort—at that period! I could dwell at length and with pleasure on many of these books, for the list includes several extraordinary productions; but my review shall be of the briefest.

Mrs. Frances Trollope came to see us in 1831. Her "Domestic Manners of the Americans" set this country by the ears for more than one decade. Although the dear lady was a very shrew in her treatment of Americans, at Niagara she was for the most part sweetly feminine and appreciative. I know of no more striking proof of the majesty of Niagara than that it tamed Mrs. Trollope. In Buffalo she was more her usual self:

"Of all the thousand and one towns I saw in America, I think Buffalo is the queerest looking; it is not quite so wild as Lockport, but all the buildings have the appearance of having been run up in a hurry, though everything has an air of great pretension; there are porticos, columns, domes, and colonnades, but all in wood. Everybody tells you there, as in all their new-born towns, and everybody believes, that their improvement, and their progression are more rapid, more wonderful, than the earth ever before witnessed; while to me, the only wonder is, how so many thousands, nay millions of persons, can be found, in the nineteenth century, who can be content so to live. Surely this country may be said to spread rather than to rise.

"The Eagle Hotel, an immense wooden fabric, has all the pretension of a splendid establishment, but its monstrous corridors, low ceilings, and intricate chambers, gave me the feeling of a catacomb rather than a house. We arrived after the *table d'hôte* tea-drinking was over, and supped comfortably enough with a gentleman, who accompanied us from the Falls; but the next morning we breakfasted in a long, narrow room, with a hundred persons, and any thing less like comfort can hardly be imagined."

There is no better book for a bumptious American to read, even today, than Mrs. Trollope's. If he can peruse it and keep a serene temper, he is fit for the kingdom of heaven. Mrs. Trollope gave us a dose of bad medicine, but it was good for us.

Her fame rather overshadows that of Captain J. E. Alexander of the 42d Royal Highlanders, F. R. G. S., and much else besides, whose "Trans-Atlantic Sketches" (London, 1833) belongs to Niagara letters. He gives a long, graphic account of Francis Abbott, the hermit of Niagara; as also does F. W. P. Greenwood, D. D., in whose "Miscellaneous Writings" (Boston, 1846) will be found a long account of a visit to Niagara in July, 1831.

In 1832, I note the following visitors to our region, who wrote books about us: Rev. Isaac Fidler ("Observations," etc.), a missionary, resident for a time at "Thornhill, Yonge Street, near Toronto"; Godfrey T. Vigne ("Six months in America"), who contributes his quota to the cheerful nonsense of Niagara, with a really fine frontispiece of the Falls, from his own drawing; E. T. Coke ("A Subaltern's Furlough"), a lieutenant of the 45th Regiment who came to Buffalo in August of this year by canal, and studied the "bustling" town, Indian reservations, battlefields, etc., in several excellent chapters; Joseph Bouchette ("The British Dominions in North America"), whose two-volume quarto work, dedicated to William IV., contains a careful topographical description of the region; and John Eyre, whose "Beauties of American Travel," are strongly evangelical. Of about this period was the visit of Prince Maximilien von Wied-Neuwied, whose elaborate "Voyage" contains a Niagara chapter; it is, in the original edition, a very scarce book.

In the next year—1833—at least eight bookwriters arrived: C. D. Arfwedson ("The United States and Canada") came by canal to Buffalo; experienced the pleasures of stage travel on the Niagara frontier, and wrote at length of what he saw—fortunately so, for he was a good observer; so, in a way, was E. S. Abdy ("Journal") who visited General Wadsworth at Geneseo and Red Jacket's widow on the Buffalo Reservation; and who, at the Falls, objected strongly to the work of one who had built "a wooden bridge and a circular building, like a shot tower, directly over one of the falls. . . . The name of this Vandal is I believe, Porter"! Captain Hamilton, author of "Cyril Thornton," notes in his "Men and Manners in America," that the epithet of "Horseshoe" as applied to one of the Niagara cataracts, is no longer applicable, as it is a semi-hexagon—yet other people have persisted in seeing it as a horseshoe, for years after! Hamilton's pages are useful to the student of anti-Masonry in Western New York. A bright chapter on Niagara is contained in the "Impressions of America" of Tyrone Power, a gifted, popular actor, who found himself in Buffalo on the Fourth of July, 1833, when the streets were full of tipsy Indians. In this year N. P. Willis paid one of his visits to Niagara in the interests of American scenery; and Patrick Sherriff, a literary farmer, making his "Tour through North America," wrote that "the banks of the Niagara from the Ferry to the Pavilion is the loveliest and most interesting portion of the globe"! John Neal, a poet of the Niagara, tells in his "Wandering Recollections" of his Niagara experiences in 1833.

The "Journal" of Frances Anne Butler—the lovely Fanny Kemble, adored by an earlier generation—is by no means least among the books of this year, 1833. Approaching Buffalo in July, by canal, she tells us how, near Lockport, "I saw a meek-eyed, yellowish-white cart-horse, standing with a man's saddle on his back. The opportunity was irresistible, and the desire too—I had not backed a horse for so long. So I got up upon the amazed quadruped, woman's fashion, and took a gallop through the fields, with infinite risk of falling off, and proportionate satisfaction." Her journal continues:

"We reached Lewistown about noon, and anxious enquiries were instituted as to how our luggage was to be forwarded, when on the other side; for we were *exclusive extras;* and for creatures so above common fellowship there is no accommodation in this levelling land. A ferry and a ferry-boat, however, it appeared, there were, and thither we made our way. While we were waiting for the boat, I climbed out on the branches of a huge oak, which grew over the banks of the river, which here rise nearly a hundred feet high. Thus comfortably perched, like a bird, 'twixt heaven and earth,' I copied off some verses which I had scrawled just before leaving Lockport. The ferryboat being at length procured, we got into it. The day was sultry; the heat intolerable. The water of this said river Niagara is of a most peculiar colour, like a turquoise when it turns green. It was like a thick stream of verdigris, full

VISITORS WHO WROTE BOOKS.   43

of pale, milky streaks, whirls, eddies, and counter-currents, and looked as if it were running up by one bank, and down by the other. I sat in the sun, on the floor of the boat, revising my verses. . . . Arrived on the other side, i. e., Canada, there was a second pause, as to how we were to get conveyed to the Falls. . . . An uneasy-looking, rickety cart without springs was the sole conveyance we could obtain, and into this we packed ourselves. . . . The sound of the cataract is, they say, heard within fifteen miles when the wind sets favourably; today, however, there was no wind; the whole air was breathless with the heat of midsummer, and, though we stopped our waggon once or twice to listen as we approached, all was profound silence. There was no motion in the leaves of the trees, not a cloud sailing in the sky; everything was as though in a bright, warm death. When we were within about three miles of the Falls, just before entering the village of Niagara, ——— stopped the waggon; and then we heard distinctly, though far off, the voice of the mighty cataract. Looking over the woods, which appeared to overhang the course of the river, we beheld one silver cloud rising slowly into the sky,—the everlasting incense of the waters. A perfect frenzy of impatience seized upon me: I could have set off and run the whole way; and when at length the carriage stopped at the door of the Niagara house, waiting neither for my father, D———, nor ———, I rushed through the hall, and the garden, down the steep footpath cut in the rocks. I heard steps behind me; ——— was following me; down, down I sprang, and along the narrow footpath, divided only by a thicket from the tumultuous rapids. I saw through the boughs the white glimmer of that sea of foam. 'Go on, go on; don't stop,' shouted ———; and in another minute the thicket was passed; I stood upon Table Rock. ——— seized me by the arm, and, without speaking a word, dragged me to the edge of the rapids, to the brink of the abyss. I saw Niagara. Oh, God! who can describe that sight?"

And thus, breathless as it were, at the brink of the chasm, the dramatic Fanny leaves us—and drops the subject.

Dr. Walter Henry, a British military surgeon, tells in his most readable volumes ("Events of a Military Life") something of his experiences at Niagara in 1834. I quote a few lines to show his estimate of the emotional effect of the scene:

"I have visited the Falls of Niagara four times; and on three of these occasions in company with ladies—for the view of any thing grand or sublime in nature or art is not worth two pence in selfish solitude, or rude male companionship, unembellished by the sex; and I have noticed that the predominant feeling at first is the inadequacy of language to express the strength of the emotion. One of the ladies alluded to, of a refined mind and ingenuous nature, after gazing for the first time, with a long and fixed expression, on the sublime object before her, looked for an instant in my face and burst into tears. There are others so constituted as to be fascinated by the spectacle to such a dangerous and overpowering extent, as to feel a strong desire to throw themselves into the abyss. A lady of good sense and mature age assured me, that as she stood on the edge of the Table Rock, this impulse became so strong and overmastering, that she was obliged to recede rapidly from the brink, for fear of the consequences. Here the mind must have been momentarily deranged by the awful grandeur of the scene. I am now of a calm and subdued temperament, the result of long effort and much reflection on the silliness of giving rein to strong feelings and emotions. But when, on my first visit, I proceeded through the Pavilion garden towards the Table Rock, and beheld an ocean moving over the precipice, and flashing and gliding into the enormous milk-white pool below, without any apparent effort, and with all the ease of a quiet rivulet stealing through a meadow, all mental restraint gave way, and my inmost spirit burst out in loud and enthusiastic admiration."

The year 1834 brought several other book-writing travelers, among them two Doctors of Divinity, the Rev. Andrew Reed and the Rev. James Matheson, who collaborated on a "Narrative of the visit to the American churches . . . from the Congregational Union of England and Wales." Their studied, precise volumes contain conscientious descriptions of the Niagara scene—written, too, with genuine intensity of feeling. These clergymen were among the first of our visitors to protest against the ruin of Niagara by vandal money-seekers: "Niagara does not belong to them. Niagara does not belong to Canada or America. Such spots should be deemed the property of civilized mankind; and nothing should be allowed to weaken their efficacy on the tastes, the morals and the enjoyments of all men."

The Hon. Charles Augustus Murray, whose "Travels in North America," were dedicated to Queen Victoria; and the somewhat scholarly and too pedantic Francis Lieber, author of "Letters to a Gentleman in Germany, written after a trip from Philadelphia to Niagara," visited our region in 1834. Greece he compares to a great epic, "while Niagara is a powerful ode, a rhapsody in which Nature herself has seized the mighty harp and plays a rapturous tune. . . . There is not once, in Dante's whole poem, even an allusion to watery torment and horror, and yet how would he have seized upon the sight [of Niagara] and wrought it into poetry." A more eminent visitor of that year was Harriet Martineau, who found much to comment on in "lawless" Buffalo, where women were subject to insult. She gives us a long chapter on Fort Erie, and records the impressions of two visits at the Falls.

I must be content with mere mention of these writers of the next year: Michel Chevalier (*"Lettres sur l'Amerique du Nord"*), who writes a chapter dated "Buffalo, 9 July,

1835," and affords us not merely description, but some study of economic conditions: the Rev. F. A. Cox, and the Rev. J. Hoby, two "D. D.'s" who attended a camp-meeting near Niagara Falls, as described in their "Baptists in America"; and Don Ramon de la Sagra, author of *"Cinco Meses en los Estados-Unidos."* There also came in that year Dr. William Fleming, whose "Four Days at the Falls of Niagara," privately printed at Manchester, Eng., is a dainty and attractive little book, illustrated with exquisite copper-plates. There are at least two editions of it.

The year 1836 sent hither a learned German, Dr. J. G. Büttner, who discourses much about the Seneca Indians in his two-volume *"Briefe aus und über Nordamerika."* A notable Englishman, Sir Francis Bond Head, lieutenant governor of Upper Canada, who was sent out to Canada to struggle with the Mackenzie upheaval, found his pleasure in letters; and in several of his books, his "Narrative," "The Emigrant," etc., offers his quota of Niagara literature.

Two literary Americans—rare birds at that day—came to Niagara this year: Willis Gaylord Clark, whose "Literary Remains" contain an anecdotal account of his journey by stage through Western New York, and experiences at Buffalo and the Falls; and Caroline Gilman, who writes of our region at length in her "Poetry of Traveling." Pretty nearly forgotten now, those long-gone devotees of *belles-lettres;* yet it is not unprofitable to peruse their pages, if only to realize the improvement in our standards of taste and literary expression.

The year 1837, marked by business disturbance and political excitement, sent at least five British book-writers to the banks of the long-suffering Niagara. D. Wilkie, a Scot, records in his "Sketches of a Summer Trip to New York and the Canadas," his experiences by canal to Buffalo. At

Niagara he indulges in a romance, with some matter-of-fact reporting. T. R. Preston, a Government office-holder at Toronto, tells in his "Three Years' Residence in Canada" how Niagara should properly be studied:

"The way in which I found that I could best comprehend the magnitude and character of the stupendous cataract, was by lying flat upon the ground in its near vicinity, mentally dissecting as it were while so recumbent, and then forming combinations of the particles *ad infinitum*. I know not if this suggestion be, or not, a novel one; but in my own case, its adoption was the result of accident, as I found that, when close upon them, I could not regard the Falls for many minutes together in an erect posture, without succumbing to an attracting influence, which I can compare only to the fascination exercised by the loadstone or the eye of the rattlesnake. I, therefore, adopted the alternative of prostrating myself (which answered the twofold purpose of reverence and convenience), and was in such wise enabled to contemplate, for hours together, without apprehension for my personal safety, the stupendous monument of ages that stood reared before me."

No advice of this kind is found in the interesting pages of Mrs. Jameson's "Winter Studies and Summer Rambles," but her Niagara chapters are important for the history of the period. Useful, too, are the scientific observations of Charles Daubeny, M. D., F. R. S., etc., professor of chemistry and botany at Oxford, who tells in his "Journal of a Tour," etc., how he studied mineral springs two miles below the cataract, and the burning spring above. His report on the geology of the Falls region is contained in the Transactions of the Ashmolean Society of Oxford.

More to the popular taste were the pages of Captain Marryat, whose three-volume "Diary in America" is to be found in various editions, English and American. Captain Marryat thought that "perhaps the wisest if not the best description of the Falls of Niagara is in the simple ejaculation of Mrs. Butler," but he indulged in much whimsical writing, of which the following is an amusing sample:

"As I stood on the brink above the falls, continuing for a considerable time to watch the great mass of water tumbling, dancing, capering, and rushing wildly along, as if in a hurry to take the leap and delighted in it, I could not help wishing that I too had been made of such stuff as would have enabled me to have joined it; with it to have rushed innocuously down the precipice; to have rolled uninjured into the deep unfathomable gulf below, or to have gamboled in the atmosphere of spray, which rose in a dense cloud from its recesses. For about half an hour more I continued to watch the rolling waters, and then I felt a slight dizziness and a creeping sensation come over me—that sensation arising from strong excitement, and the same, probably, that occasions the bird to fall into the jaws of the snake. This is a feeling, which, if too long indulged in, becomes irresistible, and occasions a craving desire to leap into the flood of rushing waters. It increased upon me every minute; and retreating from the brink, I turned my eyes to the surrounding foliage, until the effect of the excitement had passed away. I looked upon the waters a second time, and then my thoughts were directed in a very different channel. I wished myself a magician, that I might transport the falls to Italy, and pour their whole volume of waters into the crater of Mount Vesuvius; witness the terrible conflict between the contending elements, and create the largest steam-boiler that ever entered into the imagination of man."

In 1838 I note but one book: "A Journey in North America described in familiar letters to Amelia Opie," by Joseph John Gurney, a Quaker, who writes that in Buffalo "we were received in the hospitable house of the only Friend's family resident there." In 1839 came George Combe, one-time phrenological expert, whose two-volume account of his American travels devotes the usual pages to our region, with more than the usual errors of description. He found Navy Island the largest in the river; was delighted to find a phrenological society in Buffalo, and while here helped a doctor dissect a brain. "I was told that the phrenologists were so numerous and influential, that they would experience little difficulty in getting phrenology introduced into the public schools as a philosophy of mind, if they had a work suitable for the purpose. They have only one zealous opponent, a Presbyterian clergyman who preached against the science." The chief value of Combe's book, in its local aspect, is found in his study of the Indians near Buffalo. With the briefest mention of J. S. Buckingham's comprehensive "Eastern and Western States of America," which gives an especially good account of Buffalo, hotels, steamboats, etc., and which has several philosophizing, poetizing pages on Niagara, and Lt. Col. A. M. Maxwell's "Run through the United States during the autumn of 1840," I end my notes on this most prolific of decades.

Why so many authors should have visited the Niagara region in the decade of the 30's, and why, in succeeding decades they came in diminishing numbers, I leave (for the moment) to the discerning reader. Although there were fewer, from '40 to '50, there were several of distinction. There was Sir Richard H. Bonnycastle, Lieutenant Colonel of Royal Engineers, and of the Militia of Upper Canada, who was long in the Niagara district as engineer and roadmaker, and whose two volumes ("The Canadas in 1841") are pleasant reading. There was Joseph Sturge, Quaker of Birmingham, whose "Visit to the United States in 1841," though largely devoted to problems of international peace, emancipation of the negro, and kindred matters, has some appreciative pages on Niagara. There was the Earl of Carlisle, a guest of the hospitable Wadsworths, as he was of Mr. Van Buren and other eminent citizens. His imaginative temperament found expression not merely in verse, but in discourse of which the following is characteristic: "Living at Niagara was not like ordinary life. Its not overloud but constant solemn roar, has in itself a mysterious sound: is not the highest voice to which the Universe can ever listen, compared by inspiration to the sound of many waters? The whole of existence there has a dreamy but not a frivolous impress; you feel that you are not in the common world, but in the sublimest temple."

Mrs. Eliza A. Steele's "A Summer Journey in the West" (New York, 1841), contains a short chapter on Buffalo and a long one on Niagara Falls.

Very many visitors at Niagara have been put into a serious, often a deeply devotional frame of mind, by contemplation of the cataract. Not so Augustus E. Silliman (a brother of the distinguished Benjamin D. Silliman), whose "Gallop among American Scenery" is a marvel of bad style —interjectional, exclamatory, a literary curio. The author visited, apparently in 1842, Fort Erie, Lundy's Lane and Niagara, of which he writes at length. In that year came John Robert Godley, whose two volumes of "Letters from America" are by no means free from the superior, condescending tone often employed by British writers on America. Most notable of all Niagara writers at this period—perhaps most quoted of them all after Hennepin—was Charles Dickens, whose sojourn in Buffalo and at the Falls is the theme of many pages in the "American Notes." A much-admired description of the cataract includes the following paragraphs:

"Between five and six next morning, we arrived at Buffalo, where we breakfasted; and being too near the Great Falls to wait patiently anywhere else, we set off by train, the same morning at nine o'clock, to Niagara.

"It was a miserable day; chilly and raw; a damp mist falling; and the trees in that northern region quite bare and wintry. Whenever the train halted, I listened for the roar; and was constantly straining my eyes in the direction where I knew the Falls must be, from seeing the river rolling on towards them; every moment expecting to behold the spray. Within a few minutes of our stopping, not before, I saw two great white clouds rising up slowly and majestically from the depths of the earth. That was all. At length we alighted: and then for the first time, I heard the mighty rush of water, and felt the ground tremble underneath my feet.

"The bank is very steep, and was slippery with rain, and half-melted ice. I hardly know how I got down, but I was soon at the bottom, and climbing, with two English officers who were crossing and had joined me, over some broken rocks, deafened by the noise, half-blinded by the spray, and wet to the skin. We were at the foot of the American Fall. I could see an immense torrent of water tearing headlong down from some great height, but had no idea of shape, or situation, or anything but vague immensity.

"When we were seated in the little ferry-boat, and were crossing the swoln river immediately before both cataracts, I began to feel what it was; but I was in a manner stunned, and unable to comprehend the vastness of the scene. It was not until I came on Table Rock, and looked—Great Heaven, on what a fall of bright-green water!—that it came upon me in its full might and majesty.

"Then, when I felt how near to my Creator I was standing, the first effect, and the enduring one—instant and lasting—of the tremendous spectacle, was Peace. Peace of Mind: Tranquility: Calm recollections of the Dead: Great Thoughts of Eternal Rest and Happiness: nothing of Gloom or Terror. Niagara was at once stamped upon my heart, an Image of Beauty; to remain there, changeless and indelible, until its pulses cease to beat, for ever.

"Oh, how the strife and trouble of our daily life receded from my view, and lessened in the distance, during the ten memorable days we passed on that Enchanted Ground! What voices spoke from out the thundering water; what faces, faded from the earth, looked out upon me from its gleaming depths; what Heavenly promise glistened in those angels' tears, the drops of many hues, that showered around, and twined themselves about the gorgeous arches which the changing rainbows made!

"I never stirred in all that time from the Canadian side, whither I had gone at first. I never crossed the river again; for I knew there were people on the other shore, and in such a place it is natural to shun strange company. To wander to and fro all day, and see the cataracts from all points of view; to stand upon the edge of the Great Horse Shoe Fall, marking the hurried water gathering strength as it approached the verge, yet seeming, too, to pause before it shot into the gulf below; to gaze from the river's level up at the torrent as it came streaming down; to climb the neighbouring heights and watch it through the trees, and see the wreathing water in the rapids hurrying on to take its fearful plunge; to linger in the shadow of the solemn rocks three miles below; watching the river as, stirred by no visible cause, it heaved and eddied and awoke the echoes, being troubled yet, far down beneath the surface, by its giant leap; to have Niagara before me, lighted by the sun and by the moon, red in the day's decline, and grey as evening slowly fell upon it; to look upon it every day, and wake up in the night and hear its ceaseless voice: this was enough.

"I think in every quiet season now, still do those waters roll and leap, and roar and tumble, all day long; still are the rainbows spanning them, a hundred feet below. Still, when the sun is on them, do they shine and glow like molten gold. Still, when the day is gloomy, do they fall like snow, or seem to crumble away like the front of a great chalk cliff, or roll adown the rock like dense white smoke. But always does the mighty stream appear to die as it comes down, and always from its unfathomable grave arises that tremendous ghost of spray and mist which is never laid: which has haunted this place with the same dread solemnity since Darkness brooded on the deep, and that first flood before the Deluge—Light—came rushing on Creation at the word of God."

Susan Margaret Fuller's "Summer on the Lakes" begins at "Niagara, June 10, 1843," but this gifted woman has contributed but slightly to our local literature. A visitor of 1844 was Eliot Warburton, author of numerous works, among them "Hochelaga, or England in the New World," in which he dismisses Niagara with this summing up: "See it from Table Rock, gaze thence upon it for hours—days if you like—and then go home. As for the Rapids, Cave of the Winds, Burning Spring, etc., you might as well enter into an examination of the gilt figures on the picture-frame, as waste your time on them."

Contrast with this the careful study made of our river in 1845 by Francis Parkman; to what good use, every reader of his histories knows.

George Moore's "Journal . . . with Notes on Canada and the United States . . . in 1844" devotes several pages to Buffalo and the Falls, which he visited in October, 1843. In the next year came Frederick Von Raumer, whose work I know only in Turner's translation, "America and the American People" (New York, 1846). The author, professor of history in the University of Berlin, was at Niagara Falls in July, 1844. The Rev. Edward Waylen's "Ecclesiastical Reminiscences of the United States" (London, 1846) has a Niagara chapter of about this date.

Something of our region, in varying quantity and quality, will be found in the Rev. G. Lewis' "Impressions of America and the American Churches" (1844); in William Savery's "Journal" of that year—another of the useful records by members of the Society of Friends; in Alexander Mackay's "The Western World" (1846) in three volumes, dedicated to Richard Cobden; and in William Cullen Bryant's "Letters of a Traveler," the poet's visit being in the last named year. I have not noted anything for 1847, but in 1848 there came at least two writers: the Rev. James Dixon, D. D., whose "Personal Narrative of a Tour," etc., is chiefly an exposition of the state of Methodism in America at that time; and Archibald Prentice, editor of the Manchester (Eng.) *Times,* member of literary and philosophical societies, and a clear, sensible writer. He found himself interested in Buffalo, then with 35,000 inhabitants; and of Niagara, he expressed himself as follows:

"A short ride on the railway brought us from Buffalo to the village of Niagara and the Cataract Hotel, close to the back of which are the great falls. I was soon on the point of rock on the American side, where they are in full view. It takes some boldness to avow that I was less awe-struck than tourists generally profess to be; but I was delighted with the exceeding beauty of the scene. Close at hand the falling river was broken into millions of resplendent diamonds; farther off it was a perpendicular fall of snow; in the middle it was the rush of the green ocean wave into a chasm opened in the great deep; and again in the distance was the gentle snow-fall; all illuminated by a brilliant sun, and all gentle and lovely. There was no rage, no discord, no tumultuous chafings of the immense flood. There was the quietness as of the conscious possession of power; perfect harmony; perfect beauty. I saw no death of the stream as it fell—no tremendous 'ghost of spray and mist.' No voices spoke to me from out the thundering water. There was the majestic, softened by the beautiful;—calm, gentle, tranquil, exceeding loveliness."

A literary visitor of 1849 was Major John Thornton, author of a "Diary of a Tour through the Northern States of the Union and Canada." What Buffalonian today can recognize his city in the following picture: "Buffalo has a most imposing appearance as viewed from the lake. The practice of roofing the cupolas, domes, roofs, etc., with bright tin, has a most dazzling effect when the sun's rays are reflected from them"! Robert Baird's "Impressions and Experiences of the West Indies and North America" is not without local interest. The author spent a week at the Falls in 1849, and although he records that the distance to Buffalo is eleven miles, he gets most of his facts straight and gives a full, leisurely account of his experiences and reflections. Much relating to Buffalo and Niagara is to be found in *"Minnen fran en sjuttonarig vistelse i Nordvestra Amerika,"* by the Rev. Gustav Unonius; his book, published at Upsala, Sweden, in 1862, records events of a tour in 1849.

A gifted English woman, Mrs. Houston, author of "Hesperos, or Travels in the West," thought Buffalo in 1849 "showy" but not substantial. At Niagara she resented the presence of the town, as too near the scenery. In September, 1849, James F. W. Johnston looked us over. His two-volume work, "Notes on North America," discusses the causes of Buffalo's growth, and the regional geology.

I note but one foreign visitor in 1850, but that one most welcome. Then it was that Frederika Bremer came, I believe with James Russell Lowell and his wife. In Buffalo she was asked: "'Does Buffalo look according to your expectations?' To which I replied that I had not expected anything from Buffalo." She wrote delightfully of Niagara, as the reader will find, who, if not able to enjoy Miss Bremer in the Swedish, can not fail to do so in Mary Howitt's admirable translation of "The Homes of the New World." Were I writing a book on my present subject instead of trying to compress it into as few pages as possible, I should dwell at length on the poetic prose of this gifted writer.

George Francis Train gives us a Niagara incident unique, as might be expected, and altogether romantic. In 1850, when an ardent youth, he saw at Syracuse a beautiful girl, a stranger. Train gazed, and vowed to a friend: "I never saw her before but she shall be my wife." With supreme impudence, and in the spirit that perhaps wins battles, he follows the maiden and her elderly escort. They take train, he does the same, heedless of destination. He seats himself near the goddess; a refractory window (herein may lie a reason why they always are refractory) furnishes an excuse for gallant assistance. The ice is broken, introductions follow. At Oswego, the young lady embarks for Niagara. Train takes the same boat. Let him continue:

"And so we arrived at Niagara together. Dr. Wallace was kind enough to permit me to escort his charge about the Falls, and I was foolish enough to do several risky things in a sort of half-conscious desire to appear brave—the last infirmity of the mind of a lover. I went under the Falls and clambered about in all sorts of dangerous places, in an intoxication of love. It was the same old story, only with the difference that our love was mutually discovered and confessed amid the roaring accompaniment of the great cataract. We were at the Falls forty-eight hours, and before we left we were betrothed."

When they were married, the next year, "my wife," says Train, "was only seventeen. She was very beautiful," as indeed we may well believe from her published portraits. His experience ("My Life in many States and in Foreign Lands") is unique so far as the chronicles of literature record, but nothing is clearer in the history of Niagara than that it has always been a favored resort of Dan Cupid as well as the shrine of Hymen.

The decade of the '50's, like that just reviewed, brought us a score and more of authors. In 1851, we have J. J. Ampere of the French Academy, whose *"Promenade en Amerique"* devotes poetical pages to Niagara, with some graphic paragraphs on Buffalo; and Moritz Busch, author of *"Wanderungen zwischen Hudson und Mississippi,"* published some years later in Stuttgart.

George William Curtis visited Niagara in the summer of 1851, writing from there a series of letters to the New York *Sun*, which afterwards were embodied in his delightful volume, "Lotus Eating." The clearness of his perception may be shown by one brief quotation: "Disappointment in Niagara must be affected, or childish." The next year came Alexander Marjoribanks, gathering material for his "Travels in South and North America." While at Niagara he marvels as much at the suspension bridge as at the Falls. The "Autobiography" of the Rev. Abel C. Thomas, printed in Boston in 1852, has an account of the author's preaching on Table Rock.

Another world-wide tourist, William Parish Robertson, author of a "Visit to Mexico and the United States," in two volumes, records at Niagara: "I came too late to say anything which could be new or interesting, *'Tout est dit, et l'on vient trop tard,'* as La Bruyère pathetically complains when he commences his *'Caracteres.'*" Still another visitor of this summer of 1852 was Edmund Patten, author of "Glimpse at the United States," etc. And not to be overlooked is Mrs. Susanna Moodie's "Life in the Clearings," etc. (London, 1853), with its good account of the Niagara neighborhood.

The year of 1853 brought to our shores William H. H. Kingston, in whose "Western Wanderings," in two volumes, may be found abundant and good writing descriptive of our region. W. E. Baxter, Member of Parliament, made one of his numerous tours through the United States in this same year. A series of lectures given by him on his return to England was published under the title "America and the Americans." He has pleasant things to say of Buffalo, and of Niagara one very good thing: "Niagara must be visited in silence and alone." William Chambers, author of "Things as they are in America," was especially interested in the summer of '53 in the geology of the Niagara region. His analytical mind experienced a sentiment of disappointment which "I think," he says, "may be mainly traced to the ranting and exaggerated descriptions which have deceived the imagination and led to undue expectations." It is interesting to note that in this year there came to Niagara Charles Weld, a half-brother of the Isaac Weld who 55 years before had been one of the earliest to visit and describe our region. The younger brother, at the time of his American tour vice president of the Royal Dublin Society, writes with much discernment and intelligence of the phenomena of Niagara. About the time of his visit came also two other notable Britons: the Hon. Amelia M. Murray, who, in her "Letters from the United States, Cuba and Canada," tells of her visit to Niagara in October, though her pages are chiefly devoted to an analysis of American social customs. In this year also came the Rev.

VISITORS WHO WROTE BOOKS. 59

John Sinclair, Vicar of Kensington and much else; his "Sketches of Old Times and Distant Places," printed in London as late as 1875, has a readable account of a Niagara sojourn in 1853.

The Rev. Robert Everest, chaplain to the East India Company, records in his "Journey through the United States and part of Canada" that as he was on the street in Buffalo, then a town of 60,000, "a plain man passed alone with an umbrella in his hand—Millard Fillmore."

I note three wandering authors in 1855, whose works relate to this region: William Ferguson, in whose big book, "America by River and Rail," will be found his description of sight-seeing on board the first Maid of the Mist and his sage reflection regarding the cataract: "Many say you can't describe it, then do very well"; and Ivan Golovin, the object of whose "Stars and Stripes," published in London the next year, was "to show that the United States are pursuing a wrong way in their politics and morals." This reforming Russian paused long enough in his career of national correction to declare that the period spent at Niagara embraced the most happy moments of his life. A third traveller of this year was J. G. Kohl, whose impressions are to be found in his *"Reisen in Canada u. durch die Staaten von New York & Pensylvanien."*

A trifling reporter was Thomas Wilson, author of "Trans-Atlantic Sketches," his visit hereabout being in 1859. Of slight importance is the "Sketches of the South and West, or Ten Months Residence in the United States," by Henry Deedes, also of this year. Far worthier our attention is the volume of still another traveling Quaker, William Tallack, who writes pleasantly of the Niagara in his "Friendly Sketches of America." Here, too, may be mentioned John White's "Sketches from America," the visit being about this time, though the book was published in London in 1870.

The one most notable visit of the decade ending with 1860, was that of the young Prince of Wales. Several books record his American travels. Among those most worthy the attention of the curious reader is "The Prince of Wales in Canada and the United States," by Nicholas Augustus Woods, special correspondent of the London *Times*. This work contains a long, picturesque account of the Prince's visit to Niagara, the exhibitions of Blondin, etc. A briefer account of the royal tour, by Gardner D. Engleheart, private secretary to the Duke of Newcastle, was privately printed in 1860, with a few exquisite illustrations from the author's drawings.

The Earl of Southesk (K. T., F. R. G. S.), in his "Saskatchewan" (Edinburgh, 1875), makes record of his visit to Niagara in May, 1859. He was little pleased with the scene. "It is too huge," he says, "and the disgustingly obtrusive civilization that crawls over its sides turns my very heart sick. . . . A narrower, higher cataract would strike more sharply on the mental vision, than low-statured, wide-spreading Niagara. . . . The Canadian side is not strikingly offensive, but the American side teems with glaring wooden structures hanging over the very precipice. . . . Some wretched person has built a mock ruin on a little island that actually overhangs the Fall"—and more in the same strain.

A war-time visitor was Anthony Trollope, who in 1858-1861 made several stops at Niagara. The last visit, thirty years after his mother's famous sojourn, gave us a very good chapter in his "North America." The attitude of his mind is shown by the following excerpt:

"Of all the sights on this earth of ours which tourists travel to see,—at least of all those which I have seen,—I am inclined to give the palm to the Falls of Niagara. In the catalogue of such sights I intend to include all buildings, pictures, statues and wonders of art made by men's hands, and also all beauties of nature prepared by the Creator for the delight of His creatures. This is a long word; but as far as my taste and judgment go, it is justified. I know no other one thing so beautiful, so glorious and so powerful."

One of our visitors, in 1854, was a truly remarkable traveler, the Viennese scholar, Ida Meyer Pfeiffer, who spent most of her life in roaming the world. She had been twice around the globe—not the trifling jaunt then that it is now—when she came to the Niagara in August, 1854. Though she had seen so much she seems to have saved her superlative emotions for these falls. August 10th she writes:

"This was a day never to be forgotten in the annals of my life—one of those which brilliantly rewarded me for all the toils and hardships by which they were purchased; for on this day I beheld one of the most sublime and wonderful scenes of God's beautiful world—the falls of Niagara! What the eye sees, what the soul feels, at this spectacle, can never be described: painter and poet would despair of success in such an attempt. Did a man meet his mortal enemy on this spot, he must at once forgive him; and should one who has doubted of the existence of God come to this, one of the noblest of His altars, he must, I think, return converted and tranquilized. Oh! that I could have shared with all my friends, with all mankind, the emotions awakened by this wonder of creation."

Another great traveler who first saw Niagara in that year was Bayard Taylor. His volume entitled "Home and Abroad," tells of his visits, especially of one in 1860; and touches well upon an affectation of tourists: "I read last winter in one of the papers a most admirable description of the falling of the water, entitled 'Niagara, but Not described.' The writer knew all the time he was describing it."

In 1862 our Niagara author is Samuel Phillips Day ("English America"). The next year apparently brought but one, Lucien Biart, whose book, *"A travers l'Amerique,"* was "crowned" by the French Academy and has had several editions. The author writes lightly and brightly of Niagara in winter. The next year came another Frenchman, Auguste Laugel, author of *"Les États-Unis pendant la Guerre."* The French never fail to write attractively of Niagara, and Laugel is no exception, though he declares that he has never seen a good picture of it. Another French author, Jules Marcou, made five visits to Niagara, 1848-'50. In September, 1863, he came again, and wrote agreeably of his experiences under the title *"Le Niagara quinze ans après."* Late in the war—1865—a distinguished English writer who had been war correspondent in America, W. Howard Russell, visited Niagara, in the preparation of his "Canada, its Defences, Condition and Resources." He was an entertaining writer. In an earlier book, "My Diary North and South" (1863), he devotes a whole chapter to Niagara, which he first visited in 1862. With him I close the meagre list of author travelers in our region during the Civil War. The reasons for this meagreness are too obvious to call for comment. Nor is the rest of the decade of the '60's any richer in production. We have Oscar Comettant's *"Voyage Pittoresque et Anecdotique,"* etc.; and F. Barham Zincke's "Last Winter in the United States," in which he tells how he was snowbound at Niagara in the winter of '67-'8. Captain W. F. Butler was at Niagara in September, 1867. In his "Great Lone Land" he writes that "Niagara was a place to be instinctively shunned," and unfolds an enterprising Yankee's plan for drying up the Falls! F. French Townshend's "Ten Thousand Miles of Travel, Sport and Adventure" (London, 1869), contains an account of his visit to Niagara in 1868.

Belonging by association and American interest to the Civil War period is Thomas Hughes—the beloved "Tom" of Rugby—who came to America for the first time in 1870, and saw Niagara in September of that year. One reads of it in his "Vacation Rambles," chattiest, most genial of books. His principal impression—at least his principal Niagara record—was of the current baths: "We had a bath in the rush just above the Falls; you have a little room through which a slice some four feet wide of the water is allowed to rush; you get in at the side, in the back water, and then take hold of a short rope fixed close above the rush, and let the water seize and tear at you, which it does with a vengeance, tugging as if it would carry off your legs and pull you in two in the middle. You can get out of it in a moment by just slewing yourself round, and the sensation is marvelously delicious."

In the decade of the 70's—I think as early as 1871—came Henry James; not then so distinguished as now, but master (as he does not always clearly demonstrate) of an incomparable style. Of all the writers who have seriously addressed themselves to the task of describing Niagara Falls, Henry James is, in my judgment, easily first. He is among writers what Church is among painters—thoroughly poetic and thoroughly sincere. He saw Niagara when it was yet in the hands of the Philistines, and in elaborated sentences he called for its rescue. Then, goaded by "the importunities from hackmen and photographers and vendors of jim-cracks," he passes into a holy rage, declares them all "simply hideous and infamous," and calls on the

State to buy the landscape. Few voices were raised for this redemption, earlier than his. And when he does gain solitude and silence, how he adores it! Always an analyst, he goes like the great artist, at once to its heart. We may smile a little at his phrases, with just a hint of bestowing approval on the Creator as well as on His works: "The perfect taste of it is the great characteristic. It is not in the least monstrous; it is thoroughly artistic and, as the phrase is, thought out. In the matter of line it beats Michael Angelo." The more he studies, the more he approves, and presently—he cannot conceal it—the poet-soul of him is in love with it: "Nothing was ever more successfully executed"—this he says, of the crest of the fall; "it is as gentle as the pouring of wine from a flagon—of melody from the lips of a singer. . . . If the line of beauty had vanished from the earth elsewhere, it would survive on the brow of Niagara." He even approved of the Terrapin tower, still standing at the date of his visit, and which to many visitors was an offense; but this critic thought its builder "deserves a compliment," for he had set up a little but useful standard for comparison. Henry James at Niagara was as far from the hysterical panegyrist as a Tyndall, let us say, is far from the welling emotions of a Mrs. Sigourney, or the emotional attitudinizing of a Dickens; but his study of it (to be found in "Portraits of Places") sets the high-water mark, I think, in all the flood of descriptive writing on this subject.

Speaking generally, from the Civil War to the end of the century, the literature of travel touching our region is well-nigh negligible in value. Some notable visitors have come, some pleasant pages have been written; but more and more there is a disposition to treat Niagara as a twice-told tale. In 1872, I note the visit of Lady Dufferin, who has left a pleasant record in "My Canadian Journal" of her visit to

Niagara with General Sir C. Hastings Doyle, Lieutenant Governor of Nova Scotia, and Sir Edward Thornton, then British Minister at Washington. With Colonel Sir Cassimir S. Gzowski—the distinguished engineer of the International Bridge—Lady Dufferin visited Buffalo, where, she writes, "one gets such an impression of wealth and comfort that one is astonished." Another visitor of that year was Julius George Medley, Lieutenant Colonel of Royal Engineers, Fellow of the University of Calcutta, etc., from whose "Autumn Tour in the United States and Canada" one gets the impression that he thought it something of a bore to write of Niagara and hardly worth while to trouble either himself or his readers with serious description.

A picturesque wanderer of 1874 was Henri Rochefort, returning to France from his political exile—he had escaped from the penal colony of New Caledonia. No livelier book was ever written than his "Story of My Life," in which he tells characteristically of his brief sojourn at Niagara in May of the year named. "All around the Falls," he says, "which are really majestic, though one feels inclined to believe that they have been put there to attract foreigners of every nationality—is a perpetual sort of St. Cloud fête. The banks on the sides of the rapids are crowded with pedlars and even fair-stalls. Everything is on sale, especially bracelets of German lapis-lazuli and Vesuvian lava; that is to say, the products of numerous industries that have nothing to do with Niagara and its Falls. . . . A wild-beast showman absolutely insisted on my purchasing a bear, which turned sadly about in its cage just as I had done in mine only a few months earlier"! Rochefort viewed "the grand cascade" from the middle of the suspension bridge; it finishes, he says, "by giving you the impression of being an immense stick of marsh mallow or barley sugar twisting round a bobbin of an Algerian stall at a suburban fair"—about the most extraordinary impression in our whole category. He lodged at the Clifton House, and when the manager brought the visitors' book, "I contented myself with tracing this burlesque phrase: 'This fall is profound, but my own is still greater! (Signed) The Shadow of Napoleon III.'"

The "Western Wanderings" of J. W. Bodham-Whetham, though touching our region, is of no special value; nor is the jaunty and journalistic "Letters sent Home" by William Morris (author of "France and the French," etc.). Musicians are seldom authors, but Jacques Offenbach, who came to Niagara in 1875, wrote lightly, somewhat ecstatically, of what he saw, in "America and the Americans." A poetical gentleman of Spanish blood, Guillermo Prieto, wrote poetically of us in 1877, his book, *"Viaje á los Estados-Unidos,"* being published in Mexico. In that year came also William Saunders ("Through the Light Continent"), and H. Hussey Vivian, M. P., F. G. S., in whose "Notes of a Tour in America" I am struck by the following passage: "It (the fall) impressed me with a sense of its own grandeur, and the impotence of man, more than anything I ever saw, more than the eruption of Vesuvius, the crashings of a continental thunder-storm, or an ocean gale." And after all that, he was disappointed in the Great Lakes. In our list should be included Charles Marshall's "The Canadian Dominion," and Willis Nash's "Oregon," and William Morris's "Letters sent Home," all of which have chapters on Niagara as seen in the '70's.

Walt Whitman, in his "November Boughs" tells of his first visit to Niagara in 1848. It is just about the tersest Niagara chapter I have come upon:

VISITORS WHO WROTE BOOKS.

"Got in the cars and went to Niagara. Went under the Falls—saw the whirlpool and all the other sights."

Many years after, in June, 1880, he saw Niagara again and wrote of it in characteristic fashion:

"For really seizing a great picture or book, or piece of music, or architecture, or grand scenery—or perhaps for the first time even the common sunshine, or landscape, or may-be even the mystery of identity, most curious mystery of all—there comes some lucky five minutes of a man's life, set amid a fortuitous concurrence of circumstances, and bringing in a brief flash the culmination of years of reading and travel and thought. The present case about two o'clock this afternoon gave me Niagara, its superb severity of action and color and majestic grouping, in one short, indescribable show. We were very slowly crossing the Suspension bridge—not a full stop anywhere, but next to it—the day clear, sunny, still—and I out on the platform. The falls were in plain view about a mile off, but very distinct, and no roar—hardly a murmur. The river tumbling green and white, far below me; the dark high banks, the plentiful umbrage, many bronze cedars, in shadow; and tempering and arching all the immense materiality, a clear sky overhead, with a few white clouds, limpid, spiritual, silent. Brief, and as quiet as brief, that picture—a remembrance always afterwards."

Mere mention may suffice for W. G. Marshall's handsomely illustrated "Through America" (1878); Lady Duffus Hardy's "Through Cities and Prairie Lands" and "Between Two Oceans"—her Niagara visit being about 1880; David Pidgeon's "An Engineer's Holiday," of the same year; T. S. Hudson's "Scamper through America" (1882); Alberto Lombardo's *"Los Estados-Unidos"* (1882); and the work of still another Mexican, Don Juan Bustamante y Campuzano, secretary of legation at Washington, who in his *"Del Atlantico al Pacifico,"* tells of his visit to Niagara in August, 1882. In 1883 came Thomas Greenwood ("A Tour in the States and Canada—Out and Home in Six Weeks"); in 1884, the Marquis of Lorne ("Memories of Canada and Scotland"); in 1885, Alberto G. Bianchi, who in *"Los Estados-Unidos"* describes the tour of a party of Mexicans; and in 1886, Charles Bigot, whose little book, *"De Paris au Niagara"* has the good French gift of picturesqueness. At Niagara the author regrets that he is not a word painter like Zola or Loti. Loti indeed would give us a Niagara page or two worth while. Sir Henry Irving's "Impressions of America" (1884), written by Joseph Hatton, has a pleasant Niagara chapter. Frederic Daly's "Irving" also touches our region.

Most of these recent books offer little of value, especially in comparison with the elaborate chapters of earlier decades. Sir Edwin Arnold tarried at Niagara in the autumn of 1889, and in "Seas and Lands" writes of it in poetical vein. B. Kroupa, author of "An Artist's Tour" (1890), is content at Niagara to complain of excessive fees. C. L. Johnstone's "Winter and Summer Excursions in Canada" (1894) devotes but a few paragraphs to our region, and those not accurate. A notable visitor of 1894 was S. Reynolds Hole, Dean of Rochester, who in his "Little Tour in America" is clerically discursive and anecdotal, and calls Niagara "the most wonderful place in the world." Most matter-of-fact was Lady Theodora Guest, whose "Round Trip in North America" brought her to Niagara in 1894; she wrote that it was "a marvelous mass of water, but that it has no other advantage—no fine scenery, no weather and no fine flowers." The last decade of the Nineteenth Century may close, so far as our review is concerned, with Mrs. Schuyler Van Rensselaer, whose study of Niagara is found in the *Century Magazine*, June, 1899; with Dr. Auguste Lutaud

("*Aux Etats-Unis*") ; and with Rudyard Kipling, who in his "American Notes" (1899) takes no heed of Niagara, but pays his respects to Buffalo in a—for him—most gracious fashion.

The foregoing perhaps tedious record takes on an aspect of interest when considered as a whole. Let us consider for a moment these travel-books, relating in part to the Niagara. The list could be extended, but we lose little by shortening it. Ignoring a few of the least value, we have about 190 books of travel, written in the Nineteenth Century, which record, often at great length, the writers' impressions of Niagara Falls, Buffalo and the adjacent region. By far the largest part of these books are by English men and women. There is a fair sprinkling of Scots, a few French, Germans, Mexicans; but probably 90 per cent. of the lot were English. Most of the descriptive literature of Niagara, in the Nineteenth Century, was published in London. Some of the authors were officials in Canada, some were specially interested in emigration, or slavery, or other phase of American life; some were correspondents for British journals; and some were tourists—early specimens of the genus globe-trotter, with the book-writing habit. Good and bad, take them through the century, their pages give us data not elsewhere recorded, from which we get a fuller knowledge and a clearer idea of conditions hereabouts, during the century, than from any other source.

The production of travelers' books relating to the Niagara during the Nineteenth Century could be very simply shown in diagram, after the edifying fashion of the zigzag dotted line which in Government weather charts expresses the variation of temperature, or which is often used to indicate the fluctuation of the stock market. Let a base line say of ten inches represent the century—a decade to an inch. Starting with one author in 1800, a gradually ascending line indicates the half dozen or so who had appeared by 1810. By 1820, with 17 more books, the line reaches twice as high. It climbs but little, prior to 1830; but from 1830 to 1840 it jumps to twice its former height; a veritable little alp of literature. In the next ten years it falls almost to the point of 1830; and with some variations it gradually declines, until, at 1900, we have no more litera-

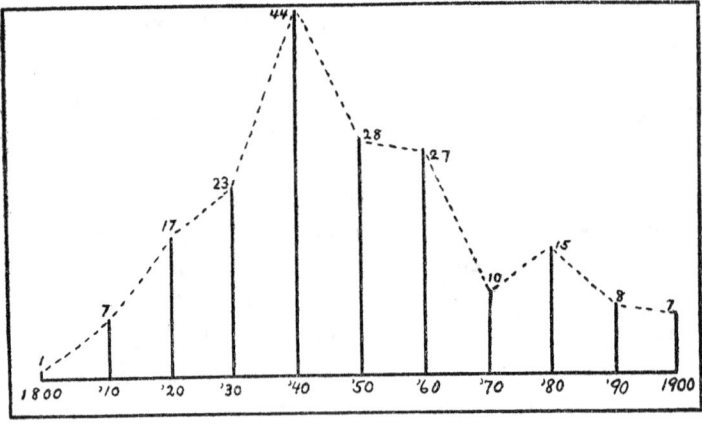

Diagram illustrating the distribution by decades of 187 authors who visited and wrote of Niagara Falls, 1800 to 1900. The bottom figures indicate the decade; those at the top the number of visiting authors for each decade. It strikingly shows the effect of increased facilities of travel, in the '30's, and the restrictive effect of the Civil War.

ture descriptive of Niagara in the new books of travel than we had in the first ten years of the century. Travel books are still being written; but the tourist—especially the Briton—no longer makes the Niagara his chief objective in America. Nowadays he is usually hurrying across the continent to the far Northwest or Japan, and is content to see Niagara from a car window, or ignore it altogether.

The literature of travel affords not merely an array of

facts, but illustrates the singular behavior of the human mind in contemplating the superlative in Nature. About one-half of the literary visitors at Niagara record that at first sight they were deeply disappointed. The other half declare that the falls quite came up to expectations. Very many visitors feel under obligations to the occasion, and indulge in affectedly fine writing. They become studiedly sentimental. This is strikingly true of writers from say 1830 to 1860. It was not merely the women, whose natures lead us to expect emotional expression, but often the men as well, who indulged in apostrophe and exclamation, in posing and phrasing, as silly as anything in the literature of our language. After a time affectation ceased to be good form and literary hysteria went out of fashion. I have sometimes wondered whether the experiences of the Civil War did not have a chastening and elevating effect on our national literature. But the simpler, sincerer expression which present taste prefers is by no means confined to American writers, although in our present study it is most evident in American books, because from about 1860 there was a marked falling off in books descriptive of this region, by foreign authors; whereas much of the best that had been written about it is by Americans of our own generation. When we recall that the Niagara panorama, scenic and human, has employed the pens of James Fenimore Cooper, of Nathaniel Hawthorne, Bayard Taylor, George William Curtis, Charles Dudley Warner, Henry James, and William Dean Howells (I am not forgetting many others of varying quality, from N. P. Willis to Mark Twain), it becomes plain that although probably the greater bulk of descriptive literature has been furnished by British commentators, yet the essential and worthiest literature of the region has of late years been penned by Americans.

The memoirs or biographies of celebrities contain many an interesting allusion to or account of their visits to Buffalo and Niagara Falls, which are not to be found in their books, published during their life-time. Fitz-Greene Halleck in 1820, Catherine M. Sedgwick in 1821, John Neal in 1833, Harriet Beecher in 1834, Ralph Waldo Emerson in 1849 or 50—and so on down the decades. Charles A. Dana came to Buffalo, a little boy, in 1812. Here he learned to speak the Seneca; and his biographer, James H. Wilson, says that when he first saw Niagara Falls he was so impressed by them that "he composed an ode on their grandeur which had considerable merit but as it has long been lost this statement must be taken on faith." Annie Fields, in her "Life and Letters of Harriet Beecher Stowe," gives "Hattie" Beecher's impressions of Niagara, which she visited in 1834: "I felt as if I could have gone over with the waters; it would have been so beautiful a death, there would be no fear in it," etc. This was two years before she married Professor Stowe, and eighteen years before "Uncle Tom's Cabin" made her the most famous of American women authors. George Ticknor was at Niagara in 1827 and again in 1845, when he wrote a long description to G. T. Curtis in Boston:

"The finest thing we have seen yet, and one of the grandest I ever saw, was a thunder-storm among the waters, as it seemed to be, the other night, which lighted up the two cascades, as seen from our piazzas, with most magnificent effect. They had a spectral look, as they came out of the darkness, and were again swallowed up in it, that defies all description and all imagination."

Theodore Winthrop visited Niagara in August, 1851, and wrote (to friends) amusingly of his experiences. He lost his luggage and had to borrow a shirt!

VISITORS WHO WROTE BOOKS.

Henry David Thoreau was at Niagara in the spring of 1861, on his way to Minnesota. It is incredible that he did not write of the Falls; he probably did, but if the letter has been published I have overlooked it. He died in less than a year after this first and only tour to the West. His health was failing before he saw this region.

Edmund Clarence Stedman came to Niagara in the summer of 1865, and while there wrote characteristic letters to his mother, and to his close friend, Bayard Taylor. The following extract from a letter to Taylor shows that even poets, if in poor health and "out of sorts," may find even Niagara tiresome and tame:

CATARACT HOUSE, NIAGARA, July 16, 1865.

... Well, here we are, on our way to Sault Ste. Marie, for which we start tomorrow, and go, as it seems to a sick man, in his "moods," out of sight and sound of humanity. ... These Falls of Niagara improve on acquaintance, but still, I feel nothing of the *awe* in their presence which greater minds profess to have felt. The fact is, one can pour over a so much loftier and louder-sounding torrent in his soul, that these seem rather lathery and tame. I catch myself wondering whether all these rascally hackmen and publicans, who talk so loudly of them, don't, in their heart of hearts, think them a humbug —a sort of springe to catch woodcocks. If this is the largest thing of the sort in the world, what a little Peddlington sort of a ball this world is, anyhow! Probably, though, I see them too late in life—(saw them some years ago, for an hour only). When quite young, the first sight of the ocean impressed me beyond measure. For years I dreamed of that white surf—the infinite laughters—the unended gloom behind. Even now I am lost, and *lifted,* by the seashore. There is nothing like it. Niagara is measurable. The roar of the cataract is that of a great mill-dam. But the ocean makes you think it has no limit. ...

Here at Niagara the best thing in my mind is my mother's quatrain to the eagle—you might have written it—

> Where the great Cataract sends up to Heaven
> Its spraying incense of perpetual cloud,
> Thy wings in twain the sacred bow have riven,
> And onward sailed, *irreverently proud!*

There is a fine swoop and curve to that last line. . . .

Temperament accounts for much, in the impressions made by Niagara upon visitors. Goldwin Smith, who must often have viewed the Falls, says nothing of them in his "Reminiscences," save to quote (twice, in varying language) a remark by Richard Cobden to a friend about to visit America, and who asked if Niagara was worth a special journey. Cobden's reply was: "There are two sublimities in Nature: one of rest, the other of motion; the sublimity in rest is the distant Alps, the sublimity of motion is Niagara." Cobden's journal of his first American visit, quoted from in Morley's "Life of Cobden," has a long account of his visit to Niagara in June, 1835. "Thank God," he exclaims, "that has bestowed on me health, time and means for reaching this spot, and the spirit to kindle at the spectacle before me!" His enthusiasm does not disturb his judgment, and he is nicely critical in a rather amusing fashion:

" . . . The view from the platform overhanging the Horseshoe Fall, when you look right down into the abyss, and are standing immediately over the descending water, is horrible. I do not think people would take any pleasure in being placed in this fearful position, unless others were looking on, or unless for the vain gratification of talking about it. . . . We crossed to the American side and took a bath, for there is not one on the Canada side. The ferryman told us of a gentleman who swam over three times. I felt less disposed than ever to quit this spot, so full of ever-increasing attraction. Were I an American, I would here strive to build me a summer residence. . . .

Timothy Flint, pioneer, missionary, author and editor, wrote at some length of Niagara Falls before he had seen them, in his "Geography and History," etc., and at length in various of his works after his visit in 1828. His biographer, John E. Kirkpatrick, says of that visit:

"He arrived at Niagara Falls at half past one at night. Instead of going to bed as his fellow passengers did, he spent the remainder of the clear moon-lit night viewing the Falls, a spectacle which it had been almost the first remembered wish of his heart to see. He saw it 'in a temperament, at a time and under circumstances just such' as he would have chosen. . . . He says:

"'He must have been obtuse of brain and of heart who could have thus contemplated this spectacle alone in this repose of nature, under the light of the moon, and the blue stars twinkling in the cloudless dome of the firmament, and not have thoughts which the poverty of language can never clothe in words.'"

The reader who seeks a detailed account of our region as it was in 1828, can hardly do better than to consult Flint's account of his visit, contained in his "Tour," first printed in the *Western Monthly Review* (Cincinnati, 1828), of which he was editor.

James T. Fields, in 1875, lectured in St. James Hall, Buffalo—where, by the way, Dickens read—and had a winter view of Niagara in a gale. In October, 1876, he was here again. "The scene at the Falls," he writes, "was never more impressive." On this visit, he sprained his ankle in Buffalo, and lectured sitting down. Samuel Bowles, for many years editor of the Springfield (Mass.) *Republican*, visited the Falls in 1854; the descriptive letters which he then wrote are to be found in his "Life and Times," by George S. Merriam. Chancellor James Kent visited the Falls as early as 1802; his "Memoirs and Letters," edited by his great-grandson, William Kent, contains the great jurist's impressions of Niagara. William Dean Howells has written much of Niagara, nowhere better than in "Niagara Revisited," first published in the *Atlantic Monthly*, May, 1883. It was reissued in Chicago the next year as an illustrated book, but owing to business complications the work was suppressed, very few copies ever getting into circulation, the result being that this little book is not only one of the rarest of Mr. Howells' works, but one of the rarest—and best—of Niagarana.

Notes of this sort could no doubt be much extended, but 1 forbear. Our review is far from exhaustive, and therein illustrates the observation that nothing bibliographical is, ever was or ever will be, complete. My object has been to show what attention the Niagara region has received from authors who have visited it. Numerous other authors I leave for mention in considering other aspects of our subject.

It should be noted, however, that our best modern writers of Niagara are no longer content merely to describe the scenery. That is used as the background against which are studied the fashions and foibles—the spirit—of the passing young man and woman. And this brings me to a consideration of our home region and its literature as utilized by the writers of fiction.

THE NIAGARA REGION IN FICTION

I HAVE sometimes thought it might not be wholly unprofitable to make a study of the fiction of our country, in its relation to history. From the earliest development of American literature, we have had the historical novel; not always so called, but still a thing easily recognized, in spite of its manifold forms. Cooper's tales, whatever else they may be as literature, are indubitably historical novels, for they present a fabric of fiction along with an attempt to portray, with some degree of fidelity, conditions and types which somewhere existed, and which characterized some period of American history.

Once, under a rash impulse, I undertook to compile a list of all novels that could be grouped according to definite periods in American history. My zeal soon abated, for I found, not only that the task, in its main outlines, had already been accomplished by expert library-workers, far better than I could hope to do it; but that there were serious difficulties in assigning certain works to any particular period. In the hands of the romancer, history ceases to be history.

My slight study of the subject discovered, among other things, that there is a tendency on the part of the storytellers to pick out the war periods for their fiction. Long lists may be made of novels dealing with the French and

Indian wars, the Revolution, the War of 1812, the Civil War; and in between these great epochs, lesser periods have their quota of fiction; for example, Shea's Rebellion in Massachusetts, the Patriot war on the New York and Canada border; the Fenian invasion, and many another episode. Every armed conflict in our history is made to figure in some work of fiction; for the story-teller—the soft-handed man of the pen—dearly loves (at his desk) the clash of steel and the smell of powder. The periods of peace have made little appeal to him. In a few instances, notably in the fiction of recent years, we have political strife substituted for warfare, or the strain and rivalry of athletic contest. There is significance, too, in the fact that many modern novels deal with attempts to get rich quickly, with financial and speculative adventures. Even the trashiest of these tales is historical in the sense that it reflects a taste and characteristic of the present day; but speaking broadly, if the *mise-en-scène* must be peaceful, the story-teller generally drops all attempt at an avowed historical setting, and is wholly occupied with a romance of his own devising.

The Niagara region, rich in its history, is by no means correspondingly rich in historical fiction. It would be strange indeed if the romantic actualities of this unique river had not appealed to those who invent romance; but the inadequacy of the fiction, in proportion to the fact, becomes more and more apparent as one studies it. It is true of fiction, as of poetry, that its quality is independent of the sublimity or beauty of natural scenery, or of the human crisis, which may have inspired it. As I have attempted to show in another study ("Niagara and the Poets") it is in the nature of things that a nameless brook should have its Tennyson, and a Niagara go unsung. As long as fiction is fiction, its highest quality must depend on the subjective treatment of human character. The physical setting is secondary.

Regarding as "Niagara region" the territory through which our river runs, and the adjacent regions which under historical or present conditions have become associated with it, we ask, How have the writers of romance enriched its literature?

The first period in our history—that of the occupancy of these lands by aborigines prior to the sway of the Iroquois, has been utilized by George Alfred Stringer in his tale "The King and the Cross," wherein conflicts between peoples more or less legendary—the so-called Eries or Neuters or Kah-quahs of whom history really knows nothing—are set down with the circumstantiality of yesterday's ball game.

The Indian and the missionary figure in countless tales. The earliest published romance of which I have knowledge relating to the Niagara region, deals with the period of French occupancy and may therefore stand next to "The King and the Cross" in our chronology. This is the "*Aventures du Sieur C. Le Beau, avocat en parlement, ou voyage curieux et nouveau, parmi les Sauvages de l'Amerique Septentrionale,*" etc., published in Amsterdam in 1738. So far as I am aware, this curious book has never been published in English. Under the guise of his own adventures, Le Beau indulges in extraordinary romancing. According to his own testimony this youth, a native of Rochelle, went to Paris in 1729, and in the same year was tempted from his legal studies into a voyage to Canada. Shipwrecked in the St. Lawrence, he reached Quebec in sad plight, June 18, 1729. Finding employment in the *bureau du castor* he made his home with the Recollect Fathers for more than a year, then ran away from sober pursuits, and with two Indians took to the woods. His narrative puts the time of his arrival at Niagara in June, 1731, and under sufficiently fantastic conditions. He was accompanied by his mistress, an Abenaki maiden, with whom he had exchanged clothes, resorting to this and other disguise to avoid arrest as a deserter by the French. He makes a long story of his encounter with soldiers at Fort Niagara, and of his final sanctuary in Seneca villages. Le Beau's book, despite its veracious air and accuracy on some points, is not history. It is therefore fiction. The author apparently came to Canada and had some experience among the Indians; and when he wrote his book, chose so to enlarge upon what he had really seen and experienced, still holding to a thread of fact, that the result has little interest as fiction, and no value whatever as history. Travelers who *will* write have been doing the same thing, from Le Beau's day to this.

There are many romances that deal with La Salle—all wretchedly cheap and tawdry in comparison with the actual romance of his life. William Dana Orcutt's book, "Robert Cavelier," is perhaps the latest attempt to utilize La Salle in fiction; but we can hardly rate it as a successful one.

And how ignorant—or incompetent—the story-writers are! They seek a picturesque, striking, gallant figure. La Salle is all that. They invent scenes and incidents utterly out of keeping with his character. And they one and all seem oblivious to the extraordinary fact, which history shows, that for some four years, in the very midst of his ardent and brilliant exploits, La Salle disappears, and of his whereabouts and his deeds in that time practically nothing is known. In September, 1669, La Salle parted from his companions, between the head of Lake Ontario—present Hamilton—and the Grand river. Their understanding was, that he would return to Montreal. But if he did, no record of it is known. He disappears; nor does he reappear, so far as trustworthy records show, until the autumn of 1674, when we find him reëmbarking for France. To be sure, Perrot's "Journal" says he was met, with a company of Indians, hunting far up the Ottawa. Others claim that he descended the Ohio, that he discovered the Mississippi, thus forestalling the claims of Joliet and Marquette. These conflicting claims, unsupported by credible documents, leave the matter wholly a mystery. For at least two of the four years which form a so strange hiatus in an otherwise glaringly-conspicuous career, there is a complete blank. What a splendid opportunity for invention—what a challenge to the romancer! Can it be that the story-tellers acknowledge their inability to invent a career for La Salle in 1670-71 which shall be consistent with the probabilities, and in keeping with his character? For the present we must leave it as one of the neglected opportunities in American fiction.

A rather recent book (1901), dealing cleverly with an early period, is Samuel Merwin's tale, "The Road to Frontenac." It weaves a romance into the known history of the Lake Ontario region in the time of Denonville, and touches upon that soldier's exploits among the Senecas and on the Niagara in 1687. But the interest centers at the other end of the lake, at old Fort Frontenac, now Kingston.

Of like character is Wm. R. A. Wilson's story, "A Rose of Normandy" (1903), in which he strives, not very successfully, to add to the romance with which history endows La Salle, Tonty, and their comrades. "A Daughter of New France," by Mary C. Crowley (1901), deals chiefly with Cadillac and the founding of Detroit, but relates somewhat to our region, and is written with most admirable knowledge of the history of the period. Here perhaps may be mentioned Mary Hartwell Catherwood's "The Story of Tonty," and William O. Stoddard's "On the Old Frontier."

A fair maid, a rough soldier, a few bloody deeds and tense adventures, and the inevitable outcome of a much-disturbed wooing—all told with singular affectation of supposed archaic speech—these are the essential and unvarying materials from which this kind of fiction is concocted.

James Fenimore Cooper must have recognition in our local fiction. "The Pathfinder," the sub-title of which is "The Inland Sea," is a tale of Lake Ontario during the old French war, with Niagara episodes. "The Spy," a part of which was written at Lewiston, is a tale of the Revolution, the scene of action being principally in Westchester county, but it includes an episode of the War of 1812 on the Niagara. In much the same way a very different sort of Niagara episode during the War of 1812 is introduced in Charles Lever's rollicking "Confessions of Harry Lorrequer."

The historical novels of Major John Richardson relate chiefly to the region of the Lakes, the Detroit, and, in less degree, to the Niagara. Born at Queenston in 1796, Richardson was truly a son of the Niagara region, though most of his life was spent away from it. In his "Eight Years in Canada" he gives us a touching account of his experiences and emotions on revisiting his old home on the Niagara, in 1838. His most famous novel, "Wacousta," is a tale of Pontiac's War. The Niagara region figures more in "The Canadian Brothers," first published in Montreal in 1840. One episode in it gives us the story of the battle of Queenston, and, naturally enough, there is a glorification of British arms. Seeking a wider market, Richardson republished this story in New York, changing the title to "Matilda Montgomerie," and leaving out the Queenston episode—a pitiable subversion of the dignity of authorship to the needs of the author. The theory of course was that citizens of the United States would not buy a story that sympathized with the triumph of the British at Queenston. We are all quite as absurd in some of our "theories" and prejudices, today.

In "Matilda Montgomerie" a chapter or so is devoted to adventures in the vicinity of Buffalo—which *Sambo,* one of the characters, calls "Bubbalo town." Although Richardson is praised for the excellence of his style, no one not imbued with the antiquarian taste, is likely to be attracted to his pages.

Our region has not been wholly overlooked by the dramatists. The old French tragedy of " *Hirza*" opens at Niagara Falls. I regret that I cannot name the author, nor, with precision, the date of production. Written in the stately verse of Racine, it belongs alike to the fiction and the poetry of our region:

> "Triste Niagara, séjour craint de nos Dieux;
> Rocs menaçants, et vous, ô torrents furieux,
> Qui, des monts inégaux couvrant les vastes cimes,
> Tombez en mugissant d'abîmes en abîmes,
> Devant vous fut brisé le calumet, de paix"; etc.

It deals with the wars of the Iroquois and the Illinois, and with the armed encroachments of the French and English; and in its heroics and grandiloquence is about as far as possible from a true depiction of the American aborigine.

More than one drama has been written—and acted—the scene of which was at least in part at Niagara. Of this class was "The Battle of Chippewa," which a traveling Buffalonian saw enacted at New Orleans in 1822. Still another, "A Trip to Niagara," etc., a three-act farce, was written in 1830 for the Bowery Theater, New York, by William Dunlap, dramatist, lecturer, historian, portrait painter and founder of the National Academy of Design. "A Trip to Niagara" brings the characters to Buffalo, where one of them, an Englishman, exclaims: "So, this is Buffalo! And I'm on the shores of Lake Erie! And what do I see after all: A town like other towns, water like other water, and people like other people—only made worse by democracy. I have not seen a well-behaved man since I came into the country, only a wild half Indian." There is a scene at a Buffalo hotel, and another at the Falls, where Cooper's *Leather-Stocking* soliloquizes: "This looks as it used to do, they can't spoil this, yet a while." To judge from the printed play, "A Trip to Niagara," was a tame entertainment, even when helped out, as it no doubt was, with as effective a display of scenery as the artist-author could devise.

Here, too, should have mention *"La Catarata del Niagara,"* a three-act drama, in verse, by Don Vicente Riva Palacio, perhaps in collaboration with Don Juan A. Mateos. It is contained in the joint publication of their dramatic works, issued in Mexico City, 1871. The first and second acts are set in Mexico, in the house of one *Doña Rosa;* the third act shifts to Niagara, the time being 1847.

A considerable shelf, perhaps five feet long, could be filled with stories of the War of 1812. My studies of American history have well nigh convinced me that that war was fought, not to maintain our rights on the high seas, but to stimulate the development of American letters by supplying picturesque material for budding romancers. The only drawback to that theory is that the straightforward unadorned record of the old sea duels, like that of the Constitution and the Guerrière, has more thrills in it than the romancers can invent. But for well-nigh a century, the novelists have hovered about this period, like bumble-bees in a field of clover. The war on the Lakes and the Niagara frontier has had a share of their attention. There are boys' books with Perry for hero—always with the introduction of things more or less impossible to the character. The events of 1812-'14 on the Niagara have been much used by Canadian story-writers. There is "Hemlock," by Robert Sellars (Montreal, 1890), which follows many of the events of the war in our district, and is none the less worthy because its point of view and sympathies are so notably Canadian. A work of greater merit is "Neville Trueman, the Pioneer Preacher, a Tale of 1812," by W. H. Withrow, published in Toronto in 1886. The fictitious characters mingle with the real, at Queenston Heights, Fort George, the burning of Niagara, Chippewa and Lundy's Lane. It is a simple tale, with no affectations; and it makes a record which we are glad to have of high character and worthy impulses. There were true patriots in Canada in those days, and it is wholesome to read of them, no matter on which side of the river one may live. In this class belongs Amy E. Blanchard's tale, "A Loyal Lass, a Story of the Niagara Campaign of 1814." The list might be much extended.

There is a considerable group of books, mostly by British writers, which should have place in our review. In the guise of fiction, they chronicle the condition of things in Upper Canada and the Niagara District, during the early years of settlement. Such a work is John Galt's three-volume novel, "Bogle Corbet, or the Emigrants," published in London in 1831. I believe too that "Laurie Todd," Galt's most famous novel, touches more or less the Niagara neighborhood.

The exploits of the Patriot War on this border, as told by most historians, certainly contain much fiction, for no two chroniclers agree. I recall however but one avowed romance with that affair as its theme—"The Prisoner of the Border, a Tale of 1838," by P. Hamilton Myers. Half a century ago, when this story was published, Myers had great vogue and his stories were popular.

There are many novels which touch this region in some degree. H. A. Stanley's stirring tale, "The Backwoodsman," is a pretty successful treatment of the old New York frontier during the Revolution, and deals with Indians and white men who belong to our local history. Judge Tourgee's "Button's Inn" is a tale of the old Chautauqua portage. C. R. Edwards' "Story of Niagara," published nearly forty years ago, is an attempt to put into fiction some of the frontier smuggling experiences; and "Where Waters Beckon," by Joanna E. Wood (1902), is a sickly sentimental offering, dealing with so-called love, soul-affinities, a retreat in the woods of Foster's Flats, otherwise Niagara Glen, and a few suicides. It is a story of Buffalo as well as of Niagara, but we can make no boast on that. The tragic story of Francis Abbott, a recluse who lived for a time on one of the islands above the Falls, and was drowned in 1829, has been written, not only by James Bird, in a trustworthy narrative, but also by "the author of 'Mettallak,'" as a work of fiction founded on fact," entitled "Francis Abbott, or the Hermit of Niagara, a Tale of the Old and New World." (Boston, 1846.)

Even the Erie Canal has its romances. If I remember aright, some of J. T. Trowbridge's juvenile tales deal with his own youthful experiences on the canal in Western New York. But the classic in this field is perhaps "Marco Paul's voyages and travels on the Erie Canal" (New York, 1852), one of Jacob Abbott's once popular series of juveniles, of a sort long out of favor; yet it would be hard to find a more vivid account of packet-boat travel on the Erie canal than is given in this quaint little volume.

A noteworthy romance of our region is *"La Virgen del Niagara,"* by Jose Rivera y Rio, published, an octavo of 592 pages!—in Mexico in 1871. Well known are Mrs. Julia Ditto Young's tale, "Adrift, a story of Niagara," published in 1889; and Mrs. Linda de K. Fulton's "Nadia, the Maid of the Mist," also a story of Niagara published in 1901. Israel Zangwill's volume of "Ghetto Tragedies," "They that Walk in Darkness," contains "Noah's Ark" (first published in *Lippincott's*), a story into which are woven, for the most part with a fair degree of accuracy, the principal facts regarding Major Mordecai Manuel Noah's proposed City of Refuge for Jews on Grand Island. E. W. Thomson's "John Bedell, U. E. Loyalist," is a slight story, the scene being laid on the Niagara.

Of juveniles which touch our region, or have their scenes largely laid hereabouts, there are many. There is "Emily and Clara's Trip to Niagara Falls," by the editor of *"The Youth's Casket,"* the story being published in Buffalo in 1864. Of wider fame was "The Rapids of Niagara," a duodecimo of 436 pages, by Susan Warner, author of "The Wide Wide World," a famous old story in its day. "The Rapids of Niagara," of the goody-goody variety, is volume six in Miss Warner's "Say and Do series." She brings her characters to Niagara, and embellishes the highly moral tale with a full-page view of the falls.

Of a more virile sort are several boys' books of recent years. I note Edward Stratemeyer's "Marching on Niagara, or the Soldier Boys of the Old Frontier"; several of the books in Everett T. Tomlinson's "War of 1812" series; "Oliver Optic's" "Out West, or Roughing it on the Great Lakes," "Through by Daylight, or the Young Engineer of the Lake Shore Railroad," etc., etc. Some of the old-time "yellow-covered literature"—the dime novels of our boyhood—were of this class. In later years the limit was perhaps reached in "The Adventures of Uncle Jeremiah and Family at the Pan-American Exposition," by "Paul Pry, Jr.," which delectable creation of the literary art opens with the cheerful slogan, "Put me off at Buffalo!"

Of short stories, with the scene laid at the Falls or on Lake Erie, there are so many that I make no attempt to enumerate them. I must, too, ignore in this review the considerable number of "Indian legends," mostly invented by writers of Caucasian blood, who have thought the great cataract a fit place for "legends," and have concocted them to meet the supposed demand. One of the latest and best productions of this character is a dainty little volume by Paul Carus: "The Chief's Daughter, a legend of Niagara" (Chicago, 1901).

One of the most extraordinary works of fiction I have ever seen, "The Canadian Girl, or the Pirate of the Lakes, a Story of the Affections, by the Authoress of 'The Jew's Daughter,'" was published in London, with steel-plate engravings, in 1838. In its pages may be found all the emotions, all the virtues, and especially all the vices, iniquities and atrocities of evil, known to man. The *Pirate* was a bad man, as no doubt a good pirate should be, but he always talked—I mean, conversed—in the polished English of Pope and Addison. I despair of giving any idea of the plot, short of quoting the whole book, and as it has 716 pages, that might disturb my own book-making plans. I can merely call attention to certain passages which make "The Canadian Girl" a part of our local literature.

It is edifying to read, of the Niagara, that "the country through which the river flows is more populous, and in a higher state of cultivation, than any other part of North America. Its wild fruits are abundant, and of the rarest and finest sorts, and the salubrious nature of the climate is seen in the healthy countenances of the inhabitants." This is truly gratifying to local pride, though we remember that Audubon thought the people hereabouts "lank and sallow." Some pages of scenic description are offered, punctuated with the emotions of the characters in the story. Of *Lady Hester,* for example, we are assured that at Niagara Falls,

"her eye scarce knew where to rest—she was astounded. The gigantic liquid sheet of emerald and of silver, 'horribly beautiful!'—its semicircular front, nearly three-quarters of a mile broad, grandly shrouded by revolving columns of mist that rose perpetually from the thundering gulf—inspired her with sublime admiration."

Lady Hester spreads her surprise and admiration over several pages; while *Letitia,* the fair and tender *Letitia,*

"after the first surprise and enchantment had a little subsided in her youthful breast, was eminently pleased with the sight of thousands of water-fowl, who, coming from northern lands in search of a milder climate, swam, or flew on whistling wings a little over, the Niagara river to the brink of the Falls, there advancing in the air about the mists fronting the stupendous sheet of water, and lingering in the neighborhood with evident joy and wonder; ducks of many species, the teal, the widgeon, the shallard, and the swan, were among these migratory birds. . . . Frequently were some of the interesting creatures borne down by the glassy current into the gulf and drowned. Letitia particularly grieved for two noble swans, which came on boldly past Goat Island, then became entangled in the confused and dashing waves of the rapids, and were presently precipitated together over the precipice. She was in tears, but a fresh succession of novel objects rendered her regret no more than momentary."

"The *Earl*, who had little relish for the sublimities of nature, had chiefly interested himself with calculating the altitude of the two cataracts and their curvilinear length, and coming to the conclusion that these great falls were not so large as many others in different parts of the world, he decided that they had no particular claim to praise"—a highly original conclusion. The geographical knowledge shown by our author is full of surprising revelations. For example, note this passage:

"The strong steamer, in which were the pursuers of the Pirate, had been all this time beating about Lake Erie, it having been supposed that he was hiding about some of the promontories on the coast, which indeed was really the case. The Fearless [the pirate craft] moved only by night on the lake. . . . But now the hunted vessel had been driven near the mouth of the lake, where the American beach was extremely wild, presenting a dark and gloomy picture; huge black rocks, like the shattered ruins of a sterile world, lay scattered in naked majesty many successive miles along the side of the lake, whose waters rushed in between them, and lashed their barren sides with furious and unceasing roar. Behind, was spread a country no less wild and stern."

This, the reader is reminded, is a description of the shore in the vicinity of Buffalo; dost recognize the portrait?

Not long ago, on a book-hunting excursion, I lighted on what I am inclined to hold as the gem of all Niagara region fiction—a trim little book of the old-fashioned demi-octavo size—just right for the coat pocket—bound in shabby leather, and printed at Exeter—I don't know what Exeter—in 1831, with this title: "Tonnewonte, or The Adopted Son of America. A tale, containing scenes from Real Life, by an American." Soon after, I ran across an earlier, very likely the original, edition, printed at Watertown, N. Y., in

1825. Here is one of the very rare local Americana, which, for many years, I had never so much as heard of; then, in widely different places, within a few months of each other, I find two different editions! So it goes in this sport of book-hunting.

Would that I knew the identity of "An American," that I might hang a lasting wreath on her—I'm sure it's her—tombstone. The English is of the dear old style, in which all the characters converse under all circumstances in finished phrases of perfect propriety. In these pages the sun never sets; but frequently "the fiery luminary sinks beneath the western horizon." A character is introduced, not after drinking tea, but "after partaking the refreshing beverage imported through such perils from the East, that herb so famous in the annals of American independence." There you have a fine literary way of saying tea.

The story opens in New York City in the autumn of 1776 with an incident of the yellow fever scourge of that year. A French child, bereft and abandoned, becomes the *protégé* of an American family who, after various domestic adventures of no consequence, migrate in 1807 into the valley of the Tonawanda in Western New York. There is something of worth in the story of this migration; the author evidently follows in some essentials the actual experiences of families known to him—or her. Beyond Utica—"an inconsiderable village"—"the road began to grow wild indeed! It was cut through the wilderness, while on each side of them arose in sombre majesty the immense trees of the forest, some of which had probably been growing since the first subsiding of the deluge." They fall in with an Irish pedlar—or, to be more faithful to our author's style, "a pedlar whose brogue declared him a native of Hibernia"—who being on his way to Buffalo, undertakes to help them on their road to Tonnewante. In the new home, crude frontier conditions become well nigh idyllic. The hero, the French foundling of early years, *Theodore de Clermont* (there's a Tonawanda name for you!) just naturally falls in love with the forest flower, *Evelina*. Although the author does not speak of her as a young woman, but as an amiable female or lovely being, she was, I think, the *bona-fide* "Sweet Evelina" for whom in youthful days we have all declared, in more or less mellifluous accents, that our love would never-never-die. But alas! just as the love of *Theodore* and *Evelina* seeems about to be consummated, Theo's long-lost father arrives, *en tour* to Niagara, and the young man is taken back to France. There he struggles on through a hundred pages all cluttered up with marquises, counts and viscounts, estates lost and regained, and especially tangled with the ensnaring wiles of *Mademoiselle Sophia des Abbayes*. It does look for a few chapters as though this lovely female would make a Tonawanda old maid out of *Evelina;* but the author knew all along that the noble *Theodore de Clermont* would renounce lands and ladies, and returning to Tonawanda, after a few adventures, say to *Evelina,* as he takes her hand: "Could I but be assured of possessing this, with the approbation and blessing of our indulgent father, earth, I would not envy thee, all thou hadst else to bestow." He says a page or two more in the same pure Tonawanda dialect, and *Evelina* melts into his embrace. The historical character of the romance is maintained, in the last chapter, by the statement that "the execution of the proposed canal has greatly enhanced the value of their property, and *Mr. de Clermont* is not only one of the happiest men in the State of New York, but bids fair also to be one of the wealthiest landholders in the Union." A beautiful touch appears on the last page, where we read that

THE NIAGARA REGION IN FICTION. 93

"Col. de Clermont is thought of as a candidate for Congress." Could anything, in history or fiction, be more American!

It was Frank Norris, you may remember, who in the opening paragraph of his story, "The House with the Blinds," wrote that some cities were places where things could happen—"cities that have come to be picturesque—that offer opportunities in the matter of background and local color." In his view, "there are just three big cities in the United States that are story cities"—New York, of course, New Orleans, and, best of the lot, San Francisco. "Fancy a novel," he adds, "about Chicago, or Buffalo, let us say, or Nashville, Tennessee." And do you remember how "O. Henry," happiest of modern short story-writers, "took him up," and wrote a splendid story of Nashville, exclaiming at the end of it, as by way of challenge: "Has anything happened at Buffalo?" Oh, for an "O. Henry," or a Frank Norris, to make them happen. That Norris later wrote a very famous novel—"The Pit"—about Chicago, is ground for encouragement that even Buffalo may yet inspire the romancer—or rather, let us say, may furnish the not wholly unromantic setting for the story-teller who brings his inspiration to bear upon Buffalo.

This city is indeed not wholly barren in romance. If I remember rightly, Elbert Hubbard made it the scene of his early story, "The Man," and made Police Justice King, under thin disguise, a character in it. Robert Barr's story of the Fenian invasion of Canada in 1866, "In the Midst of Alarms," opens "in the marble-floored vestibule of the Metropolitan Grand Hotel in Buffalo." An early novel on the same theme, and one of some historical value, is "Ridgway," by *"Scian Dubh,"* the *nom-de-plume* I believe of a Buffalo Irishman named McCarroll. "Ridgway," which was published in this city in 1868, is genuinely a Buffalo book; and although no high quality can be claimed for it as a romance, it has the great excellence of fidelity to the spirit and temper of the time with which it is concerned.

Were I asked to give precedence to any one work of fiction dealing with the Niagara region I should think first of Chateaubriand's *"Atala."* Artificial to the last degree, opposed to every tenet of the realistic school, no more resembling fact than moonlight resembles the day, it is none the less a vivid poetic masterpiece. But with *"Atala"* aside, I should come down to very modern days, and hesitate between "Their Pilgrimage," by Charles Dudley Warner, and "Their Wedding Journey," by William Dean Howells. Mark Twain's remarkable contribution to Niagara literature—the "First Authentic Mention of Niagara Falls," being extracts from Adam's Diary—I am not forgetting, but I am willing to. But both Warner and Howells are a delight. Both employ the same method—they use the Niagara setting as a background upon which they study the foibles and characteristics of everyday people. And see how Warner vividly pictures the scene, but all incidentally, as a background for the romance of his lovers:

"When they returned the moon was coming up, rising and struggling and making its way slowly through ragged masses of colored clouds. The river could be plainly seen now, smooth, deep, treacherous; the falls on the American side showed fitfully like patches of light and foam; the Horseshoe, mostly hidden by a cold silver mist, occasionally loomed up a white and ghostly mass. They stood for a long time looking down at the foot of the American Fall, the moon now showing clearly the plunge of the heavy column—a column as stiff as if it were melted silver—hushed and frightened by the weird and appalling scene. They did not know at that moment that there where their eyes were riveted, there at the base of the fall, a man's body was churning about, plunged down and cast up, and beaten and whirled, imprisoned in the refluent eddy. But a body was there. In the morning a man's overcoat was found on the parapet at the angle of the fall. Some of them remembered that in the evening, just before the park gate closed, he had seen a man approach the angle of the wall where the overcoat was found. The man was never seen after that. Night first, and then the hungry water, swallowed him. One pictures the fearful leap into the dark, the midway repentance, perhaps, the despair of the plunge. A body cast in here is likely to tarry for days, eddying round and round, and tossed in that terrible maelstrom, before a chance current ejects it, and sends it down the fierce rapids below.

"The walk around Goat Island is probably unsurpassed in the world for wonder and beauty. The Americans have every reason to be satisfied with their share of the fall; they get nowhere one single grand view like that from the Canada side, but infinitely the deepest impression of majesty and power is obtained on Goat Island. There the spectator is in the midst of the war of nature. From the point over the Horseshoe Fall our friends, speaking not much, but more and more deeply moved, strolled along in the lovely forest, in a rural solemnity, in a local calm, almost a seclusion, except for the ever-present shuddering roar in the air. On the shore above the Horseshoe they first comprehended the breadth, the great sweep, of the rapids. The white crests of the waves in the west were coming out from under a black, lowering sky; all the foreground was in bright sunlight, dancing, sparkling, leaping, hurrying on, converging to the angle where the water becomes a deep emerald at the break and plunge. The rapids above are a series of shelves, bristling with jutting rocks and lodged trunks of trees, and the wildness of the scene is intensified by the ragged fringe of evergreens on the opposite shore. Over the whole island the mist, rising from the caldron, drifts in spray when the wind is favorable; but on this day the forest was bright and cheerful, and as the strollers went farther away from the Great Fall, the beauty of the scene began to steal away its terror. The roar was still dominant, but far off and softened, and did not crush the ear. The triple islands, the Three Sisters, in their picturesque wildness appeared like playful freaks of nature in a momentary relaxation of the savage mood. Here is the finest view of the river; to one standing on the outermost island the great flood seems tumbling out of the sky. They continued along the bank of the river. The shallow stream races by headlong, but close to the edge are numerous eddies, and places where one might step in and not be swept away. At length they reached the point where the river divides, and the water stands for an instant almost still, hesitating whether to take the Canadian or American plunge. Out a little way from the shore the waves leap and tumble, and the two currents are like race-horses parted on two ways to the goal. Just at this point the water swirls and lingers, having lost all its fierceness and haste, and spreads itself out placidly, dimpling in the sun. It may be a treacherous pause, this water may be as cruel as that which rages below and exults in catching a boat or a man and bounding with the victim over the cataract; but the calm was very grateful to the stunned and buffeted visitors; upon their jarred nerves it was like the peace of God."

In the work of both Howells and Warner, the poet, the artist and the humorist always contend, and the outcome is not merely vivid word-painting, but a just and genial philosophy. I find nothing worthier in the fiction of our region.

A DREAMER AT NIAGARA

IN 1791 a young Frenchman landed at Baltimore, hastened by stage over a bad, newly-made road to Philadelphia, and sojourned a week at an inn, awaiting the return to the capital of General Washington. The President returned.

"I saw him go past in a carriage drawn by four prancing horses, driven four-in-hand. Washington, according to my then ideas, was necessarily Cincinnatus; Cincinnatus in a chariot somewhat upset my republic of 296 B. C. Could Washington the Dictator be anything save a boor, driving his oxen with a goad, and holding the tail of his plough? But when I went to carry my letter of recommendation to him, I found once more the simplicity of the ancient Roman.

"A small house, resembling the neighboring houses, was the palace of the President of the United States; no sentries, no footmen even. I knocked, and a young maid-servant opened the door. I asked if the general was at home; she replied that he was in. The servant asked my name, which is difficult to pronounce in English, and which she could not remember. She then said softly, 'Walk in, sir,' and led the way down one of those narrow passages which serve as an entrance hall to English houses; she showed me into a parlor where she asked me to wait until the general came.

"I felt no agitation; greatness of mind or fortune in no way overawe me; I admire the first without being crushed by it; the second calls forth my pity rather than my respect; no man's countenance will ever disconcert me.

"After a few minutes the general entered the room; tall in stature, of a calm and cold rather than a noble bearing, he resembled his engraved portraits. I handed him my letter in silence; he opened it and glanced at the signature which he read aloud, exclaiming:

"'Colonel Armand!'"

"This was the name by which he knew the Marquis de La Rouërie and by which the latter had signed himself.

"We sat down. I explained to him as best I could the object of my journey. He replied in monosyllables in English and French, and listened to me with a sort of astonishment. I remarked this, and said to him, with some little animation:

"'But it is less difficult to discover the Northwest Passage than to create a people, as you have done.'

"'Well, well, young man!' he exclaimed, giving me his hand.

"He invited me to dinner for the next day, and we parted."

This youth was François Auguste, vicomte de Chateaubriand, scion of an old family in decadence. The French Revolution completed the wreck. Chateaubriand, who had held a commission in the French army since 1788, found himself in the spring of 1791, ready for any adventure that would take him out of France. Being of a poetic mind, he decided to discover the Northwest Passage. Nothing could be more delightful than the naïveté with which he planned to accomplish the impossible: "I proposed to travel westward, so as to strike the northwest coast of America above the Gulf of California; from there, following the outline of the continent, and always keeping the sea in sight, I intended to explore Behring's Straits, double the northernmost cape of America, descend on the east along the shores of the Arctic Ocean, and return to the United States by way of Hudson's Bay, Labrador and Canada." From this it will be seen that Chateaubriand was not only the Prince of Dreamers, but still very young. What wonder that Washington, remembering his own frontier campaigns of forty years before, should have looked upon this youth of 21, innocent of any knowledge whatever of America, with amazement.

Our hero ate his dinner, as appointed, with the President; and a few days later journeyed up to Albany, still thinking of the Northwest Passage. "What means had I," he afterwards wrote, "to carry out this prodigious peregrination? None at all. Most of the French travellers have been isolated men, left entirely to their own resources; it is but rarely that the Government or any company has employed them. Mackenzie and many others after him have to the profit of the United States and Great Britain, made conquests upon the immensity of America, with which I had dreamed of aggrandizing my native land. In case of success, I should have had the honor of bestowing French names upon unknown regions, of endowing my country with a colony upon the Pacific Ocean, of taking away the rich fur-trade from a rival Power, and of preventing that Power from opening out a shorter road to the Indies, by placing France herself in possession of that road."

He was still dreaming of the Northwest Passage when the Hudson-river packet finally set him down at Albany. There he hunted up a veteran fur-trader, Swift by name; to whom, as to Washington, the scheme of conquest was explained. Mr. Swift, as gently as a trader could, meanwhile thinking no doubt that the youth was a crazy fool, made what Chateaubriand calls "some very reasonable objections." "He told me that I could not undertake a journey of this importance at first sight alone, without assistance, without support, without letters of recommendation to the English, American and Spanish stations by which I should be obliged to pass; that if I had the good fortune to cross so many solitary tracts of country, I should arrive at frozen regions where I should perish of hunger. He advised me to begin by acclimatizing myself, suggested that I should learn the Sioux, Iroquois and Esquimaux languages, and live among the *coureurs* and the agents of the Hudson's Bay Company. Having gained this preliminary experience, I might then, in four or five years, with the assistance of the French Government, proceed on my hazardous mission."

This advice, which we must admit seems sound, Chateaubriand says annoyed him. "Had I trusted to my own judgment, I should have set out then and there to go to the Pole, as I might go from Paris to Pointoise." He concealed his vexation, hired a Dutch guide and two horses, and still nursing a secret purpose to arrive at the Pole and amaze the world, he set out for Niagara Falls.

In a general survey of the tourist literature of our region, and of the travellers who have made it, I have yielded to the temptation to linger a little over this journey of Chateaubriand. He saw things none saw before, nor have they been recorded since. In the Onondaga country he saw "false ebony-trees" and heard the "cuckoo of the Carolinas"—this was perhaps the catbird. It is related of him that on one occasion he landed from a boat on Lake Ontario, and ran into the woods to enjoy the luxury of the wild unstinted freedom of Nature in all her glory of forest and flowers; and in the ecstacy of excitement, he was hugging the trees, he tells us, when he heard a loud and rumbling roar, which alarmed and brought his mind back to earth from elysium, and caused him to run to his comrades in the boat to see what was the matter; but the alarm, he said, had been causeless; *"it was only the tide coming in!"*

A DREAMER AT NIAGARA.

In his romance of *"Atala"* Chateaubriand introduces an episode at the Falls of Niagara, in which one reads: "Pines, wild walnut trees, rocks of the most fantastic shapes, adorn the scene; eagles, borne away by the current of air, descend whirling round to the bottom of the gulf; and carcajous, suspended by their long tails from the extremities of the declining branches, watch to seize on the bodies of elks and bears floating in the abyss." Who among us has seen the carcajou—elsewhere we learn it is the "spotted carcajou"—hanging by his tail among the other wonders of Niagara?

The whole of his narrative of the visit to Niagara is too long to introduce here. The following extracts will afford some idea of his adventures, of the poesy with which his mind endowed even commonplace things, and of the rhythmic charm of his diction, which survives a translation into English:

"We rode towards Niagara. When we had come a distance of eight or nine leagues of our destination, we perceived, in an oak grove, the camp-fire of some savages, who had settled down on the bank of a stream where we ourselves were thinking of bivouacking. We took advantage of their preparations: after grooming our horses and dressing ourselves for the night, we accosted the band. With legs crossed tailor-wise, we sat down among the Indians around the blazing pile, and began to roast our maize cakes.

"The family consisted of two women, two infants at the breast, and three braves. The conversation became general, that is to say, interspersed with a few words on my side, and many gestures; after that, each fell asleep in the place where he sat. I alone remained awake, and went to sit by myself on a root trailing by the bank of the stream.

"The moon showed above the tops of the trees; a balmy breeze, which the Queen of the Night brought with her from the East, seemed to go before her through the forests, as though it were her cool breath. The solitary luminary climbed higher and higher in the sky, now pursuing her even way, again surmounting clusters of clouds, which resembled the summits of a snow-clad mountain chain. All would have been silence and repose, but for the fall of a few leaves, the passing of a sudden gust of wind, the hooting of the wood-owl; in the distance was heard the dull roar of the Falls of Niagara, which, in the calm of night, extended from waste to waste and expired in the lonely forests. It was during those nights that an unknown muse appeared to me; I gathered some of her accents; I marked them on my tables, by the light of the stars, as a vulgar musician might write down the notes dictated to him by some great master of harmony.

"The next day, the Indians armed themselves, the women collected the baggage. I distributed a little gunpowder and vermillion among my hosts. We parted, touching our foreheads and breasts; the braves shouted the order to march, and walked in front; the women went behind, carrying the children, who, slung in furs on their mothers' backs, turned their heads to look at us. I followed this progress with my eyes until the whole band had disappeared among the trees of the forest.

"The savages of the Falls of Niagara in the English dominion were entrusted with the police service of the frontier on that side. This outlandish constabulary, armed with bows and arrows, prevented our passage. I was obliged to send the Dutchman to the fort of Niagara for a permit to enter the territory of the British government. This saddened my heart a little, for I remembered that formerly France had ruled in both Upper and Lower Canada. My guide returned with the permit: I still have it; it is signed, 'Captain Gordan.' . . .

"I stayed two days in the Indian village. . . . The Indian women busied themselves with different occupations; their nurslings were slung in nets from the branches of a tall purple beech. The grass was covered with dew, the wind issued all perfumed from the woods, and the cottonplants of the country, throwing back their capsules, looked like white rose-trees. The breeze rocked the cradles in mid-air with an almost imperceptible movement; the mothers stood up from time to time to see if their children were asleep and had not been awakened by the birds.

"From the Indian village to the cataract was some three or four leagues: it took my guide and me as many hours to reach it. Already at six miles distance, a column of vapour indicated the situation of the weir to my eyes. My heart beat with joy mingled with terror, as I entered the wood that concealed from my view one of the grandest spectacles which nature has offered to mankind. . . .

"We dismounted. Leading our horses by the bridle, we passed through heaths and thickets until we came to the bank of the Niagara river, seven or eight hundred paces above the falls. As I never ceased going forward, the guide caught me by the arm; he stopped me on the very edge of the water, which passed with the swiftness of an arrow. It did not seethe, but glided in one sole mass to the slope of the rock; its silence before its fall contrasted with the uproar of the fall itself. The Scriptures often compare a people to the mighty waters; here it was a dying people which, deprived of its voice by the agony of death, went to hurl itself into the abyss of eternity.

"The guide continued to hold me back, for I felt, so to speak, drawn on by the stream, and I had an involuntary longing to fling myself in. At one time, I would turn my eyes up the river, to the banks; at another, down to the island which divided the waters. Here the waters suddenly failed, as though cut off in the sky.

"After a quarter of an hour of vague and perplexed admiration, I went on to the falls. The reader will find in the *'Essai sur les révolutions'* and in *'Atala'* the two descriptions which I have written of the scene. Today, high-roads run to the cataract; there are inns on the American side, and mills and factories overhang the chasm.

"I was unable to utter the thoughts that stirred me at the sight of so sublime a disorder. In the desert of my early life, I was obliged to invent persons to adorn it; I drew from my own substance beings whom I did not find elsewhere, and whom I carried within myself. In the same way, I have placed memories of *Atala* and *René* on the edge of the cataract of Niagara, as the expression of its sadness. What meaning has a cascade which falls eternally in the unfeeling sight of heaven and earth, if human nature be not there, with its destinies and its misfortunes? To be steeped in this solitude of water and mountains and not to know with whom to speak of that great spectacle! To have the waves, the rocks, the woods, the torrents to one's self alone! Give the soul a companion, and the smiling verdure of the hill-slopes, the cool breath of the water, will all turn into charm: the journey by day, the sweetest repose at the end of the day's march, the gliding over the billows, the sleeping upon the moss, will call forth from the heart its deepest tenderness. I have seated *Velléda* upon the shores of Armorica, *Cymodocea* beneath the porticos of Athens, *Blanca* in the halls of the Alhambra. Alexander created towns wherever he hastened: I have left dreams behind me wherever I have dragged my life.

"I have seen the cascades of the Alps with their chamois and those of the Pyrenees with their lizards; I did not go sufficiently high up the Nile to meet its cataracts, which are reduced to rapids; I will not speak of the azure zones of Terni or of Tivoli, graceful fragments of ruins or subjects for the poet's song:

'Et praeceps Anio ac Tiburni lucus.'

"Niagara eclipses everything. I gazed upon the cataract the existence of which was revealed to the old world, not by puny travelers like myself, but by missionaries who, seeking solitude for the love of God, flung themselves upon their knees at the sight of some marvel of nature and received martyrdom while completing their hymn of admiration. Our priests greeted the fine sights of America and consecrated them with their blood; our soldiers clapped their hands at the ruins of Thebes and presented arms to Andalusia: the whole genius of France lies in the double army of our camps and our altars.

"I was holding my horse's bridle twisted round my arm; a rattlesnake came and rustled in the bushes. The startled horse reared and backed towards the falls. I was unable to release my arm from the reins; the horse, still more terrified, was dragging me after it. Already its fore-feet were off the ground; cowering over the edge of the abyss, it maintained its position only by the strength of its loins. It was all up with me, when the animal, itself astonished at its fresh peril, gave a sudden turn and vaulted inwards. Had my soul left my body amidst the Canadian woods, would it have carried to the Supreme Tribunal the sacrifices, the good works, the virtues of the Pères Jogues and Lallemant, or empty days and wretched idle fancies?

"This was not the only danger I encountered at Niagara. A ladder of creepers was used by the savages to climb down to the lower basin; it was at that time broken. Wishing to see the falls from below, I ventured, in the face of my guide's representations, down the side of an almost perpendicular rock. In spite of the roar of the water which seethed below me, I kept my head and climbed down to within forty feet of the bottom. When I had reached so far, the bare and vertical rock gave me nothing to lay hold of; I was left hanging by one hand to the last root, feeling my fingers open beneath the weight of my body; few men have spent two such minutes, as I counted them. My tired hand let go; I fell. By an unparalleled stroke of good fortune, I found myself upon the pointed back of a rock upon which I ought to have been smashed into a thousand pieces, and yet I felt no great hurt; I was at half a foot from the abyss and had not rolled into it; but when the cold and the damp began to penetrate me, I saw that I had not come off so cheaply; my left arm was broken above the elbow. The guide, who was watching me from above and saw my signals of distress, ran off to fetch some savages. They hoisted me with ropes along an otter's path, and carried me to their village. I had only a simple fracture: two splints, a bandage and a sling were enough to effect my cure. I stayed twelve days with my surgeons, the Niagara

Indians. I saw tribes pass which had come down from Detroit or from the districts lying south and east of Lake Erie. I enquired into their usages. . . . I wished to hear my hosts' songs. A little Indian girl of fourteen, called Mila, and very pretty (the Indian women are pretty only at that age), sang something very pleasant. . . .

"The tribe of the little girl with the bead departed; my guide, the Dutchman, refused to accompany me beyond the cataract; I paid him and joined a party of traders who were leaving to go down the Ohio; before setting out, I took a glance at the Canadian lakes."

It is not my present purpose to touch upon Chateaubriand's subsequent adventures in America. According to his own account—repeated with some variation in his various works—he traveled from Niagara to Pittsburgh, thence went down the Ohio and Mississippi to Natchez, with more or less vague wanderings into Florida. Returning north by way of Knoxville, he sailed the 10th of December, arriving again in France January 2, 1792.

Do you ask: "What of it?" Merely this: That there now has come along one of these mousing, burrowing, insistent literary gentlemen, who has scheduled Chateaubriand's dates, mapped his alleged route, hunted out the circumstances of his interviews and visits and adventures, and finally through the respectable medium of the *Revue d'Histoire littèraire de la France,* declares with convincing circumstantiality that the distinguished author of *"Atala"* and *"René"* and *"Mémoires d'Outre-Tombe"* and above all of the *"Voyage en Amérique,"* could not by any possibility have made the American travels he claims to have made. This merciless searcher after facts, M. Joseph Bédiér, shows that it is extremely doubtful if Chateaubriand ever was received by Washington, and that it is quite certain that he did not make the travels in the South which he has so poetically described. M. Bédiér does indeed leave us the Niagara episode; though he is much troubled to make Chateaubriand's description agree with the facts.

The facts undoubtedly are, that Chateaubriand came to America, and to Niagara. He may have visited Pittsburgh, but he certainly did not travel as widely as he claims to have done. He supplemented his own observations and experiences by drawing on the writings of others. M. Bédiér devotes many pages to parallel publication of passages from Chateaubriand and from many authors and early travellers in America on whom he drew. He seldom appropriated their language, but he stole their ideas, and set them forth more beautifully, more poetically, than the first writers could.

After all, it is Chateaubriand the poet that we are thankful for, for he has endowed the literature descriptive of American scenery and aborigines with a charm and grace which no other writer gives.

In after years, he loved to identify himself with America, in whimsical, poet's fashion. Soon after his return to France, serving under arms with his brother, the latter was asked,

" 'Where does your brother the chevalier come from?'

"I was still bronzed by the American sun and sea air," he tells us. "I wore my hair uncurled and unpowdered"; and to the question which had been put to his brother, the poet replied, "From Niagara."

" 'From the cataract!'

"I was silent.

" 'Monsieur is going—?'

" 'Where there is fighting.' "

The days that followed were evil ones. Many of the poet's relatives went to the guillotine; four of them, including his brother, were "all immolated together, on the same day, at the same hour, on the same scaffold."

I have referred to *"Atala,"* which he tells us was written wholly in America, "in the huts of the savages," and for which, by the way, Gustave Doré has drawn the most impressive picture of Niagara Falls in existence—the artist never having seen them! How narrowly that romance escaped destruction, Chateaubriand records in the *"Mémoires"*:

At Trèves, "I sat down, with my musket, among the ruins; I took from my knapsack the manuscript of my travels in America; I arranged the separate sheets on the grass around me; I read over and corrected a description of a forest, a passage of '*Atala*,' in the fragments of a Roman amphitheatre, preparing in this way to make the conquest of France. Then I put away my treasure, the weight of which, combined with that of my shirts, my cloak, my tin can, my wicker bottle, and my little Homer, made me throw up blood.

"I tried to stuff '*Atala*' into my cartridge-box with my useless ammunition; my comrades made fun of me, and pulled at the sheets which stuck out on either side of the leather cover. Providence came to my rescue; one night, after sleeping in a hayloft, I found when I awoke, that my shirts were no longer in my sack; the thieves had left the papers. I praised God; that accident assured my fame and saved my life, for the sixty pounds that pressed upon my shoulders would have driven me into a consumption."

Returning to France in 1792, he was wounded at the siege of Thouinville. We next find him in London, where he passed several years in exile, supporting himself wholly by his literary labors. During this time he wrote his famous essay on Revolutions. After the 18th *Brumaire*, he was allowed to live again in Paris, where, in conjunction with

LaHarpe and others, he established the *Mercure de France* and the *Journal des Debats.*

He was at this time a Bonapartist, and declared in one of his applications that the Emperor was one of those men whom God, when He is weary of punishing, sends upon the world in token of expiation. The "Genius of Christianity," beyond doubt the most celebrated and generally read of all his reflective works, appeared in 1802, in London, at a period admirably adapted to its success. Bonaparte wished to restore the Church, and a book which twenty years before would have found few to defend it, now attained an immense popularity. The sincere religious feeling which pervades it, mounting at times into the lofty atmosphere of poetry, found its way to the heart of the public, then recovering from the fatal extreme to which it had been hurried. The next year, during his residence in Rome as Secretary of the Embassy under Cardinal Fesch, he wrote "The Martyrs," and in the same year was appointed on a mission to the Valais, which station he resigned after the death of the Duc d'Enghien. In 1806 he traveled to Jerusalem, by way of Cyprus and Rhodes, returning through Egypt, Tunis and Spain. His *"Itinéraire"* is one of the finest specimens of descriptive writing in the French language. At this date the fame of Chateaubriand had become European, and he was recognized as one of the first living authors of France.

In 1811 he was elected a member of the French Institute, in place of Chenier. After the banishment of Napoleon, he published a pamphlet entitled "Bonaparte and the Bourbons," which Louis XVIII was accustomed to say was worth more to him than an army. This decided his position as a royalist, which political view he held during the remainder of his life. He remained in Ghent during Napoleon's second brief reign, as Minister to Louis XVIII, and after the final restoration of this monarch was made a viscount and a peer of France. From this time until 1829, he held various important positions under the Government; beside serving as Minister to Berlin, Extraordinary Ambassador to London, and to the Congress of Verona, and Minister to Rome. The most important of his literary productions, in addition to his editorials in the *Journal des Debats*, were his "Notes on Greece," and a very popular essay on the abolition of the Censorship, in which he affirmed that without freedom of the press a representative government was worth nothing. His complete works were published in 1829, the publishers L'Avocat and LeFevre having offered him the enormous sum of 550,000 francs for the copyright.

When the July Revolution took place, he advocated the claims of the Duke of Bordeaux, and refused to give the oath of loyalty to Louis Philippe, which obligated him to resign his title of Peer. For the last years of his life he devoted himself largely to the compositions of his delightful Memoirs. There is a fine pen-picture of him in his declining days, leonine in aspect, seated in a chair as on a throne, reading from his *"Mémoires"* in the salon of his dearest friend, Mme. Recamier.

Anything like a survey of his literary work and place would lead us too far afield. "With me," he somewhere says, "began the so-called romantic school, a revolution in French literature." Nothing could be more true. Victor Hugo has admirably summed it up. "Chateaubriand," he says, "stood on the threshold of this century and stamped it with his seal. The literary generations that have followed are all his children. Gustave Flaubert, the De Goncours, Alphonse Daudet, studied and formed their style on the inimitable prose of his '*Mémoires d'Outre Tombe*,' the most exquisite work, perhaps, in all the French language. The works of Chateaubriand," Hugo adds, "are as dead as the readers they charmed, but his influence is a leading factor in the book-making of our day, and will last as long as the French tongue is spoken or read."

THE NIAGARA IN ART

IF one were asked to say what has been the most pictured subject in all the world, he might perhaps pause for reflection.

If this rather broad query were narrowed to the one subject of natural scenery, still one might hesitate to declare whether this mountain or that valley, or what wonder of rushing stream, pouring cataract, or mountain height, had received most attention from the artists of brush and pencil.

The quest is no doubt an idle one, since the only precise answer must rest upon statistics,—in regard to a matter on which no statistics exist. The question, however, now that I have for the first time put it fairly to myself, is not without suggestiveness. As one attempts to survey in thought what mankind has done by way of picture-making, since the first rude scratches with stick or stone or coal, on stone, or hide, or bark or clay, he soon eliminates all primitive picture-making, and all practice of pictorial art, down to this very day, in all lands of Islam, of Buddha, of Confucius, of all the

" . . . lesser breeds without the law."

With all the millions of Mohamedans, picture-making is a forbidden—at least a disapproved—occupation. No Mongol, Malay, African—no red, brown, black or yellow race has ever cultivated art for art's sake or any other reason.

The Aryan is the world's picture-maker; and of all the Aryans, the pictorial art has flourished widest and highest in Christian lands.

If these statements appear reasonable, may we not go at once to the end of this train of thought, and declare that the Christ figure and Christianity's great symbol of the Cross, have been and are more drawn and painted than any other subjects which appeal to the mind of man? True, in world history, Christianity is not old. But if the peoples of earlier epochs practiced picture-making, knowledge of their work, for the most part, has not survived. All the picturings of the Egyptians, the Assyrians, and all the civilizations of the past, are, so far as we know them, few and negligible, as indeed is the picture-making of China, Corea and Japan.

If the reader concur in these deductions he will perhaps reflect that through all the centuries in which painting as a fine art was developing, the greatest painters found their greatest inspiration in the Christ. Great painters there were in Greece and Rome before the Christian era; but how few their works and how limited their distribution and influence in comparison with the works of the great masters whose canvases of the Christ personality, albeit presented in a myriad ways, have not been lost to the world; but in these latter days are perpetually being multiplied by copyists and engravers, by painters and photographers, many million fold.

I think we may safely maintain some such deductive reasoning. The same course of thought brings me to conclude that of all human subjects the Buddha is the most sculptured. Images of Buddha exist by the thousand thousand, where you will scarcely find one Buddha picture.

If we eliminate subjects of divine attributes, and seek to determine what individual in all the world has been most portrayed in pictures, there is again a wide range for choice, with perhaps equally good arguments in several directions. It has been the perverse lot of many great men to live too early to be much portrayed. Modern newspapers afford proof that the frequency with which one's portrait is made public is not of itself a sufficient guarantee of greatness. Julius Cæsar might be rated greater than—shall we say—William J. Bryan; yet the world rejoices in a thousand portraits of the latter Public Character, where it has one of the former—and that one dubious.

Considering then, the modern processes of picture-multiplication, we see at what a disadvantage were the great of the earth before the days of the press—the modern prolific press—and the camera. Thus it comes about that your Member of Congress or your Alderman may be far more abundantly portrayed than Alexander the Great. Of famous moderns, I should hazard that Napoleon, Queen Victoria, Washington and Lincoln have been among the most pictured. Indeed, when one calls to mind the wide realm of Great Britain and the fine loyalty that animates the typical subject of that crown, whether in India, Australia or other ends of the earth; especially when one remembers the long reign of their most beloved sovereign, reaching well down into the days of vast multiplication of portraits; the conclusion is inevitable that more portraits have been painted, engraved, photographed and printed of Victoria than any other person who ever lived.

The reader who wonders what all this has to do with my subject, is reminded that one of the greatest histories ever written, Diedrich Knickerbocker's "New York," begins with the creation of the world. The method is useful, though now fallen into neglect. I can not aspire to such thoroughness, and will come at once to the point which all that has gone before is intended to establish, namely: that no other place on earth has been so much pictured as Niagara Falls.

We prove it by elimination of all other places. No other scenic point in America, which can be called a wonder, has been so long known to the public or so much resorted to. Europe abounds in scenes of beauty or grandeur, often with the added attraction of human associations; yet there never has been such abundant picturing of alp or valley, of Coliseum or Parthenon, as our Niagara has known for two centuries.

We begin, of course, with Hennepin. He was not the first white man who saw the Niagara Falls, but he is the first who wrote at length of them, and in connection with whose writings a picture appeared. The so-called Hennepin view, reproduced in modern prints without number, is well-nigh as familiar as yesterday's photograph. It is customary to speak of it with great respect, if not admiration; and it is accepted, I think, as pretty good evidence of a former condition of the cataract, before the deep recession appeared in the Horseshoe, and while yet there was a third fall.

I have great respect for historical evidence, and great admiration for Father Hennepin, whose gifts as romancer have never been half appreciated. But I confess, the more I contemplate this first picture of the falls, the more skeptical I grow regarding it. The reader will remember that Hennepin and the main body of La Salle's expedition sailed into the Niagara river, December 6, 1678. A small party of LaSalle's men, whose names we do not know, had been sent on in advance, and although there were other routes to the west, probably passed up the Niagara. Father Hennepin's activities in the neighborhood continued until August,

1679, when the Griffon sailed. He passed eastward, by the Niagara route, in Easter week, 1681, in which year he returned to Europe. Three years later, in Paris, he published his first book. In that—the *"Louisiane"*—the story of the expedition is told, and the great cataract is described, but there is no picture of it, nor was any published until 1697, eighteen years after he had seen it.

Now consider that picture, as a sketch. The point of view is very high. The artist looked down on the falls. He was so high that he saw the Niagara river all the way to Lake Erie, and he saw the lake, and mountains on either side of it. Any one who could see all this, was seeing in imagination and in memory, and not very good memory at that. It is plain, I think, that the first picture of Niagara Falls was not engraved from any sketch or drawing "made on the spot." It couldn't be, and be so wrong. But it is just about what one who was not an artist might produce from recollection of scenes he had been through a score of years before; especially if he were not trying to make a true picture—a work of art—but merely to give a bird's-eye view of the Niagara "streight," as the old chronicles have it, from the Falls to Lake Erie. Beyond some such purpose, I think Father Hennepin is to be absolved from responsibility for the first Niagara picture. It was no doubt drawn for the engraver, and engraved on the copper, by French or Flemish artists who had never been in America. The details are theirs, not Hennepin's. They may, indeed, have constructed this and the other illustrations which appeared at the same time in the "New Discovery" wholly from the data given in Hennepin's text. None of the pictures has any particular resemblance to anything that existed; and they all show how impossible it is to draw an object correctly from some other man's description.

Much has been made of the third or western fall shown in this primitive sketch; but do not those who argue from it the existence of a separate fall at that point, overlook Hennepin's own statement that Niagara consisted of two falls? Probably the portion that appears to descend crosswise of the great fall, was but the extreme right of it, very badly drawn. The river no doubt ran higher and stronger at that point then than now; the rocks made an elbow of it; and the recession of the V-shaped cleft, now deep in the Horseshoe, had probably begun. There is no hint of it in the Hennepin picture, but it is shown, well-nigh as conspicuous as now, in a picture made only seventy years after Hennepin's was published. We will presently consider that picture.

The Hennepin picture was for many years the world's only pictorial presentment of the cataract. It was much copied, especially for use in the ponderous folio compilations of voyages and travels which now often form a substantial foundation for accumulations of old books in antiquarian shops. As was to be expected each engraver departed a little more from the original and from the truth. For 150 years after Hennepin there continued to be published views of Niagara, inspired not by the cataract itself, but by this grotesque old copperplate of 1697. There was thus evolved a certain typical view of Niagara, resembling Niagara not at all, showing two straight downfalls of water into a basin of surf-like flouncy foam; with Goat Island reduced to a huge pillar of rock, and this rock, like the abutting shores, elaborately drawn in a built-up box-like form of cleaveage and fracture suggestive possibly of granitic or igneous formation, but as far as possible from the smooth sedimentary and practically horizontal strata of the Niagara region. The surface of shores and island, in this

THE NIAGARA IN ART.   119

type of view, is adorned with wonderful trees—each a long slightly curved stem set from tip to base with recurrent boughs, the unique effect being that of a long dart or javelin with many barbs. Beyond are the usual mountains and lake, and in the foreground are stalwart naked savages pointing out the wonders of the scene to a group of amazed Frenchmen, some in military uniform, others in priestly robes. On the brink a small dog vociferously barks. I have been unduly concerned about this dog, for he appears, then disappears, in these old engravings with singular uncertainty. On the Canadian side a path is shown, with natives carrying burdens on their heads up and down the steep portage.

This whole group of seventeenth and eighteenth century engravings, often identical in many respects while varying in small details, is a curious illustration of dull imitation. The most curious thing about it is that this species of Niagara picture continued to be published long after truer and in some cases splendid studies of Niagara had been drawn and published.

There exist numerous very early engravings of Niagara Falls, which are now matters of curiosity rather than works of art. Among the most curious are plates engraved with two or more subjects, the Niagara cataracts among them. A large vignette on some of Herman Moll's famous maps shows the Falls—the conventionalized Hennepin picture—with a colony of busy beavers in the foreground, gnawing down trees and building dams. One might almost infer from the picture that Niagara Falls were a beavers' dam. Of this sort, too, is the picture of Niagara Falls that ornaments the map which accompanies the American travels of Prince Maximilien Wied-Neuwied (1832-34). In front of the cataract, on a low riverside plateau, mounted Indians are pursuing a herd of bison. Most striking, most artistic, and perhaps most rare of these combination engravings, is a copperplate signed S. LeClerc, an artist whose span of life was from 1637 to 1714. Here we have a Niagara which if anything is straighter and higher than Hennepin's. Out of a cloud above the left of the fall emerges Elijah in a chariot of fire. At least, so declares a title at the lower margin: *"Elie enlevé dans un char de feu"*—but the artist has given Elijah not merely a glorious burst of flame but a fine pair of steeds which are prancing above the yawning abyss of the cataract. The upper margin of the picture bears the legend: *"Chute de la rivière de Niagara."* The picture provokes speculation as to whether the artist sought to combine the two greatest marvels, one of earth, the other of translation from earth to heaven; whether he sought to fix the locality from which Elijah made his ascent; or indeed, whether Le Clerc were responsible for the whole engraving. A variation of touch, of stroke and tone, suggests that two hands may have worked on it. If the work is wholly LeClerc's its production must have been after 1697, the year in which the Hennepin picture appeared, and before 1714, the year of his death.

Of this sort, too, is an aquatint, published to commemorate the death of Washington. In front of Niagara Falls stands the Goddess of Liberty; at her side a grotesque figure, apparently a negro, weeps over a memorial tablet; and above the cataract flies an American flag of thirteen stripes and thirteen stars.

Still another extraordinary Niagara is an exquisite little plate forming a frontispiece of the old French tragedy of *"Hirza."* Here an impossible Niagara—we could not know it was Niagara except that the text says so—forms a background for a rocky tomb and a display of heroic aborigines

—all utterly impossible. No doubt one can find other curious old engravings in which our falls are used as a background, a mere setting, a stage property, for whatever subject the artist was engaged upon. In such compositions, verisimilitude to nature is not looked for, or desired. To copy nature without imagination—without ideality—is to make no very lofty flight in the realm of art. One of the most effective "Niagaras" ever painted is the weird, suggestive cataract, glimpsed through a very nightmare of gloomy pines and cedars, which was drawn by Gustave Doré to illustrate Chateaubriand's *"Atala."* Doré never saw the Falls, nor did he need to. His fancy could supply just the sort of Niagara required to harmonize with and express the spirit of *"Atala."*

Early in the eighteenth century certain map-publishers —Popple, Homanno of Nuremberg and perhaps others, embellished their maps of North America with engravings of Niagara Falls, but these, like Le Clerc's picture, were obviously based on Hennepin's original. After Hennepin, I do not find any picture of the falls, that can in any measure be ascribed to one who had seen them, until 1751. In February of that year the *Gentlemen's Magazine* published "A view of the Fall of Niagara," designed to accompany Peter Kalm's letter about the Falls, written at Albany, Sept. 2, 1750, and published in the *Gentlemen's Magazine* of January, 1751. Kalm's description, by the way, appears to have been the first account of Niagara originally written in English. Hennepin's and La Hontan's descriptions had been translated into English before Kalm wrote, but although he was a Swede, this Niagara letter was written in English, to a friend in Philadelphia—the beginning of English literature on the subject! He probably had nothing to do with the making of the picture which appeared in the

Gentlemen's Magazine a month after his letter; but whoever engraved it evidently referred to his description for data. Like the Hennepin picture it is a birdseye view, and shows the river above the falls, and Lake Erie in the distance. The surrounding mountains are still there, but the ship, which the Hennepin picture shows on the lake, has disappeared. So have the great rock and the "third fall" at the extreme right. Several islets appear in the Canadian channel, opposite Goat Island; great birds hover over the river; men are climbing up a ladder on the face of Goat Island; and two other men, as the legend states, are "passing over ye east stream with staves." These changes from the Hennepin picture are all suggested by Kalm's report.

After Kalm, engravings multiplied, but for many years were all more or less of the Hennepin type—always excepting Pierie. An early German copperplate, "Wasserfall von Niagara," has the whole scene reversed, with the third or cross-fall on the left (now the New York) side! Andrew Ellicott's drawing, engraved by Thackara & Vallance, 1790, although a great advance toward truth, over the Kalm and Hennepin views, is still vastly inferior to the Pierie picture of many years before.

The world had no idea of what the Niagara really looked like until 1774, when there was published in London a splendidly executed copperplate from a drawing made in 1768 by Lieutenant William Pierie of the Royal British Artillery. This soldier-artist, of whom I regret I know nothing further, was probably stationed at Fort Niagara and improved his leisure by studying the cataract.

Several of the most interesting early engravings of the falls are from drawings by British soldiers. To one of them, the work of Captain Thomas Davies—the engraving

THE NIAGARA IN ART.   123

being dedicated to General Amherst—is ascribed the date 1760, antedating by a few years the work of Pierie. Davies was far from being an artist; and yet his bad, crude drawing, with a rainbow like half of a cartwheel, comes nearer to depicting the Niagara scene than all the Hennepin-suggested pictures that have gone before.

We may say, in a sense, that Niagara art began with Hennepin; but in its higher sense, it began neither with Hennepin nor Davies, but with Pierie. His point of view is on the high land back of the present Queen Victoria park. The scene embraces both falls. The distant shores, flat and true to nature, close in the horizon. The Horseshoe is shown not as a straight curtain of water, nor yet, as in Davies', by a great semi-circular sweep, but approximately as it is today, with a wedge-shaped cleft tending up-stream. It is almost a century and a half since this study was made. The wedge has extended a little and is, perhaps, sharper. The flood of water is less, so that now we have bare rocks at either side of the greater fall where formerly the flood swept. Yet the contour of the cataract is today approximately what it was in 1768.

I am free to confess that I do not care particularly for the Niagara Falls as we know them today. The vicinage of the cataract appeals to my imagination less and less with each succeeding year of protection and improvement. Here is no note of criticism upon the intelligent work of Niagara's governmental guardians. Far from it. Much of the beauty of the environment has been preserved, and some of it, now vanished, will perhaps be restored when power companies cease from troubling; but if preserved and guarded, Niagara is not and never can be the Niagara of the wilderness. We tend inevitably in our care of such a place to curb and pave, and smooth out, to bridge and trim and to wall, to improve this roadway and that bit of lawn; in short, while protecting it so far as may be from vandalism, these works are necessary to fit it for the use and delight of the multitude. Whoever knows Europe, can recall scores of places which once must have been the very heart of wild beauty—back, let us say, in the days of Cæsar,—but are now and for many years hemmed about with all the devices of protection, perhaps gates of admission, with hotels at nicely-groomed points of view, with refreshment booths and paths and permits in perfect propriety.

Keenly as I feel the beauty and serenity of the great sweep of green waters, I find less and less in the prim and parked environs that appeals to me. The Niagara I would have delighted in was that which Pierie saw. How one would have enjoyed standing at his elbow upon that sightly height, or sitting at his side on rock or log, looking down into and over the great cedar swamp where now are the lawns and paths and playgrounds of the park; while beyond poured the green flood of the great river, fed by thousands of miles of wilderness-rimmed lakes. This of a truth was the Niagara known to the red man and to the missionary, to La Salle and all the gallant train of the remote adventurous days.

I have no doubt that as Lieutenant Pierie worked over his sketches he was the butt of joke and jibe of soldier comrades who could find better sport in the wilderness than the tame drawing of pictures. Who they were or what their worth, we do not know. Forgotten every one of them. But Pierie we remember with gratitude, and prize the work into which he put not only skill as a draughtsman, but to which he gave that admirable fidelity which marks him as a lover of beauty and of truth.

When Lieutenant Pierie wrought, Niagara belonged

wholly to his King. Almost a century later the missionary Livingston was to discover in the heart of Africa the only cataract on earth which rivals Niagara, and was to christen it, with fine loyalty, after England's Queen. Today the Victoria Falls, on the Zambesi, are drawing enterprising travelers to the British possession of Rhodesia, as Niagara was the attraction for far-wandering Britons of a century before.

In another study I have made note of Isaac Weld, Jr., and his Niagara visit of 1796. Weld was an Englishman, a landscape painter by profession, but not a great artist. Among the numerous copperplate engravings from his own sketches which embellish his volume of travels, are three of Niagara. These appear to much better advantage in the original quarto edition of 1799 than in later octavo issues. They are not beautiful or technically striking, these studies of the falls. Weld was very matter-of-fact, or, as the modern phrase is, was a realist, and nothing at all of an idealist. None of his drawings quite gives adequate height to the cataract, nor have they any quality of suggestion or impressiveness. None the less they are a useful pictorial record of Niagara aspects at the end of the 18th century. In a rather apologetic note regarding his own drawings, the artist says: "Those who are desirous of becoming more intimately acquainted with the stupendous cataract, will soon be gratified," at least so he has been given to understand by the artist in whose hands they at present are, "with a set of views from the masterly pencil of Captain Fisher of the Royal British Artillery, which are allowed by all who have visited the Falls of Niagara to convey a more perfect idea of that wonderful natural curiosity than any paintings or engravings that are extant." I regret that these wonderful pictures are not known to me.

Still another English artist was John Maude, whose visit to the Falls of Niagara in 1800 was not published until 1826. His book is, I think, somewhat sought after by collectors of Americana, not more for the value of his narrative than for the attractive copperplate engravings from his own paintings. There are occasionally offered by dealers, at pretty stiff prices, copies of Maude with colored plates, inserted manuscripts, and other souvenirs of personal association, supposed to make peculiar appeal to the collector. Maude's narrative has a certain value, but I cannot say much for his pictures. His "General View of the Falls from the United States side" absurdly minimizes their height. His beautifully engraved "Horseshoe" shows that cataract with a rim in smooth unbroken curve, which we know has not been its condition at any rate since the days of Pierie. It is incredible that any sober-minded man could so prevaricate with brush or pencil. How could he have looked at it and drawn it as he did!

Some of the early engravings, of various dates, are exceedingly curious. I have seen one, of unknown age, "drawn by Heath, engraved by Metz." It is of the Hennepin type, with mountains in the distance, palm-like trees, and wagon-tracks on the American side. Goat Island is exceedingly attenuated—it looks to be a fragile rock pillar several hundred feet high and a few feet wide. In this wonderful engraving the American fall is as wide as the Canadian, and there is no hint of "horseshoe" or any curve in either. Equally marvelous—more so, indeed, considering its later date—is a view of Niagara by W. M. Craig, engraved by T. Wallis. The river is seen above the fall, like a Scotch loch, surrounded with close, high, sullen hills. A barren rock stands for Goat Island, and the face of the fall is mostly hidden by a vast cloud that drifts across the picture, starting from the base of the fall on the extreme left and suggesting the smoke from a bon-fire of damp leaves on a windy day. A few aborigines appear in the foreground, looking like negroes, with black skins and white loin-cloths. Still another amusing "Niagara," bearing the imprint "Rawdon, Clark & Co.," shows three falls and two Goat Islands, with Indians in canoes cheerfully being carried over! A singular picture, with some artistic merit, was "painted by Wall, engraved by Archer." It is a view of the Falls from below, and either the painter or the engraver has managed to make the whole face of the fall look frozen, although it is not a winter picture. To note but one more of these curios, there is a birdseye view of the Niagara river from Erie to Ontario, "showing the situation and extent of Navy Island and the towns and villages on the banks of the river," etc., drawn by W. R. Callington, a Boston engineer, "from an actual survey made in 1837." The picture was no doubt occasioned by the Mackenzie Rebellion, which accounts for the prominence given to Navy Island. The whole thing is bad and inaccurate, not the least curious feature being two good-sized islands at the outlet of Lake Erie—a pictorial reminder, but not a true one, of vanished Bird Island.

The old books of American travel, especially those written by Englishmen, contain many views of Niagara, often pretty bad, sometimes merely curious, but occasionally engraved from drawings or paintings of manifest worth. The large folding drawings of Niagara and other subjects, by George Heriot, Deputy Postmaster General of British North America, which accompany his quarto work of "Travels through the Canadas," etc., published in 1807, have chiefly, perhaps, an antiquarian interest, though the author must be rated among the artists. Of greater interest are the sketches made at Niagara by Alexander Wilson, the Scotch-American poet-naturalist, who walked from Philadelphia to Oswego, coming thence by boat to Niagara Falls, and back again, and told the story of it all in verse. His Niagara drawings were engraved and published in the *Portfolio* of 1810. The Niagara drawings signed "Bonfils," which are to be found in Hector St. John de Crévecoeur's *"Voyage dans la Haute Pensylvanie,"* etc. (Paris, 1801), may have place in our list; as perhaps should A. Hervieu's etching of Indians at Niagara, with the falls as a background, which accompanies Tyrone Power's "Impressions of America." The field of book illustration is practically boundless, yet here one sometimes finds real gems of Niagara art. The numerous Niagara paintings of Mrs. John Graves Simcoe, wife of the first Lieutenant Governor of Upper Canada, have lately been published in Canada, with her diary, covering her residence on the Niagara, 1792-93. While they have a considerable historical value, their art quality does not call for consideration.

The early woodcuts of Niagara are for the most part negligible, except as curios; though it may be noted that one of them was by Peter Maverick, who is regarded as the first American wood engraver. A woodcut in Prior's "Universal Traveler" (London, 1823), has the Canadian fall on the American side of Goat Island! A modern woodcut that should have mention was a two-page picture in *Harper's Weekly*, Aug. 9, 1873, showing "How different people see the Falls," viewing them with the eye of the artist, the poet, the business-man, etc.

Of exceptional character are the Niagara drawings made in 1827 by Captain Basil Hall of the British Navy. He used a "camera lucida," which gave him an image of the object to be drawn; all he had to do was to limn the outlines as the sun and his lens set the copy. While this was not great art it was ingenious—there being no photographs then—and it was useful as a record.

The first American artist of distinction to visit the Falls and to paint them was, I believe, John Vanderlyn, whose old home at Kingston on the Hudson still stands, an object of interest to visitors, not merely because of its association with the artist, but because of its age. It is one of Kingston's famous old stone houses, built by Dutch settlers early in the eighteenth century, its walls withstanding the burning of the town by the British in 1777. Young Vanderlyn came to Niagara in 1802. That he studied the cataract and its vicinity seriously and to good purpose is attested by his numerous paintings. Two of these, evidently the original sketches in oil, are preserved in the old Senate House in Kingston. Another, a canvas of some eight feet or so in length by four and a half in height, is owned by one of the old Kingston families. It is a most curious picture of the Falls, in that it scarcely shows the cataracts. The point of view is high up on the bank of the Canadian side, opposite the upper rapids. The American fall is shown in the distance but nothing is shown of the face of the Canadian fall; looking down the river from this point, one sees only the line of its crest. The rapids, the islands, indeed, the topography of much of the surrounding country, is admirably represented. In the foreground runs the Canadian portage road, along which toils the ox-team of a pioneer. Several buildings are shown; Indians rest at the roadside; and athwart the landscape thrusts a great dead tree, on a limb of which sits an eagle, overlooking the scene. It is a singular composition; although painted with skill and intelligence, its chief interest today is historical rather than artistic.

Vanderlyn is known by other views of Niagara which he painted, and of which he published fine aquatints, in London in 1804. One of these, "A view of the Western Branch of the Falls of Niagara, taken from Table Rock," etc., is about 30 by 21 inches in size. It was engraved by F. C. Lewis, and inscribed "to the Society of Fine Arts in New York." It shows the angle of the Horseshoe, less deeply worn than now. Of like size is a companion picture, "Distant view of the Falls, including both branches, with the islands and adjacent shores, taken from the vicinity of the Indian Ladder." This picture, engraved by Merigot, was also published in London in 1804 by Mr. Vanderlyn himself.

Of a later period are the paintings of F. Richardt, engraved by A. H. Payne, and the drawings of Lieutenant-Colonel Cockburn, engraved by J. Edge, or in aquatint by C. Hunt. These and numerous other now rare views of the Niagara were published by Ackermann, of London, from 1830 to the middle of the century. The enterprising house of Ackermann did much to spread abroad a true knowledge of the great cataract. There is one general view of Niagara Falls from the Canada side, or, as the engraved inscription has it, "from above the English ferry," which is sometimes to be found delicately colored, and is indeed a work of art worth the several pounds sure to be asked for it.

Other excellent plates, "plain or colored,'" were published in the first half of the 19th century by McLean of the Haymarket, London, from the paintings of Major Henry Davis of the 52d Light Infantry. The date of this soldier-artist's visit to Niagara is not clear, but apparently in the 30's or 40's. A copy of his "Great Horseshoe Fall," a most realistic picture, bears date 1818; but this I take to be an error, perhaps for 1848.

Among the early publications of the distinguished house of Goupil is a finely colored "Rapids of Niagara," drawn from nature by August Köllner.

More than half a century ago Washington Friend, an English artist of merit, whose panorama of American scenery was exhibited throughout England, made a series of studies of Niagara which were among the best of the period. Some of these have been reproduced in colors by English publishers of guide books. Perhaps Friend's most famous works are two large paintings, one a general view of the falls, the other showing the Canadian fall, which I believe are owned by the royal family of Great Britain. Some years ago, when a notable art collection was placed on view at Burlington House, these Niagara pictures by Washington Friend were conspicuously hung with an announcement that they were loaned for public inspection by the Prince of Wales—the late Edward VIIth. Judging from the photogravure reproductions made of them at the time, they are well-painted studies of Niagara, depicting the scene with useful fidelity.

Among Friend's Niagara views which have been published not the least interesting at this date are pictures of the whirlpool and Queenston Heights, places of great former beauty but now much changed by the intrusion of modern "improvements."

My reference to Edward VIIth reminds me that Her Royal Highness, the Princess Louise, has painted the Horseshoe Fall, evidently with no little skill. An engraving of her work accompanies an article on "Niagara" by Joseph Hatton in the London *Art Journal* of 1885.

Pictures of Niagara Falls were vastly multiplied by the development of chromo-lithography. The processes of engraving upon stone were well adapted to such a subject, either in colors or in single tint. Prior, say, to 1825 or thereabouts, the published views of our natural scenery were almost entirely either copperplate or engraved on steel, but from the date named down to the development of photo-engraving there has been a great production of lithographs, among them some of the worst as well as some of the best pictures of the Falls which we have. Notable among the earlier lithographs are the Niagara views painted by W. Vivian and drawn on the stone by T. M. Baynes; and the Paris lithographs—a fine Niagara series—from the drawings of Blouet. Both of the above artists made many Niagara studies, their work being published in London and Paris in the 30's.

Of about that period, perhaps, are the colored views "painted and engraved upon stone by W. J. Bennett." If the collector finds old colored lithographs of Niagara with large and vari-colored goats in the foreground—the artist's ingenious method of indicating that his point of view was Goat Island—he may be pretty sure that it is a "Bennett."

Lieutenant De Roos, who traveled here in 1826, illustrated his book with his own very good drawings, lithographed. Another British officer, Lieutenant E. T. Coke, made his own sketches at Niagara, which were drawn on stone by T. M. Baynes, for "A Subaltern's Furlough."

Of American artists whose Niagara studies were lithographed, may be mentioned A. Vaudricourt, whose interesting lithographic views of the cataract (1845-46) occur in various forms, sometimes small, but best about 30 by 14 inches. Vaudricourt is said to have utilized for his drawings the daguerreotypes of F. Langheim. Is there any other instance of the employment of the daguerreotype in landscape work? Woodcuts made from Langheim's daguerreotypes of Niagara are to be found in Appleton's Guide

Book (of the United States) published in 1846; and possibly elsewhere.

If one may judge from existing prints of the Niagara subject, the lithographic art gained high excellence in Paris while yet the London and American productions were still mediocre or worse. I cannot speak of German or Italian works of this period—say prior to 1840—with much knowledge or any enthusiasm. Such early pictures of Niagara as I have seen produced in those countries are too crude and insignificant to include in our review. Possibly I am overlooking real works of art—if so, may I have the pleasure of discovery. But certain it is the early French lithographs of Niagara are by all odds the most pleasing; and among them I should rank as of chief importance the pictures of Jacques-Girard Milbert. He is of sufficient importance in the art story of Niagara to warrant us in dwelling briefly upon his career.

He was artist, author, and naturalist. Born in Paris in 1766, he died there in 1840. He had won gratifying recognition, and held numerous posts of distinction—had been professor of design in the National School of Mines; had accompanied, as chief draughtsman, a Government expedition to the antipodes; and had sojourned two years in the remote Isle of France, now Mauritius, studying its physical and social conditions,—when in 1815 he came to America in the official train of the French consul to New York. For eight years he traveled through this country, engaged in scientific research and in sketching, which pursuits brought him to Niagara Falls in the summer of 1818. Ten years later there was published in Paris the narrative of his American travels, in two handsome quarto volumes; the interest of which was vastly augmented by a folio volume of his drawings. The work is entitled *"Itinéraire pittoresque du fleuve Hudson et des parties latérales de l'Amerique du Nord."* I know of no translation or other edition. Milbert's drawings were transferred to the stone by many artists, some of them of reputation. The names of Adam, Bichebois, Deroy, Dupressoir, Jacottet, Joly, Sabatier, Tirpenne and Villeneuve, are given as art-collaborators for the production of this work—an item of Niagara art and history which now for many years has been rather hard to come across, though stray pictures from the collection occasionally are to be found in the hands of London or Paris dealers. There is never any difficulty in recognizing a Milbert. His Niagara studies are not only well drawn, but have a delicacy which makes them pleasing and attractive, apart from their historical value—it will soon be a century since the artist drew them! The Paris publishers, Henri Gaugain & Co., gave to the work a worthy typographic setting; the folio drawings are printed in tint, and the titles of the subjects are in French, German, English and Latin. A fine copy of Milbert is for the collector of Americana—in the field of early art—a rather choice possession, well nigh rivalling in scarcity, if not in purchase value, the "Voyage," etc., of Prince Maximilien von Wied-Neuwied of a later date. The Prince's American travels were in the early 30's; the Paris publication of his work was a decade later. As the accompanying royal folio atlas of some 80 plates includes studies of our falls by M. Charles Bodmer, the artist of the expedition, we should include him, if not the enterprising prince himself, among the artists of Niagara. The Prince was at Niagara in June, 1834, when, he says, "Mr. Bodmer took his general view of this sublime scene, which is the best I have yet met with in every respect perfectly faithful to nature."

The Niagara drawings of W. H. Bartlett are worthy of

notice for several reasons. They form an important part of one of the most notable art works ever issued devoted in part to the scenery of the Niagara region—the "American Scenery," handsomely published in London by Virtue in 1840, though many of the engravings bear an earlier date.

Bartlett was a young English artist, who, in his later years, won great popularity for his illustrations of Egypt, Jerusalem, and other regions of picturesque and storied interest. His Niagara studies were made in the latter part of the decade of the 30's, a period, by the way, peculiarly rich both in the art and literature of the Niagara region, due in part, no doubt, to the fact that the opening of the Erie Canal and the building of railroads for the first time had made travel to the banks of the Niagara comparatively easy.

The London publishers who directed Bartlett's work engaged for the literary part of the venture N. P. Willis, whose place in American letters was perhaps rated higher then than it would be now. Willis' work is by turns clever and commonplace. But the chief value of the volumes lies in the 120 engravings, all from Bartlett's drawings. His studies were engraved by many different hands, so that the artist's work received a somewhat varying presentation in the metal. Yet, as one turns the pages of this still beautiful and attractive work, it is impossible to say that any one of the engravers failed to do justice to the original picture. The work includes eight engravings of scenes on the Niagara, with perhaps as many more studies of the Lakes, the Erie canal, etc., of local interest.

Several of Bartlett's drawings, aside from their art quality, have a definite value as historical records; thus the outlet of Niagara river with Lake Ontario in the distance is one of the very few pictures that show the lower gorge and the original monument to General Brock. But one other contemporary drawing known to me shows it better, and that is Bartlett's own study of Queenston Heights and the first Brock monument, made from the old Lewiston landing. That picture in some of its detail is worth whole chapters of reminiscences and record by way of recalling the conditions of that time. The drawing of the lower gorge has a peculiar charm in that it preserves for us the wildness of that beautiful reach of river before it was encroached upon by the works of man. It is true that the artist, or the engraver, or the two in wicked collusion, have given us a lovely sunset fair and square in the north; but one cannot be too critical; perhaps the sun did set north of Toronto in the late 30's; and at any rate, artists have a perpetual license to take liberties with the celestial bodies.

Genuinely edifying to the inquirer as to early conditions at Niagara, is Bartlett's view of the landing on the American side. It shows the rowboat, small but staunch, which served as ferry for many years; and it shows the log runways, the windlass, and the rough zigzag steps up the cliffs, which long ago disappeared. For these and like data Bartlett's picture is the best source of information I know of, even if he does give us a glimpse of the falls coming like an ocean from the sky.

And this brings me to Bartlett's chief fault as an historical artist. He is a little prone to impose upon us by a subtle magnifying of his subject. It is very easy to draw the Niagara, as for instance his marvelous "View from Table Rock," and then by introducing human figures drawn say to one-half or one-quarter scale, vastly to magnify the height and grandeur of the scene. But if his studies are open to this suspicion, or to a general charge of over-prettiness—which fault, if it be a fault, perhaps lies with the steel plate itself—they must also be credited with genuine merit as works of art and in many instances with definite value as historical records.

It was these beautiful volumes on "American Scenery," the first creditable work of the sort that had been undertaken, that first fairly made known to the world the chief scenic features of the eastern and northern United States. What has since developed as the greatest scenic portion of our country was then practically unknown. In the seventy and more years that have elapsed since these drawings were published, there have been many works on similar lines, of varying merit, some of them enlisting the talent of genuine artists; but I know of none which is a better Niagara record or a more pleasing one than these old-time drawings of W. H. Bartlett.

More than one artist appears to have re-engraved Bartlett's pictures. A New York publisher, Hermann J. Meyer, in 1854 issued a Niagara series with German text; most of the pictures were suspiciously like Bartlett, though far inferior to the originals. The collector will sometimes run across a beautiful plate, "Under the Horseshoe," drawn by J. C. Buttre and published in New York. It suggests Bartlett's study of the same subject, yet in the treatment of the water is wholly different—and better than Bartlett.

In the roll of Niagara art the name of Thomas Cole has long been eminent, if not preëminent. Though born in England, Cole spent most of his life in America and is a sort of landmark in the earlier development of American painting. He first visited Niagara in 1829. Of that visit his biographer, Louis L. Noble, records a not unusual experience: "He was disappointed. Lifted by no rapture, burdened by no sense of overpowering grandeur, he gazed upon it almost without an emotion above that of surprise at himself. . . . Its failure to affect him at once lay in its very greatness. . . . Niagara to Cole was, by his own declaration, far less than the mountains. They were symbols of the eternal majesty, immutability and repose, which no cataract could ever be. . . . Niagara was great in its loneliness." How much of this expresses Cole's mind, and how much the mind of the Reverend Mr. Noble, one cannot say. Many a man has been lost to posterity through the philosophizing of his biographer.

It is recorded that Cole made many drawings of Niagara at this time—the spring of 1829. He sketched it "at various points, particularly from below, and upon Table Rock, and from a projection on the eastern brink, where the eye commands, at a glance, the entire sweep of the cataract with the rugged cliffs of Goat Island. For the study of water, especially under all its circumstances connected with torrent-motion, Niagara far exceeded, in his opinion, all other places. A favorite study was a singularly fine swell, beautifully breaking back upon itself, in the rapid below the bridge crossing to the island. Well nigh twenty years afterward, he pointed it out to a friend, the same 'thing of beauty' which he had studied with more pleasure and effect than almost any other single object at the falls. Footing it down the river with sketch-book in hand, the Whirlpool afforded fine opportunities for water-studies, and the heights of Queenston opened to his view an expanse of forest-tops, then unbroken but by the mighty river, and bounded by the distant Ontario, which he did not fail to secure for future purposes."

When or where he painted his great picture of the Falls is not clear. Writing from London, May 1, 1831, he says: "I hope to arrive in America November next. With me I shall bring several pictures, and most likely the Falls of Niagara." I find no record of his painting Niagara at a later period. Cole was but 28 years old when he first studied the cataract. Sixteen years later, when he had won high rank in the art world, he again visited Niagara Falls, with his wife. The following page from his journal is appropriate here, as it shows the attitude of an artist mind towards the Niagara subject:

"*September* 4, 1847.—On Tuesday last, Maria and I returned from an excursion to Niagara. Niagara I have visited before. Its effect on my mind was perhaps as great as when I first saw it. But I am convinced that, sublime and beautiful as it is, it would soon cease to excite much emotion. The truth is, that the mind dwells not long with delight on objects whose main quality is motion, unless that motion is varied. Niagara, stupendous and unceasing as it is, is nevertheless comparatively limited,—limited in its resources and duration. The mind quickly runs to the fountain head of all its waters; the eye marks the process of its sinking to decay. The highest sublime the mind of man comprehendeth not. He stands upon one shore, but sees not the other. Not in action, but in deep repose, is the loftiest element of the sublime.

"With action waste and ultimate exhaustion are associated. In the pure blue sky is the highest sublime. There is the illimitable. When the soul essays to wing its flight into that awful profound, it returns tremblingly to its earthly rest. All is deep, unbroken repose up there—voiceless, motionless, without the colors, lights and shadows, and ever-changing draperies of the lower earth. There we look into the uncurtained, solemn serene—into the eternal, the infinite—toward the throne of the Almighty.

"The beauty of Niagara is truly wonderful, and of great variety. Morning and evening, noon and midnight, in storm and calm, summer and winter, it has a splendour all its own. In its green glancing depths there is beauty; and also in its white misty showers. In its snow-like drifts of foam below, beauty writhes in torment. Iris, at the presence of the sun, at the meek presence of the moon, wreathes its feet with brighter glories than she hangs around the temples of the cloud. Yet all is limited. It cannot bear comparison with that which haunts the upper abysses of the air. There is infinity in the cloud-scenery of a sunset. Men see it, though, so commonly, that it ceases to make an impression upon them. Niagara they see but once or so, and then only for a little while; hence the power it exerts over their minds. Were there Niagaras around us daily, they would not only cease in most cases to be objects of pleasure, but would, very likely, become sources of annoyance.

"But great, glorious, and sublime Niagara—wonder to the eye of man—I do not wish to disparage thee. Thou hast a power to stir the deep soul. Thy mighty and majestic cadence echoes in my heart, and moves my spirit to many thoughts and feelings. Thy bright misty towers, meeting the vault on high, and based upon the shooting spray beneath, are images of purity. Thy voice—deep calling unto deep, with a might that makes the hoary cliffs to tremble,—leads back the soul to Him, speaking upon Sinai's smoking summit. Thy steep-down craggy precipices are the triumphal gate through which, in grand procession, pass the royal lakes and captive rivers. The soul is full of thee. Favoured is the man who treads thy brink. Thankful should he be to God for the display of one of His most wonderful works. But they are blessed who see thee not, if they will accept the gift which God vouchsafes to all men, which, in beauty and sublimity, does far surpass Niagara—the sky. O that men would turn from their sordid pursuits, and lift their eyes with reverential wonder there."

Cole's picture, in its day acclaimed a masterpiece, has now a two-fold interest in the historic sense; it is a beautiful record of a pristine forest Niagara that has long ago vanished; and it is in itself an example of a method and manner of painting—one might almost say, of seeing Nature —no longer favored, perhaps not attainable by modern artists. I should add, that I only know Cole's "Niagara" through engravings. I have made considerable inquiry, especially of the directors of the principal art collections in America, but none of them has been able to inform me in whose hands the original painting now is. In 1831 it was owned by Joshua Bates. Engravings of Cole's "Niagara" were published by Walker, in Boston, in 1832. It was also engraved by T. S. Woodcock and published in Baltimore by Robert Reid.

Lord Morpeth, afterwards the Earl of Carlisle, visited Niagara Falls and wrote poetry about them. He also made many friends in America, one of the best being W. H. Prescott, the historian. Carlisle appears to have asked him to procure a painting of the cataract, with what result is shown by the following extract from one of Mr. Prescott's letters:

BOSTON, U. S., January 27, 1851.

MY DEAR CARLISLE: I wrote you from the country that, when I returned to town, I should lose no time in endeavoring to look up a good painting of the Falls of Niagara. I have not neglected this; but though I found it easy enough to get paintings of the grand cataract, I have not till lately been able to meet with what I wanted. I will tell you how this came about. When Bulwer, your Minister, was here, I asked him, as he has a good taste in the arts, to see if he could meet with any good picture of Niagara while he was in New York. Some time after, he wrote me that he had met with "a very beautiful picture of the Falls, by a Frenchman." It so happened, that I had seen this same picture much commended in the New York papers, and I found that the artist's name was Lebron, a person of whom I happened to know something, as a letter from the Viscount Santarem, in Paris, commended him to me as a "very distinguished artist," but the note arriving last summer, while I was absent, I had never seen Mr. Lebron. I requested my friend, Mr. ———, of New York, on whose judgment I place more reliance than on that of any other connoisseur whom I know, and who has himself a very pretty collection of pictures, to write me his opinion of the work. He fully confirmed Bulwer's report; and I accordingly bought the picture, which is now in my own house.

It is about five feet by three and a half, and exhibits, which is the most difficult thing, an entire view of the Falls, both on the Canada and American side. The great difficulty to overcome is the milky shallowness of the waters, where the foam diminishes so much the apparent height of the cataract. I think you will agree that the artist has managed this very well. In the distance a black thunderstorm is bursting over Goat Island and the American Falls. A steamboat, the "Maid of the Mist," which has been plying for some years on the river below, forms an object by which the eye can measure, in some degree, the stupendous proportions of the cataract. On the edge of the Horseshoe Fall is the fragment of a ferry-boat which, more than a year since, was washed down to the brink of the precipice, and has been there detained until within a week, when, I see by the papers, it has been carried over into the abyss. I mention these little incidents that you may understand them, being somewhat different from what you saw when you were at Niagara; and perhaps you may recognize some change in the form of the Table Rock itself, some tons of which, carrying away a carriage and horses standing on it at the time, slipped into the gulf a year or more since.

I shall send the painting out by the "Canada," February 12th, being the first steamer which leaves this port for Liverpool, and as I have been rather unlucky in some of my consignments, I think it will be as safe to address the box at once to you, and it will await your order at Liverpool, where it will probably arrive the latter part of February.

I shall be much disappointed if it does not please you well enough to hang upon your walls as a faithful representation of the great cataract; and I trust you will gratify me by accepting it as a souvenir of your friend across the water. I assure you it pleases me much to think there is anything I can send you from this quarter of the world which will give you pleasure. . . .

And believe me, dearest Carlisle,

Ever faithfully yours,

W. H. PRESCOTT.

It may be well to remind the reader that the historian Prescott was nearly blind; and, incidentally, to correct his statement about the horses and carriage. The great fall of Table Rock occurred at noonday, June 25, 1850. The driver of an omnibus, who had taken off his horses for their midday feed, and was washing his vehicle, felt the preliminary cracking, and escaped, with the horses; the empty omnibus being carried into the gulf below. Of Lebron, or his work, I find no record.

It is now more than half a century since Frederic Edward Church painted Niagara Falls. When his picture was first exhibited, in New York in 1857, it was declared to be the greatest Niagara painting ever made. That appeared to express the consensus of the most capable critical opinion of the day. In the half century and more that has passed since, countless canvases have undertaken to express the spirit of the Niagara scene; but as I studied Church's picture, recently, in the Corcoran Gallery at Washington, I could but echo the verdict of 1857. I know of nothing that surpasses it, nothing that ranks with it. Frederic E. Church is still first in the ranks of Niagara artists.

It is not a vast canvas—seven or eight feet or so, by three and a half. One rather forgets just what it shows; but long after he may find his mind dwelling in quiet delight on the vision of a sublime onward movement of emerald water, which falls majestically into an impenetrable abyss. Something of the greatness of this picture lies in its simplicity, in its freedom from distracting and belittling accessories. One draws from it something of the thrill and uplift of spirit that comes to the rightly-attuned soul in contemplation of any great expression of nature—a sweep of ocean billows, or a night full of stars.

The genius of Church, as expressed in this picture, had due recognition in his time. Ten years after the "Niagara" was painted, it won a prize at the Paris Exposition of 1867. It was widely exhibited in Europe; and returning to America found a fit and fortunate abiding place in the Corcoran Gallery. The capital of the nation is an appropriate place for the greatest painting of Niagara Falls.

It is related of Church that during the summer he spent at Niagara, he painted very little. "He passed many days there, not busily sketching all the time, but wandering about with his eyes and his heart brooding on the cataract, sitting sometimes for hours, studying the shifting splendors of the spectacle; and having made his sketches, came home, and in two months of devotion produced this picture." His method is commended to artists who are under the cloud of realism. Church's picture, ignoring everything but the heart and soul and essence of the scene, is the most real— and the most poetic—picture of Niagara ever painted.

Fortunately, as is not always the case with a great picture, there exist excellent chromo-engravings of Church's "Niagara." They are hard to find, nowadays, and have to be well paid for; but the original engraving, made soon after the picture was painted, is, if in good condition, a prize worth paying well for. There is also, in the National Gallery of Scotland, at Edinburgh, another "Niagara" by Church.

The half century and more that has elapsed since Church achieved his masterpiece, has not, so far as I am aware, produced anything on the Niagara theme that eclipses it in

THE NIAGARA IN ART.

merit. Niagara has been—and still is—much painted, but the studies of it that could command wide attention as works of art, are surprisingly few. Many of America's best art galleries—most of them, in fact—contain no Niagara.

It is pleasant to be able to record that on at least one occasion the Commonwealth of New York has taken official cognizance of Niagara as an art subject. Prior to the Columbian Exposition, the State commissioned P. C. Flynne, then resident at Niagara Falls, to paint a picture of the cataract for exhibition in the New York Building at Chicago. The completed work is probably one of the largest of the Niagara paintings now exhibited, the canvas being eight by fifteen feet. It embraces both the American and Canadian falls; and if it reveals no particular inspiration, it is at any rate skilfully and intelligently painted. In 1894 the artist presented it to the State of New York, and since that time it has held a conspicuous place in the Senate lobby of the Capitol. It may be noted that the unfinished mural work of William M. Hunt, in the Capitol at Albany, was to have included some treatment of the Niagara theme.

Louis R. Mignot, a New York artist, exhibited at the Columbian Exposition a study of Niagara which long since probably found its way to some private collection. Although the "Niagaras" in public galleries are few, there are beyond question many, often of great excellence, cherished in private hands.

A little reflection suggests that the real Niagara—not the wearisome depiction of detail, but the poetic soul of the green flood—should appeal with peculiar force to the artist of marines. I incline to the belief that of all the myriad of Niagara studies the very few which have superlative art excellence find their merit purely in the study of the movement, color and mass effects of the water. This phase of Niagara is akin to the ocean and it is no great surprise, though a matter of satisfaction, that one of the greatest of marine painters found his way to the banks of the Niagara, not to draw the detail of the scenery, but to paint a masterpiece of the moving waters. This was Mauritz Frederick Hans de Haas. The name de Haas has an honored place in the art annals both of America and Europe. At least three artists of distinction have borne it. Maurice, to Anglicize his first name, was born in Rotterdam in 1832. His earlier life and study were in that city and the Hague. In 1851 he was painting water-colors in London. Becoming a pupil of Louis Meyer,—then recognized as the greatest marine painter of Europe—he developed a style of marked character and excellence. His work pleased not only the artists, but the public, and his pictures—nearly always marines—were welcomed for the principal art exhibitions of Europe. He was given the curious appointment of artist to the Dutch Navy; and royalty in the person of Queen Sophia of Holland bought one of his best known paintings ("Dutch Fishing Boats"), and bestowed upon the artist special marks of her favor. In 1859, soon after his marriage, he came to New York, being induced thereto, it is said, by his friend and patron, August Belmont. From that date until his death in 1895, he was a conspicuous and honored figure in the American art world, a member of the National Academy of Design and the winner of many medals. On coming to Niagara, he spent some time in a study of its attractions; but, ignoring the great cataract, found a subject worthy of his genius in the rapids above the falls. There may be readers of this page who can recall having seen at the International Exposition in Paris, in 1878, de Haas' superb picture of these rapids. It was the subject of much comment and criticism, especially in the art press, and it is entitled to rank, I think, among the greatest works of this master of marine painting.

It was a reflective French visitor at Niagara—M. Auguste Laugel, author of *"Les Etats-Unis pendant la Guerre"* (Paris, 1864)—who thought that the only artist who could have painted the scene, the only one capable of rendering *"la terrible majesté de ce spectacle,"* was Ruysdaël. "He would doubtless have chosen a day when the waters were darkest, when great sweeping clouds throw heavy and threatening shadows, when the pines bend under a cold and furious wind." I do not agree with M. Laugel in this. Ruysdaël's *penchant* was for the melancholy moods of Nature; whereas in my thought the characteristic aspect of Niagara is bright and peaceful.

Countless modern artists—those of note as well as amateurs—have painted or engraved Niagara. Harry Fenn's masterpiece is his "Niagara." Joseph Pennell has made excellent studies of it. J. Henry Hill, about 1889, etched a large plate of the Canadian Fall, producing a beautiful, genuinely artistic picture. Two studies in oil, one a summer, the other a winter view of the cataracts, by W. C. Bauer, are to be included among the thoroughly good modern work on this subject. These canvases were recently in the hands of a New York dealer. Notable, too, are the Niagara paintings of F. V. Du Mond, reproduced in photogravure to illustrate William Trumbull's poem, "The Legend of the White Canoe." So are J. Hamilton's engraving on steel from T. Taylor's drawing, and the steel plate engraved by Jones, from Frankenstein's painting. This last, published many years ago in Philadelphia, gives a good general view of the Falls, from Hennepin's Point. An earlier painting, showing the rapids above the American

Fall, and Judge Porter's first bridge, was engraved and published in London in 1831. One of the most striking of all the published pictures is a large colored lithograph, after John Bornet's original, showing both falls, published by Goupil in 1855. But it is obviously impossible to enumerate all the work—even all the good work—on this subject.

Many pictures of the Niagara Falls have been published in Buffalo, but few of them are of a character to be included in these notes. Mention may be made of the drawings of F. Holloway, showing the American fall from the Ferry and the Horseshoe from Table Rock; these were published in this city about 1860. A portfolio of Niagara Falls views, lithographed by Hall & Mooney and published from Steele's Press in 1844, has little art merit, most of the views being badly redrawn from Bartlett. William H. Beard painted the old Lewiston bridge, his picture being lithographed in 1850; but I do not find that he or Buffalo's pioneer artist, James H. Beard, ever painted the Falls.

Several artists, whose work is particularly well known in the Niagara region, have in recent years produced pictures of the Falls which should have mention in our interview. In the Historical Building at Buffalo hang Reginald C. Coxe's study of the Rapids, and his large and very lovely canvas of the Luna Fall.

Here also is Raphael Beck's fine painting of the Falls, a general scene from much the same point of view as Thomas Cole's. Like Cole, Mr. Beck has painted a primitive Niagara with no buildings, bridges or other signs of the white man's intrusion.

Among the many interesting pictures, old and modern, good and bad, preserved at Niagara Falls, the visitor is sure to study the fanciful, clever paintings depicting "The Red Man's Fact"—an Indian maid being swept over the fall in a sacrificial canoe; and "The White Man's Fancy," in which the personified Spirit of the Cataract beckons in the mist. These paintings, made widely familiar by process-reproduction, were painted by James Francis Brown, resident for some years at Niagara Falls and at Buffalo.

Of all the artists who have studied Niagara none approaches in comprehensive thoroughness the work of Amos W. Sangster. In the local annals of the region Mr. Sangster may fairly be styled *the* artist of the Niagara. A lifelong resident of Buffalo, he gave his productive years to painting and etching, usually of nearby subjects. Lake Erie, I think, was his chief delight. He painted, with uncommon skill, its shores and waters, in storm and calm. His marines, harbor views and kindred subjects, have long been deservedly popular. It was in the early 80's or thereabouts that he conceived the laborious project of illustrating the Niagara river from lake to lake. Many difficulties were overcome, and the work was issued in folio parts, bearing date 1886, though its completion was a year or so later. It was dedicated to the artist's personal friend, Grover Cleveland, then President. The work includes an ample descriptive text, and was well printed. The great feature of it is Mr. Sangster's art—one hundred and fifty-three etchings on copper, from his own drawings, many of them being full-page plates. The illustration of the river and the falls is thorough and in the main satisfactory; and some of the large plates rank among the best we have of the cataract.

Numerous artists, some of established repute, have visited the Falls, and painted them, in recent years, but of the ultimate destination of their canvases I can only write, in some cases, on newspaper authority. I well recall, a few years ago, a sojourn at Niagara of Gilbert Munger, who years before had been there and painted Niagara Falls by commission from Emperor William I. of Germany. For this picture, it is recorded, he was decorated by his Emperor.

Then there was P. Calderon Cameron, a Scotch artist, who painted two vast pictures of Niagara Falls in winter. The first one, after exhibition in this country and Europe, was sold to H. H. Warner of Rochester—and of patent medicine fame,—for, it was stated, $30,000. The huge canvas finally met its fate in London, where it was ruined in a fire. The artist had created some sensation in painting this picture, by having himself suspended by means of a tackle reaching half way down the precipice, so that he might make his studies in mid-air. After the destruction of his picture, Mr. Cameron came again to Niagara—I think about 1890—and set up his easel on the ice bridge in the gorge below the cataract. The second painting, as finally completed, in a specially-built studio at "River Rest," near New Brunswick, N. J., was ten feet high and twenty-one feet long. It was described by a newspaper writer at the time of its completion as "a study in greys." Its present whereabouts, or ultimate fate, I do not know.

Another very large painting of the Falls was made about 1889 by M. Hottes, a Virginian, who claimed to be the first cadet sent from that State to West Point after the Civil War. Turning from the arts of war to gentler pursuits, he studied painting in Munich, being a fellow-student of William M. Chase. I confess ignorance of his work except in regard to his great Niagara—great at least in dimensions, for it covered 190 square feet of canvas, and was completed in the spring of 1890, in a large hall in Rochester. Mr. Hottes had begun his masterpiece in the old Museum building on the Canadian side of the Falls; but after some months of work he concluded that the mist and dampness of that place were detrimental to his picture. He thereupon moved it to Rochester, where it was completed. It was a general view of the cataract on a bright summer day, and according to contemporary criticism in the Rochester press was "a great work, and would do credit to any artist of the day." What has become of it? It would seem as if such large paintings as this and Cameron's could hardly be lost if they have real artistic worth.

These notes on Niagara in art would be sadly incomplete without some mention of the Niagara panoramas. The younger generation knows nothing of this form of entertainment. In fact, one has to be older than he likes to be, to remember it at all—and even at that, unless he be a veritable patriarch, he will know little of the panorama except in its last years. The genuine old-fashioned panorama was a popular form of edifying entertainment more than a century ago. It continued, in this country, down to the Civil War period; perhaps, in rural and remote towns, it lingered yet longer. The writer's earliest recollections, which hazily embrace such events as the siege of Vicksburg and the death of Lincoln, also include, as of about that time, a wonderful evening spent in contemplation of a panorama of "The Streets of New York," as shown in a certain village hall. Still vivid in memory is the row of smoking oil lamps which stood on the edge of the little stage as footlights, and cast their uncertain beams on the thoroughfares of the metropolis as they unrolled from a great cylinder of canvas planted upright at the left of the stage, and as slowly were rolled up again on the right. There was much creaking and an occasional hitch, as the *deus ex machina* wearied at the crank. Most of what that panorama showed is forgotten; but still vivid is a picture of a fallen horse, probably on Broadway, with the crowd characteristic of such an incident. What the lecturer may have said of the splendors of New York has wholly faded; but very distinctly is recalled his praise of this scene, which was declared to be "one of the great masterpieces of American art," as perhaps it was. Midway in this marvelous entertainment the curtain went down, while the cylinders of canvas were changed and new ones set up— much as pressmen now handle their rolls of printing paper for the press; meanwhile the orchestra—a young woman at a melodeon—relieved the tedium of the wait with musical "pieces," sacred and patriotic. The climax came toward the close, when the canvas, creaking on its rollers, showed a regiment of blue-coated soldiers marching past the old Astor House; and the girl at the wheezy melodeon played with all her soul and both hands and feet, "When Johnny comes marching Home Again," and the crowded audience of perhaps two hundred village people joined in chorusing the "Hurrah!" Oh, yes, the old panorama was not such a bad entertainment after all, especially if one were a little boy with all the world yet to see. Grand opera sometimes since has offered much less entertainment.

Long before "The Streets of New York" toured the country in great canvas rolls, there were panoramas of Niagara. Indeed I suspect that Niagara panoramas were the first ones seen in America, although in Europe, in the eighteenth century, there were shown panoramas of battles and of religious subjects. But before our Great West was known, Niagara was America's greatest wonder, and it was early painted, not so much for American contemplation as for exhibition abroad. Thus, in the autumn of 1832, we find Robert Burford, an English artist of speculative bent, faithfully sketching the Falls and vicinity. He returned to London, where a panorama of Niagara was painted from his drawings and exhibited at a building called the Panorama, in Leicester Square. The canvas probably was not great in extent, since (as we learn from a surviving pamphlet which advertised the show) the "Siege of Antwerp" was exhibited there at the same time. The painting itself is probably long ago dust or ashes; but a folding sketch, which shows its main features, is preserved and is of no slight historical value. It indicates the location of buildings long since gone if not forgotten, among them Forsyth's hotel, the old stairway, the guide's house, etc., on the Canadian side; and Whitney's hotel on the American. What is now known as Luna Fall is here named Montmorency!

Burford's panorama was apparently used to promote public interest in a projected City of the Falls, which it was proposed to build on the Canadian Heights above the cataract. The prospectus of this city which was offered to the London investor of 1832 was in a literary way as great a work of art as the panorama. It was pictured as the prospective rival of the most famous European resorts, "where the most secluded privacy can be enjoyed in the midst of the most refined society, yet so regulated, that Economy, Recreation and Pleasure are united—where the well-dressed and well-conducted, without reference to rank or wealth, may, and do, mingle with Lords, Grandees and Princes." Although the Canadian City of the Falls has not developed quite on the lines emphasized in the prospectus of 1832, it has grown into a comfortable community with a national pleasure-ground of surpassing beauty and industrial features which would vastly have surprised the promoters in the days of Burford's panorama.

Other panoramas of which I have record were Brewer's, shown in American cities in the '50's, made up, apparently, of canvases of "Niagara River and Falls in summer and winter," the Mammoth Cave and the Prairies; and the

Baker-street Bazaar in London, where in this decade of the '50's, was exhibited the "Grand Moving Mirror of American Scenery, painted on 25,000 feet of canvas, comprising the Falls of Niagara, the Mammoth Cave of Kentucky," etc. Possibly those two art-expositions were identical.

The name of G. N. Frankenstein may not hold a familiar place on the roll of American art. Little seems to be recorded of him. Cincinnati claimed him, I believe; and, if the Press can be believed (and why not?), his achievements in the realms of art were of the most notable. His one accomplishment in which we are interested was the making of one hundred original paintings of Niagara Falls, as studies for his panorama of the great cataract. The New York press of 1853, in which I find some mention of him, did not lack in praise. His genius was regarded as beyond question. We can only judge now of the quality of his work, by what was said of it at the time. At any rate, he had the high virtue of industry, for he was often at Niagara, from about 1840 to 1852. In *Harper's Monthly* of 1853, may be found some account of his work, with many woodcuts from his paintings, and a picture of the artist himself, in winter garb, standing in the snow before his easel, diligently painting the winter scene. "The artist whose labors we have so largely borrowed," writes the editor, "has made the study of the great cataract a labor of love. He has summered and wintered by it. He has painted it by night and by day; by sunlight and by moonlight; under a summer sun, and amid the rigors of a Canadian winter, when the grey rocks wore an icy robe and the spray congealed into icicles upon his stiffened garments. The sketches from which we have selected have grown up under his hands for a half score of years." If one may judge by all this heralding, Frankenstein's panorama was a real work of art; but whatever its merit, it no doubt long ago passed into the limbo of the forgotten.

There may have been yet other panoramas of our cataract; but it must suffice to notice the latest, if not the last, which was for a time famous as the Cyclorama of Niagara. It was an enterprise chiefly promoted by several gentlemen of Buffalo, who put a generous amount of money into it, and for a time enjoyed the prospect of rich returns. That these were not realized has nothing to do with the art side of the affair, which is the only side suitable for consideration here. It came about that Paul Philippoteaux, a very clever French artist, son of a yet more eminent sire, Felix Philippoteaux, was commissioned to paint Niagara Falls. He was an artist of established reputation; the pupil of Cabanel and Leon Cogniet, the winner of first medals at the *Écoles des Beaux Arts* and of the *Prix de Rome* competitions. He had already painted several cycloramas, among them the long-popular Battle of Gettysburg, when in 1886, he was engaged for the "Niagara." Of several assistants who shared with him the making of the gigantic picture, Adrien Shulz, at any rate, is entitled to notice. He was a Parisian, pupil of Dardoize and Hanoteau, and his pictures had for many years been features of the Salon.

In the spring of 1888 the Cyclorama of Niagara was opened to the London public, in York Street, Westminster. As was to be expected, considering the artists, it was genuinely a work of art. The painting was delightful, the manner of exhibition—the spectators viewing it with all favorable accessories of light, from the midst of the great circle which it formed—was pleasing and effective; and for a time the London public flocked to see it. The canvas was four hundred feet long—or rather, when set up, four hundred feet in circumference; and fifty feet high. Here were twenty thousand square feet of Niagara beauty, majesty and power made visible even to the stay-at-home British public, at a shilling a head. So successful was it, for a time, that M. Philippoteaux painted a second Niagara. This was sold to an English company, with a view to exhibition on the continent. Whatever was the fate of that painting, the present chronicler knows not. Many and vexatious business troubles arising, the original painting was brought to America, and exhibited, with discouraging returns, at Chicago. I have not traced its subsequent fortunes. It has not been exhibited for some years, and is probably in the oblivion of storage.

The principal public art collections of America contain few paintings of the Niagara cataract or rapids. The Corcoran Gallery at Washington easily leads the list with its incomparable Church. The Pennsylvania Academy of Fine Arts at Philadelphia has an interesting miniature of Niagara Falls, from the capable brush of William Russel Birch. George Loring Brown painted a "Niagara by Moonlight," which sketches of that artist state is owned in Malden, Mass.; and in the Detroit Museum hangs Mortimer L. Smith's "Niagara Falls in Winter."

The Carnegie Institute, Pittsburgh; the Albright Art Gallery, Buffalo; the City Art Museum of St. Louis; the Boston Museum of Fine Arts; the Art Museum of Worcester, Mass.; the Art Institute of Chicago; the Cincinnati Museum; and the Metropolitan Museum of Art, New York City, contain in their collections no paintings of Niagara Falls.

That they do not is hardly matter of surprise. What may be termed the great passages in Nature, do not necessarily inspire great art. Our art galleries probably would be searched in vain for pictures of the Mississippi or the

Amazon, the Falls of the Zambesi, Mount Everest or—shall we say—Mount Blanc or Washington. These things make no particular appeal to the artist, because of the qualities which give them preëminence in geography.

It used to be said of Niagara Falls, as no doubt of other unusual phases of Nature, that "they cannot be painted." This attitude of mind is illustrated by the following passage from C. F. Arfwedson, who toured hereabouts three-quarters of a century ago:

"Long before I arrived at Niagara, I had often and repeatedly been told that it is not in the power of man to describe and paint these falls in true colors. I even met with Americans who went so far as to consider it a sacrilege to attempt to depict Niagara by word, pen, or pencil. One day—I still have a lively recollection of my surprise—I happened to pass a bookseller's shop in New York, in company with a native American; several excellent drawings of Niagara were exposed in the window for general inspection. I stopped, and drew his attention to them, expressing, at the same time, my delight at the various engravings. Uncertain whether I actually meant what I said, he eyed me a long while with a penetrating look, and exclaimed at last, with a sneer, 'You have not seen Niagara!' and then cut short his conversation. This remark hurt me at the time, and I was almost resolved to follow the example of a certain traveller, who heard so much said of the waterworks at Philadelphia that he determined not to see them at all. Luckily I did not act upon the same principle at Niagara; but my curiosity became so excited, that I can only compare it to the sensation I felt when entering Rome for the first time, or wandering in the streets of Pompeii. In truth, there are no words expressive enough, no pen gifted with sufficient inspiration, no pencil endowed with an adequate share of poetical imagination, to describe Niagara as it actually is."

In a more confident vein is the following comment by Anthony Trollope:

"I came across an artist at Niagara who was attempting to draw the spray of the waters. 'You have a difficult subject,' said I. 'All subjects are difficult,' he replied, 'to a man who desires to do well.' 'But yours, I fear, is impossible,' I said. 'You have no right to say so till I have finished my picture,' he replied. I acknowledged the justice of his rebuke, regretted that I could not remain till the completion of his work should enable me to revoke my words, and passed on. Then I began to reflect whether I did not intend to try a task as difficult in describing the Falls, and whether I felt any of that proud self-confidence which kept him happy at any rate while his task was in hand. I will not say that it is as difficult to describe aright that rush of waters, as it is to paint it well. But I doubt whether it is not quite as difficult to write a description that shall interest the reader, as it is to paint a picture of them that shall be pleasant to the beholder."

As for mere *painting,* the work of a Church proves that the Falls can be painted, not merely with realism, but with subtlest spirit. In a word, then (to be done with this): Is it not true of the painter as the poet, that he carries his greatness with him, and does not find it lying in wait at this or that specially distinguished spot of the earth? The photographer, I grant, comes grandly into his own at a Niagara Falls; but Nature's highest appeals are largely independent of the accidents of rock and water. The painter's noblest art never can find its supreme expression in merely depicting the physical, no matter on how grand a scale it is presented in Nature.

JOHN VANDERLYN'S VISIT TO NIAGARA FALLS IN 1802

THE first American artist to visit and paint Niagara Falls, so far as I have been able to learn, was John Vanderlyn. In preceding pages (129-130) I have made brief note of his work. As there has come into my hands a hitherto unpublished narrative of his visit to Niagara in 1802, it seems appropriate, in printing it, to add some further facts regarding his eventful career.

There exists no published biography of Vanderlyn. Many years ago the story of his life was written, either by himself or from his dictation, but while in the hands of a New York publisher the manuscript was destroyed by fire. Much material was then lost which could not be replaced; there still exists, however, much regarding him which it is hoped may yet be put before the public by a competent and sympathetic hand. Vanderlyn was a striking figure in the art history of America, and his relations with Aaron Burr and other celebrities of his day give to his career an exceptional interest.

James Parton, in his "Life and Times of Aaron Burr," has told the story of Burr's first meeting with Vanderlyn:

"The interest which Colonel Burr took in the education of youth has been before alluded to. He always had a *protégé* in training, upon whose culture he bestowed unwearied pains and more money than he could always afford. The story of Vanderlyn, the most distinguished *protégé* he ever had, was one which was often related in these later years.

"He was riding along in a curricle and pair, one day during his senatorial term, when one of his horses lost a shoe; and he stopped at the next blacksmith's to have it replaced. It was a lonely country place, not far from Kingston, in Ulster county, New York. He strolled about while the blacksmith was at work, and, returning, saw upon the side of a stable near by, a charcoal drawing of his own curricle and horses. The picture, which must have been executed in a very few minutes, was wonderfully accurate and spirited, and he stood admiring it for some time. Turning round, he noticed a boy a little way off, dressed in coarse homespun.

"'Who did that?' inquired Burr, pointing to the picture.

"'I did it,' said the boy.

"The astonished traveler entered into conversation with the lad, found him intelligent, though ignorant, learned that he was born in the neighborhood, had had no instruction in drawing, and was engaged to work for the blacksmith six months. Burr wrote a few words on a piece of paper, and said, as he wrote:

"'My boy, you are too smart a fellow to stay here all your life. If ever you should want to change your employment and see the world, just put a clean shirt in your pocket, go to New York, and go straight to that address,' handing the boy the paper.

"He then mounted his curricle and was out of sight in a moment. Several months passed away, and the circumstances had nearly faded from the busy senator's recollection. As he was sitting at breakfast one morning, at Richmond Hill, a servant put into his hand a small paper parcel, saying that it was brought by a boy who was waiting outside. Burr opened the parcel, and found a coarse, country-made *clean shirt*. Supposing it to be a mistake, he ordered the boy to be shown in. Who should enter but the Genius of the Roadside, who placed in Burr's hand the identical piece of paper he had given him. The lad was warmly welcomed. Burr took him into his family, educated him, and procured him instruction in the art which nature had indicated should be the occupation of his life-time. Afterward, Burr assisted him to Europe, where he spent five years in the study of painting, and became an artist worthy of the name."

Regarding this story, of which there are several versions, one of Vanderlyn's friends sent a letter of correction to the historian, Parton, when his Life of Burr was first published; the letter is appended to the later editions of that work. The writer was Robert Gosman, now deceased, son of the Rev. Dr. John Gosman, who in 1808 became the pastor of the old Dutch church in Kingston, and was its first pastor to preach in the English language. Robert Gosman wrote with an intimate knowledge which could not be questioned, and I can do no better than to quote a portion of his letter correcting Parton, as it forms our most authoritative statement as to the early years of the first American artist who painted Niagara Falls:

"RONDOUT, N. Y., February 11, 1858.

" . . . Vanderlyn honored me with his confidence during the last five years of his life. I minuted, at his request, from his own lips, the principal events of his career. As is ever the case with the aged, the incidents of his earlier life were most vividly recalled. The circumstances of his first acquaintance with Colonel Burr, and the friendship and favor with which that eminent man honored him, were favorite subjects of discourse; and I recorded many anecdotes illustrative of the character of 'his best friend.' This but added to the strength of a conviction I had had for many years, that the popular idea of Burr's character was erroneous, and would be corrected in time. But to my purpose, which was to correct the anecdote as to Vanderlyn in your recent biography of Colonel Burr. That is related by you, in the main, as it had been in circulation for many years. But it is an invention purely.

"Vanderlyn was born at Kingston, in 1775. His grandfather, a Hollander, was a portrait painter of decided talent, though he did not make painting a profession; his father had the same taste and bias; and from his earliest years John Vanderlyn showed the direction of his powers. The Vanderlyn family were in comfortable circumstances and highly esteemed. John was educated at Kingston Academy, then an institution of high standing, and was a proficient in the classics. At the age of seventeen he passed a year in New York, and had, in a paint and color shop, and at an evening drawing-school, some very seasonable advantages. He turned his attention to oil painting the summer afterwards, copying at home two of Stuart's portraits lent by a friend, one being that of Colonel Burr. This copy was purchased by the then representative in Congress from this district, who was a warm friend of Colonel Burr, and who mentioned the fact to the Colonel at the session of 1795, the latter being then in the Federal Senate. 'Colonel Burr never forgot anything,' as Vanderlyn frequently said, and he did not forget that his friend had spoken very warmly of the decided talent of the youthful painter.

"In the summer following, Vanderlyn, when at New York, received a note without signature, asking him to call at a certain place. He did so; it was the office of Colonel Burr; and at the instance of J. B. Prevost, who was there, and who said the note was in the Colonel's handwriting, Vanderlyn proceeded to the residence of Burr, at Richmond Hill. The young artist was warmly met by Colonel Burr, became an inmate of his house for several weeks, fulfilling orders which came through his friend; and in the autumn of 1795 he was placed under the instruction of Gilbert Stuart, at Philadelphia.

"Vanderlyn remained with Stuart about a year, when the latter told Colonel Burr he had taught him all he could, and said he was then ready for Paris. Colonel Burr provided his young friend with the means; Vanderlyn went to Paris in 1796, remaining there between four and five years, and enjoying all the advantages of its admirable schools in art. . . .

"On the occasion of Burr's Parisian sojourn (1810-11), he assisted Vanderlyn pecuniarily, instead of the latter assisting him. Vanderlyn was always in straitened circumstances, and never more so than at that time. He was generous to a fault, but rarely had a louis which was not mortgaged ten deep. The 'Marius at Carthage' was the only picture he ever exhibited at the Louvre, or indeed anywhere else in Europe; though he painted his 'Ariadne,' and made some remarkable copies from Correggio and other masters during his abode there.

"I have the honor to be, very respectfully yours,
"ROBT. GOSMAN."

The omitted portions of Mr. Gosman's letter relate to current charges against the character of Aaron Burr, with which we are not in the present connection, interested.

Returning to America in 1801, Vanderlyn found himself in a high tide of favor. He was welcomed as a youth of great accomplishments and still greater promise. In Washington he became a member of the household of Aaron Burr, who was then Vice President; and there and in New York he was made much of, socially, and received many requests to paint portraits. He refused all commissions at this time, however, but painted the portraits of Burr and his daughter Theodosia, both in profile and both now widely known through engravings. He was apparently the most popular if not the most capable artist in America when in the autumn of 1802 he set out with a friend for Niagara Falls. The narrative of that tour was taken down in later years, from the artist's dictation, by the late Robert Gosman. The original manuscript is now owned by the Rev. Roswell Randall Hoes, chaplain in the

United States Navy, stationed at Norfolk, Va.; through his courtesy the Buffalo Historical Society is enabled to give it, herewith, its first publication:

JOHN VANDERLYN'S NIAGARA VISIT IN 1802.

In the latter part of September, 1802, Vanderlyn, with a young nephew, took his way to Niagara Falls. He purchased a horse and hired a chaise, and with as little baggage as was compatible with the supposed exigencies of a journey through a wilderness comparatively, and his sketching materials, proceeded from Kingston, up the west bank of the Hudson. Our travellers followed the ordinary route from Albany to Schenectady, thence ascending the valley of the Mohawk to Utica.

It was on the first of October that, in passing over the then high hill at Little Falls, the first sketch taken on this journey was made. Here the artist caught a fine view of the Genesee Flats, with a grandly rugged foreground, and the turbulent Mohawk eddying and foaming among the rocks, partially hidden by huge tangled and rough forest trees clinging to its precipitous banks.

Utica was then a small town, just emerging from the condition of a trading post and frontier station; and having lost the picturesque character and attributes of a garrison town without, as yet, having acquired the grace or comforts of advanced civilization. There was however a very comfortable tavern, for the travel to "the Genesee country" was becoming very great.

Simeon DeWitt, the State Surveyor General, had already passed over the country with his Lempriere in hand, erasing the Indian nomenclature, and giving to townships and villages, names ludicrous in their misapplication, and provoking the most biting comparisons. Rome then existed, but it was an aggregation of small temporary dwellings redolent of discomfort, and a half century could not efface from the artist's memory a most vigorous remembrance of the activity and sleeplessness of the Roman fleas.

Passing from Rome to Onondaga Hollow, the travellers met an Indian, a drunken Onondaga, bottle in hand, singing as a refrain "We sell all dis," and sweeping an imaginary boundary line. A few coppers persuaded the semi-savage to halt whilst the artist took his rapid sketch. The after history of this sketch is so curious, that it deserves note. A year or two afterwards Vanderlyn met, at a friend's, in Paris, an ecclesiastic—of Italian birth, we believe—of very benevolent turn and warmly commiserating the condition of the American aborigines. The little he knew of them seemed to be drawn from the history of Jesuit missions. He anxiously enquired of Mr. Vanderlyn, on learning that he was an American, as to the condition of the Indians in New York. The artist quietly replied that he could give his reverence an answer briefly, directly and professionally, if he would call at his lodgings next day. The good father did call, and Vanderlyn, without a word, put into his hands this sketch of the drunken Oneida as a statement in brief of the condition of his race. It is equally complimentary to the penetration of the priest and the force of the artist's pencil, that he took the reply to its fullest extent at a glance. He judiciously dealt out his anathemas, not on the poor savage, but on his tempters and destroyers, laid down the sketch with a sigh, and, though he and Vanderlyn met frequently afterwards never reverted to the subject.

After dipping into Oneida Hollow the travellers ascended a hill whence they caught a glimpse of Oneida lake, and an inadequate sketch was added to the memorials of the tour. Till reaching Manlius, the highway had been tolerable, but thence it was so decidedly bad, even for a backwoods road, that the "chaise" was abandoned, with a bargain to have it sent back to Albany, another horse was purchased, and the residue of the journey to Niagara made on horseback. Their first day's travel as cavaliers was marked by meeting a lawyer of Vanderlyn's acquaintance, and the *rencontre* was attended with the usually disastrous consequences of such meetings. The lawyer tendered his advice as to a short-cut road; it was followed; and the natural consequence was that they consumed several hours in toiling to a deserted clearing at its end, bringing about a catastrophe equivalent to a nonsuit, and compelling a retracement of their steps and proceedings *de novo*.

The artist spoke of his sensations on this, his first experience of the painful solitude of an unbroken forest. Any sound would have been a relief—any sight breaking the sameness of the long walls of trees hemming them in, a blessing indeed. There was no breeze to stir the foliage; and the hot noontide sun pouring upon the expanse of decaying vegetable matter, engendered an oppressive and sickening atmosphere. The dead level of the road was peculiarly wearisome to a wayfarer from a land of mountains and valleys, and once it was seriously debated whether it would not be best to turn back to the Hudson. In all his subsequent journeyings, Mr. Vanderlyn declared, he never passed through a more repellant country, and said he was convinced it would not be settled for a century.

At Cayuga Bridge the travellers were most kindly entertained by Gen. John Swartwout. Thence they skirted the sandy beach to reach Geneva, then a small village on the hill above the lake. The lake did not strike the artist very forcibly, for with his mind intent upon the grander aspects of nature towards which he was wending, the placid beauty of that charming sheet of water with all its unbroken sylvan surroundings seemed tame and lifeless.

From Geneva to Canandaigua, the travellers made their sore way over "a corduroy road," or a road made of logs laid crosswise in the swampy soil, its inequalities unmitigated by the slightest covering of earth. A little girl at Canandaigua, said Mr. Vanderlyn, described it more accurately than he had ever heard it, by calling it "the bump, bump road."

At Canandaigua the travellers were hospitably received by Mr. Thomas Morris, to whom they were introduced by a letter from Colonel Burr. Their host at parting gave Mr. Vanderlyn letters to Judge Hamilton of Queenston, Canada, and other Canadian gentlemen, which were exceedingly useful. Mr. Morris highly commended the idea of the artist to visit Genesee Falls *prior* to Niagara, "for," he remarked, "after seeing the latter, Genesee is hardly worth a glance. But," said he, "it is a place which will be known hereafter, for there is a capital water power."

The travellers turned off to Genesee Falls, now the site of the city of Rochester. The germ of the present thriving town with its dozen giant mills, consisted of a solitary farm house and a primitive grist mill. The Genesee river falling over three ledges formed three distinct falls. Now the whole stream is diverted to furnish power for the mills, and all the primitive aspect of the scene is lost. A finished pen and ink sketch of the Falls of the Genesee by the artist's hand, is still in existence. Mr. Vanderlyn and comrade found homely but bounteous entertainment at the farm house spoken of, and as a farther act of hospitality, their host got up a raccoon hunt by torchlight, which proved highly successful.

From the junction of the cross road to Genesee Falls and the main route, to the next inn was twenty miles, twelve of it being unbroken forest. Night closed upon them as the travellers were toiling wearily over the log causeway of a morass, for they were unhappily in the heart of "the endless swamp of Tonawanta." It was moonlight, and though this aided their progress, it sadly bewildered them by giving in the fantasies of light and shade, hints to imagination which detected crouching beasts of prey in the gloom, and pictured imaginary houses in the distance. There was no lack of strange sounds in this wilderness, the hoot of an owl being occasionally blended with the scream of a panther. More jaded in mind than body, the travellers reached a clearing and saw a cheering light, just as they had decided to try and perch in a tree till daybreak. The haven of rest proved to be a rude log house, where they were received at midnight and with backwoods kindness treated to the best the cabin afforded. No incident of moment occurred prior to the arrival of Mr. Vanderlyn and his nephew at New Amsterdam, now more appropriately called Buffaloe. The place was then little more than a cluster of log huts, so uninviting that the travellers crossed to Canada, where they found the evidences of an older and more thriving country and got comfortable quarters at a stone farm house.

From this point, Chippewa, even then a small village though little more now, was twenty miles distant. The cloud of mist from Niagara greeted the pilgrims some eighteen miles from the cataract and its roar was heard two miles. Vanderlyn remained at Niagara twelve days, having reached [there] about mid October. After a day of needed rest at Chippewa the artist took up his comfortable quarters at Burden's farm house hard by the cataract—so near in fact—say 800 yards—that a constant tremor pervaded the house and all its belongings, rendering a new comer rather nervous till custom caused it to be unnoticeable. A fork stuck into the floor would quiver like an aspen.

In 1802 there was no crossing for miles above and below the Falls, and all Vanderlyn's sketches were therefore taken from the Canada shore. The only descent to the water was by "the Indian Ladder," thus perilous enough to deter the timorous from its trial. "Table Rock," which is so noticeable a feature in Vanderlyn's views, was then unmutilated by the wear of the elements, and the gunpowder experiments which have at length destroyed it. Nature had then no divided empire with art, for save an occasional clearing, and a farm house or log cabin here and there, Niagara doubtless appeared very much as it did when Father de Smet, in 16.., stood upon its banks, and the glories and magnificence of the scene were revealed to the first intelligent European to whom they were revealed.

The companion engravings afterwards given as the fruits of this tour by Mr. Vanderlyn, were a "General View," and a "View of the Great Fall." The first was taken three fourths of a mile below the cataract near the Indian Ladder, which is directly opposite "the American Fall." From the semi-circular sweep of the shelf, this General View gives a surpassing idea of the magnitude and proportions of Niagara. The sketch for the Great, or Horse Shoe Fall, was taken from Table Rock.

A day or two elapsed before the artist employed his pencil. He said it required that time at least to give him any idea of the proportion of the elements of the scene. The absence of grand scenery, of towering rocks or mountain heights as standards of comparison, rendered it impossible at first to seize an idea of the magnitude of the scene. He said that in truth he was disappointed—a feeling which is confirmed by most who see Niagara at first, the reality not coming up to the imagination all indulge. Added to this, the tremor of the rocks, and the roar and motion of the mighty waters had a confusing effect, distracting, dizzying and bewildering, for a time. The man overcame the artist. He forgot his errand; sitting several hours as if under a spell, lost to himself, taking in no distinct idea of the scene, and only conscious of an arena of overwhelming grandeur and power in full and turbulent vigour.

The narrative ends abruptly, nor have we any further record of the sojourn at the Falls, or the return journey. If Mr. Vanderlyn ever dictated it, it was perhaps destroyed in the fire referred to.

The reader will have noted a few errors in the account of the journey. The "Genesee Flats" should no doubt read "German Flats." According to credible testimony it was not Simeon DeWitt, but a subordinate in his department, who is responsible for the classic names of places throughout central New York. The drunken Indian referred to as an Onondaga, and again as an Oneida, may have been either. The Thomas Morris met at Canandaigua was no doubt the son of Robert Morris, the financier of the Revolution, whose land interests in western New York were to some extent looked after by Thomas. Father de Smet was never at Niagara, so far as we know, and was of the nineteenth, not the seventeenth century; the allusion is undoubtedly to Father Hennepin, in 1678.

On his return from Niagara to Kingston Vanderlyn evidently applied himself to his several paintings of the Falls, as already noted. He returned to Europe in 1803, published his famous companion studies of Niagara in London in 1804; and after a sojourn in Paris, where he painted a portrait of Washington Irving, settled in Rome, where he did his most notable work. Living in a house that had been Salvator Rosa's, he painted his famous picture, "Marius amid the Ruins of Carthage." It was exhibited at the Louvre in 1808, where it received a gold medal offered by the Emperor Napoleon, in a competition shared in by twelve hundred artists. It is significant of the artist's varied fortunes that this medal was twice pawned for the necessities of life, and was finally redeemed and preserved by members of the family of Bishop Kip, in San Francisco, who at last accounts were the owners of the "Marius."

After two years in Rome, Vanderlyn again returned to Paris, where he worked, with splendid results, until 1815. Besides painting many portraits, and copies of great works of Raphael, Titian and Correggio in the Louvre, he painted his original "Ariadne of Naxos," afterwards purchased by Durand and engraved by him "in one of the best plates ever produced in America." When, some years later, the "Ariadne" was exhibited in America, it aroused a no small storm of protest in certain quarters, simply because it was a nude study, something the American public has been curiously slow to learn to look upon with proper vision.

It was during this sojourn in Paris that Vanderlyn befriended Aaron Burr, who after his duel with Hamilton found it advisable for a time to live abroad. In Europe he was shunned by Americans, but Vanderlyn remained true to his former benefactor.

Returning to America, the artist entered upon a series of calamitous and disappointing years. Although some portrait commissions came to him, there was on the whole but little demand for his services. He missed the appreciative art "atmosphere" of Europe, and as one project after another miscarried, his nature changed and he became morose and resentful. He had dreamed of founding in America a National Gallery of Art, but failed to enlist funds or even kindly interest. Although his sitters for portraits included many of the great men of the day—Madison, Monroe, Calhoun, Clinton, Jackson, Randolph and others—he claimed that the rivalry of Stuart and Trumbull deprived him of a just recognition. He turned his talents to panorama painting, secured a concession from the Corporation of New York for a building, and in the rear of the present City Hall, erected the New York Rotunda, where for some dozen years were exhibited very excellent panoramas, largely his own work, as well as various of his smaller canvases. The financial outcome of this enterprise was disastrous; in 1829 the city refused to renew his lease, and deeply in debt, he turned again to portrait painting. So embittered was he by his experiences that some years later, when elected to membership in the Academy of Design, he refused to accept the honor.

Among his constant friends were Joseph Allston and Gulien C. Verplanck, through whose efforts, in 1832, he was commissioned by Congress to paint a full-length portrait of Washington, for the House of Representatives. This work, when completed, gave such satisfaction that the Government paid him $2500, instead of the $1000 originally stipulated. In 1837 he was commissioned to paint, for

$12,000, one of the panels for the rotunda in the Capitol. He gladly accepted the commission, chose for his subject, "The Landing of Columbus," and went to Paris to execute the work. But age and disappointment had sapped his powers. The work was mostly painted by clever French artists employed by Vanderlyn. The composition is said to have been his, but the completed picture was a great disappointment to all capable judges of art, and detracted rather than added to Vanderlyn's reputation. Before being placed in the Capitol it was exhibited throughout the East; and it may be noted that it is the original from which was engraved the plate long used by the Treasury Department on the back of the five-dollar bills of the United States currency.

In his youth some of Vanderlyn's successful attempts were in the way of historical compositions, among others, "The Death of Jane McCrea"; but in later life he made no attempt in this field. One of his latest portraits was of President Taylor, now in the Corcoran gallery, in Washington. His portraits of Burr and R. R. Livingston are owned by the New York Historical Society. His "Ariadne" is owned by the Pennsylvania Academy of Fine Arts. Several of his canvases, among them the "Niagaras" previously noted, and a number of excellent portraits, are preserved in Kingston.

John Vanderlyn's end was a touching one. I quote from a sketch of him printed in the New York *Evening Post*, July 11, 1903:

"One morning in September, 1852, he landed from a Hudson river steamboat in a feeble condition, and set out to walk to Kingston, two and a half miles distant. Fatigue soon overcame him, and he was found sitting by the roadside by a friend from whom he begged a shilling for the transportation of his trunk, adding that he was sick and penniless. He secured a small back room in the village, and the friend spoken of went quietly about among a few of his acquaintances with a subscription list for his maintenance. Funds for the purpose were promptly pledged, but they were never needed. A few mornings after his arrival Vanderlyn was found dead in bed. . . . He rests now in the old Wiltwyck cemetery in Kingston, with neither stone nor mound to mark his grave."

The same capable biographer sums up his artistic merits and defects as "those of a painter trained in the school of David—splendid draughtsmanship and skill in composition marred by frequent want of feeling for color." Although his range of subject was wide, his production was limited, and the only canvases I have learned of, from his brush, which depict American scenery, are the early pictures I have described of Niagara Falls, painted while yet the world's only pictorial acquaintance with the great cataract was through the inadequate sketches of early travelers, and one or two worthy works by Europeans. But the pioneer American artist of Niagara is John Vanderlyn.

THE NIAGARA IN SCIENCE

IN no field of literature regarding the Niagara region do we arrive at more definite and gratifying results than in science. Our poetry may be uninspired, our part in fiction dubious, our art in large measure negligible; but in science at any rate Niagara stands for something definite—something splendid and fruitful.

Without attempting a scientific treatise I propose to bring together sundry available facts which will show what Niagara represents, or what has been accomplished by its aid, in the various branches of physics and of natural history; with something of its associations with distinguished scientists.

The first men to visit the Falls, in anything like a scientific spirit, were Canadian officers who came to Niagara in May, 1721. Before that date the white visitors had included missionary priests, soldiers and traders; and although the latter at any rate would no doubt contemplate the place with a practical eye, and objurgate the interruption to navigation, yet their scientific attainments did not go beyond some slight devices for ameliorating the toil of the portage. But in the spring of 1721, there came to the Niagara men of another stamp: Charles Le Moyne, Baron de Longueuil, lieutenant governor of Montreal; with him the Marquis de Cavagnal, son of the Governor-General of Canada, Captain de Senneville, M. de Laubinois, commissary of ordnance, Ensign de la Chauvignerie the interpreter, De Noyan, commandant at Frontenac, and others, with a numerous train of soldiers and servants. The main object of the visit was to treat with the Senecas; an incidental object was to measure the Falls. There is no mention of their having been measured, up to this time. An unofficial report says that the French officers used a cod-line and a stone of half a hundred weight, and they found the perpendicular height *"vingt et six bras"*—that is, twenty-six fathoms, or 156 feet. This first measurement was probably taken from what we know as "Prospect Point," where the height today is not far from what it was found to be in 1721.

The Rev. Father Bonnecamp, with De Celoron's expedition, at Niagara in 1749, reports its height to be "133 feet, according to my measurement, which I believe to be exact."

Peter Kalm, the first professional naturalist to write of Niagara, reported in 1750 that "those who have measur'd it with mathematical instruments find the perpendicular fall of the water to be exactly 137 feet. Mons. Morandrier, the King's engineer in Canada, assured me, and gave it to me also under his hand, that 137 feet was precisely the height of it"; but he adds, that those who have tried to measure it with a line, "find it sometimes 140, sometimes 150 feet, and sometimes more."

Andrew Ellicott, brother of Joseph, who was the "Father of Buffalo," was a distinguished civil engineer, a man of scientific habit of thought, and the first American surveyor to measure the Falls. He found "the perpendicular pitch 150 feet," to which he added 58 feet for the descent in the upper rapids, and 65 feet for the lower rapids, a total descent of 273 feet "in the distance of about seven miles and a half."

Andrew Ellicott's description is really one of the landmark-documents in the history of the region. It is not long, but compact with precise data. It was widely reprinted, and served to make general a new standard of information regarding physical phenomena at Niagara. He noted the formation of clouds, from the ascending spray; and the striking effect of the water "puffed up in spherical figures, nearly as large as common cocks of hay; they burst at the top and project a column of spray to a prodigious height; they then subside, and are succeeded by others, which burst in like manner."

This interesting phenomenon has been commented on by many writers from Ellicott's day to this; the accepted explanation being that air carried down by the mass of falling water is at first compressed, then, as the pressure is lessened, expands and forces itself upwards, producing the "haycock," "cone" or "geyser" effect as it bursts through the water and escapes. One of the best treatises on this subject, entitled "The Upward Jets at Niagara," by W. H. Barlow (F. R. S., etc.), is a paper read before a meeting of the British Association; it appears in the publications of that body, and also in the *Journal* of the Franklin Institute, Philadelphia, 1877. The author, who was one of the judges at the Centennial Exposition, visited the Falls in 1876.

Initial curiosity as to the height of the Falls being satisfied, scientific thought was more and more concerned with the history of Niagara and its gorge. In the eighteenth century the science of geology did not exist, in the modern comprehension of the term; yet very early men were speculating and announcing theories as to the formati n of the gorge.

One of our earliest writers on the scientific aspects of Niagara was Dr. Benjamin Smith Barton of Philadelphia. Among the papers which he contributed to the *Proceedings* of the American Philosophical Society was one entitled "Notes on the Falls of Niagara," written (but not published) in 1799. Ten years before that he had communicated to the society "An account of an earthy substance found near the Falls of Niagara and vulgarly called the Spray of the Falls, together with some remarks on the Falls," by Robert McCauslin, M. D. Dr. McCauslin had then resided at Niagara for nine years, and as early as 1781 had measured the height of the cataract, with the aid of "the acting engineer," perhaps of Fort Niagara. He reported the American fall at 143 feet, the Canadian at 163. In view of the early date and the thorough acquaintance with the region which Dr. McCauslin had, it is well to quote from his remarks on the recession of the Falls:

"This retrocession of the Fall does not by any means go on so quickly as some have imagined. During nine years that I have remained at Niagara, very few pieces of rock have fallen down which were large enough to make any sensible alteration in the brink; and in the space of two years I could not perceive, by a pretty accurate measurement, that the northeast brink had in the least receded. If we adopt the opinion of the Falls having retired six miles, and if we suppose the world to be 5700 years old, this will give above $66\frac{1}{2}$ inches for a year, or $16\frac{2}{3}$ yards for nine years, which I venture to say has not been the case since 1774. But if we accede to the opinion of some modern philosophers and suppose that America has emerged much later than other parts of the world, it will necessarily follow that this retrograde motion of the Falls must have been quicker, which is a supposition still less consonant to the observations of late years."

In New York—then the seat of Government—in the winter of 1790, Andrew Ellicott told of Niagara to his friend William Maclay, one of the United States Senators from Pennsylvania. Senator Maclay considered what had been told him, and in his journal, February 1, 1790, wrote as follows:

"Mr. Ellicott's accounts of Niagara Falls are amazing indeed. I communicated to him my scheme of an attempt to account for the age of the world, or at least to fix the period when the water began to cut the ledge of rock over which it falls. The distance from the present pitch to where the Falls originally were, is now seven miles. For this space a tremendous channel is cut in a solid limestone rock, in all parts one hundred and fifty feet deep, but near two hundred and fifty at the mouth or part where the attrition began. People who have known the place since Sir William Johnson took possession of it, about thirty years ago, gave out that there is an attrition of twenty feet in that time. Now if 20 feet equals 30 years, then 7 miles or 36,960 feet equals 55,440 years!"

To most modern readers the deductions of McCauslin and Maclay would seem to be harmless enough. Yet the Christian world of that day was not able to listen to anything which opened the way to doubt of the then accepted interpretation of Scriptural statements. When Dr. McCauslin wrote, and for many years after, no man could declare that the rocks at Niagara showed the earth to be of greater age than the literal reading of Genesis made out, and maintain his integrity as a Christian or even a believer in the Christian's God. Half a century after McCauslin Sir Charles Lyell gave to the geological problems at Niagara the most intelligent study thay had, up to that time, received. Yet a large part of the world was still incapable of accepting his conclusions, which pointed to the world's great age. Dr. J. L. Comstock, a prolific author on natural history topics, in his "Outlines of Geology" (3d ed. New York, 1837) reviews Lyell's earlier theories at length, and sums up as follows:

"Suppose the cataract of Niagara now at the outlet of Lake Erie and moving into it at the rate of 50 yards in 40 years, or a little more than a yard per year, we would inquire of Mr. Lyell how long a period would be consumed in draining it to the bottom, and whether the escape of its waters thus sudden 'would cause a tremendous deluge,' as he asserts. The title of Mr. Lyell's book being 'An attempt to explain the former changes of the Earth's surface, by reference to causes now in action,' is itself an attack on the sacred Scriptures, but we are happy to believe that Christianity is in little danger from his arguments."

The Niagara Falls have been used both to prove, and to disprove, the Biblical account of the Deluge. In 1837 George Fairholme published in London a substantial volume entitled: "New and conclusive physical demonstrations, both of the fact and period of the Mosaic Deluge, and of its having been the only event of the kind that has ever occurred upon the earth." As he construed the Scriptural testimony, he found that the Deluge occurred some 4000 years ago; whereupon, with all possible ingenuity, he interprets all geological data so as to harmonize with his theory. As a result, all his calculations arrive at conclusions exactly corresponding with the Mosaic chronology. Although he had never seen the Falls of Niagara he had at hand descriptions of them by several travelers, and these were adequate for his purpose. He contemplated the seven miles of gorge cut by the river from Queenston to the cataract, and finds "distinct evidences" that the recession of the falls has occupied less than 5,000 years. He devotes many pages to his argument. "As the operation of Niagara began," he says, "at Queenston, on that same day when the shallow basin of Lake Erie first overflowed its margin, we are thus led, by all the laws of inductive reasoning, to the origin of the whole American continent, as a dry land, at a period not more remote than about four or five thousand years." And again, speaking of the erosion produced by streams, he observes: "Their ceaseless friction affords us the key to the fact of a commencement; and in the remarkable case of Niagara, this the greatest of all cataracts, seems to have been purposely appointed, to confound the reasoning of the skeptic, and to open a more secret cabinet, distinctly disclosing to us the very date of this event."

Even in Fairholme's day the science of geology had made such progress that fair-minded men, with a knowledge of the subject, were unable to reconcile Biblical chronology with the testimony of the rocks. The conflict that arose between the students of nature and the adherents of theological teaching was one of the bitterest phases in the long conflict between theology and science. When geologists began to assert that the rocks proved that the earth was more than five or six thousand years old, the strict adherents to the Book of Genesis called them infidels, and atheists. Nor is this strife by any means a matter of the remote past. Many years after Fairholme proved it all—presumably to his own convincement—another Englishman felt called upon to prove it all over again. This was Philip Henry Gosse, whose "Omphalos," published in London as late as 1857, seeks to reëstablish the tottering structure of Mosaic chronology. He developed a theory originally put forward by Granville Penn, and styled "prochronism." "In accordance with this," says Andrew D. White, summarizing the views of Gosse (in his "Warfare of Science with Theology"),

"all things were created by the Almighty hand literally within the six days, each made up of 'the evening and the morning,' and each great branch of creation was brought into existence in an instant. Accepting a declaration of Dr.

Ure, that 'neither reason nor revelation will justify us in extending the origin of the material system beyond six thousand years from our own days,' Gosse held that all evidences of convulsive changes and long epochs in strata, rocks, minerals and fossils are simply *'appearances'*—only that and nothing more. Among these mere 'appearances,' all created simultaneously, were the glacial furrows and scratches on rocks, the marks of retreat of rocky masses, as at Niagara"—

all these and many more manifestations of great time, we are asked to believe came into being in an instant; asked to believe, as Dr. White puts it, "that Jehovah tilted and twisted the strata, scattered the fossils through them, scratched the glacial furrows upon them, spread over them the marks of erosion by water, and set Niagara pouring—all in an instant—thus mystifying the world 'for some inscrutable purpose, but for His own glory.'"

William Priest, a musician whose volume of American travels was published in London in 1802, did not visit the Niagara region, but has the following interesting allusion:

"An American writer has been endeavoring to investigate the age of the world, from the Falls of Niagara! According to his calculation (which, by the way, is not a little curious) it is 36,960 years since the first rain fell upon the face of the earth."

I have not been able to identify this "American writer."

From Andrew Ellicott's day to this the geologists have been studying Niagara and figuring out its age, with amazing diversity of result. The literature of Niagara geology is vast—probably exceeded by that of no phase of our subject except possibly the War of 1812. No one who devotes himself to the science of geology can omit Niagara from his studies, and anything like an exhaustive mention of those who have written on the subject is here out of the question.

In his "Partial Bibliography of the Geology of the Niagara," etc., A. W. Grabau (1901) gives the names of 61 authors who have written 194 books or papers on the subject. Grabau's list is but a beginning and might be greatly extended. He takes note only of scientists of distinction. To the student of the subject in its historical aspect many other writers, especially the earlier ones, must be taken note of, for we trace through them the gradual growth of knowledge and adjustment of theories. The problems of the "age" of the cataract, and of its rate of recession, have always been of great interest because their solution would establish a relation between the periods of geologic time and the centuries of human chronology.

Soon after Andrew Ellicott had made his measurements of Niagara, came the French *savant* C. F. Volney. Our grandparents knew Volney's "Ruins" as a classic. His "Views" contains a long account of his investigations at Niagara, which he visited in 1796—a memorable year, in which Great Britain relinquished her hold on the "American" side of the Niagara and the Lakes. DeWitt Clinton was studying the rocks at Niagara in 1810, and in 1822, under the pseudonym of "Hibernicus," wrote at length of the geology of the region in his "Letters on the Natural History and Internal Resources of the State of New York." He called the cataract "a great manufactory of clouds and rainbows," and adds: "It serves as a barometer as far as Buffalo. If the spray spreads from the north it is a sign of a northerly wind; a southeast wind indicates rain."

Amos Eaton wrote prior to 1825. Robert Bakewell, an eminent Englishman, studied the Niagara problem as early as 1829, and estimated the age of the Falls—that is, the time of recession from the escarpment at Lewiston—to be 12,000 years. Lyell, in 1841, visited Niagara, wrote delightfully of it, and decided that its age was about 35,000 years. Compare this with the 55,440 years of Maclay and Ellicott, and the "less than 5,000 years" of Fairholme!

In 1831 G. W. Featherstonhaugh made certain general observations on the ancient drainage of North America, and applied the operating principle to the origin of the cataract of Niagara. He especially controverted Mr. James Geddes, a distinguished engineer, who in a paper in the *Proceedings* of the Albany Institute, had taken the ground that the Niagara had not cut its gorge back from the Queenston ridge to its present position, but that the river had found the ravine already existing, and flowed through it.

A truly great name in Niagara study is that of James Hall, for many years New York State Geologist. It was he who in 1842 set the first stone monuments by which the recession of the Falls has ever since been measured. Professor Hall's work of 1842, and subsequent surveys, supplied exact data, so that there is little guess-work about the retreat of the Falls in the last seventy years. The rate of recession has been shown to vary remarkably, the American fall, from 1842 to 1875, averaged .74 of a foot a year; from 1875 to 1886, only .11 of a foot; from 1886 to 1890 its rate rose to 1.65 feet, making an average per year, for the period 1842 to 1890, of .64 of a foot. The Horseshoe wears away much faster; from 1886 to 1890 at the rate of 5.01 feet; and for the whole period, 1842 to 1890, an average of 2.18 feet per year.

Dr. Julius Pohlman of Buffalo was the first scientist to base his calculations on these known rates of recession. He reasoned that a portion of the gorge was pre-glacial in origin, and reduced the length of the post-glacial or recession period to 3,500 years. Warren Upham, taking the same data but reasoning differently, made the age of the

THE NIAGARA IN SCIENCE. 185

gorge "between 5,000 and 10,000 years." J. W. Spencer, whose writings on this subject are held in esteem, puts the age of the gorge at 32,000 years; and F. B. Taylor, also a learned and prolific writer on Niagara, places the length of the recession period, tentatively, at 50,000 years. Professor G. F. Wright makes elaborate calculations and gets 10,000 years as the answer; and Professor C. H. Hitchcock figures it all out, with delightful precision, at 18,918 years.

Never was there a more palpable case of the disagreement of doctors. We may as well leave it, as A. W. Grabau, a thorough student of the subject, leaves it in his valuable "Guide to the Geology and Paleontology of Niagara Falls and Vicinity" (Albany, 1901)—that is, with a few generalities:

"All such estimates are little more than personal opinions. . . . The leading questions concerning the extent of the pre-glacial erosion in this region, and the changes in volume of water during the lifetime of the Niagara, which are of such vital importance in the solution of this problem, are by no means satisfactorily answered. Nor can we assume that we are familiar with all the factors which enter into the equation. There may be still undiscovered causes which may have operated to lengthen or shorten the lifetime of this great river, just as there may be, and probably are, factors which make any estimates of the future history of the river and cataract little more than a mere speculation. We may perhaps say that our present knowledge leads us to believe that the age of the cataract is probably not less than 10,000 nor more than 50,000 years."

Of prime interest are Robert Bakewell's "Observations on the Whirlpool and on the Rapids below the Falls of Niagara" *(Am. Jour. Sci. and Arts,* New Haven, 1847), with curious illustrations. Mr. Bakewell, then a resident of England, was at Niagara for six days in 1829. In 1846, after he had made his home in the United States, he spent eight days more at the Falls, studying the geology and physical geography of the place. The paper referred to derives much of its value from the author's ability to compare his own observations at two intervals seventeen years apart. His son also wrote on the same subject.

I have alluded to Professor James Hall's work of placing markers in 1842. In 1837 he had been appointed by Governor Marcy to investigate the geology of the Fourth (N. Y. State) district, including the Niagara region. The result of his work, as presented in his "Geology of New York, Part IV.," etc. (Albany, 1843), is perhaps even now the most valuable single work we have on the geology of the Niagara region.

Sir Charles Lyell, greatest of English geologists, made a leisurely visit at Niagara in 1841. His studies of the region ("Travels," etc., London, 1845) are conspicuous for their thoroughness and sagacity, and his descriptions of scenery and narrative of travels are still entertaining and profitable reading, even for the unscientific. Not only in the "Travels," but in other of his writings, especially his "Principles of Geology," will the student find much relating to our region.

Other notable English scientists who have written of their Niagara experiences include Sir Andrew C. Ramsay, who came in 1859; John Tyndall in 1872; Thomas Henry Huxley in 1876. The last named, with his wife, visited Buffalo, to attend the meeting of the American Association for the Advancement of Science. Here they were the guests of Mr. O. H. Marshall, who afterwards visited them in England. A week was spent at Niagara, "partly," writes Professor Huxley's biographer, his son Leonard,

"in making holiday, partly in shaping the lectures which had to be delivered at the end of the trip. As to the impression made upon him by the Falls—an experience which,

THE NIAGARA IN SCIENCE. 187

it is generally presumed, every traveler is bound to record—I may note that after the first disappointment at their appearance, inevitable wherever the height of a waterfall is less than the breadth, he found in them an inexhaustible charm and fascination. As in duty bound, he, with my mother, completed his experiences by going under the wall of waters to the Cave of the Winds. But of all things nothing pleased him more than to sit of an evening by the edge of the river, and through the roar of the cataract to listen for the under-sound of the beaten stones grinding together at its foot."

Professor Tyndall's visit, in November, 1872, gave to Niagara literature one of its most delightful chapters. The reader is recommended to turn to it, in the "Fragments of Science," where he can enjoy the whole of it. No aspect of the scene escaped Mr. Tyndall's attention. He soon concluded "that beauty is not absent from the Horseshoe Fall, but majesty is its chief attribute." With the veteran guide, Tom Conroy, he made his way along the foot of the Horseshoe Fall, below Terrapin Point, to a point seldom visited and only by the active; the place has since been named "Tyndall's Rock." In his record of the experience he does not content himself with formal observations on the force of the currents or the erosion of the rocks. Scientist that he was, and accustomed to deal only with exact facts and known quantities, he takes note not only of external phenomena, but of a "certain sanative effect" which the spray and thunder of Niagara wrought on himself. "Quickened by the emotions there aroused, the blood sped exultingly through the arteries, abolishing introspection, clearing the heart of all bitterness, and enabling one to think with tolerance, if not with tenderness, on the most relentless and unreasonable foe."

I know of no more significant utterance in all the realm

of Niagara literature. Coming from a sentimentalist, it would scarce command our attention. Uttered by a Tyndall, it has the impressiveness of a new revelation of the eternal and benignant gospel of nature.

In 1886 the American Association for the Advancement of Science met for the third time in Buffalo, thus gathering on the banks of the Niagara America's foremost living geologists and physicists. As fruit of that meeting, or of subsequent studies then inspired, there are many books and countless papers in scientific journals. Among the more prolific and authoritative of recent writers on Niagara geology I must be content with the mere mention of Herman Leroy Fairchild ("The Birth of Niagara"), E. L. Garbett, G. K. Gilbert of the U. S. Geological Survey—author of many monographs on the subject, W. D. Gunning ("The Past and Future of Niagara"), Aug. S. Kibbe ("Report of the Survey to determine the Crest Lines of the Falls of Niagara in 1900"), J. S. Newberry, N. S. Shaler ("Aspects of the Earth"), J. W. Spencer—author of many papers relating to Niagara geology and kindred topics, Warren Upham ("The Niagara River since the Ice Age"), Alexander Winchell, R. S. Woodward ("On the Rate of Recession of Niagara Falls"), and G. Frederick Wright, among whose numerous useful writings mention should be made of the "New Method of Estimating the Age of Niagara Falls" and "The Niagara Gorge as a Geologic Chronometer."

Dr. John Bigsby, in a paper published in 1824 (*Amer. Jour. Sci. and Arts*) describes minerals and other specimens found at Niagara Falls in June, 1819.

Nobody has measured the flow of Niagara, but many engineers and scientists have computed it. One of the earliest to do so was Z. Allen, in co-operation with E. R. Blackwell. In his report of their work ("On the Volume of the Niagara River," etc., *Am. Jour. Sci. and Arts, New Haven,* 1844), Mr. Allen writes:

"Whilst passing a few days at the Falls of Niagara in the summer of 1841, it occurred to me to make the necessary admeasurements for ascertaining the quantity of water precipitated by the grand cataract. . . . For this purpose the services of Mr. E. R. Blackwell of Black Rock, a most skillful and accurate engineer, were engaged by me."

There is a full-page map (by Blackwell) of a section of the Niagara river opposite Black Rock, with thirty-eight soundings extending in three ranges across the river, with localities, etc., indicated. Mr. Allen computed the total horse-power of Niagara Falls at 4,533,334.

An exceptional phase of Niagara study is Professor William H. Brewer's "Earth Tremors at Niagara Falls." (*Yale Sci. Monthly,* May, 1896.) It is an account of observations made at Niagara Falls through a period of forty-five years. The heaviest vibrations were found to be on either side of and near the Horseshoe Fall. They disappeared in places in the soft shales below the limestone, although they were evident in the harder limestone and sandstones. Passing down the gorge, the vibrations decreased in intensity, becoming too faint to be perceived between the suspension bridges, but increasing again on nearing the rapids. The theory has been promulgated that crystals are more common in the rocks near the Falls than elsewhere, their formation being promoted by the jar of the cataract; but Professor Brewer found no evidence of this.

There is probably no connection between earth tremors at Niagara Falls, and earthquakes; but Professor Brewer's paper reminds me of a report made by Dr. Charles E. West "On an Earthquake in Western New York," Oct. 23, 1857. Dr. West's report of it, made at a meeting of the American Association for the Advancement of Science, held in Baltimore in May, 1858, says in part:

"It occurred in Buffalo, at a quarter past three o'clock, p. m., and was violent compared with other earthquakes in the Northern States. I was seated in a chair with my head leaning against the mantel of the fireplace when the shock occurred, and so great was its violence as to throw me forward to my feet. . . . A farmer living in Aurora, a town sixteen miles southeast of Buffalo, was digging potatoes in his field, at the time of the earthquake, and so powerful was the shock that he instinctively leaned upon his hoe-handle, and while in this posture he observed the dirt shake back and forth over his hoe, which was partially buried in the soil."

Further evidence is presented from Port Hope, Ont., Lockport, Buffalo, Jamestown, Warren, Pa., Erie, Pa., and other points. Other earthquake tremors have been reported —or imagined—in this region, but this one of Oct. 23, 1857, is the only one supported by credible testimony. Dr. West, it is unnecessary to remind the older residents of Buffalo, was the first principal of the Buffalo Female Seminary, a gentleman of wide repute for his scholarly attainments and love of truth. It might be shown, perhaps, that some of the supposed earthquake tremors were coincident with the fall of great rock-masses at the cataract, and either caused the fall, or were caused by it. This was the case on January 7 and 8, 1889, when the fall of heavy rock masses in the cleft of the Horseshoe produced earth tremors that were felt for some miles around.

In 1804, Dr. Benjamin Smith Barton, in his *Medical and Physical Journal*, reported that an "earthquake occurred at the Falls of Niagara, on the 26th of December, 1796, about six o'clock in the morning. It seemed to proceed from the northwest, and did not last more than two seconds. But it was sensibly felt for fifty miles around the Falls." This also, in all probability, was due to the fall of rock.

The sound of Niagara—its roar, or if you please, its thunder, or as one poet prefers to put it, its silence—has occasioned much curious comment. The very earliest visitors had as much to say about the great noise, and the distance at which it could be heard, as about any visual aspect of the scene. Niagara was, naturally, discovered by the ear before it was by the eye; and as we have noted, some of the early missionaries reported having heard it, without going to see it. The distance at which its sound could be heard was always matter of curious report and speculation.

J. T. Trowbridge, in that pleasant autobiography, "My Own Story," speaks of his boyhood in Lockport, where, he says, writing of the Falls, "often in the still autumn weather, I listened to their continuous, low, hardly distinguishable roar, a sound that always breathed a quiet joy into my soul." This was in the '40's, and the distance was some eighteen miles. Tom Moore the poet, in 1804, claimed to have heard the Falls at Buffalo. This is corroborated by the Hon. Lewis F. Allen, an early resident of Buffalo, who told me not many years before his death in 1890 that many a time, seated on the veranda of his house on Niagara street near Ferry, in the calm of a summer evening, he had heard the roar of the Falls. What with whistles and bells and horns, the noise of trains and electric cars, the din of pavement and factory, the civic "shouting and tumult," all that make up the composite Voice of Cities, it has been many a day since the cadence of Niagara has been audible in Buffalo. But the sound is constant at the source; and I have no doubt that if we would all keep still, and the wind were in the right quarter, Niagara's roar could again be heard, as Tom Moore said, "upon Erie's shore."

In the early years of the long-distance telephone it was thought to be a notable feat to make the roar of Niagara audible in New York City. It is still an impressive thought that audiences assembled in distant cities can, by the aid of well-perfected instruments, distinctly hear its deep music.

Ole Bull, who came to America in 1843, soon saw the Falls. In the autumn of 1844, resting at Bristol, R. I., he wrote down his "musical thoughts" of Niagara. His wife, who is his biographer, says that he had "spent many days at the Falls at different times, and saw them in all lights—in sun and storm." "One evening great forest fires added their blaze and glare to the silvery shimmer of the moonlit rapids, and the lurid light with the grand rush and roar of the waters made a deep impression upon him." It was at Niagara that he made the acquaintance of George Ticknor and his family, with whom the musician ever after maintained a pleasant acquaintance and friendship.

The "Niagara," which he played for the first time in New York in the winter of 1844, was disappointing to the general public, though favorably commented on by the press. It was of the class of compositions which make no appeal to the unimaginative. After it had been explained to the public —after writers gifted with phrases if not with true interpretative insight had given to the public a tangible explanation of what they thought that Ole Bull thought he was expressing in terms of the violin—then the public professed to like it, and to see—or hear—a great deal of exquisite sentiment in it, pertaining in an emotional way to the cataract of Niagara. N. P. Willis was one of those who undertook to record Ole Bull's emotions so that others, less gifted, might share them. Thus he wrote, in part:

"We believe that we have heard a transfusion into music —not of 'Niagara,' which the audience seemed *bona fide* to expect, but of the *pulses of a human heart at Niagara.* We had a prophetic boding of the result of calling the piece vaguely 'Niagara,'—the listener furnished with no 'argument' as a guide through the wilderness of 'treatment' to which the subject was open. This mistake allowed, however, it must be said that Ole Bull has, genius-like, refused to misinterpret the voice within him—refused to play the charlatan, and 'bring the house down'—as he might well have done by any kind of 'uttermost,' from the drums and trumpets of the orchestra.

"The emotion at Niagara is all but mute. It is a 'small, still voice' that replies within us to the thunder of waters. The musical mission of the Norwegian was to represent the insensate element as it was to him—to a human soul, stirred in its seldom reached depths by the call of power. It was the *answer* to Niagara that he endeavored to render in music—not the *call!*"

Another of Ole Bull's interpreters, most richly endowed with imagination, was Lydia Maria Child, who in her once-famous "Letters from New York" wrote as follows:

"You ask me for my impressions of Ole Bull's 'Niagara.' It is like asking an æolian harp to tell what the great organ of Freiburg does. But . . . I will give you the tones as they breathed through my soul. . . .

"I did not know what the composer intended to express. I would have avoided knowing if the information had been offered; for I wished to hear what the music itself would say to me. And thus it spoke: The serenely-beautiful opening told of a soul going peacefully into the calm, bright atmosphere. It passes along, listening to the half-audible, many-voiced murmurings of the summer woods. Gradually, tremulous vibrations fill the air, as of a huge cauldron seething in the distance. The echoing sounds rise and swell, and finally roar and thunder. In the midst of this stands the soul, striving to utter its feelings.

> 'Like to a mighty *heart* the music seems
> That yearns with melodies it cannot speak.'

"It wanders away from the cataract, and again and again returns within sound of its mighty echoes. Then calmly, reverentially, it passes away, listening to the receding chorus of Nature's tremendous drums and trombones; musing solemnly as it goes, on that vast sheet of waters, rolling now as it has rolled, 'long, long time ago.'

"Grand as I thought 'Niagara' when I first heard it, it opened upon me with increasing beauty when I heard it repeated. I then observed many exquisite and graceful touches, which were lost in the magnitude of the first impression. The multitudinous sounds are bewildering in their rich variety. . . . There is the pattering of water-drops, gurglings, twitterings, and little gushes of song. . . . It reminded me of a sentence in the 'Noctes Ambrosianae,' beautifully descriptive of its prevailing character: 'It keeps up a bonnie wild musical sough, like that o' swarming bees, spring-startled birds, and the voices of a hundred streams, some wimpling awa' ower the Elysian meadows, and ithers roaring at a distance frae the clefts.'

"The sublime waterfall is ever present with its echoes, but present in a calm, contemplative soul. One of the most poetic minds I know, after listening to this music, said to me: 'The first time I saw Niagara, I came upon it through the woods, in the clear sunlight of a summer's morning; and these tones are a perfect transcript of my emotions!' In truth, it seems to me a perfect disembodied poem; a most beautiful mingling of natural sounds with the reflex of their impressions on a refined and romantic mind. This serene grandeur, this pervading beauty, which softens all the greatness, gave the composition its greatest charm to those who love poetic expression in music; but it renders it less captivating to the public in general, than they had anticipated. Had it been called a Pastorale composed within hearing of Niagara, their preconceived ideas would have been more in accordance with its calm, bright majesty."

"Over everything stands its doemon or soul," says Emerson, "and as the *form* of the thing is reflected to the eye, so is the *soul* of the thing reflected by a melody. The sea, the mountain-ridge, Niagara, super-exist in precantations, which sail like odours in the air; and when any man goes by with ears sufficiently fine, he overhears them, and endeavors to write them down, without diluting or depraving them."

After all this, one can but wish that we had Ole Bull's own explanation of his "Niagara" music.

The sound of the cataract appeals particularly to the poets and the scientists, and therein, perhaps, reveals their kinship. Most poets are not scientists, in the practical sense of the term; but every true scientist is a poet, in his appreciation of nature's processes and revelations. Frederick Almy touches the matter with fine discernment in his paper on "What to See" at Niagara ("The Niagara Book"):

"Mr. Howells speaks in his book of the *repose* of Niagara. Another paradox is its silence. The sheets of falling water are so unchanging to the eye that the motion seems no more actual than when the breeze runs through a field of grain. It moves without moving. In some such way the unchanging volume of sound soon leaves on the ear a strange sense of silence. Now and again, however, as some more compact mass of water makes its fall, a new note strikes the ear, and under all is the heavy beating of the air as if of sound too low for the range of human hearing. It has always seemed to me as if much of the voice of Niagara might be to us inaudible."

Eugene M. Thayer, in a notable paper on "The Music of Niagara" *(Scribner's Magazine,* February, 1881), analyzes the voice of the cataract as it appealed to his trained musical sense. He writes the chords of its harmonies, and finds them four octaves lower than the lowest range of our piano keyboards. His study is exceedingly suggestive and profitable to read. Mr. Thayer often visited Niagara Falls and was a well-known figure at that resort. His passion for the place suggested in some of its phases the morbid infatuation of Francis Abbott, the Niagara "hermit" of many years before. Mr. Thayer committed suicide by shooting, at Burlington, Vt., June 27, 1889.

Much might be written of the bird-lovers at Niagara. In 1804 there came to our river the Paisley poet-weaver who had turned poet-naturalist, Alexander Wilson. He had walked from Philadelphia to Oswego, coming thence to the Niagara by the lake. In my paper on "Niagara and the Poets" I have dwelt at some length on Wilson's adventures, and on his work as a poet; in the present connection we need recall him only as naturalist.

The Niagara visit was four years before the publication of the first volume of his "American Ornithology," but he was already diligently collecting material for it. At the Falls he was much impressed by the numbers of the white-headed or bald eagles. The most striking of all the plates in his great work is the colored engraving showing this bird, about one-third life size. "In the background"—to quote Wilson's own description,

"is seen a distant view of the celebrated cataract of Niagara, a noted place of resort for these birds, as well on account of the fish procured there, as for the numerous carcasses of squirrels, deer, bear and other animals that, in their attempts to cross the river, above the Falls, have been dragged into the current, and precipitated down that tremendous gulf; where among the rocks which bound the rapids below they furnish a rich repast for the vulture, the raven and the bald eagle. . . . There rises from the

THE NIAGARA IN SCIENCE.

gulf into which the Fall of the Horseshoe descends, a stupendous column of smoke, or spray, reaching to the heavens and moving off in large black clouds, according to the direction of the wind, forming a very striking and majestic appearance. The eagles are here seen sailing about, sometimes losing themselves in this thick column, and again re-appearing in another place, with such ease and elegance of motion, as renders the whole truly sublime."

Wilson's prose, especially when he attempts fine writing, is apt to grow feeble. In his famous poem, "The Foresters," descriptive of this tour to Niagara, he has told of the eagles in verse:

> "High o'er the wat'ry uproar, silent seen,
> Sailing sedate, in majesty serene,
> Now midst the pillared spray sublimely lost,
> Swept the gray eagles, gazing calm and slow
> On all the horrors of the gulf below;
> Intent, alone, to sate themselves with blood,
> From the torn victims of the raging flood."

Wilson, like Audubon, and Charles Lucien Bonaparte, who continued Wilson's work, makes numerous references to Niagara Falls as the habitat of birds which he describes.

John James Audubon was at once author, artist and naturalist. As America's greatest ornithologist I find his most fitting place among the scientists. In his journal—a fascinating narrative of one of the most interesting of careers—he tells of his visit to Niagara in the summer of 1824. He had crossed the State from Albany, part of the way by canal, as yet unfinished to Buffalo. I quote from his journal:

"*August 24.* Took passage for Buffalo, arrived safely, and passed a sleepless night, as most of my nights have been since I began my wanderings. Left next morning for the Falls of Niagara; the country is poor, the soil stiff white clay, and the people are lank and sallow. Arrived at the hotel, found but few visitors, recorded my name and wrote under it, 'who, like Wilson, will ramble, but never, like that great man, die under the lash of a bookseller.'

"All trembling I reached the Falls of Niagara, and oh! what a scene! my blood shudders still, although I am not a coward, at the grandeur of the Creator's power; and I gazed motionless on this new display of the irresistible force of one of His elements. The falls, the rainbow, the rapids, and the surroundings all unite to strike the senses with awe; they defy description with pen or pencil; and a view satisfied me that Niagara never had been and never will be painted. I moved towards the rapids, over which there is a bridge to Goat Island, that I would like to have crossed, to look on the water which was rushing with indescribable swiftness below, but was deterred from the low state of my funds. Walking along the edge of the stream for a few hundred yards, the full effect of the whole grand rush of the water was before me. The color of the water was a verdigris green, and contrasted remarkably with the falling torrent. The mist of the spray mounted to the clouds, while the roaring below sounded like constant heavy thunder, making me think at times that the earth was shaking also.

"From this point I could see three-quarters of a mile down the river, which appeared quite calm. I descended a flight of about seventy steps, and walked and crouched on my hams along a rugged, slippery path to the edge of the river, where a man and skiff are always waiting to take visitors to the opposite shore. I approached as near the falling water as I could, without losing sight of the objects behind me. In a few moments my clothes were wet. I retired a few hundred yards to admire two beautiful rainbows, which seemed to surround me, and also looked as if spanning obliquely from the American to the Canadian shore. Visitors can walk under the falling sheet of water, and see through it, while at their feet are thousands of eels lying side by side, trying vainly to ascend the torrent.

"I afterwards strolled through the village to find some bread and milk, and ate a good dinner for twelve cents.

Went to bed at night thinking of Franklin eating his roll in the streets of Philadelphia, of Goldsmith traveling by the help of his musical powers, and of other great men who had worked their way through hardships and difficulties to fame, and fell asleep hoping, by persevering industry, to make a name for myself among my countrymen.

"*Buffalo, August 25.* This village was utterly destroyed by fire in the War of 1812, but now has about 200 houses, a bank, and daily mail. It is now filled with Indians, who have come here to receive their annuity from the Government. The chief Red Jacket is a noble-looking man; another, called the Devil's Ramrod, has a savage look. Took a deck-passage on board a schooner bound to Erie, Pennsylvania; fare, one dollar and fifty cents, to furnish my own bed and provisions."

Thus far the journal; but this was not Audubon's only visit to Niagara. The fortunate reader who has access to Audubon's great work, the "Ornithological Biography," will find therein a pleasant chapter on Niagara, describing another visit, apparently in 1820. The following is extracted from it:

"After wandering on some of our great lakes for many months I bent my course toward the celebrated Falls of Niagara, being desirous of taking a sketch of them. This was not my first visit to them, and I hoped it would not be the last.

"Artists (I know not if I can be called one) too often imagine that what they produce must be excellent, and with that foolish idea go on spoiling much paper and canvas, when their time might have been better employed in a different manner. But digressions aside—I directed my steps towards the Falls of Niagara, with the view of representing them on paper, for the amusement of my family.

"Returning as I then was from a tedious journey, and possessing little more than some drawings of rare birds and plants, I reached the tavern at Niagara Falls in such plight as might have deterred many an individual from obtruding himself upon a circle of well-clad and perhaps well-bred society. Months had passed since the last of my linen had been taken from my body, and used to clean that useful companion, my gun. I was in fact covered just like one of the poorer class of Indians, and was rendered even more disagreeable to the eye of civilized man, by not having, like them, plucked my beard, or trimmed my hair in any way. Had Hogarth been living, and there when I arrived, he could not have found a fitter subject for a Robinson Crusoe. My beard covered my neck in front, my hair fell much lower at my back, the leather dress which I wore had for months stood in need of repair, a large knife hung at my side, a rusty tin box containing my drawings and colors, and wrapped up in a worn-out blanket that had served me for a bed, was buckled to my shoulders. To every one I must have seemed immersed in the depths of poverty, perhaps of despair. Nevertheless, as I cared little about my appearance during those happy rambles, I pushed into the sitting-room, unstrapped my little burden, and asked how soon breakfast would be ready.

"In America no person is ever refused entrance to the inns, at least far from cities. We know too well how many poor creatures are forced to make their way from other countries in search of employment, or to seek uncultivated land, and we are ever ready to let them have what they may call for. No one knew who I was, and the landlord looking at me with an eye of close scrutiny, answered that breakfast would be on the table as soon as the company should come down from their rooms. I approached this important personage, told him of my avocations, and convinced him that he might feel safe as to remuneration. From this moment I was, with him at least, on equal footing with every person in his house.

"He talked a good deal of the many artists who had visited the Falls that season, from different parts, and offered to assist me, by giving such accommodations as I might require to finish the drawings I had in contemplation. He left me, and as I looked about the room, I saw several views of the Falls, by which I was so disgusted, that I suddenly came to my better senses. 'What,' thought I, 'have I come here to mimic nature in her grandest enterprise, and add my caricature of one of the wonders of the world to those which I here see? No. I give up the vain attempt. I will look on these mighty cataracts and imprint them where they alone can be represented—on my mind!'

"Had I taken a view, I might as well have given you what might be termed a regular account of the form, the height, the tremendous roar of these Falls; might have spoken of people perilling their lives by going between the rock and the sheet of water, calculated the density of the atmosphere in that strange position, related wondrous tales of Indians and their canoes having been precipitated the whole depth; might have told of the narrow, rapid and rockbound river that leads the waters of the Erie into those of Ontario, remarking *en passant* the Devil's Hole and sundry other places or objects; but supposing you had been there, my description would prove useless, and quite as puny as my intended view would have been for my family; and should you not have seen them, and are fond of contemplating the most magnificent of the Creator's works, go to Niagara, reader, for all the pictures you may see, all the descriptions you may read of these mighty Falls, can only produce in your mind the faint glimmer of the glow-worm compared with the overpowering glory of the meridian sun.

"I breakfasted amid a crowd of strangers, who gazed and laughed at me, paid my bill, rambled about and admired the Falls for a while, saw several young gentlemen *sketching on cards* the mighty mass of foaming waters, and walked to Buffalo, where I purchased new apparel and sheared my beard. I then enjoyed civilized life as much as a month before I had enjoyed the wildest solitudes and the darkest recesses of mountain and forest."

More than one bird-lover has since pursued his favorite study in the vicinity of the great cataract, and has written of it. The Duke of Argyll, not many years ago, spent some time at Niagara, and in a series of pleasantly-written articles in the *Youth's Companion,* made special note of the birds he had seen in the neighborhood of the Falls.

I must not forget the visit of Professor Louis Agassiz, who gave a course of scientific lectures at Niagara Falls in the summer of 1848. He was really the leader of a party of scientists, who made an excursion from Boston to the north shore of Lake Superior, June to August, 1848. The narrative of the tour, written by J. Elliot Cabot, gives an account of the party's sojourn at the Falls, of their scientific explorations in the neighborhood, and of Professor Agassiz' evening lectures on the phenomena of the region. Agassiz saw at Niagara for the first time a living gar-pike, the only representative among modern fishes of the fossil type of *Lepidosteus*. From this type, he tells us, he had learned more than from any other, of the relations between the past and present fishes. Incidentally we learn from Mr. Cabot's narrative, that rattlesnakes were still abundant at Niagara Falls and pigs roamed the streets of Buffalo.

Niagara has ever been beloved of the botanists. Her constant baptism of spray no doubt has something to do not only with the growth of an exceptionally large number of species, but with the profusion of individuals. Goat Island in particular is prolific of flowering annuals; and although year after year its natural gardens have been despoiled in May and June by the hordes of school children who call their wholesale pulling of plants "botanizing," yet most of the species persist, and, to a surprising degree, in generous and forgiving abundance.

Peter Kalm was the first botanist to study the flora of the

Falls. Students of the science today need only a reminder to make them associate two of our most interesting wild plants with the great Swedish botanist. Both are named for him. One is *Lobelia Kalmianum;* the other, the rarest of the St. Johnsworts in this latitude, *Hypericum Kalmii;* and both of these plants are to be found today at Niagara Falls, as no doubt they were in 1750, by Kalm himself. Another rarity that has in recent years been found near the Horseshoe Fall, Canadian side, is *Daphne mezereum,* but we cannot ascribe to it association with any early flower-loving visitor.

It is probable that F. A. Michaux, whose "North American Silva," published in 1807, was the first work of value relating to our native trees, visited Niagara. Though I do not find allusion to the Falls in his work, he frequently notes, in his description of species, that he observed them "on the shores of Lake Ontario" or Erie.

Among the published letters of Alexander Wilson is the following:

PHILADELPHIA, July 8, 1806.

To MR. WILSON AT THE FALLS OF NIAGARA.

Dear Sir: This will be handed to you by Mr. Michaux, a gentleman of an amiable character, and a distinguished naturalist, who is pursuing his botanical researches through North America, and intends visiting the Cataract of Niagara. The kindness I received from your family in 1804 makes me desirous that my friend, Mr. Michaux, should reside with you during his stay at Niagara; and any attention paid to him will be considered as done to myself, and suitable acknowledgments made in person by me on my arrival at Niagara, which I expect will be early next Spring.

You will be so good as give Mr. Michaux information respecting the late rupture of the rock at the Falls, of the burning spring above, and point out to him the place of descent to the Rapids below, with any other information respecting the wonderful scenery around you.

In the short stay I made, and the unfavorable weather I experienced, I was prevented from finishing my intended sketch equal to my wishes; but I design to spend several weeks with you, and not only take correct drawings, but particular descriptions of every thing relating to that stupendous Cataract, and to publish a more complete and satisfactory account, and a better representation of it, than has been yet done in the United States.

I had a rough journey home through the Genessee country, which was covered with snow to the depth of fifteen inches, and continued so all the way to Albany. If you know of any gentlemen in your neighborhood acquainted with botany, be so good as to introduce Mr. Michaux to them. . . .

I cannot say who was the Mr. Wilson at Niagara Falls, or whether Mr. Michaux used this letter; but he probably did. His father, André Michaux, also studied the flora and silva of America, but did not come into the Niagara region. Alexander Wilson's project of revisiting the Falls was never carried out. His original sketches, made in 1804, were completed by an artist, engraved by George Cooke of London, and illustrated his poem of "The Foresters," as it originally appeared in the Philadelphia *Portfolio,* in 1809-10.

John Bartram, the first American botanist—spoken of by the great Linnæus as "the greatest natural botanist in the world," made his way in 1743, with Lewis Evans, from Philadelphia to Fort Oswego on Lake Ontario. Such a journey through the wilderness was no slight undertaking, and no doubt these naturalists felt on reaching the lake that they had pushed far enough into a region of doubtful hospitality. They did not come on to Niagara. Amos Eaton, eminent in his time both as botanist and geologist, studied those sciences at Niagara, which he visited as early as 1824. Asa Gray knew the Niagara region prior to 1834 when he published his "Notice of some new, rare or otherwise interesting plants from the Northern and Western Portions of the State of New York." Whoever has used Gray's "Manual" will recall his frequent citation of Niagara Falls as habitat of uncommon species, though no doubt many of his specimens were had in exchange, as perhaps his data were secured, from local correspondents.

Constantine Rafinesque, an enthusiastic but most eccentric naturalist, visited Niagara Falls in 1826, studying and collecting with impartial zest its plants, birds, animals, fishes and rocks. A meager account of his sojourn there is contained in his "Life of Travels and Researches in North America and South Europe," published in 1836.

To those of us who live within the sound of Niagara no student of the regional flora will ever attain quite the place long held by Judge George W. Clinton. For many years he was, preëminently, Buffalo's naturalist. Botany was his delight, and no one knew better than he all the herbal and sylvan treasures of Niagara's banks. He especially loved the Whirlpool woods, not then as now despoiled and devastated, but a wonderful wild nook, where great tulip and sassafras trees grew. Foster's Flats, too—now politely named Niagara Glen—with its walking-fern (*camptosorus rhyzophyllus*), its rare *Aspidiums* and *Pellaeas,* and other lovely shy things in the vegetable world, was a favorite forage-ground. As David F. Day wrote of him: "The thick woods, the shaded dells and the wild fastnesses about the Falls of Niagara and at Portage become known to us as they had never been known before." Judge Clinton wrote of his botanical studies in his "Notes of a Botanist," which delighted many readers during their newspaper publication. His successor in this special field was Mr. Day, who like

Judge Clinton, studied much but wrote and published all too little.

Every natural phenomenon, every scientific phase of the Falls, has been written of. Some of the minor writings in this field are most interesting. For instance, Charles A. Carus-Wilson has written (*Nature,* vol. 47) of the Niagara spray clouds, which "exhibit an ice bow in clear frosty weather." He notes the absence of mock suns, which are accounted for by supposing the presence of hexagonal ice crystals; and he offers the theory that the ice crystals in the Niagara spray clouds are not hexagons but rhombs.

More appealing, perhaps, to popular appreciation are the color observations of H. G. Madan (*Nature,* Dec. 21, 1882), who finds in the American fall "a perfect and permanent illustration of contrast-colors. The pure, green, even sheet of water is trimmed, as it were, at regular intervals, by broad bands of foam, which although of course really white, appear of a delicate rose-pink hue. . . . The effect heightens the beauty of the beautiful fall, and I am surprised that no poet has made capital out of it." It would seem to be rather "capital" for the artists.

May I close these notes, which could be much extended, by recording one observation of my own, of Niagara Falls as a cloud-maker.

I had occasion to go to Lewiston on an early morning train. Seated on the river side of the car, I enjoyed the prospect of the fresh and dewy landscape. It had been a windless night, and banks of fog were still sleeping above the fields along the river. As the train reached that fair stretch of stream, north of Tonawanda, I observed a long, heavy cloud lying on the northwest horizon. The sun was yet low in the east, and the level beams made sharp contrasts of light and shade on the cloud. As a bend in the road opened an unobstructed view of the heaviest and lowest-hanging portion of this cloud, it was discovered to reach earthward with a mightly tap-root, the lower end of which was hid by intervening trees.

I rubbed my eyes to make sure there was no illusion, and resurveyed the celestial field. A few little clouds were at rest here and there on the horizon's rim, but in no quarter any heavy cloud, except this one, whose arms stretched out, vaporous and dark, across the Niagara peninsula for miles on the one hand toward Lake Erie, and toward Lake Ontario on the other; and whose middle part was joined to earth by this sharply-defined pillar of vapor. It was not until, a mile or so below the Falls, where the road skirts the edge of the gorge and gives the traveler a fleeting but unobstructed view of the cataract, that this earthward-reaching cloud was seen to be nothing but the uprising vapor of the Falls. During the still hours of the night, undissipated by the sun, it had poured upward and spread out on a supporting stratum of air until it shadowed the country for many miles.

Returning, a little later in the day, there was to be seen only a distant-drifting cloud and the shifting spray that vanished from sight as it rose in the warm air. The sun and the morning breeze had broken the tie that held the cloud to the cataract which had given it birth.

Men looked at the cataract for many years before the idea of utilizing its energy occurred to them. The earlier visitors viewed it, as all the universe was viewed before the slow rise of a knowledge of nature developed the natural sciences, as merely an extraordinary manifestation of Divine power. As Nature's story became better known and geology more and more an exact science, Niagara was studied with a view of reading from this torn page of the earth some portion of its history. The great cataract was seen to be one of the world's chronometers, measuring with its ceaseless beat the progress of the ages. Men ceased to dispute over the Mosaic account of creation, ceased attempting to prove by the phenomena of Niagara that the Deluge was universal and that it occurred exactly when the pre-scientific interpretation of the Pentateuch made out that it should have occurred. Gradually through the decades, these themes of earlier strife and difference lost their importance. The pulpit ceased to assail as infidel the geologist who dared assert that the recession of Niagara proved the earth of a far greater age than the six thousand or so Mosaic years. Gradually the age of the earth and the erosion of the Niagara gorge were taken as facts—as things demonstrated.

And all the time, while artists and poets and critics were painting and rhapsodizing, more and more men of a practical turn were thinking of the tremendous power of Niagara. No miller who had ever regulated the flow of a little stream to turn his mill-wheel could look upon Niagara without reflecting on the tremendous waste of energy. A small mill or two were set by Niagara's margin in the pioneer days. Later, when settlement had advanced and capital was available, came the era of construction of hydraulic canals, diverting a small fraction of the flood, yet by its aid building up no inconsiderable a city of many manufactories.

All this time the literary world was having its small say. Hundreds of travelers wrote hundreds of uninspired books, and would-be poets measured their emotions in mediocre verse. Deeply religious natures, such as Mrs. Sigourney, Margaret Fuller, Harriet Martineau and Fredrika Bremer, were brought by Niagara into moods of exalted devotion. Irritating British critics, disliking America and Americans, of the type of Basil Hall and Mrs. Trollope, found Niagara a new excuse for hostile demonstrations. A few men, true poets and analysts at soul—Dickens, Hawthorne, Henry James, and other choice spirits—labored to reveal to us the real Niagara. And all this time the great river was pounding away at its rocks and hurling its measureless millions of tons into the abyss to no purpose whatever save as a means of æsthetic gratification. But as it is a law of Nature that man's higher attainments come in the process of evolution from those that are lower, so is it in the relation of man to Niagara: as the latest expression of his appreciation of it, he has begun to use it, without destroying it or marring its beauty, for the good of mankind.

The greatest thing that can be recorded of Niagara, in no matter what aspect it is studied, is, that we have in some measure learned to utilize it for human good. With Niagara as the starting point, as the inspiration, all the rivers of the world, big and little, which offer any available power, are being brought into new service for humanity. Already a thousand waterfalls—of mighty cataracts and of sylvan cascades—are "harnessed," as the phrase is; and the record of it is the latest and greatest chapter in the story of Niagara.

When the historian comes who can write knowingly and authoritatively of this phase of the subject, he will accord eminence, if not absolute precedence, to Sir Carl Wilhelm Siemens. His name will always be associated with Niagara Falls. This renowned physicist and inventor found in our cataract his greatest spur to achievement. In many papers, mostly contained in his collected "Scientific Works" (3 vols., London, 1889) will be found record of his accomplishments in this connection. In volume two is a paper, "On the transmission and distribution of energy by the electric current," read at the meeting of the Physical Society (British), February 22, 1879. In volume three is his address as president of the Iron and Steel Institute, delivered March 20, 1877. This paper, first published in the *Journal* of the Iron and Steel Institute for 1877, was, I believe, the first formulation by a scientist, and first presentation to a scientific body, of a method of electrically transmitting Niagara's power for use. In these and other addresses of Sir William, are given, more or less *in extensu,* his observations on waste energy at Niagara, and the electrical transmission of power therefrom.

In the "Life of Sir William Siemens" (Anglicising his name) by William Pole (London, 1888) is set forth evidence to show that Siemens was the first to propose the utilization of Niagara power by electrical transmission. "This subject," says his biographer, "formed a favorite study of Dr. Siemens; and it seems to have first strongly impressed itself on his mind when, in the autumn of 1876, he went to America and visited the Falls of Niagara. In all his many journeys in different countries nothing made such a deep impression on him as this wonderful natural phenomenon. The stupendous rush of waters filled him with fear and admiration, as it does every one who comes within sound of its mighty roar." Dr. Siemens in his own account says nothing of "fear and admiration," but observes that the vast amount of falling water accomplished nothing save by its weight and concussion to raise, by a minute fraction of a degree, the temperature of the St. Lawrence river! "But," continues Dr. Pole,

"he saw in it something far beyond what was obvious to the multitude; for his scientific mind could not help viewing it as an inexpressibly grand manifestation of mechanical energy. And he at once began to speculate whether it was absolutely necessary that the whole of this glorious magnitude of power should be wasted in dashing itself into the chasm below?—whether it was not possible that at least some portion of it might be practically utilized for the benefit of mankind? He had not long to think before a possible means of doing this presented itself to him. The dynamo machine had just then been brought to perfection, partly by his own labors; and he asked himself, Why should not this colossal power actuate a colossal series of dynamos, whose conducting wires might transmit its activity to places miles away? This great idea, formed amid the thunderings of the cataract, accompanied him all the way home, and was meditated on in the quiet of his study. He submitted it to the test of mathematical calculation, and so far convinced himself of its reasonable nature, that he determined when a fitting occasion arrived, to make it known. That occasion arrived in the spring of 1877, when he had to give an opening address as President of the Iron and Steel Institute."

For many years, many schemes were devised, and plans proposed, for securing some part of the Niagara power. When the development of electrical science made it possible not only to catch this power but to carry it to distant places, new conceptions evolved as to what was possible. But in the earlier plans electricity played no part. As early as 1830 George Catlin constructed a model of the Falls, to scale. Men were even then figuring on using its power, and Catlin's model may have stimulated their fancies, but it seems to have been chiefly used for exhibition, as any painting might have been.

As late as 1878 a company was formed to transmit from the Falls to Buffalo "a constant supply of compressed air," to be used as a substitute for steam in factories.

In the years immediately preceding the perfection of the dynamo a great many plans were proposed for utilizing Niagara power. Buffalo being the chief power-using place on the river, most of these early schemes sought to take the power from the river at Buffalo. Some of these deserve to be chronicled for their originality, if nothing else. T. W. Clark of Schofield, Wis., proposed "to move the great cataract of Niagara back to Buffalo and drop the water through a thousand great turbine wheels located in wheel pits 240 feet deep at that city." The "moving" of the Falls was to be done by driving a great tunnel through the Clinton shale from the precipice at the cataract to the outlet of Lake Erie, 300 feet below the surface and 22 miles long. This project was to make Buffalo "the greatest manufacturing city on earth." Less benevolent was the project of one Peter Cameron, apparently a citizen of Rochester, who advocated a deep tunnel from the Falls to Lake Erie, not to build up Buffalo, but to drain Lake Erie, make Buffalo, Toledo and Cleveland inland cities and "reclaim" the floor of Lake Erie for agricultural purposes.

Still another project of the late '80's or thereabout was that of Charles M. Bartlett of Chicago, who secured patents and claimed to have ample financial backing from Chicago capitalists, for the installation at Niagara Falls of a power plant which would not mar the beauty of the scene. He proposed to cut chambers in the rock under the river back of the cataract, in which turbines could be placed. He proposed to enter the bedrock of the river at the foot of the precipice. The entrance excavation was afterwards to constitute the tail-race. Back of this he planned to penetrate upward as well as laterally, and cut room for the bottom floors of the wheel-pit:

THE NIAGARA IN SCIENCE. 213

"The lowest floor will be used as a waste-room to receive the water before it flows out through the tail-race. The second floor will be the machinery floor, on which are to be located a turbine wheel and electric dynamos to store and convert the power obtained, to use. . . . Workmen who operate the machinery will be let down by an elevator shaft sunk on shore and conecting from the bottom with the wheel-pit by tunnel. A house at the top of the elevator shaft will probably be the only structure above ground."

Buffalo was to have been Mr. Bartlett's first main point for disposing of his power. A publication of the day says: "As an inducement to New York to grant the right to operate, Mr. Bartlett will lay before the Legislature an elaborate design of electric lights, which he will agree to suspend over the brink of the Falls from the American to the Canadian shore and keep perpetually burning. The design will represent the two nations shaking hands across the chasm." Although much reported for a time, in the press, this project presently dropped out of sight, perhaps because the necessary legislative consent was not secured. In view of the subsequent action of Canada relative to "reciprocity" overtures made by the United States, the proposed electrical clasped hands above the cataract would have been at least somewhat premature.

The most amazing project of those years was that of Leonard Henkle of Rochester, who gravely produced elaborately-drawn plans and unfolded a scheme for the construction of a monstrous building, to bridge the Niagara river from Goat Island to the Canadian shore, 35 feet above the brink of the fall. It was to be 1,600 feet long, 804 feet high in the center and 606 feet at the ends, with from 40 to 50 stories! Its lower part was to be used for power-generation. The inventor proposed to install "122 pairs of twin turbine wheels, each of 6,000 horse-power, making in all

732,000 horse-power under a 28-foot head of water. It is estimated that 21,000,000 cubic feet of water pass over the Falls per minute, and by this 7,320 dynamos of 1,000 horse-power each will be run." I hesitate to quote further from Mr. Henkle's astounding prospectus. His ideas were perhaps of the sort that belong less to Niagara and science, than to dreams and visions. But in his day he had a hearing, if not always a serious one, and the press, especially of Western New York, lent itself generously to the somewhat ironical exploitation of his project. The cost of the undertaking was estimated at $38,000,000, and the chief promoter was quoted at one time as saying that $17,500,000 were pledged "by persons who are interested in the undertaking." Not the least striking feature of it all was the vast assembly hall which was to be provided in the very ample building, devoted to the uses not only of art and science, but especially dedicated to religion and the promotion of international amity.

The decade of the '80's was prolific in Niagara schemes. The Buffalo Historical Society preserves the original list of subscribers to a fund for a prize to be given to the winner of a competition for utilizing the power of Niagara river. It contains the signatures of 108 men and firms, chiefly of Buffalo, who from July 14, 1887 to May 23, 1888, subscribed $1,000 each to this project. The fund was to constitute "a prize or reward to be offered to the inventors of the world for the discovery or invention (and sole right to use the same), of the best appliance for utilizing, and that will utilize economically, the water power of Niagara river at or near Buffalo," etc. Numerous plans, most of them of the "crank" variety, were elicited by this offer, which was widely advertised. The more promising were submitted to a board of hydraulic engineers and other competent persons; but in the end all were rejected; so that no prizes were awarded, nor were any of the subscriptions ever called for.

Some years later, after power-development at the Falls had been successfully undertaken, Alonzo C. Mather proposed a combined bridge and power wheel construction for the Niagara river at Buffalo. His plans were regarded as far more practical than most of those that had been proposed; and as he professed to be able to finance his undertaking without popular subscriptions, municipal or State aid, and merely sought the necessary permission to build his bridge, his claims received serious and for a time favorable attention. A bill granting the desired permission passed at least two Legislatures at Albany. In 1899 Mr. Mather was again before the Legislature with a measure which had the endorsement of Buffalo's Exchanges, and of the Mayor. At this time the inventor asked only for permission to erect an experimental span, to demonstrate the soundness of his claims; but although much seemed to be offered, with vast possibilities, opposition developed and the Mather bridge bill never received a Governor's signature.

When the history of this phase of "Niagara and Science" is written, it will contain due recognition of the work of Thomas Evershed, who first suggested the utilization of Niagara power by means of wheelpits with a tunnel tail-race to the lower river. It will record the part borne by the International Commission of which Sir William Thomson (Lord Kelvin) was the president, his associates being Professor Mascart, Colonel Theodore Turrettini, Dr. Coleman Sellers and Professor W. C. Unwin. And it will give due credit to many other men of great attainments, among them George Forbes and William Birch Rankine, who in one capacity and another shared in the work of "harnessing" Niagara. When this history is written it will tell of the co-operation of the greatest engineers and electricians of our age. The literature of this subject is found today less in books than in the pages of engineering and electrical journals and the *Proceedings* of learned societies. Something of it is contained in the "Life of Lord Kelvin," by S. P. Thompson (London, 1910). The story of the gradual construction, installation and operation of power plants at Niagara Falls, already written by a thousand pens, is still being written—and still to be written. It is the most important, the most fascinating, the most splendid chapter in all the literature of Niagara.

In common with all other parts of our country, Niagara has its literature of history and locality; but in distinction from all others it has a literature which celebrates one of the world's greatest wonders. From the day of its discovery to this hour, Niagara has been a point of pilgrimage for all lovers of nature, for all devotees at the shrine of beauty and grandeur. And Niagara has spoken to each, after his kind. For the artist, she draws aside her silvery veil, and in her rainbows and her emerald tide gives him glimpses of the beauty of light, of form and of motion, which are hints from worlds hereafter. To the musician, she sounds the deep diapasons of earth's grandest organ. To the empty minded, she makes no revelation. To all high and serious minds, she brings peace, tranquillity, wholesome renewals of strength and kinship with nature. To the devout, she speaks as with the voice of God. These are some of the varied utterances which we find recorded in the literature of the Niagara region.

TWO EARLY VISITORS

THE narratives of early travels in the Niagara region have for me a peculiar attraction; partly, no doubt, because they help to fill in periods in our history for which data are scanty; and partly, perhaps, because they give us the Niagara landscape, and conditions hereabouts, before the adjuncts of civilization had so largely obliterated the things of the wilderness. Often have I echoed the sentiment expressed by Tyrone Power, an Irish actor of worth and wit, who visited the Niagara early in the last century: "How I have envied those," he says, "who first sought Niagara, through the scarce-trod wilderness, with the Indian for a guide; and who slept upon its banks with the summer trees for their only shelter, with the sound of its waters for their only réveille." One of Power's own countrymen, many years before, and no doubt unknown to the actor, had realized to the full this romantic longing. I do not recall that that early visit has been made note of, in our local annals, but it may appropriately be put on record here, especially as it concerns still another visit, which likewise merits a place in our Niagara chronicling.

Let us fancy ourselves, then, back in the year 1789. Although the Revolution was over, and the Treaty of Paris had been signed for half a dozen years, the British still held control of both sides of the Niagara, and maintained garrisons at Fort Niagara, Fort Schlosser (now included in the city of Niagara Falls), and Fort Erie. Buffalo did not exist; though for nine years the Senecas, refugees from the

Genesee country, had had their villages on Buffalo Creek; and for five years the house built by Ezekiel Lane and his son-in-law Martin Middaugh, the first white settlers on the site of the present city, had stood near the present Exchange street, east of Washington, not far from the bank of Little Buffalo Creek.

This in very brief was the local situation when there came into the region one who after enjoying to the full the wilderness life as he found it here, was to pass to a life of trouble and a most lamentable end. This was Lord Edward Fitzgerald. I am not to write his biography and so refer the reader at once to the story of Lord Edward's life and death, as written eighty years ago by Thomas Moore. For our purpose it is enough to recall that he was the first son of the first Duke of Leinster, and was born near Dublin in 1763. Given a military training, we find him serving with his regiment, the 19th, in the American Revolution. As *aide-de-camp* to Lord Rawdon, he distinguished himself in numerous engagements, particularly in the battle of Eutaw Springs, South Carolina, where he was wounded, Sept. 8, 1781. His biographer finds it "not a little striking that there should have been engaged, at this time, on opposite sides, in America, two noble youths, Lafayette and Lord Edward Fitzgerald, whose political principles afterwards so entirely coincided." After the surrender of Cornwallis, Lord Edward was sent, early in 1783, to the West Indies, where he served on the staff of General O'Hara. For the next few years he had a varied service, in different parts of the world; and in 1788 again came out to America to join the 54th regiment in New Brunswick. He had reached the rank of major, and according to report, was much esteemed in the service. A sergeant-major of the 54th at this time was the afterwards celebrated William Cobbett. In the latter's once famous "Advice to Young Men" he says that he got his discharge from the army "by the great kindness of poor Lord Edward Fitzgerald"; and he tells how, on dining one day with Mr. Pitt, on being asked by that statesman some questions respecting his former officer, he answered that "Lord Edward was a most humane and excellent man, and the only really honest officer he ever knew in the army." An old portrait of him (from which the frontispiece of Moore's life of him was engraved), happily endorses this verdict, and shows him as a bright-faced, alert, good-humored youth, the very embodiment of Irish wit and energy.

This may serve as a sufficient introduction to his Lordship the major, who with a fellow officer and a servant, in February and March, 1789, walked from Fredericton to Quebec, 175 miles through the wilderness. "We were thirty days on our march, twenty-six of which we were in the woods, and never saw a soul but our own party." In April of that year, in high health and spirits, he set out from Quebec, bound for Ireland, by way of Niagara Falls, the Mississippi and the Gulf of Mexico! Contemplating the adventure, before leaving Quebec, he wrote home that he supposed they would think him mad; but his heart was set on it. "It will not be very expensive, particularly as I go all the first part with a relief of troops that are proceeding up as far as Lake Superior. I am not quite determined whether I will go up quite so far, perhaps only as far as Detroit, from that to the Fort Pitt, and from thence to the Ohio, and down it to the Mississippi."

This was the tour on which Lord Edward set out, towards the end of April. By June 1st he was on the Niagara, where he wrote the following letter to his mother:

"Fort Erie, June 1, 1789.

"Dearest Mother: I am just come from the Falls of Niagara. To describe them is impossible. I stayed three days admiring, and was absolutely obliged to tear myself away at last. As I said before, to describe them would be impossible:—Homer could not in writing, nor Claude Lorraine in painting: your own imagination must do it. The immense height and noise of the Falls, the spray that rises to the clouds—in short, it forms all together a scene that is well worth the trouble of coming from Europe to see. Then, the greenness and tranquility of everything about, the quiet of the immense forests around, compared with the violence of all that is close to the Falls,—but I will not go on, for I should never end. . . .

"I set out tomorrow for Detroit: I go with one of the Indian chiefs, Joseph Brant, he that was in England. We have taken very much to one another. I shall entertain you very much with his remarks on England, and the English, while he was there. Instead of crossing Lake Erie in a ship, I go in canoes up and down rivers. In crossing Lake Ontario, I was as sick as at sea,—so you may guess I prefer canoeing;—besides my friend Joseph always travels with company; and we shall go through a number of Indian villages. If you only stop an hour, they have a dance for you. They are delightful people; the ladies charming, and with manners that I like very much, they are so natural. Notwithstanding the life they lead, which would make most women rough and masculine, they are as soft, meek, and modest as the best brought up girls in England. At the same time, they are coquettes *au possible*. Conceive the manners of *Mimi* in a poor *squaw,* that has been carrying packs in the woods all her life.

"I must make haste and finish my letter, for I am just going to set off. I shall be at Michilimackinack in nineteen days. My journey then will be soon over, for from that I shall soon reach the Mississippi, and down it to New Orleans, and then to my dearest mother to Frescati, to relate all my journey in the little book-room. I shall then be happy. Give my love to all. I think often of you all in these wild woods:—they are better than rooms. Ireland and England will be too little for me when I go home. If I could carry my dearest mother about with me, I should be completely happy here."

A subsequent letter may be briefly quoted, to complete the story in its local bearing:

"DETROIT, June 20 [1789].

"MY DEAREST MOTHER: It is so hot I can hardly hold the pen. My hand trembles so, you will be hardly able to read my letter. My journey quite answered my expectations. I set out tomorrow for Michillimackinack, and then down the Mississippi. I am in rude health. As soon as I get to the Mississippi I reckon my journey half over. I can say no more, for really it is too hot for anything but lying on a mat. *Entre nous,* I am in a little sorrow, as I am to part tomorrow with a fellow-traveller who has been very pleasant and taken great care of me: *Les plus courtes folies sont les meilleures.* I have been adopted by one of the Nations, and am now a thorough Indian."

According to Tom Moore, this adoption took place at Detroit, through the medium of a chief of the Six Nations, David Hill, by whom he was formally inducted into the Bear Clan. A document recording the conferment of this "wild honour," as Moore phrases it, was preserved among Lord Edward's papers; and is, in alleged Indian and English, as follows:

> "*Waghgongh Sen non Pryer*
> *Ne nen Seghyrage né i*
> *Ye Sayats Eghnidal*
> *Ethonayyere*
> DAVID HILL
> *Karonghyontye*
> *Tyogh Saghnontyon*
> 21 June 1789.

"I, David Hill, chief of the Six Nations, give the name of *Eghnidal* to my friend Lord Edward Fitzgerald, for which I hope he will remember me as long as he lives.

"The name belongs to the Bear Tribe."

Captain David Hill's letter purports to be in the Mohawk, but the orthography as given by Moore is very erroneous. According to O. H. Marshall, who commented on this letter, *"Karong hyontye"* is the Indian name of Captain David. *"Tyogh Saghnontyon"* is the name of Detroit, where the letter was written.

Lord Edward's correspondence says no more of the Niagara region, but it has not told the whole of his experiences hereabouts. For further particulars I turn to a young woman's journal of 1789, which although published some thirty odd years ago, has never been made use of, so far as I am aware, in connection with the letters of Lord Edward Fitzgerald, to illustrate conditions on the Niagara soon after the Revolution.

The young woman was Ann Powell, daughter of John Powell of Boston, in which town she was born in 1769. When she met Lord Edward Fitzgerald, and with him visited the site of Buffalo in 1789, she was twenty years old, he twenty-six. The Powell genealogy shows that her ancestors were of a distinguished line in Colonial Massachusetts. Her grandfather Powell came from England as secretary of Lieutenant Governor Dummer, and married his sister, Ann Dummer. Their eldest son, William Dummer Powell, married Janet Grant, sister of Sir Alexander Grant. They were a Loyalist family, and about 1775, being declared alien, left Boston for Canada. William Dummer Powell, eldest son of the John who was Dummer's secretary, became Chief Justice of Canada. At the time we are considering, he had been appointed a Puisne Judge;

and it was in connection with his duties in that office that the journey from Montreal to Detroit was undertaken. Thanks to his young sister, Ann, who accompanied him and kept a journal, we have a glimpse of our locality not elsewhere afforded. This journal, with a few unimportant pages omitted, follows:

FROM THE JOURNAL OF ANN POWELL.

TOUR FROM MONTREAL TO DETROIT IN 1789—VISIT TO THE SITE OF BUFFALO WITH LORD EDWARD FITZGERALD.

When I talked of keeping a journal from Montreal to Detroit, I was not aware of the difficulties attending the journey. I expected it would be tedious, and thought writing would be a very pleasant employment, and so it might have proved, had it been practicable, but the opportunities for writing were so few, that I found it would be impossible to keep a journal with any degree of regularity, so I left it wholly alone, and trusted to my memory (which never deserved such a compliment) for recalling whatever was worth communicating.

We left Montreal on the 11th of May, 1789, with a large party of our friends, who paid us the compliment of seeing us the first stage, where we took a farewell dinner.

We then went to our boats; one was fitted up with an awning to protect us from the weather, and held the family and bedding. It was well filled, eighteen persons in all, so you may suppose we had not much room; as it happened that was of no consequence, it was cold on the water, and we were glad to sit close. This mode of traveling is very tedious; we are obliged to keep along the shore and go on very slowly.

The first night we slept at the house of a "Habitan," who turned out with his family, to give us the best room, where we spread our beds and slept in peace. I entertained myself with looking at the Canadian family who were eating their supper, saying their prayers, and conversing at the same time.

The next day we reached a part of the St. Lawrence where our boats were obliged to be unloaded, and taken through a Lock, the rapids being too strong to pass; these rapids were the first of any consequence that I had seen. Perhaps you do not know what I mean by a rapid; it is when the water runs with swiftness over large rocks, every one of which forms a cascade, and the river here is all a bed of rocks. There is no describing the grandeur of the water when thrown into this kind of agitation; the sea after a tempest is smooth to it.

My brother had traveled the road before, and knew the people, and the distance from house to house.

This part of the country has been settled since the Peace, and it was granted to the troops raised in America during the war. We went from a Colonel to a Captain, and from a Captain to a Major. They have most of them built good houses, and with the assistance of their half pay, live very comfortably.

One night we reached the house of an old servant of Mrs. Powell's; the children were delighted to see her, and I was well pleased to view a new scene of domestic life. This woman, it seems, had married a disbanded soldier, who had a small lot of land, where they immediately went to live, and cultivated it with so much care, that in a few years they were offered in exchange for it, a farm twice its value, to which they had just removed, and were obliged to live some time in a temporary log house, which consisted only of one room, in which was a very neat bed, where a lovely babe of three months old, lay crowing and laughing by itself. A large loom was on one side, on the other all the necessary utensils of a famly, everythng perfectly clean.

Small as the place was, we chose to stay all night, so while Mrs. Powell was giving orders for arranging the beds, my brother and I walked out to enjoy a very fine evening. The banks of the river were very high and woody, the moon shone bright through the trees, some Indians were on the river taking fish with harpoons, a mode of fishing I had never seen before. They make large fires in their canoes, which attract the fish to the surface of the water, when they can see by the fire to strike them. The number of fires moving on the water had a pretty and singular effect.

When we returned to the house, we found the whole floor covered with beds. The man and woman of the house, with their children, had retired to their own room, and left us to manage as we pleased. A blanket was hung before my mattress, which I drew aside to see how the rest were accommodated. My brother and sister, myself, five children, and two maid servants made up the group; a blazing fire (not in the chimney, for there was none, but in one side of the room, which was opened at the top to let out the smoke, and gave us a fine current of air) showed every object distinctly.

I was in a humor to be easily diverted, and found a thousand things to laugh at. It struck me that we were like a strolling party of players.

At night we always drest a dinner for the next day. When we were disposed to eat it, the cloth was laid in the boat, and our table served up with as much decency as could be expected, if we could be contented with cold provisions. Not so our sailors; they went on shore and boiled their pots, and smoked their pipes.

One day we happened to anchor at a small Island, where the men themselves had some difficulty in climbing the banks, which were very steep. I finished my dinner before the rest of the party, and felt an inclination to walk. I took one of the maids and made one of the men help us up the bank; we strolled to the other side of the Island, and when we turned round, saw the whole of the ground covered with fire. The wind blew fresh, and the dried leaves had spread it from where the people were cooking. We had no alternative, so were obliged to make the best of our way back. I believe we took very few steps, for neither of us had our shoes burnt through.

The weather was so fine that we ventured to sleep out, and I liked it so much that I regretted that we had ever gone into the house; it is the pleasantest vagabond life you can imagine.

We stopt before sunset, when a large fire was instantly made, and tea and chocolate were prepared; while we were taking it the men erected a tent; the sails of the boat served for the top, and blankets were fastened round the sides; in a few minutes they had made a place large enough to spread all our beds, where we slept with as much comfort as I ever did in any chamber in my life. It was our own fault if we did not choose a fine situation to encamp.

You can scarcely conceive a more beautiful scene than was one night exhibited. The men had piled up boughs of trees for a fire, before our tent, till they made a noble bonfire. In the course of the evening it spread more than half a mile; the ground was covered with dry leaves which burnt like so many lamps, with the fire running up the bushes and trees. The whole formed the most beautiful illumination you can form an idea of. The children were in ecstasies, running about like so many savages, and our sailors were encamped near enough for us to hear them singing and laughing.

We had, before we left Montreal, heard of his Majesty's recovery, so if you please you can set this all down as rejoicings on that account, though I doubt whether it once occurred to our minds, yet we are a very loyal people.

On the tenth day we reached Kingston; it is a small town, and stands on a beautiful bay at the foot of Lake Ontario. The moment we reached the wharf, a number of people came down to welcome us; a gentleman in his hurry to hand out the ladies, brushed one of the children into the lake. He was immediately taken out, but that did not save his Mother a severe fright. We went to a house of a Mr. Forsyth, a young bachelor, who very politely begged we would consider it as our own. Here we staid three days, and then sailed with a fair wind for Niagara.

At Kingston we were overtaken by two officers of the artillery, one going to Niagara the other to Detroit. They both expressed themselves pleased with joining our party, and accepted an offer my brother made them, to cross the Lake in a vessel appointed for him. We were fifteen where there were only four berths. When the beds were put down at night, every one remained in the spot he had first taken, for there was no moving without general consent.

One night after we had lain down and began to be composed, Mrs. Powell saw one of the maids standing where she had been making the children's beds, and asked her why she staid there? The poor girl who speaks indifferent English answered: "I am quazed, Ma'am." Sure enough, she was wedged in beyond the power of moving without assistance. I heard a great laugh among the gentlemen, who were divided from us by a blanket partition. I suppose they were "quazed" too.

Lake Ontario is two hundred miles over. We were four days crossing it. We were certainly a very good humoured set of people, for no one complained or seemed rejoiced when we arrived at Niagara.

The fort is by no means pleasantly situated. It is built close upon the Lake, which gains upon its foundations so fast, that in a few years they must be overflowed. There, however, we passed some days very agreeably, at the house of Mr. Hamilton. We received the most polite attentions from Colonel Hunter, the commanding officer, and all his officers. Lord Edward Fitzgerald had been some months at Niagara before us, and was making excursions among the Indians, of whose society he seemed particularly fond. Joseph Brant, a celebrated Indian chief, lives in that neighborhood. Lord Edward had spent some days at his house, and seemed charmed with his visit. Brant returned to Niagara with his Lordship. He was the first, and indeed the only savage I ever dined at table with.

As the party was large, he was at too great a distance from me to hear him converse, and I was by no means pleased with his looks. These people pay great deference to rank; with them it is only obtained by merit. They attended Lord Edward from the house of one Chief to another, and entertained him with dancing, which is the greatest compliment they can pay. Short as our stay was at Niagara, we made many acquaintances we were sorry to leave. Several gentlemen offered to escort us to the landing, which is eight miles from Fort Erie [Fort Niagara].

There the Niagara river becomes impassible, and all the luggage was drawn up a steep hill in a cradle, a machine I never saw before. We walked up the hill, and were conducted to a good garden with an arbor in it, where we found a cloth laid for dinner, which was provided for us by the officers of the post.

After dinner we went on seven miles to Fort Schlosher. The road was good, the weather charming, and this was the only opportunity we should have of seeing the Falls. All our party collected half a mile above the Falls, and walked down to them. I was in raptures all of the way. The Falls I had heard of forever, but no one had mentioned the rapids. For half a mile the river comes foaming down immense rocks, some of them forming cascades 30 or 40 feet high. The banks are covered with woods, as are a number of the Islands, some of them very high out of the water. One in the centre of the river, runs out into a point, and seems to divide the Falls, which would otherwise be quite across the river, into the form of a crescent.

I believe no mind can form an idea of the immensity of the body of water, or the rapidity with which it hurries down. The height is 180 [!] feet, and long before it reaches the bottom, it loses all appearance of a liquid. The spray rises like light summer clouds, and when the rays of the sun are reflected through it, they form innumerable rainbows, but the sun was not in a situation to show the effect when we were there.

One thing I could find no one to explain to me, which is, the stillness of the water at the bottom of the Falls; it is as smooth as a lake, for half a mile, deep and narrow, the banks very high and steep, with trees hanging over them. I was never before sensible of the power of scenery, nor did I suppose the eye could carry to the mind such strange emotions of pleasure, wonder and solemnity.

For a time every other impression was erased from my memory. Had I been left to myself, I am convinced, I should not have thought of moving whilst there was light to distinguish objects. With reluctance I at length attended to the proposal of going, determining in my own mind, that when I returned, I would be mistress of my own time, and stay a day or two at least.

We were received at Fort Schlosher by Mr. Foster, of the 60th Regiment, one of the most elegant young men I ever saw. Here we were extremely well accommodated, and much pleased with the house and garden. I never saw a situation where retirement wore so many charms.

The next day we went in a batteau to Fort Erie. When we arrived there we found the commanding officer, Mr. Boyd, was gone in a party with Lord Edward and Mr. Brisbane to the other side of the river, where the Indians were holding a Council. The gentlemen all returned in the evening, and seemed so much pleased with their entertainment, that when they proposed our going with them the next day, we very readily agreed to it. I thought it a peculiar piece of good fortune, having an opportunity of seeing a number of the most respectable of these people collected together.

We reached the spot where the Council began, and as we passed along, saw several of the chiefs at their toilets. They sat upon the ground with the most profound gravity, dressing themselves before a small looking-glass; for they are very exact in fixing on their ornaments, and not a little whimsical. I am told that one of these fellows will be an hour or two painting his face, and when anyone else would think him sufficiently horrible, some new conceit will strike him, and he will rub it all off, and begin again.

The women dress with more simplicity than the men, at least all I have seen; but at this meeting there were not many of the fair sex. Some old squaws who sat in council, and a few young ones to dress their provisions; for these great men, as well as those of our world, like a good dinner after spending their lungs for the good of their country.

Some women we saw employed in taking fish in a basket; a gentleman of our party took the basket from one of them, and tried to catch the fish as she did, but failing, they laughed, at his want of dexterity. One young squaw sat in a tent weaving a sort of worsted garter intermixed with beads. I suppose she was a lady of distinction, for her ears were bored in four different places, with ear-rings in them all. She would not speak English, but seemed to understand what was said to her.

A gentleman introduced Mrs. Powell and me to her as white squaws, begging she would go on with her work, as we wished to see how it was done. She complied immediately, with great dignity, taking no more notice of us than if we were posts. A proof of her good breeding.

We then went up a steep bank to a very beautiful spot; the tall trees were in full leaf, and the ground covered with wild flowers. We were seated on a log in the centre, where we could see all that passed.

Upwards of 200 chiefs were assembled and seated in proper order. They were the delegates of six nations; each tribe formed a circle under the shade of a tree, their faces towards each other; they never changed their places, but sat or lay on the grass as they liked. The speaker of each tribe stood with his back against a tree. The old women walked one by one with great solemnity and seated themselves behind the men; they were wholly covered with their blankets, and sought not by the effect of ornaments to attract, or fright, the other sex, for I cannot tell whether the men mean to make themselves charming, or horrible, by the pains they take with their persons.

On seeing this respectable band of matrons I was struck with the different opinions of mankind. In England when a man grows infirm and his talents are obscured by age, the wits decide upon his character by calling him an old woman. On the banks of Lake Erie a woman becomes respectable as she grows old, and I suppose the greatest compliment you can pay a young hero, is that he is as wise as an old woman, a good trait of savage understanding. These ladies preserve a modest silence in the debates (I fear they are not like women of other countries) but nothing is determined without their advice and approbation.

I was very much struck with the figures of these Indians as they approached us. They are remarkably tall, and finely made, and walk with a degree of grace and dignity you can have no idea of. I declare our beaux looked quite insignificant by them; one man called to my mind some of Homer's finest heroes.

One of the gentlemen told me that he was a chief of great distinction and spoke English, and if I pleased he should be introduced to me. I had some curiosity to see how a chief of the six nations would pay his compliments, but little did I expect the elegance with which he addressed me. The Prince of Wales does not bow with more grace than Captain David. He spoke English with propriety, and returned all the compliments that were paid him with ease and politeness. As he was not only the handsomest but the best drest man I saw, I will endeavor to describe him.

His person is tall and fine as it is possible to conceive, his features handsome and regular, with a countenance of much softness, his complexion was disagreeably dark, and I really believe he washes his face, for it appeared perfectly clean, without paint; his hair was all shaved off except a little on the top of his head to fasten his ornaments to; his head and ears painted a glowing red; round his head was fastened a fillet of highly polished silver; from the left temple hung two straps of black velvet covered with silver beads and brooches. On the top of his head was fixed a Foxtail feather, which bowed to the wind, as did a black one in each ear; a pair of immense earrings which hung below his shoulders completed his head-dress, which I assure you was not unbecoming, though I must confess somewhat fantastical.

His dress was a shirt of colored calico, the neck and shoulders covered so thick with silver brooches as to have the appearance of a net, his sleeves much like those the ladies wore when I left England, fastened about the arm, with a broad bracelet of highly polished silver, and engraved with the arms of England. Four smaller bracelets of the same kind about his wrists and arms; around his waist was a large scarf of a very dark colored stuff, lined with scarlet, which hung to his feet. One part he generally drew over his left arm which had a very graceful effect when he moved. His legs were covered with blue cloth made to fit neatly, with an ornamental garter bound below the knee. I know not what kind of a being your imagination will represent to you, but I sincerely declare to you, that altogether Captain David made the finest appearance I ever saw in my life.

Do not suppose they were all dressed with the same taste; their clothes are not cut by the same pattern, like the beaux of England. Every Indian is dressed according to his own fancy, and you see no two alike; even their faces are differently painted; some of them wear their hair in a strange manner, others shave it entirely off. One old man diverted me extremely; he was dressed in a scarlet coat, richly embroidered, that must have been made half a century, with waistcoat of the same, that reached half way down his thighs, no shirt or breeches, but blue cloth stockings. As he strutted about more than the rest, I concluded that he was particularly pleased with his dress, and with himself. They told us that he was a chief of distinction.

We only staid to hear two speeches; they spoke with great gravity and no action, frequently making long pauses for a hum of applause. Lord Edward and Mr. Brisbane remained with them all night, and were entertained with dancing.

We were detained some days at Fort Erie by a contrary wind. On the 4th of June as we were drinking the King's health like good loyal subjects, the wind changed and we were hurried on board; we were better accommodated than when we crossed Lake Ontario, for the weather was so fine that the gentlemen all slept on deck. Lake Erie is 280 miles over, we were five days on our passage.

The river Detroit divides Lake Erie from Lake St. Clair, which is again separated by a small river from Lake Huron. The head of Lake Erie and the entrance into the river Detroit is uncommonly beautiful. Whilst we were sailing up the river a perverse storm of rain and thunder drove us into the cabin, and gave us a thorough wetting. After it was over we went on shore. The fort lies about half way up the river, which is 18 miles in length. In drawing the line between the British and American possessions, this fort was left within their lines; a new town is now to be built on the other side of the river, where the Courts are held, and where my brother must of course reside.

As soon as our vessel anchored, several ladies and gentlemen came on board; they had agreed upon a house for us, till my brother could meet with one that would suit him, so we found ourselves at home immediately.

The ladies visited us in full dress, though the weather was boiling hot. What do you think of walking about when the Thermometer is above 90? It was as high as 96 the morning we returned our visits.

Whilst we staid at the Fort, several parties were made for us. A very agreeable one by the 65th to an island a little way up the river. Our party was divided into five boats, one held the music, in each of the others were two ladies and as many gentlemen as it could hold.

Lord Edward and his friend arrived just time enough to join us; they went round the Lake by land, to see some Indian settlements, and were highly pleased with their jaunt. Lord Edward speaks in raptures of the Indian hospitality; he told me one instance of it, which would reflect honor on the most polished society. By some means or other, the gentlemen lost their provisions, and were entirely without bread in a place where they could get none; some Indians traveling with them, had one loaf, which they offered to his Lordship, but he would not accept it; the Indians gave him to understand that they were used to do without and therefore it was less inconvenient to them;

they still refused, and the Indians then disappeared, and left the loaf of bread in the road the travelers must pass, and the Indians were seen no more.

Our party on the Island proved very pleasant, which that kind of parties seldom do; the day was fine, the country cheerful and the band delightful. We walked some time in the shady part of the Island; and then were led to a bower where the table was spread for dinner. Everything here is on a grand scale; do not suppose we dined in an English arbor. This one was made of forest trees that grew in a circle, and it was closed by filling up the space with small trees and bushes, which being fresh cut, you could not see where they were put together, and the bower was the whole height of the trees though quite closed at the top. The band was placed without, and played whilst we were at dinner. We were hurried home in the evening by the appearance of a thunder storm; it was the most beautiful I ever remember to have seen. The clouds were collected about the setting sun, and the forked lightning was darting in a thousand different directions from it. You can form no idea from anything you have seen of what the lightning is in this country. These Lakes I believe are the nurseries of thunder storms. What you see are only stragglers who lose their strength before they reach you.

The locality indicated by Miss Powell as "the other side of the river," was, obviously, somewhere in the present bounds of Buffalo, probably on the banks of Buffalo Creek. When they "went up a steep bank to a very beautiful spot," they not unlikely gained what is now the Terrace; must have been, indeed, as the neighborhood of the Indian villages further up Buffalo Creek would not satisfy Miss Powell's description. The old man in the scarlet coat was Red Jacket. Miss Powell's narrative is corroborated by various official documents. A letter from Joseph Brant and other Indians to Governor George Clinton, dated "Canadague"—i. e., Canandaigua—"30th July, 1789," refers to this council of Buffalo Creek. Red Jacket is one of the signers with his "mark." (See "Proceedings of the Commissioners of Indian Affairs," etc., edited by F. B. Hough, Albany, 1861.) David Hill, one of the chiefs of the Six Nations, is referred to in Stone's "Life of Red Jacket," 1st ed., p. 95. Miss Powell is in error in writing that Lord Edward "had been some months at Niagara" before she arrived. His letters show that he was there in May; "some weeks" was perhaps meant.

Lord Edward finished his journey, returning to Ireland by way of New Orleans, much as planned. He has no further connection with the Niagara region or Buffalo, but the reader should have some further glimpse of his romantic career. When the French Revolution broke out he supported its principles and in 1793 went to Paris, where he married Pamela, the reputed daughter of Louis Philippe Joseph, Duke of Orleans, and Madame de Genlis. "On his return to Ireland, Fitzgerald was desirous of effecting a separation of that country from England, and induced the French Directory to furnish him with a fleet and troops. A landing was attempted on several occasions, but without success, and Fitzgerald was seized, tried and condemned to death." While he lay in prison suffering from his wounds, a soldier friend who had known him in Charleston during the American Revolution, called on him and chanced to speak of the circumstances under which they had first become acquainted; when the suffering patriot exclaimed: "Ah! I was wounded then in a very different cause. That was in fighting *against* liberty—this, in fighting *for* it." Before the time set for his execution arrived, Lord Edward died from his wounds, June 4, 1798. In her chaplet of heroes and patriots, Ireland will forever keep the memory of Lord Edward Fitzgerald.

HISTORICAL ASSOCIATIONS OF BUFFALO

I HAVE been asked to say something on the historical associations of Buffalo. At the outset, one most admit that Buffalo, like many American towns, has paid little attention to her landmarks, and has been too busy developing material interests to care whether or not anything were done to preserve the historical associations. This is so generally the case with American towns that it need call for no particular comment; but, in the point of view of the student of history, it is a matter of regret that more reminders of the past are not preserved for the future. To those who make the study of history a business, it is readily obvious that more than a sentimental value attaches to reminders of things that are gone. An old house; a battlefield, which still shows the marks of conflict; a venerable tree, in the shade of which a treaty or a council were held—any of these things is an historical document quite as much as the written manuscript or the printed page, and to the student helps make clear and vivid conditions of the past. Some things of this sort, happily, we have preserved from earlier generations; and of some occurrences of which all trace is gone we are able to determine the original site, so that after all, in some fashion, we can still read the book of Buffalo in its topography and along its water-front to pretty good purpose.

There are two ways of studying local history: one way contents itself with a mere determination of dates and sites.

Though this service has its value, I confess it scarcely appeals to me. Another aspect of local history, which I think is the more useful, is that in which we see its relations to the general history of our country. In this last relation, Buffalo is, perhaps, the least historic point on the Niagara frontier. The history of our town as a white man's settlement runs back scarcely more than a century; but the history of the Niagara river and of the lakes which it joins goes back almost two centuries farther and belongs to that romantic and picturesque chapter of American development which begins with the forest missions of the Jesuits and other holy orders, shifts soon into the period of exploration, and, finally, after a time of strategy, of forest-fort building and of wilderness campaigns, changes again from the domain of the French to the rule of the English. In all the long conflict of the old French war, ending on our frontier in 1759, and in all the troubled years that followed, down to the close of the Revolution, our river and lake bore an important part. But there was no Buffalo, nor, indeed, did the site of Buffalo figure to any extent in these early annals of the region.

I am to confine myself to the present city. A portion of it was the seat of Seneca villages, two or three of which may still be traced by experts on the banks of the Buffalo and Cazenovia creeks. Local archæologists also tell us that within the present area of Delaware Park they find remains of Indian village occupancy and burial. The motto which is engraved on a lintel in the Historical Building, "Other council fires were here before ours," is perhaps literally true, though it is little more than tradition which fixes upon the banks of the Scajaquada in the vicinity of that building a former abiding-place of the Senecas.

There is more definiteness about the tradition connected

with a stream at the other extremity of Buffalo. Smoke's creek, whose course into Lake Erie has, in recent years, been well-nigh obliterated by great steel works and other buildings, derives its name from the Seneca chief known to the English as "Old Smoke." He held a position of peculiar prominence among his people, is said to have been foremost in leading them against the American settlers at Wyoming, and was buried years after on the banks of the stream which bears his name. South Buffalo has many associations with the Indians. Here lived Red Jacket, who died in 1830 and was buried in what is now known as the "Old Indian Cemetery" on Buffam street. This little plot of ground, still shaded by fine old oaks and walnuts, was the burial-place of many of the Seneca Nation, prominent during the Revolution and in the early years of the 19th century. Here, too, was buried Mary Jemison, the white woman, whose life of captivity among the Indians is one of the most famous stories in our local history. The remains of Mary Jemison were removed in 1874 to Glen Iris, and the bones of Red Jacket and other Seneca chiefs were re-interred in Forest Lawn Cemetery by the Buffalo Historical Society in 1884 and 1894. The old Indian burying-ground has now been added to the park system of Buffalo and let us hope will be preserved with its fine trees for future generations. Near by was formerly the Indian Mission Church, built 1826, abandoned 1843. What is now known as Indian Church avenue crosses its former site. Several other points in this vicinity are of interest to the student of the Seneca Indians and their former relations to the people of Buffalo.

Two or more council houses have at different times stood on or near the banks of Buffalo creek, the last one probably being not far from the present site of the International

Railway Company's car-house on Seneca street, near its junction with Elk. But perhaps the region has no associations of more importance than those which cluster around the old mission house still standing on Buffam street. Built in 1833, it is still in good preservation, with heavy hewn black walnut beams that bid fair to stand for many a year to come. In this house, from 1833 to 1844, dwelt the Rev. Asher Wright, missionary to the Senecas, and his gifted and devoted wife. Here, in 1839, was set up the Mission Press, on which, in the Seneca language, from specially made type, were printed portions of the Scriptures, hymnals, spelling books, and Seneca lexicon, and a periodical, the *Mental Elevator,* in the Seneca tongue. The story of the work carried on for many years by Mr. and Mrs. Wright is perhaps the most beautiful record of disinterested devotion to the welfare of others to be found in the annals of Buffalo.

There are many places within the city limits which have associations, more or less important, with the Seneca Indians. Most of these need not be touched on in a brief sketch like the present. But the reader whose interest is at all drawn to this subject will do well some pleasant day to stroll through Forest Lawn Cemetery. He will note the bronze statue erected to Red Jacket and his associates; but he is not so apt to have his attention drawn to another and older, though less conspicuous, monument, nearer the east side of the cemetery, which marks the resting place of some twelve hundred bodies that were removed in 1851 from the old Franklin Street Cemetery—the present site of the City Hall—to the then new Forest Lawn. Among these remains were those of Farmer's Brother, one of the worthiest Senecas of whom history gives us record. A man of far higher character than Red Jacket, he proved himself the staunch friend of the Americans, and fought bravely in their cause during the War of 1812.

Buffalo was a poor little frontier village when that war began. The first white settlement on Buffalo creek was, apparently, in 1784; and there were squatters, frontiersmen, and renegades, of whose presence here something is known, but little that is worth our thought, until the village of New Amsterdam was surveyed for the Holland Land Company by their agent, Joseph Ellicott, in 1802. The town that grew up in the next decade was wiped out of existence by the British and Indians in 1813; so that, although we have records which enable us to fix the locality of many buildings thus destroyed, there now exists in the city no structure that was standing in the village of Buffalo when the British burned it. There is one house, now within the city limits, which was standing at the time of the burning, but it was then some three or four miles north of Buffalo on the Williamsville road. Its age gives it distinction, although no associations of great importance belong to it. It was built in 1809 by a settler, Zachariah Griffin, and the story goes that the Indians in their course of destruction with musket and firebrand were too much overcome with liquor before they reached this house to do any further damage. Oddly enough, it still stands, sound and comfortable, as a residence, although its exterior appearance is undoubtedly changed. It is No. 2485 Main street, the second house north of the Belt Line crossing. A little one story house, it is apparently of ordinary frame construction, but behind its veranda and clapboards are still the old log walls of the original structure.

I am often asked what is the oldest house in Buffalo, and it may be worth while to mention a few which are entitled to the respect we accord to age. The Griffin house, already mentioned, is, so far as I am aware, entitled to precedence. There are but two or three in the county of greater age. One of them known as the Evans homestead, at Williamsville, dates back, in its oldest part, to 1797, and has the associations which come, not only from long occupancy by a family prominent in the history of our county but from having been the headquarters of General Scott and other officers during the War of 1812. Within the city, the oldest house of distinction for many years was undoubtedly that known as the Porter mansion, afterwards the home of the Hon. Lewis F. Allen; later, stripped of its more dignified belongings, serving commercial purposes as part of an automobile factory, and finally torn down. It was formerly No. 1192 Niagara street, between the street and the river, a short distance north of Ferry street. Its site is wholly surrounded now by factory buildings; one who has not known it in its better state can form no idea of the former beauty of the place—a dignified, ample house, with beautiful grounds, originally sloping to the banks of the river. Built in 1816 by General Porter, afterwards Secretary of War, it was for many years, both during his ownership and that of Mr. Allen, often the scene of distinguished hospitality, and many famous men were guests there. Mr. Allen's nephew, Grover Cleveland, was, for a time, an inmate of his household. It is a pity that so fine an old house, with so many historical associations, could not have been preserved, as is sometimes the case with old houses in other towns, for a museum or headquarters of historical or antiquarian organizations.

There are but few buildings in the city whose age entitles them to distinction. One that remained a comfortable home until recently was No. 1118 Niagara street, built in 1819 by Col. William A. Bird. For the most part, buildings that may be called old, now standing in the city, were erected in the decade of the 30's. Two or three residences are known of an earlier period. One of the latest to go was No. 37 Church street, understood to have been built before 1830. The Wilkeson homestead, on Niagara Square, dates from about 1825. Two or three years before this date, Joseph Ellicott began the construction of a home for himself above High street, about in line with the present Washington street. The house was completed by others and passed through various ownerships; finally, some twenty odd years ago, being bought by Mr. John C. Glenny and moved in two sections to Amherst street, where it was re-erected with new wings and some other alterations, and now stands as one of Buffalo's most beautiful homes and the only structure in Buffalo directly associated with the founder of the city.

While we have lost the old houses, we have retained knowledge of their sites. Thanks to the good work of the Niagara Frontier Landmarks Association, suitable tablets are being placed on numerous sites which have associations worth preserving. One of these, on the Dun Building, marks the site of Buffalo's first schoolhouse, built in 1807; another, on the Public Library, recalls the fact that that site was occupied by two courthouses; the first one built in 1810, destroyed at the burning of Buffalo; the second one enduring until 1876. This spot, the center of the administration of justice for what was formerly Niagara county, and after the division, of Erie county, covering a period of over half a century, has many associations connected with the leaders of the bar, judges, and lawyers whose names make a long list in the annals of our city. Two Buffalo citizens, who became Presidents of the United States, figured for many years in the practice of their profession in the old courthouse—Millard Fillmore and Grover Cleveland.

One house which was spared at the burning of Buffalo in 1813, known as the St. John House, stood on ground now covered by the H. A. Meldrum stores. The earlier life of the town was active in the neighborhood of the Terrace and lower Main street, and well-nigh every foot of that region has its associations with events in our early history. Some of these sites, no doubt, will later receive attention of the Landmarks Association.

No period in the city's history is more distinctly marked than that of the War of 1812, and yet I do not know of a single construction, not even an earthwork, belonging to that time which now endures. There are many points along the water front, from Buffalo creek to Lower Black Rock, which have stirring associations with this war. The sites of several batteries are known; one, which saw but little service, was on the Terrace; another overlooked the Niagara from the edge of the bluff at the foot of Vermont street, the actual site being utterly obliterated by the construction of the Erie canal in 1825; but now, overlooked from the Front, most nearly approached a short distance south of the memorial to the 13th U. S. Infantry, in the grounds of Fort Porter. Still another battery was on a high bank just south of the foot of Massachusetts street. As in the case of the battery just mentioned, the construction of the Erie canal and later of the railroad, which cut away much of the original bank, left only empty air where formerly was this defensive work. But the edge of the bluff at the point indicated is the nearest approach on the old level. No place in Buffalo commands a finer view. A point of public resort, a memorial tablet should sometime be

ASSOCIATIONS OF BUFFALO. 245

placed here, where it would be seen by thousands, and add the historic to the present scenic interest.

Many points on the Niagara river bank have associations with this period we are considering. Especially storied is the site of the present International Railway Company's buildings, opposite School street, which cover the ground where formerly stood Fort Adams, otherwise known as Fort Tompkins. From this point to Breckenridge street was battleground on more than one occasion. At the mouth of the Scajaquada creek, on the south side, was the Sailors' Battery, which figured in several hot engagements. Here, too, during the war, were fitted out several of the vessels which constituted the fleet with which Perry won his glorious battle on Lake Erie. The present Niagara street bridge over Scajaquada creek bears a tablet which records the fact that thereabouts, on August 3, 1814, was fought the important Battle of Black Rock.

We have touched but a few of many points and many associations in this interesting part of our city. Returning to Fort Porter, we find associations of a later period, though it should be noted that Fort Porter itself has never shared in any war, although the old magazine which was destroyed some years ago—the ruins of it underlying the present parade-ground—was a picturesque structure and looked as though it might have many war-time associations. As a matter of fact, it was built in 1846-47, and, although it served the Government for some years as a storehouse, for a longer period it stood useless, having been ruined by fire. No sentimental nor historic interest attaches to it.

Although there are many points in the city which have associations with the period of this old war, I do not now recall any visible reminder of it save one—a granite boulder on the meadow in Delaware Park, which marks the burial-place of soldiers who died of camp fever during that war, in the barracks hospital which stood on the banks of Scajaquada creek, within the present area of Forest Lawn Cemetery. Their bones were removed many years ago to their present resting-place, the long trench in which they were deposited being marked at either end with a willow tree; these willows for many years were objects of distinction and beauty in the park, but yielding to time and storm, they disappeared and the present boulder with its tablet was placed there on the 4th of July, 1896.

This is, perhaps, enough by way of reminder of this old war. Later and more peaceful years have their associations as well as those of conflict. The War of 1812 destroyed Buffalo; the building of our harbor and the opening of the Erie canal created a new Buffalo. The grave of Samuel Wilkeson, marked by a rugged monument, shaded by fine trees, in a quiet part of Forest Lawn, should be known to every one who gives a thought to the history of our city; for it was Judge Wilkeson, more than any other one man, who brought about conditions which made possible the development into Buffalo's commercial greatness. As the inscription on his monument records: *"Urbem condidit."*

It was in Judge Wilkeson's house, then newly built, that officials and prominent men of the State gathered after the first passage westward through the Erie canal, in the fall of 1825. This house, already referred to, has not only been the home of three generations of men and women prominent in our community and devoted to its welfare, but has been the scene of many gatherings of significance in Buffalo's history. It faces Niagara Square, and we may as well note that this spot and the neighboring Square, now bearing the name of Lafayette, have both, from the earliest days of the town, been the scene of countless gatherings, receptions, and events of note. That most famous of early executions in Western New York—the hanging of the three Thayers—took place in Court street, a few rods west of Niagara Square. During the Civil War, the Buffalo troops rendezvoused there and made their final reviews before leaving for camp. Across the Square from the Wilkeson homestead, was for many years the residence of Millard Fillmore. It is one of the queer things in our history that this Square, so long associated with a President of the United States, contains no reminder of him, his former home even being known by another name than his; and the Square in these later days has been given the distinction of a monument to another President, whose last associations with Buffalo were of the saddest, but who is not known to have any associations whatever with this particular spot.

Probably no place in Buffalo stands for more history, both local and general, than Lafayette Square. In the old days, when it was Courthouse Square and little more than an open common, it was the scene of many conventions, meetings, celebrations, and speeches. In 1825, when Lafayette made his visit to Buffalo, he was given a reception at the Eagle Tavern, on the west side of Main street, about where the Hudson stores now are, and the square opposite was named in his honor. The only national political convention ever held in Buffalo—the Free Soil Convention of 1848—was held under a great tent in this Square. There are, too, political associations of an early period that attached to the block below, for in the famous Log Cabin campaign of 1840 Buffalo's veritable log cabin was built on the northeast corner of Main and Eagle streets, and there the citizens met to harangue, and cheer for "Tippecanoe," and drink hard cider.

Following the political associations a little further, it is well to remind the reader of at least one other site in our city which is distinguished because of the people who have labored there. Where now stands the building of the Fidelity Trust Company, formerly stood, since 1820, the three or four successive buildings owned by the Messrs. Weed, devoted in the main to the hardware business. In the upper stories of the last of these buildings, which was demolished to make way for the present structure, were, for a time, the offices of Millard Fillmore, and, at a later period, the offices of Nathan K. Hall, of Grover Cleveland, and of his partner Wilson S. Bissell. The old Weed block, therefore, sent out two Presidents and two Postmasters-general.

Not all our historic associations relate to distant years. An event of very recent years, which must have mention, was a sequence of the Pan-American Exposition and the assassination of President McKinley. The house in which President McKinley died, September 14, 1901, known then as the Milburn residence, No. 1168 Delaware avenue, will always possess for the resident and the visitor a melancholy interest. His successor, Theodore Roosevelt, took the oath of office as President of the United States, in the home of Mr. Ansley Wilcox, at No. 641 Delaware avenue, on the day Mr. McKinley died. This house, by the way, is one of the most "historic" in Buffalo. Built about 1840 as the commandant's headquarters for the military establishment known as Poinsett Barracks, it originally faced to the east, looking out on the parade ground, which extended from Delaware to Main street, surrounded by buildings, the whole military tract covering the area now bounded by North, Main, Allen and Delaware. During this period, one part of the present house was occupied by Dr. Wood, post surgeon, whose wife was a daughter of Zachary Taylor,

ASSOCIATIONS OF BUFFALO.

who became President of the United States in 1850, with Millard Fillmore as his Vice-president. After the abandonment of Poinsett Barracks and the conversion of the tract to other uses, the house now standing was given its front approach from Delaware avenue. Additions and modern improvement have been made, but the main part of the structure is still the original old house, one of the most dignified and attractive residences in our city.

We could ramble up and down Main street, and back and forth across the town at great length, recalling this and that association, passing in review virtually the whole history of Buffalo. There are many associations with places which offer to the eye no reminder, no memorial, of the past. The enduring landmarks of early days are very few.

It was not my fortune to know Buffalo until what to people in middle life may be called comparatively recent years. My residence here dates from 1881; a little more than a quarter century. To elderly persons who were born here, who are familiar with the conditions and traditions of a generation earlier than their own, the Buffalo I can have known is not an old-time Buffalo at all. For that matter, none of us who read this page can have known the old Buffalo. And we must remember that for the young people of today many things even of thirty years ago, would seem strangely antiquated. For instance, the recent Buffalo that I first knew, was a city of much less than half its present size. There were still trees around the old First Church, and residences in its rear, along Pearl street. There were a few horse-car lines. You could go out Niagara street, as far as the Prospect reservoir, where the 74th regiment armory now stands, for five cents; if you rode further, the fare was eight cents. Horse-cars took you out Main street to Cold Spring. You could go on, as far as the Sisters'

Hospital, in a bobtail car drawn by one horse, over rails at the side of the street. When business seemed to warrant, it ran once an hour. On Main street the Williamsville stage was as familiar as the Lockport trolley cars are now—but it went slower. There were still public cisterns in many parts of town, and the pumps on the Terrace, at Main and Genesee, and elsewhere, were much used. Bacteriology was in its infancy, and the microbe, though no doubt then with us, had not attained its present monopoly of ailment.

The old group of down-town churches were still the devotional meeting-places of most of the church-going population. The phrase, "The Churches," was still in common use as designation of what is now Shelton Square; no doubt some of our older residents still use it, but the reason for it is no longer apparent. The "Old First" has gone; so have St. John's, and Trinity, and the Washington-street Baptist, and the United Presbyterian, and two or three other earlier churches on Washington street. The French St. Peter's has gone, and the Wells-street chapel. Old Temple Beth Zion, originally a Methodist church, made way for the Masonic building on Niagara street. The Central Presbyterian and the Niagara-square Baptist—Congregational in its later years—are both abandoned, and the former at least may be demolished before these lines reach the reader. Of them all, there now remain, consecrated to religious use, but two, St. Paul's and St. Joseph's. A new St. Joseph's is building, but its completion will not, it is to be hoped, put an end to the older edifice, infinitely rich in associations, or to its sacred use.

Thirty years ago we had but one theatre—at least but one attended by polite society—the old Academy. There was still an occasional sailing craft in the harbor. The Board of Trade still flourished on Central Wharf; and

ASSOCIATIONS OF BUFFALO. 251

from the purlieus of Canal street the sulphurous glory had not yet wholly departed. What are now choice residence districts were still vacant land and cow-pasture. Among my own recollections of what I must call modern Buffalo, are, an attendance at ball-games on grounds between Richmond and Elmwood; and at a circus whose tents were pitched just west of Wadsworth street, about where St. John's place now runs.

As one notes the constant change, both in the business and residential sections, one comes to the conclusion that in Buffalo at least each generation practically creates its own city. If one will compare the Buffalo of today with that, say, of thirty years ago, he will be surprised to note how few of the important buildings are old. Our City Hall, it is true, dates back to 1876, and the Jail is somewhat older; but the Federal building, the Municipal building, every one of the theatres; two of the three high schools; all of the prominent hotels except the Genesee; even the historic old Mansion House has been built over; our two great armories; the Chamber of Commerce, the Y. M. C. A. building; and the "old" Y. M. C. A. building, now the home of the Y. W. C. A.; all of the conspicuous club houses—the Saturn, University, Twentieth Century, Country—all in fact except the Buffalo and the Park, and they occupy former residences so altered and enlarged as to be practically new; the Public Library, the Grosvenor, the Catholic Institute, the Historical Building, the Albright Art Gallery; most of the churches and hospitals and asylums; the banks; scores of public and private schools; miles on miles of business buildings, and thousands of residences, which really make up the Buffalo of today, have all been built within the last thirty years. Attention is called to this feature of our city merely to emphasize the point that historic association does not depend upon the preservation of the old. The associations remain with us though the face of our city constantly changes; and while we often lament the passing of a beautiful old residence or a building which has been the scene of important events, it is well to remember that after all the history of the community is embodied in the acts of its men and women.

It is with the deeds of the makers of Buffalo that the student of our history is, after all, most concerned. It would be a pleasure, were it feasible, to recall the names and achievements of many of the men and women who have lived their lives in this community and accomplished something for the world's betterment; but as one begins to recall name after name, their very number is seen to make it impracticable. Our dearest associations must always remain with the personality of those who have lived and worked, rather than with the things of brick and mortar that may withstand for a few years. The only enduring work and the most significant is the wholly immaterial memory of good lives and useful effort, things that cannot be labelled, nor kept in museums, nor marked by tablets. Is it not true of all history, that it is merely the outcome of individual character and effort?

FROM INDIAN RUNNER TO TELEPHONE

ORIGINALLY WRITTEN FOR THE MAGAZINE "OPPORTUNITY," JANUARY, 1909.

NO chapter in the story of Western New York is more important or more interesting than that which relates the development of means of intercommunication. It touches the real life of the people far more than the record of wars and politics.

Western New York has sometimes been called the "most highly civilized spot on earth." If there is a touch of irony or humor in this, the residents of Western New York need not admit it. They do have all the advantages and blessings to be found anywhere. In nothing are they more fortunate than in facilities of travel and communication by mail, telegraph and telephone.

The telephone service in our day, the highest and best development of intercommunication, is the latest of a long series of steps in our progress.

When the white man first came to know what we call Western New York, it was the home of a people highly developed, compared with most of the American aborigines. Their trails ran across and up and down the country, and their fleet-footed runners, by using the relay system, carried verbal messages from Lake Erie to the Hudson in an incredibly short time. The first whites used the old Indian trails; but they used more the natural waterways. The campaigns and marches of the French—who were the first white masters of the region—and after them of the British, were mostly made by boats which skirted the shores of Ontario and Erie, or paddled and poled up and down the streams, with arduous portages from one watershed to another.

This was the state of things so far as travel or traffic was concerned when white men first undertook to acquire the lands of Western New York.

For this sketch we will refer to Western New York as that region bounded on the east by a line running through Seneca lake. Under the old Colonial charters, both Massachusetts and New York made claim to this territory. The final adjustment of their claims led to a sale in 1788 on the part of Massachusetts of the pre-emption right to some six million acres, to Nathaniel Gorham and Oliver Phelps. They paid about a million dollars for it, but they paid in scrip which soon fell much below par. The first Western New York land deal was not a conspicuous success for the speculators. Two years later, Phelps and Gorham bought the Indian title to 2,600,000 acres, extending from about the line of Seneca lake to the Genesee river. The Indians got very little out of the bargain, as was the case in every trade with the whites.

In 1791, the western part of the great tract was resold to Robert Morris, who again sold it to a company of Dutch speculators, who, although they did not constitute a corporate company, are known in history as the Holland Land Company.

These Dutch speculators sent their surveyors and agents into the wilderness. They opened the first roads and laid out the first settlements. For the sake of its good harbor on Lake Erie, a town was begun on Buffalo creek in 1799, and with Dutch loyalty was called New Amsterdam. It soon became Buffalo.

For many years the two tracts into which Western New York was thus divided,—the Phelps and Gorham tract east of the Genesee, and the Holland Land Company's tract west of it,—present similar phases of development.

The first people to come in and take up the lands were from New England; especially in the Genesee valley was the New England immigration so large that it turned that fertile wilderness into what is still the garden region of New York State, and gave it a character for thrift, culture and morality which constituted it a second New England.

The Holland Purchase, too, had a similar influx of settlers from New England; but as time went on it received more immigrants from Europe, most of them bringing very few worldly goods. Its interests, too, were less purely agricultural, especially at Buffalo, where lake traffic drew together large numbers of sailors and others of a more or less rough and adventurous disposition. Buffalo has always been made up of many races. Rochester, the chief city of the Genesee valley region, has always remained more distinctly of New England parentage and English origin.

The first thing that marks the development of a new region after the settler has hewn the trees and built his cabin, is the opening of a road that he may be in touch with his neighbors,—neighbors none the less though perhaps many miles distant.

The first wagon track on the Holland Purchase was opened in 1798 and followed in the main the old Indian trail from Canandaigua to the Buffalo creek. In the next ten years, many roads were opened between the new settlements, usually by the agents of the Holland Land Company. One important road a hundred years ago, and still a much used highway, was not so constructed. This was the Military Road opened by United States officers stationed at Fort Niagara in 1800. They constructed it from the brow of the high land above Lewiston to Scajaquada Creek, now within the limits of Buffalo. Originally built to facilitate the transportation of troops and munitions of war from Lake Ontario to Lake Erie, it later became a convenient road for the settlers. A portion of it, today known as the Military Road, is a part of the street system of Buffalo.

Even before the roads were made, the people of Western New York asked the Government for a mail service. Before the era of settlements, when the French or British troops controlled the region, military mail was sent back and forth by boat between Oswego and Fort Niagara, and this method was followed long after the first roads were opened. In winter the mail carrier was either an athletic soldier or an Indian who ran through the forest on snow-shoes. Many an important mail has been delivered by such a carrier at Oswego, Fort Niagara and Buffalo Creek.

In 1790 there were but 175 postoffices in the United States and 1875 miles of post roads. These were mostly between old cities near the seaboard. In New York State Utica got its first mail in 1793, Canandaigua in 1794. The first mail was carried from Canandaigua to Niagara,—meaning not the present city of the Falls, but the old Fort,—in 1797. On all the early mail routes in Western New York, the carrier was a horseman who rode over the mirey and stump-crowded roads, usually with his mail in his hat or pocket, carrying food for himself and oats for his horse in saddle-bags. As settlements and roadside taverns multiplied, the food question was simplified and the saddle-bags were used for the mail. On September 30, 1804, Buffalo's first postmaster was appointed. This was Erastus

Granger, for many years one of the most prominent men in Western New York. At that time there were no postoffices nearer to Buffalo than Batavia on the east, Niagara to the north and Erie to the southwest. The post route from Canandaigua to Niagara was changed in that year so that the carrier rode his horse by way of Buffalo creek, leaving there the packet of letters and papers for Buffalo and for the occasional schooner on the lake. Buffalo received its mail once in two weeks until 1805; then, until 1809, it had a weekly service. In 1810 a change to "stage-wagon" service was established from Buffalo eastward and the mail used that method. Andrew Langdon—grandfather of a prominent citizen of Buffalo of that name—drove the first stage from Albany to Buffalo.

The war of 1812 to 1815 was a great setback to the development of Western New York. It stopped immigration, it impoverished many of the settlers who had already taken up lands, and checked the development of all improvements.

From about 1815, for ten years or so, the interest of the people in this section largely centered on the construction of the Erie canal. Open from the east as far as Rochester in 1823 and to Buffalo and Lake Erie in the fall of 1825, it became for a period the main highway of freight shipment and of travel; but it did not carry the mail. When the canal was opened, in October, 1825, the news was carried by the booming of cannon, one after another, across the State from Lake Erie to the Hudson, in one hour and twenty minutes.

The era in which the canal was without rival was short. Eight years after the first boat had left Buffalo for the east, a railway was opened from Buffalo to Black Rock. It was a most primitive construction, the rail being of wood covered with a strap of iron and the motive power a team of horses; but it was the beginning of the great railway era. In 1836, however, a real railroad with a steam locomotive whch drew the queer old cars over a wonderfully rough track was opened from Buffalo to Niagara Falls. It carried the mail and there was no lack of people willing to take chances and travel on the new-fangled line. The chain of railways across New York State from Albany to Buffalo was completed in 1843. Built in sections with connecting links added at intervals of years, and representing many companies and various interests when completed, it was found to keep very nearly the line of the old stage road, which in turn had gradually evolved from the earlier roads of the settlers, and these had followed, wherever practicable, the ancient trails of the Indians.

Whoever rides today in the luxurious coaches on the rapid-moving trains across the state, passes, for the greater part, through the same valleys, skirts the same hills—but does not see the same forests—which marked the way along which the Iroquois runner hastened two hundred years ago.

From the time railroads were first built, they carried the mails, but it was not until many years later that the rate of postage was so reduced that communication by mail ceased to be an expense which was felt by the average individual. In the earlier years, domestic postage ranged from 6½c to 25c. Towards the close of the War of 1812, this maximum rate of 25c was increased 50 per cent., so that a letter of any considerable length sent from one part of New York State to another was likely to cost either the sender or the receiver 37½c. No envelopes were used. The correct way of folding, sealing and addressing the sheets of paper is now one of the lost arts. The modern envelope and cheap postage practically revolutionized domestic correspondence.

The railway era was quickly followed by the Age of Wire. Before people in New York State had overcome their timidity enough to travel generally on the railways, they began to hear of Morse's new-fangled "magnetic telegraph." Nothing in the history of the world did so much to revolutionize intercommunication as this invention. Next to the inventor himself, none did more to make it practicable than two men of Western New York. It was Millard Fillmore of Buffalo, afterward President of the United States, who, as a member of Congress in 1842, procured for Morse the Government appropriation for the construction of an experimental line. Morse's idea was to bury the wires. It was Ezra Cornell of Ithaca who first suggested stringing them on poles. Mr. Cornell made a fortune out of the idea and hastened the day when telegraph communication was made well nigh universal.

The Civil War had a curious effect on the development of the telegraph. Prior to the war it was used sparingly, partly because of its cost, partly because many people mistrusted its accuracy. But the demand for prompt reports from the front during the war led the great newspapers of the country to make the first extensive use of the wire for news reports. The business public soon followed. Boards of trade and commercial interests generally made little or no use of the telegraph until about the time of the Civil War. Now the bulk of their business is transacted by wire.

Extensive as telegraphic communication has become, it has never reached every corner of every county, and practically every household, as has the telephone. This is the more wonderful when we recall that the practical use of the telephone is scarcely more than a quarter century old.

Although the telephone was in use more than thirty years ago, it was for some years chiefly confined to great cities and short distances. It is not too much to say that now all of Western New York is brought into instantaneous communication by a network of wires.

While these advances have been taking place, Western New York itself has been transformed. When the first Federal census was taken, in 1790, the white population of old Ontario county, which then embraced all of the territory we are considering, was 1085. The fourteen counties into which old Ontario has been divided, had at the Federal census of 1900 a population of 1,469,360, now beyond question in excess of a million and a half. With the possibilities of wireless communication and other yet undreamed-of improvements, who can doubt that the coming decades will show changes in our means of intercommunication as marked and wonderful as those of the past?

SOME THANKSGIVING CONTRASTS

A SUNDAY AFTERNOON ADDRESS AT THE HISTORICAL BUILDING.

I ASK you to join with me in considering briefly the historical aspect of Thanksgiving, the American feast and holiday which most of us—I hope all of us—are to celebrate this week. I have no thought of preaching a Thanksgiving sermon. Our point of view in these talks, as you know, is always that of the student of history. As such let us take note of certain significant changes in the character and observance of this day we call Thanksgiving.

And first, let me call attention to certain contrasts in the proclamations establishing the day. I hope you have all read the short proclamation issued a few days ago by Governor Hughes. I was much struck on reading it with its significant difference from many of the formal proclamations which have preceded it. "With profound appreciation," says the Governor, "of the obligations of liberty and of our dependence, for the maintenance of our institutions, upon a proper sense of the responsibilities of citizenship and upon the cultivation of those qualities of character which will enable us to discharge them." And again he says: "Let us devote our lives to the attainment of the best of which we are capable in all good works, delighting in our fellowship and in the joyous service of brotherhood."

And then he goes on and in the usual way recommends a religious observance of the day.

But such language as Governor Hughes uses, such ideas and ideals as inspired that language, would have been absolutely impossible and incomprehensible to the old Colonial governors whose proclamations instituted the observance of the day.

Contrast with these words of Governor Hughes the following from the Connecticut proclamation of 1650: "Every person *shall* duly resort and attend thereunto upon such public fast days and days of thanksgiving as are to be generally kept by the appointment of authority," and for failure to obey this mandate the Connecticut citizen was liable to a fine of five shillings. This illustrates the early idea of commanding the people, not merely to attend service, but to pray and to fast and to rejoice.

More than one hundred years later, in Massachusetts Bay Colony, a man was liable to fine or other punishment if he worked on days appointed for fasting and prayer. In 1696, William Veazie of Boston was pilloried for plowing on a fast-day.

For many years such was the conception and the custom. Gradually, as the nation expanded, the ideas underlying this thanksgiving institution shifted. It would be an interesting inquiry to trace year by year the evolution of the modern conception; but for our purpose let us cite only one other, a proclamation by Governor Seward, made some fifty years ago, in which, after reviewing the blessings of the people, he says: "I *recommend* to my fellow citizens that they abstain on that day from secular employments." It was no longer a peremptory order, but a recommendation. Governor Seward's proclamation was by no means exceptional; his point of view was that of his time; but note how far he had travelled from the old compulsory mandates of 1650. And now, half a century after Seward, we find the Governor of New York State neither ordering nor formally recommending, but heartily reminding the citizen and the individual of his obligations to government and to others. Nothing more perfectly illustrates the growth of the feeling of personal responsibility, than such a proclamation as we have this year from Governor Hughes.

Again, notice the contrasts in the observance of the day. It has come to be a custom that no governor of a State issues a Thanksgiving proclamation until the President of the United States has issued one. By custom the institution has taken on a national character. In its origin, as you know, it was purely local, and for many years it continued a variable and irregular institution. Three of the early Presidents, Washington, John Adams and Madison, issued proclamations to the people, calling on them to observe certain days with fasting, prayer and thanksgiving; but after Madison no President of the United States issued a proclamation for a national thanksgiving until Abraham Lincoln. This seems the more remarkable because at different periods in our history, when most of the states and territories had practically settled upon one day in the year for thanksgiving observance, requests had been presented to the President that the institution of Thanksgiving might be given a national character. This feeling manifested itself always during or after some national crisis or calamity. The most notable Thanksgiving in the early history of the country followed the treaty of peace concluding the War of 1812. After the great financial crisis of 1837-'38, after the Mexican War, and at different times during the long period of bitter agitation over slavery, special fast days, sometimes combined with the feature of thanksgiving, were ordained by the governors of different states. But there was a feeling at Washington that such matters belonged to the states.

A Buffalo President had offered to him, urged upon him, the opportunity to establish this most symbolical day of American observance, but he failed to improve the opportunity. This was Millard Fillmore. While he was President in 1852, a strong movement was started to give to Thanksgiving a national character by having it proclaimed by the President and observed on the same day throughout the Union. Prior to that time, the different states named their own days, so that a Massachusetts man might celebrate Thanksgiving in Boston, and, perhaps, being later in Connecticut or New Jersey, might celebrate another Thanksgiving with the citizens of those states.

Among the manuscripts in the possession of this Society, formerly belonging to President Fillmore, are certain interesting letters written to him by representatives of public journals and by organizers and educational workers, explaining to him at great length how he might add to the luster of his administration, by creating a national Thanksgiving Day. Mr. Fillmore's reply was that such matters were the prerogative of the several states. And such, apparently, was the view of his successors until the day of Lincoln.

I have said that the popular demand for this observance always followed a period of crisis or calamity, so that you may readily believe that the greatest of our nation's crises, the Civil War, turned the minds of the people more strongly than ever before in their history to the formal observance of this institution. President Lincoln issued several proclamations creating days of prayer and fasting during the Civil War.

In 1863 he appointed August 6th as a special Thanksgiving because "there have been vouchsafed to the Army and Navy of the United States victories on land and on the sea so signal and so effective as to furnish reasonable grounds for augmented confidence that the Union of these States will be maintained, their constitution preserved and their peace and prosperity permanently restored." The people were not asked to give thanks because the North had won victories over the South, but "for augmented confidence that the Union of these States will be maintained." I cannot forbear to call attention to one striking thing which this quotation illustrates—the beauty and purity of Mr. Lincoln's English. How came he to be master of a diction that rivals in its rhythmic appeal to the ear, and in its precise and forceful use of our speech, the most exalted passages in the Prophets, the prayer of St. Crysostom, or the best of English anywhere? Was the gift his because he was absolutely sincere, and wrought, as well as wrote, in the midst of times that taught, no less than they tried, the souls of men?

But President Lincoln died before the whole country had fairly come to consider itself once more as a Union. So that it was his successor, President Johnson, who had the distinction of issuing the first Thanksgiving proclamation for a national observance throughout the country. From Andrew Johnson's day to this we have had an annual Thanksgiving proclamation from the President.

Nothing better illustrates the changed conditions since Thanksgivings were first observed in this country than a list of some of the things for which thanks were specially ordered at different periods.

Our ancestors gave thanks for not starving to death. This, in a word, was the occasion of those first New England Thanksgivings.

For rain.
For the end of a too rainy season.
For the arrival of provision ships.
For deliverance from pirates.
For defeat of enemies in war.
For safe arrival of persons of rank or quality.
For the birth of an heir to the British throne. This, of course, in the English colonies.
For the establishment of the Constitution.

Some of these promptings to thanksgiving may be dwelt on a little. For instance, the gratitude for rain. That caused the second American Thanksgiving, in July, 1623. This was no harvest-home, but a triumph of the faith of the community. From May to the middle of July there had been no rain. The Pilgrims stood it as long as they could, then set apart "a solemn day of humiliation." In the morning, when they began to pray, according to the old chronicle, "it was clear weather and very hot, and not a cloud or any sign of rain to be seen." Strenuous religious services were kept up for nine hours; towards evening it began to rain—and the shower lasted fourteen days. They were no mere dilettanti, these Pilgrim fathers, when it came to praying. Then they changed their fast to a thanksgiving.

You may be a bit skeptical as to a thanksgiving because of defeat of enemies in war. A manuscript preserved in the archives of the Hague shows that in 1644 the New Yorkers marched to Greenwich, Conn., shot or burned alive five or six hundred Indians, including women and children; they then marched back to New York—and sat down to a Thanksgiving dinner! And did the New England colonists have a Thanksgiving season after the virtual annihilation of the Pequots?

It has always been true that men give thanks at the

defeat of their enemies. One of the most notable Thanksgiving Days in the history of our country was October 9, 1760, which was appointed by Colonial Governors "a day of Public Thanksgiving for the success of his Majesty's Arms, more especially in the intire Reduction of Canada." Clergymen everywhere (except in Canada), and especially in Boston, preached long sermons full of exultation at the overthrow of the power of France in America; and these were the good old-fashioned double-barreled sermons, which began with a long discourse in the morning, stopped for a noon breathing spell, and wound up with two or three more hours of exhortation in the afternoon. To many an eager, restless youth in those days, the real Thanksgiving must have begun when the minister's "amen" released him from all these hours on hard benches.

One of those old Thanksgiving sermons has come down to me. It was preached on this same October 9, 1760, morning and afternoon, by Jonathan Mayhew, a most eminent D. D. of his time, in the West Church, Boston. His text was: "Thou art my son. . . . Ask of me, and I will give the Heathen for thine inheritance, and the uttermost parts of the earth for thy possession." The devout inference, of course, was that the Lord had taken Canada away from the wicked French, and had put it in the possession of the good English, as a part of the general scheme of advancing His kingdom on earth. That was, of course, the only way that Minister Mayhew and his people could look at it; that is the way we always look at the defeat of an adversary. The curious thing about it is that these same people, a few years later, were holding Thanksgiving services in gratitude to the Almighty for their own deliverance from the English!

As to the establishment of the Constitution, it is interesting to recall that in 1789 a joint commission of the two houses of Congress waited upon Washington "to request that he would recommend to the people of the United States a day of public thanksgiving and thanks to God, especially for affording them an opportunity peacefully to establish a constitution of government for their safety and happiness." There have been other occasions in our history when Congress has asked the President to proclaim fast or thanksgiving days—three times during the War of 1812.

The modern evolution of Thanksgiving day observance has carried us a long ways from the original institution. Every schoolboy knows, probably with more certainty of information than his elders, that what is now a national observance is an outgrowth of the Pilgrim Thanksgiving. As a religious observance it antedates the coming of the Pilgrims; fasts and feasts are as old as the Hebrew faith, if not as old as the race itself. But the first American Thanksgiving followed that first Pilgrim harvest of 1621; on which joyful occasion, thanks to "King" Massasoit, the turkey was brought in, and entered upon the most exalted career attained by any bird, not even excepting the eagle. We give the eagle vague respect, but we love the turkey.

I have spoken of the second American Thanksgiving. The third American Thanksgiving of formal observance was in 1631, because of the safe arrival of provision ships. Gradually, the festival became established, and extended to other colonies; but Thanksgiving has always been pre-eminently a New England institution. Other parts of the country have varied in their regard for it. Where there is a strong element of New England settlers, Thanksgiving is made much of. It was the great day of the year in Boston for a century and a half before New York paid much attention to it. New York, with different traditions, always exalted Christmas and New Year's. The Bostonians for long years frowned on the Christmas festivities, which savored so much of ritualism and, as the old preachers used to put it, "of popery." New York and the southern colonies have adopted Thanksgiving from New England. New England has warmed up to a merry Christmas; and these and the whole country have handed the earlier day over to feasting, visiting and sports, with less and less of religious observance.

Thanksgiving Day and Fast Day sermons are really pretty lively reading—if they are old enough. Our country got through the Colonial and the Revolutionary period with an alternation of fasts and thanksgivings which truly gauges the varying fortunes of the struggle. But when we were once fairly launched in the critical period that followed, and then so soon carried into another war with Great Britain, our troubles began in earnest. The American politician arrived as he never had before, and that "menace of malice," which one of our Presidents mentioned in one of his Thanksgiving proclamations, showed itself as never before. Fast days multiplied, and there were few Thanksgivings.

A very curious chapter of American history could be written from data contained in the Fast Day and Thanksgiving Day sermons preached during the decade from 1810 to 1820. New England did not support President Madison's policy. When Congress declared war, June 18, 1812, the first thing that the Governor of Massachusetts did was to proclaim a day of fasting, humiliation and prayer. Other governors did the same, in addition to the annual spring fast, usually a Sunday in April, which was a regular observance at that time. So violent was the adverse criticism on Madison's policy, that, although the President did not swerve from his course, he fell in with the spirit of his opponents—or perhaps felt that the emergency called for it—and proclaimed a national fast. This was on August 20, 1812. But before that time the New England ministers had "sailed into him," hot and heavy. He was denounced as the enemy of his country and the tool of France. Pulpit politics, then as now, were not conspicuous for discretion. But no minister today would be apt to go to the intemperate extremes of language and denunciation of the National Executive that characterized many a fast day sermon of these wrathy New England parsons. They usually prefaced their remarks by saying that it was not their custom to talk politics in the pulpit, but that the day was exceptional. Many a Thanksgiving sermon nowadays has a like introduction. Freedom of speech meant free speaking, in the New England pulpit in the good old days.

The Reverend John Smith, pastor of the church in Salem, N. H., told his congregation: "Whether Great Britain is friendly to the American interest or not, she is friendly to her own interest, and in defending herself she guards our liberties. Could our twenty ships effect any real injury to the thousand ships of the British navy, it would be like taking away the rampart of our own defense. Could the wildest imagination conceive of anything like victory over England, in the same event might be seen the complete ruin of our own country." What a shock to this good man must have been those glorious sea-duels that were so soon to demonstrate American superiority. He urged the young men not to enlist, and declared the war not merely "an alliance with France," but "making war with the Lamb and with the saints," "uniting with Antichrist"—an epithet at the time often given to Bonaparte—"combining with the deluded nations, that wander after the beast, . . . and finally go to perdition." Dr. Dwight's fast-day sermons in the chapel of Yale College proved to the boys, with absolute logic, that the war would put this country in an abject alliance with France. "We are linking ourselves," said William Ellery Channing, in his fast-day sermon at the Federal street church, Boston, July 23, 1812, "with the acknowledged enemy of mankind, with a government which has left not a vestige of liberty where it has extended its blasting sway." The Reverend John Gardiner, at Trinity Church, Boston, on the same day said: "Let no considerations whatever, my brethren, deter you at all times and in all places from execrating the present war. It is a war unjust, foolish and ruinous. . . . As Mr. Madison has declared war let Mr. Madison carry it on." Scores of New England's ministers harangued their congregations in this strain.

Outside of New England, especially in Philadelphia, the Episcopal ministers were equally violent against President Madison. All through the war, the fast-day sermons preached by New England ministers were practically another hostile campaign against the struggling American forces. The preachers did not hesitate at personalities towards the President. The Reverend Elijah Parish, at Newburyport, fulminating on the certainty of an alliance with France, exclaimed: "Have not the Rulers at Paris and Washington, since the commencement of the war, been one as much as 'the great red dragon' and 'one of his horns' are one? Which sooty slave in all the ancient dominion, has more obsequiously watched the eye of his master, or flew to the indulgence of his desires, more servilely, than the same masters have waited and watched, and obeyed the orders of the great Napoleon? Are not the bonds of this alliance already stronger than death?" These clergymen feared not only political bondage to France, but the spread throughout America of French atheistical views. Only now and then did a minister, on these fast-day occasions when politics were permitted, stand up for his President. Such a one was the Reverend John Giles, Presbyterian, of Newburyport; and such another was Solomon Aiken, pastor of the First Church in Dracutt, who issued "an address to Federal clergymen on the subject of the war," and vigorously showed them which way lay true patriotism. "Some of you," he said, "treat our Christian rulers with more freedom than what Michael thought decent, or even dared, to treat the devil."

These fast-day exhibitions of public feeling gradually gave way to a more reconciled state of mind, as the fortunes of war favored us more. And when President Madison proclaimed April 13, 1815, as a National Thanksgiving Day, even his pulpit critics who had opposed him most bitterly and hampered his policy all they could throughout the war, found a good deal to be thankful for. With the exception of the Thanksgivings of 1863-'64, that of April 13, 1815, was the most notable in the history of the United States.

In one of President Roosevelt's Thanksgiving proclamations there is a striking sentence. Each generation, he says, in the more than the century and a quarter which have passed since this country took its place among the nations, "has had its peculiar burdens, each to face its special crisis, and each has known years of grim trial, when the country was menaced by malice, domestic or foreign levy, when the hand of the Lord was heavy upon it in drouth or flood or pestilence, when in bodily distress and anguish of soul it paid the penalty of folly and a froward heart." President Roosevelt wrote his own proclamations; there can be no doubt of that. He is a historian; and when he sweeps the past years in a single sentence, he is thinking of specific things in our history. "Menaced by malice" is no mere phrase. American progress has always been more delayed and endangered by internal strife than by any act of other nations. We are more at peace now, among ourselves, than ever before. Curiously enough, the bitterest strife of past years finds its most intemperate record in fast-day and Thanksgiving-day sermons.

Nothing is more significant, in the history of our people, than the decline of the fast. Good Catholics and orthodox Hebrews continue faithful in the observance of fasts prescribed in their churches. There are fasts for the Protestant Episcopalians; but taking that denomination as a whole, there is less insistence on abstaining from food than formerly. As for the multitude of sects, for the most part, they do not fast. The tendency of the time is simply that of all peoples who are prosperous. The last great fasts in American history were observed in the dark days of the Civil War. If this country should be once more plunged into such deep trouble, the fast day would no doubt reappear as essentially a national observance. The first national Thanksgiving proclamation was issued by President Lincoln in 1863; the second in 1864, after the triumphs of the Union forces. There was a spirit of earnestness in the Thanksgiving services then that has disappeared from them now. This is no reproach; it is human nature. We are too prosperous to observe days of supplication and fasting, too free from great calamity to be anything more than just placidly thankful. The so-called decline of Thanksgiving is but an index of national well being. It does not mean that the people are grown irreligious.

Turning to recent years, it is instructive to observe how

the keynote, the special bequest of different Thanksgivings varies, as shown in the proclamations.

Thus in 1883, Grover Cleveland, then Governor of the State, found as a special cause for the people's gratitude, "that the supremacy of law and order has been complete," and "we have advanced in all that pertains to the material, social and educational interests of our people." The year before this Governor Cornell had mentioned as a special blessing that the "tide of immigration to our shores has been unprecedented." This view would hardly prompt a special thanksgiving today.

Governor David B. Hill, in 1885, called upon the people to give thanks because "political rights have been enjoyed without infringement from any source."

Governor Flower, in 1893, found special reason for gratitude because the "State had been spared serious conflict between employers and employes."

Each of these shows in a measure the issue which had engaged the attention of the public and on which, more or less, party lines had been drawn, or a subject of general discussion and common concern.

In 1889 Governor Roosevelt in a proclamation, which was as unconventional and individual as are all of his utterances, saw reason for thanksgiving because "each man has been permitted to live his life and do his work as seemed best to him, provided only that he in no wise interfered with the liberty and well being of his fellows." "It is right," he added, "that we should give thanks for the prosperity that has come to the nation and for the way in which this great people in the first flush of its mighty manhood is moving forward to meet its destiny and to do without flinching every duty with which that destiny brings it face to face."

The Thanksgiving proclamations of President Roosevelt and Governor Hughes, and some other of the present governors of States, well establish, from an historical point of view, the fact that this country is absolutely at peace, undisturbed by any menace to its prosperity. Whenever that menace has arisen, the thought of those in authority has found definite expression, so that we may see in the old proclamations just what were the evils from which deliverance was sought or the specific blessings for which the nation's gratitude was due.

If the future historian of this country were to have no other sources of information than the Thanksgiving proclamations, he could not write much of a history, but he could state with confidence two important facts:

First: That the American people (notwithstanding the clamor of political strife, the conflicts of labor, and all the difficult problems of our day) are at this time really very prosperous and with ample grounds for happiness and gratitude.

Second: That the idea of personal responsibility—the national valuation of individual conduct towards the state as towards one's fellows—has come to the front, as never before in the history of this Nation.

ON THE NIAGARA FRONTIER WITH HARRIET MARTINEAU

THERE recently came into the possession of the Buffalo Historical Society the original manuscript of a long letter written by Harriet Martineau, at Niagara Falls, in 1834. It was addressed to her friend the Rev. Charles Brooks, at "Hingham near Boston, Massachusetts." As it has never been published, and as it is in part an interesting bit of Niagara literature, I deem it worthy a place in these records. The letter itself is something of a curiosity; written in a light angular hand on thin paper, covering both sides of the folded sheets and then cross-written, from side to side and from top to bottom, in a very maze of thrifty and exasperating chirography. The only portion of the sheets not closely criss-crossed, is a space on the back for the address—for this was before the days of envelopes, and the precious pages were folded after a fashion which is now a lost art, and fastened with red wafers.

Few of our early visitors—especially of our early English visitors—have been so affable, so gracious without condescension, as Harriet Martineau. When she came to America in the summer of 1834, she was thirty-two years of age, and for ten years had had a growing reputation as a writer and a vigorous, remarkably clear-minded young woman. Her first book, "Devotional Exercises for the use of Young Persons," was not of a sort likely to gain wide popularity. In 1830 she won three prizes offered by the Central Unitarian Association for as many essays "designed to convert respectively the Catholics, the Jews and the Mohammedans. The essays," observes an acute biographer, "probably converted nobody, but brought in forty-five guineas." She had won some measure of popularity by her stories, and genuine respect for her ability by her "Illustrations of Political Economy" and "Illustrations of Taxation," when, in 1834, she sailed for America. Here she was less interested in the obvious phases of our society and our scenery, than in the great problems which then engaged the thought of political and social leaders in the United States. On her return to England in 1836 she published her well-known work, "Society in America," and followed it in 1838 with the three-volume "Retrospect of Western Travel." She designed in this latter work to picture the scenery and the lighter phases of her journeyings; but at her lightest Miss Martineau was never anything but serious; and her criticisms of slavery, as she had observed it in her travels, won for her "Retrospect" some pretty harsh criticism. Had she come to us twenty years later she would have found the Abolition movement better organized, and would have been greeted by warm sympathizers.

I revert to her "Retrospect" because it is one of the best books we have, for its period. It pictures America to us as it was seen in 1834 by a person who was absolutely without prejudice and who never became hysterical. Miss Martineau was very deaf, and thereby may have been spared some small unpleasantnesses; but she seems to have had a singularly judicial cast of mind. She loved justice as well as she loved philosophy; and the lapse of more than three quarters of a century has not taken from her pages their worth or attractiveness. In later years her work grew more and more grave. In 1853 she published a condensation of Comte's "Positive Philosophy," followed by a "History of England during the Thirty Years' Peace" and other works of learning and merit. Her voluminous "Autobiography" is one of the most candid records we have of an ardent life pledged to high ideals. Able biographers have long since sought to do justice to this gifted, high-minded woman. I here merely seek to recall to the student of our regional history her visits and what she wrote of us.

The "Retrospect" contains a lively chapter on Buffalo, and another and longer one on Niagara Falls. Miss Martineau visited the Falls in October, 1834, and again in June, 1836. It was during her first visit that she wrote the letter I am about to quote from. First, however, I wish to copy from her pages a narrative of the burning of Buffalo, told to her by one who had shared in the experiences described. It is a record worthy a place in Buffalo's annals of the War of 1812. I give it as Miss Martineau wrote it down—seated, she tells us, with a friend, "a lady of Buffalo, who happens to be a good walker," on the ruins of Fort Erie; and I reserve a word or two of comment or correction until the end:

At the time of the War of 1812, Mrs. W. lived in Buffalo, with her father, mother, brothers, and sisters. In 1814, just when the war was becoming terrific on the frontier, her father and eldest brother were drowned in crossing the neighboring ferry. Six months after this incident, the danger of Buffalo was so great that the younger children of the family were sent away into the country with their married sister, under the charge of their brother-in-law, who was to return with his wagon for the mother and two daughters who were left behind, and for the clothes of the family. For three weeks there had been so strong an apprehension of a descent of the Indians, the barbarous allies of the British, that the ladies had snatched sleep with their clothes on, one watching while the others lay down. It was with some difficulty, and after many delays, that the wagon party got away, and there were still doubts whether it was the safer course to go or stay. Nothing was heard of them before night, however, and it was hoped that they were safe, and that the wagon would come for the remaining three the next morning.

The ladies put out their lights early, as they were desired; and at eight, two of the three lay down to sleep; Mrs. W., then a girl of sixteen, being one. At nine, she was called up by the beating of a drum, the signal that the Indians were at hand. No description can give an idea of the loathing with which these savages were then regarded,— the mingled horror, disgust, dread and hatred. The Indians were insidious, dangerous, and cruel beyond example, even in the history of savage warfare. These poor ladies had been brought up to hate them with a deadly hatred; they were surrounded with persons burning with the injuries inflicted by Indian revenge and barbarity; for weeks they had lived in hourly dread of death by their hands; their strength was worn, and their nerves were shaken by the long suspense; and now the hoarse drum woke them up with news that the hour was come. A deadly sickness overspread their hearts as they started from their beds. They looked from their windows, but could see nothing through the blank darkness. They listened, but they knew that if the streets had been quiet as death, the stealthy tread of the savages would have been inaudible. There was a bustle in the town. Was the fight beginning? No. It was an express sent by the scouts to say that it was a false alarm. The worn-out ladies composed their spirits, and sank to sleep again.

At four, they were once more awakened by the horrid drum, and now there was a mustering in the streets which looked as if this were no false alarm. In the same moment, the sister who was watching what passed in the street, saw by torchlight the militia part asunder and fly, and Mrs. W., who was looking through the back window, perceived in the uncertain glimmer that a host of savages was leaping the garden-fence,—leaping along the walks to the house, like so many kangaroos,—but painted, and flourishing their tomahawks. She cried out to her mother and sister, and they attempted to fly; but there was no time. Before they could open the front door, the back windows came crashing in, and the house was crowded with yelling savages. With their tomahawks, they destroyed everything but the ladies, who put on the most submissive air possible. The trunks containing the clothing of the whole family stood in the hall, ready to be carried away when the wagon should arrive. These were split to fragments by the tomahawk. These wretches had actually met the wagon, with the rest of the family, and turned it back; but the brother-in-law, watching his opportunity, wheeled off from the road when his savage guards were somewhat engaged, and escaped.

The ladies were seized, and as Mrs. W. claimed protection, they were delivered into the charge of some squaws to be driven to the British camp. It was unpleasant enough, the being goaded on through such a scene by savage women, as insolent as the men were cruel; but the ladies soon saw that this was the best thing that could have happened to them; for the town was burning in various directions, and soon no alternative would be left between being in the British camp and in the thick of the slaughter in the burning streets. The British officer did not wish to have his hands full of helpless female prisoners. He sent them home again with a guard of an ensign and a private, who had orders to prevent their house being burned. The ensign had much to do to fulfil his orders. He stood in the doorway, commanding, persuading, struggling, threatening; but he saved the house, which was, in two days, almost the only one left standing. The whole town was a mass of smoking ruins, in many places slaked with blood. Opposite the door lay the body of a woman who in her despair had drunk spirits, and then defied the savages. They tomahawked her, in sight of the neighbors, and before her own door, and her body lay where it had fallen; for there were none to bury the dead.

Before the fire was quite burned out, the Indians were gone, and the inhabitants began to creep back into the town, cold and half dead with hunger. The ladies kept up a large fire (carefully darkening the windows), and cooked for the settlers, till they were too weary to stand, and one at a time lay down to sleep before the fire. Mrs. W. often during those dreary days used to fasten a blanket, Indian fashion, about her shoulders, and go out into the wintry night, to forage for food,—a strange employment for a young girl in the neighborhood of a savage foe. She traced the hogs in the snow, and caught many fowls in the dark. On the third day, very early in the morning, six Buffalo men were enjoying a breakfast of her cooking, when the windows were again broken in, and the house once more full of savages. They had come back to burn and pillage all that was left. The six men fled, and, by a natural impulse, the girl with them. At some distance from the house, she looked behind her, and saw a savage leaping towards her, with his tomahawk already raised. She saw that the next instant it would be buried in her skull. She faced about, burst out laughing, and held out both her hands to the savage. His countenance changed, first to perplexity; but he swerved his weapon aside, laughed, and shook hands, but motioned her homewards. She was full of remorse for having quitted her mother and sister. When she reached her door, the house was so crowded that she could neither make her way in, nor learn anything of their fate. Under the persuasion that they lay murdered within, she flew to some British dragoons who were sitting on the ground at a considerable distance, watching the burning of the remainder of the town. They expressed their amazement that she should have made her way through the savages, and guarded her home, where they procured an entrance for her, so that she reached the arms of her patient and suffering mother and sister. The house was, at length, the only one left standing; and when we returned, Mrs. W. pointed it out to me.

The settlers remained for some time in the woods, stealing in to a midnight warming and supper at the lone abode of the widow and her daughters. The ladies had nothing left but this dwelling. Their property had been in houses which were burned, and their very clothes were gone. The settlers had, however, carried off their money with them safely into the woods. They paid the ladies for their hospitality, and afterwards for as much needlework as they could do; for every one was in want of clothes. By their industry these women raised themselves to independence, which the widow lived some tranquil years to enjoy. The daughter who told the story is now the lady of a Judge. She never boasts of her bravery, and rarely refers to her adventures in the war; but preserves all her readiness and strength of mind, and in the silence of her own heart, or in the ear of a sympathizing friend, gratefully contrasts the perils of her youth with the milder discipline of her riper age.

The "Mrs. W." of this narrative was Sarah, daughter of Gamaliel and Margaret St. John, who became the wife of Samuel Wilkeson. Miss Martineau's dates are wrong, the events described being at the burning of Buffalo, December 30, 1813, and days following. Certain other inaccuracies may best be corrected by referring the reader to the narratives of Mrs. Wilkeson's sisters, Mrs. Sidway and Mrs. Skinner, published in volume IX., Publications of the Buffalo Historical Society.

Miss Martineau tarried in Buffalo long enough to note several things of significance. She thought Buffalo an undesirable place of residence, because of the many rough characters that gathered here. "It is the rendezvous of all manner of persons; the passage through which fugitives pass from the States to Canada, from Canada to the States, and from Europe and the Eastern States into the wild West. Runaway slaves come here, and their owners follow in hopes of recapturing them. Indian traders, land speculators, and poor emigrants come here, and the most debased Indians, the half-civilized, hang about the outskirts. . . . The place is unavoidably a very vicious one." For her other observations in Buffalo, at Fort Erie and Niagara Falls, I must refer the reader to her own pages; and submit without further comment a letter which she wrote, as above described, omitting portions of no general interest, but adhering to Miss Martineau's peculiarities of style:

NIAGARA FALLS, Oct^{br} 19th, 1834.

DEAR FRIENDS (for I know Mrs. B. will let me address her thus)—I can not hope that you have been thinking of us as often as we have of you, but yet you may have begun to look for a letter to tell how we like your country & your people, so far. On our part, we hope that you are now so far settled down into your usual habits of life that a full sheet will not come in upon you as an interruption. How we did think of you both on the day of your meeting and on the next Sunday! And now we want to know what you are doing, & whether you will write to tell us. A letter addressed to us at Mr. [name illegible], Philadelphia, between the 10th & 25th of next month, will be sure to reach us & we shall be truly thankful for it. A newspaper wh I have just taken up tells me that I am now at Boston—a thing not to be believed even on such assurance while the roar of these falls is in my ears. You will not expect me to wish to be anywhere but where I am, but indeed I should like to spend an hour by your evening fireside and hear what is doing in Hingham. Well, let us hope the time will come.

If I did but know where to begin, I sh'd like to tell you what I think of what I have seen,—secure that you will not betray me by repeating as my *opinions* what can be no more than first *impressions*. I will just go on till my paper is full & leave the rest for some future time. First, let me discharge a duty, as well as give myself & you pleasure by reporting of my companion, Louisa Jeffery. I am really delighted with her, & my esteem & regard for her grow every day. Our popularity so far I consider to be much owing to the cheerfulness & pleasantness of her manners. No difficulty or fatigue seems to have any effect upon her. She is as careful of me as my mother herself cd be, & as a companion, she is all I c'd wish; so great is her good sense joined with much cultivation of mind. I believe that she is much liked wherever we have been & am sure she ought to be.

We have had *such* a month of enjoyment. We are in love with travelling; & I really hope in spite of the contradictions between what we hear & what we see to learn more of man & get more light upon social morals than I anticipated, & Mr. B. knows how much I expected. From New York we went to Paterson & saw the falls of the Passaic, & a pleasant manufacturer's family, where we were kindly entertained & taught much of what life is like in such a place. Then from New York to West Point, where we saw Washington Irving, & some curious & some interesting human specimens besides, & where I was driven half delirious by the beauty of the scene. Then up to Tivoli where we staid three days with the Elmendorfs & saw much of the neighboring country. Then to Stockbridge, where we staid with the Sedgwick clan for some time,—so happy that we scarcely expect to enjoy ourselves more in all our lives. I am sure Stockbridge can be no fair specimen of a village in any country. I never saw any thing to compare with it for its union of the charms of scenery & Society. The presence of Miss Sedgwick alone is blessing enough for any one place; but the whole clan seems worthy of her. You will rejoice to hear that we are not only to meet her again in Philadelphia, but that she & her eldest brother will travel with us all thro' the West next spring.

At Albany, we joined Dr. Julius, his two friends, Messrs. Oppenheim & Sillen, & Mr. Higham, for our journey to the falls. Miss Sedgwick w'd fain have gone, but a call of duty at home prevented her, besides that she had already taken the journey this year. At Albany, Mr. Van Buren called on me. I had letters to him at Washington, but I was glad to begin our acquaintance earlier that I might be able to unravel some of the contradictions that we hear about him wherever we go. He was kind & communicative, took pains to provide for my seeing Auburn properly, & held out the prospect of much further intercourse at Washington.

Our happy party arrived here last Tuesday after a delightful week's journey, comprehending days at Trenton Falls, Auburn, & Canandaigua. We saw all the beautiful scenery by the way, except a part of the valley of the Mohawk, wh we passed in the canal boat in the dark. Louisa & I wished to make out a week here, not being able to understand how people persuade themselves that they have seen the Falls by staying two days. Our companions c'd not remain so long, and were obliged to return by different routes; so Higham, & Oppenheim set out for New York on Friday & Dr. Julius & Mr. Sillen for Toronto yes^y. We go back to Buffalo tomorrow for some days & then proceed to take possession of Gen'l Mason's house at Detroit, where his son, who is Govr of Michigan will take care that we get a palaver with Indians, & all else that we want. Crossing the Lake to Cleveland, we go by Pittsburg to Philadelphia. We might go through all our adventures in white satin shoes, for besides that I have abundance of letters, the principal people of every place call upon me & the only fear seems to be that I sh'd be overwhelmed with kindness.

I was amused at a message from the Mayor of Buffalo (whose name I do not yet know). We arrived at dark & left early next morning, but he conveyed his regrets that he did not hear of my arrival for two hours (!) after I alighted, when he thought it w'd be too late to call, but means to await my return. The only thing of this kind that has vexed me is its having been said in the newspapers that I am rich, a mistake wh can not but cause me inconvenience.

I will talk over the Falls with Mr. B. when we meet. As you, Mr. B., have not seen them, I shall not talk here of their unimaginable beauty. It is this beauty, soft beyond all names of softness, wh strikes me much more than their *grandeur*, though I have been over them & under them, looked at them from every side.

An adventure of ours yes^y will give you an idea of what we do to see the country. We wanted to have just a peep at Ontario, as we may not live to visit it next year. So we went to Queenston by stage, with Dr. Julius, & bade him farewell there, intending to walk back (7½ miles). We got a package of sandwiches & a bottle of cider at the inn, in order to have as much time as possible for exploring. We carried our prog to Gen'l Brock's monum^t wh we ascended, full of astonishment that we had heard so little of the splendid scene wh lay below us. I w'd almost as soon have passed by the Falls in the night as have omitted this view of the strait, the lake, forests, villages & (alas!) battle grounds. The portress, a nice little Yorkshire woman, was delighted to see countrywomen, & made us eat our dinner in her cottage, where she told us all her affairs. When we had seen everything & were setting out on our walk home, a country wagon, driven by a fine lad, passed, & he asked us to let him drive us to the falls, as he was going as far as Chippewa. We were glad of such an opport^y of learning something of Canada farming so we jumped in; whereby we escaped a thorough wetting, saw a new road, & learned all that the lad c'd tell us,—he being amused all the while, instead of hav'g a solitary ride. This will do, won't it?

I am apt to forget that we are in Canada till the boarders here & our host begin their *cruel* remarks on their neighbors over the water,—the narrow limit wh sh'd not divide men's hearts. I almost think that the host must speak to please his British guests, or he c'd not be so hard as he is. They all seem to vie with each other in abusing the Americans, & agreed at breakfast this morning that Mrs. Trollope's book is the truest, & it only stops short of the truth. Some of these people are really superior people, & they say they were delighted with the States when they first travelled through them. When they appeal to us, & we can only say that we have not seen the enormities they speak of, they look at one another with smiles, as much as to say that we shall soon grow wiser. One silly man acknowledges that there is more refinement of mind & manner than among the Eng^h generally, but fears that religion has a poor chance, since so much political independence must make men think themselves independent of God! There is a new idea for you! At least it is quite new to us.

As for me,—if I may say what I feel at the end of one month,—*I am charmed*. No one thing has struck us both so much as (what I have never heard even alluded to by our countrymen) that freedom & ingenuousness of manners wh belongs *only* to a society remarkably pure in its morals. I w'd already stake all the knowledge I have of human nature on the fact that the morals of society are purer here than in any society I have ever been in. The disagreeable instinct by which the presence of profligacy is indicated has never once been awakened; & the confidence thus inspired is exhilarating to a degree I cannot describe. We cannot explain this to the boarders here and we must therefore submit to their anticipations that we shall grow wiser as we travel on. Next to this comes the universal diffusion of plenty & comfort, & the growing conviction that your gov^t is as wise & as stable as I believed it was. The more I read & hear, the more amused I am at all alarms about your political perils; & I shall probably feel this at any rate till I get to Washington. At present, I like the children, their independence & extraordinary efficiency & dexterity. I cannot judge of them in their filial relation till I have been more in private houses.

Now for what I do *not* like.—Your newspapers distress a stranger. Their carping spirit & abusive language disgust me more than anything I almost ever met with. I mean to get at the bottom of this. Then—we were on board the canal boat with a party of clergymen going to Utica—some of them missionaries; & their praying & saying grace *all day,* their stories of special judgments, & criticisms of their neighbours realized all I had ever read of bigotry & cant. But there is much like this in England. It does not belong to the country,—unless indeed it be the ignorant & silly questions wh were asked about the Chinese, & foolishly answered by a missionary from China. I can hardly imagine *any* disciple in Eng^d asking if the Chinese are cannibals. Tobacco is a grievance, of course; & now and then we are struck with a little coldness of manner: but all this is nothing in comparison with the hearty hospitality & unvarying consideration & kindness we have met with: still less with the *innocence* wh I have spoken of as the prevailing charm. As to domestic accommodations, we are only surprised at their completeness, considering how new a country we are in. Here are, in brief, my *impressions.* I shall have much more to say, & with more confidence, when I have been settled in a town for a month together.

. . . My mother writes delightfully, persuading me that she is happy without me. It was a great comfort to her while writing, she says, to remember that you were on board, dear Mrs. B.

Farewell now. Louisa sends her kind regards. Believe me ever most truly & gratefully yours

H. MARTINEAU.

Up to the hour of our leaving N. York, we were obliged to your brother for much kind attention.

The Mayor of Buffalo in 1834, whose courtesy Miss Martineau mentions, was Ebenezer Johnson.

I conclude these notes with the following letter which Miss Martineau wrote at this time to her mother. It has been published, in her "Autobiography," but deserves a place in our collection:

NIAGARA, October 14.

. . . You must not expect a description from me. One might as well give an idea of the kingdom of heaven by images of jasper and topazes as of what we have been seeing by writing of hues and dimensions. Except the hurricane at sea, it is the only sight I ever saw that I had utterly failed to imagine. It is not its grandeur that strikes me so much; but its unimaginable beauty. All images of softness fail before it. Think of a double rainbow issuing from a rock one hundred feet below one, and almost completing its circle by nearly lighting on one's head. The slowness with which the waters roll over is most majestic. There is none of the hurry and tumble of common waterfalls, but the green transparent mass seems to ooze over the edges. The ascent of the spray, seen some miles off, surprised me; it did not hang like a cloud, but curled vigorously up, like the smoke from a cannon or a new fire. We have crossed the ferry, and done more than in my present state of intoxication I can well remember or tell you of. On the spot, I felt quite sane—sure-footed and reasonable; but when I sat down to dinner, I found what the excitement had been. I could not tell boiled from roast beef, and my only resource was to go out again as soon as we could leave the table; and now I am very sleepy. I expected I should be disappointed, and told Miss Sedgwick so. She was right in saying that it was impossible. If one looks merely at a cataract, it would be easy to say, "Dear me! I could fancy a rock twice as high as that, and a river twice as broad," but I could not think any imagination could conceive of such colouring; and I was wholly unprepared for the beauty of the surrounding scenery. Fragments of rainbow start up and flit and vanish, like phantoms at a signal from the sun. We have watched the growth of this moon, "the Niagara moon"; and there she is, at her very brightest! What a pleasure there is in a wholly new idea! It never occurred to me before that there can never be a cloudless sky at Niagara. A light fleecy rack is always in the sky over the falls; and the watcher may here see the process of cloud-making. No more now. Rejoice with me that I have now seen the best that my eyes can behold in this life. . . .

Yours most affectionately,

H. MARTINEAU.

HISTORY THAT ISN'T SO

WITHOUT aspiring to the ranks of those who maintain that there is no truth in history; and conceding (to avoid argument) that there is much in what they say, I am still prompted to point out in behalf of what I conceive to be history, a few instances which really have no warrant to be so called. I would shrink from the rôle of the Schoolmaster Abroad, for to correct other people is usually as futile as it is, to me, distasteful. It is my present reflection, however, that if there is any service to be rendered by seeking out and setting down facts, an equal service may be rendered by pointing out some alleged facts which are only fiction.

There is no difficulty in doing this if one go back far enough. While it might be embarrassing to accuse a living writer of mendacity, there is no trouble at all about it if your writer has been dead for a century or so. In such a case no temper is aroused; the contention usually becomes merely a matter of mild amusement.

This is very much so with several of the early writers who described Niagara Falls. It is not likely they deliberately tried to deceive anybody; a traveler must have a marvelous tale to tell, and from the beginning Niagara has been a fount of inspiration. Father Hennepin's account of the Falls has been much quoted. Here is a somewhat later one, that of the Baron La Hontan, which I like better:

"As for the waterfall of Niagara; 'tis seven or eight hundred feet high, and half a League broad. Towards the middle of it we descry an Island that leans towards the Precipice, as if it were ready to fall. All the Beasts that cross the Water within half a quarter of a League above this unfortunate Island, are suck'd in by force of the Stream: And the Beasts and Fish that are thus kill'd by the prodigious fall, serve for food to fifty Iroquese, who are settled about two Leagues off, and take 'em out of the water with their Canows. Between the surface of the water that shelves off prodigiously, and the foot of the Precipice, three Men may cross in a breast without any other damage than a sprinkling of some few drops of water."

This is the most satisfactory description of Niagara Falls I know of. It is jaunty, off-hand, sufficiently precise, not too long—and how suggestive! That it hit the popular fancy, and even that of scholars, is shown by the following extract from an old English geography:

"Near this place (Fort Niagara) there's a waterfall in the river, which runs down from Lake Conti (Erie); 'tis about eight hundred foot high, and half a league broad. Towards the middle there's an island that leans toward the precipice, as if it were ready to fall down. All the beasts that cross the water for a mile at least above this precipice are sucked down by the stream and killed by the Fall: so that fifty Iroquese, who are planted near it, daily wait for them in their canoes. Under this cataract, three men may pass abreast without being much wet, because the current falls like a spout over their heads."

So it was not the staid and trustworthy Hennepin, but the devil-may-care La Hontan, who supplied the Niagara data for small Britons in the Eighteenth century. This shows us at what an early period the British educational authorities adopted the system which has been so well characterized by Oliver Wendell Holmes: "Ignorance of America," says the genial Doctor, "is one of the branches taught in the English public schools." That little geography

HISTORY THAT ISN'T SO.

lesson also illustrates a trait of human nature. La Hontan said the falls were "seven or eight hundred feet high." The geography maker, who drew on La Hontan for his information, made them "about eight hundred feet high." Tell a man that a mountain he has climbed is eight to ten thousand feet high, and how high do you suppose it is when he tells of his exploit? Never a foot less than ten thousand. Tell a woman that the diamond you are giving her cost between $250 and $500—and what do you suppose that diamond cost, when she shows it to her friends!

The first man who tried to measure the height of Niagara, by eye, estimated that they were from 150 to 200 feet; by the time he had told of it two or three times, he said they were about 200 feet, then 200 feet or more; and the hearer, all the while believing that he was giving a true report, made them "two or three hundred"; and so they grew with each telling. Having got up to 800 feet, the wonder is they didn't go further. Probably some one came along with a new measurement.

Oliver Goldsmith must have had other sources of information about us than that old geography, for I read in the account of Niagara given in his invaluable "History of the Earth and Animated Nature": "It may easily be conceived that such a cataract quite destroys the navigation of the stream, and yet some Indian canoes, as it is said, have been known to venture down it with safety." This bit of history carries off at a pen-stroke all the laurels of Mrs. Taylor and the redoubtable Bobby Leach.

And, as my friend the Baron would say, as for going over the Falls, the student should by no means overlook that wonderful treatise by Thomas Carlyle: "Shooting Niagara —and After," which in more than one book-catalogue— those seductive works, compiled with exceptional acumen—

I find classified with works relating to the cataract. How edifying this essay of Carlyle may prove to students of our great natural wonder, I leave for them to discover.

The literature of our region begins with a blunder. Champlain says in *"Des Sauvages"*: "At the end of this lake"—i. e., Ontario—"they pass a fall, somewhat high and with but little water flowing over." We cannot possibly believe that—the power companies had not arrived in 1603. Perhaps some of Champlain's aboriginal informants were of the cautious and conservative type, men of the stamp of the Rev. Barzillai Frost. Edward Everett Hale tells the story; and although it is quite a jump from Champlain to Hale, it may as well be recorded here. Dr. Hale is writing of the boyhood of James Russell Lowell, a portion of which was passed in the home of the Rev. Barzillai Frost:

"Imagine the boy Lowell, with his fine sense of humor, listening to Mr. Frost's sermon describing Niagara after he had made the unusual journey thither. He could rise at times into lofty eloquence, but his sense of truth was such that he would not go a hair's breadth beyond what he was sure of, for any effect of rhetoric. So in this sermon, which is still remembered, he describes the cataract with real feeling and great eloquence. You had the mighty flood discharging the waters of the vast lake in a torrent so broad and grand—and then, forgetting the precise statistics, he ended the majestic sentence with the words: 'and several feet deep.'"

And what of this, as a contribution to human knowledge:

"The Falls of Niagara river are the greatest and most sublime curiosity which this or any other country affords. . . . The noise produced by this cataract is sometimes heard 40 or 50 miles. . . . There is sufficient space between the perpendicular rock and the column of water for people to pass in perfect safety. . . . Near Burlington Bay is a volcano, subject to frequent irruptions, with a noise like thunder. The Indians sacrifice to the Bad Spirit at this place."

This description, which rather carries the impression that there is a fine popular promenade behind the falls, is not, as one might suppose, from some old and excusable author of a couple of hundred years ago, but from the sixteenth edition of Morse's "American Universal Geography," published in Boston in 1815.

As for that active volcano on Burlington Bay—somewhere in the vicinity of Hamilton, Ont.—it's quite too much for me; I leave it right there.

The spread of misinformation about Niagara began, as we have seen, as soon as men began to write of the region. The first man usually means the first lie. In contemplation of such a cataract, exaggeration was a natural tribute of the mind. La Hontan's "seven or eight hundred feet" was of a sort with the modern reporter's estimate of a crowd, or the first reports of loss of life in a casualty. People see the real thing, but it gets exalted in their imagination before they describe it. We are so accustomed to the contemporary writing of history that isn't so—in the Press—that we lose our powers for critically estimating the history of long ago. Perhaps, in cases like La Hontan's, the overstatement—the mere excess of fact, as it were—is what the critics mean when they talk of "literary perspective." The Falls were so far from Europe they had to be elevated to make the proper effect upon the reader. The Baron's motive was wholly laudable.

The early artists who illustrated Father Hennepin's books were impelled by the same motive. America was so far off, the features of its topography must be magnified and emphasized to be appreciated in Europe. So they put high mountains around Lake Erie, and up and down the Niagara, and planted thereon strange trees—the sort of tropical verdure that a man in a Paris garret or a Dutch cellar might dream of. And among these mountains and under these dreamland trees they tried to depict the strange American animals: the bison, a very queer European cow with a hump and curly hair; and from the bough above they hung a long-tailed rat—presumably an attempt to depict the opossum. Some of the early pictures of the beaver, drawn of course by artists who had never seen one, but were impressed by priests' and travelers' accounts of their wonderful sagacity, are uncannily human.

In the 1704 edition of Hennepin's *"Nouvelle Decouverte,"* there is a picture of the building of the Griffon, that famous pioneer vessel of the Upper Lakes. It was constructed, you will remember, on the American shore of the Niagara near the present village of La Salle. According to the old French or Flemish artist, there were high mountains with precipitous sides over on the western bank, which is now Canada. Alas, the leveling influences of time in democratic communities—these mountains are all gone now. The Griffon itself, we learn from this precious picture, was put together under the shade of a tree which looks like a huge feather-duster, or a sheaf of corn-leaves tied to a pole. The early artists were fond of this tree; it appears in many plates illustrating Seventeenth-century travels in America. I too am a lover of trees, and in years past have roamed over every foot of ground of the Niagara shores; but I found no trace of the Hennepin feather-duster tree. Still, the species is not extinct. I have but to turn to a certain shelf of old books, where La Salle and Hennepin and Tonty and other worthies hold converse with each other, and lo!

as I turn the leaves, the feather-duster tree is found as abundant and flourishing as ever.

And speaking of the Griffon. Our local newspapers are little enough addicted to history; yet the story of La Salle's small craft is a favorite, and allusions to it are not infrequent, though rarely—I may as well say, never—with accuracy. Editors and contributors seem to have agreed that the Griffon was the first white man's vessel on the Great Lakes. Over and over again I find it so stated; and not merely in newspapers, but in school-books. What then of the brigantine in which La Salle's party sailed across Lake Ontario in December, 1678, bringing on her material for the construction of the Griffon? She was afterwards wrecked on the Lake Ontario shore. She was appropriately named the Frontenac, and, obviously, to her belongs the distinction of priority.

There has long been a variety of opinion and disagreement as to the place where the Griffon was built. It was Mr. O. H. Marshall who found and set in order the evidence which fixes the spot near the present site of La Salle. I think this is proved, although there are statements in some of the old chronicles which I cannot reconcile with this view. That the matter has occasioned the writing of considerable "history that isn't so," is readily seen by examining any shelf of books on that period of American history. Jared Sparks, in the early editions of his "Life of La Salle," says the boat was built "at Chippewa creek, on the Canadian side of the river." Parkman, prehaps accepting Sparks as trustworthy, said the same thing in his "Life of Pontiac." These statements are changed, in recent editions. John S. C. Abbott, who is not to be classed with Sparks or Parkman, but whose unreliable pages have had wide reading, says, in his "Adventures of La Salle and his Companions," that the ship-yard "was about six miles above Niagara Falls, on the western side of the river, at the outlet of a little stream called Chippewa creek." Schoolcraft, in his "Tour to the Lakes," said the Griffon was built "near Buffalo." Governor Lewis Cass, in an address before the Historical Society of Michigan, claimed that "the Griffon was launched at Erie"; and Bryant & Gay's "History of the United States" has the amazing statement that the Griffon was built at Fort Frontenac, which it locates on Lake Erie!

A statement which is made from the best available evidence, even if afterwards shown to be wrong, is entitled to respect. But it is a reprehensible thing for author or publisher to persist in error, after the truth has been established.

Some of the statements relative to the much written-of episode of La Salle on the Niagara are—to me—inexplicable. What for instance can be made of this, which occurs in the article "Fort Niagara," contained in that nearest approach of the human mind to omniscience, the latest edition of the Encyclopaedia Brittanica:

"A fort built (1675) by Gabriel Edouard, chevalier de Nouvel (1636-1694), was soon destroyed, as were Fort Conti and the trading-post built by La Salle in 1679."

I leave that for students of our regional history who like "nuts to crack," along with another, a simple inquiry: How did Point Abino get its name?

La Salle is often but erroneously called Chevalier; not merely by amateurs in historical study, but by more than one writer of reputation. Thus the story of La Salle, by John S. C. Abbott, in the "American Pioneers and Patriots" series, is entitled "The Adventures of the Chevalier De La Salle," etc. It would seem to require exceptional carelessness to mistake La Salle's family name, Cavelier, for "Chevalier," indicating the rank of knighthood. Cavelier was ennobled, but never knighted. The patent of nobility granted him by Louis XIV., May 13, 1675, states that he, his wife and their lawful issue shall be "deemed and reputed noble, bearing the rank of Esquire, with power to reach all ranks of knighthood and gendarmerie." But La Salle never married and found a grave in a Texas swamp, with no higher rank of nobility than "Sieur." His companion Tonty was knighted before he appears on the Niagara, and is entitled to be called "Chevalier."

It has long been customary to write of Father Hennepin as the discoverer of the Niagara. If discovery is to be ascribed to the expedition of which he was a member, ought not the leader of that expedition to have the credit? Yet we are not warranted in saying that La Salle discovered the Falls. We do not know what white man first saw them. It is a good guess, with some plausibility, that Etienne Brulé was that man; but there is nothing to prove it. Many years before Hennepin came this way, Jesuit missionaries had written of it. Father Jerome Lalement had referred to the Falls, by name, thirty-seven years before Hennepin saw them; and thirty-one years before, another missionary, Father Paul Ragueneau, had told of "a waterfall of frightful height" between Erie and Ontario. Hennepin may very likely have read their descriptions. We may be sure that much information about the great cataract was current before the party including Hennepin arrived in December of the year 1678.

By the way, is Hennepin responsible for our present perverse spelling of "Niagara"? Before him it was "Ongiara" and "Onguiaahra," the two (Huron or Neuter) forms pronouncing much the same. Hennepin was not the student of the native dialects that his predecessors, the Jesuits, were. Which was the more likely to be correct?

And now, to this wrong name, "Niagara," we have long given a wrong pronunciation. It was formerly spoken "Ni-[or Nee]-ah-ga-ra." To speak it with a syllable ending in hard "g"—"Ni-*ag*-a-ra"—is to do violence to the genius of the Seneca language. "Ni-ag-a-ra" is a harsh and ugly word. "Nee-ah-ga-ra" is soft and pleasant. I have elsewhere ("Niagara and the Poets") called attention to a line in Goldsmith's "Traveler" which shows that in his day the word was correctly spoken:

"And Nia-*ga*-ra stuns with thundering sound."

The scansion and rhythm would be lost with our present perverted pronunciation.

So we are not only wrong in our name of the falls, but wrong in our pronunciation of that wrong name!

There exists a curious narrative of the discovery of Niagara Falls. Many years ago it was widely printed, in more than one language. Not long ago I found it in French, in the first volume of the *Magazin de Bas-Canada, Journal Littéraire et Scientifique,* etc., published in Montreal in 1832. After I had taken the trouble to copy and translate it, I found that it was essentially the same story that had appeared in the *Museum of Foreign Literature and Science,* Philadelphia, October, 1831, which had taken it from *Fraser's Magazine.* No doubt it may turn up in a score of old-time magazines and reviews, to say nothing of the newspapers. It is a veracious, rather straightforward narrative, too long to be given here in full, but of which the following summary may suffice.

Among the first missionaries who were sent from England to convert the American aborigines to Christianity, were Joseph Price and Henry Wilmington. It is related with some detail, but a lack of dates, that these young Englishmen, after a passage of thirteen weeks from Plymouth, landed at Boston, "then a very small but thriving village," fired with a desire to carry the gospel to the Indians. At the end of May they set out, provided with compasses and fowling-pieces. "It was their intention to visit a distant tract of country, of which nothing was known except vague reports of sheets of water so immense that, but for the circumstance of their being fresh, they might have been led to suppose they were on an island." After some days, having passed "the ultimate farm," they plunged into the forest "which had most likely never been trodden by the feet of civilized man." After various woodland incidents they reached "a large and rapid river." "In about a week after, they reached a chain of mountains," beyond which were encountered friendly Indians who were surprised "at beholding people so different in colour to themselves, and armed with what appeared to them only polished sticks." A flock of wild geese passing high overhead, the Indians futilely shot arrows at them, whereupon Price and Wilmington promptly brought down two with their guns—no slight exploit even for expert woodsmen and hunters, which these missionaries could hardly claim to be. They sojourned with the Indians at their village "on the Oneida." This is the first name which helps to localize the story, but as we go on it appears that "the Oneida" is the designation not of a lake but of a river. Price preached a sermon, until the Indians refused to listen any more. Then he proposed to Wilmington that they verify a rumor, heard in Boston, of great inland waters. They set out, the chief Maiook—or Mayouk, a work suggesting "Mohawk"—guiding them to a river which he said "would carry them to the great basin."

But few of his people had been there, but an old man in his youth had gone many days in his canoe, coming to an enormous river which fell from a fresh-water lake. While hunting he had heard a great noise of water, but fear had turned him back.

The missionaries were given a guide—one account says Maiook went with them. They have adventures in a burning wood; reach Lake Ontario and for days coast along its shore, finally coming to "a great and rapid river," which they ascended until rapids were encountered, when they continued along the bank. Price told a young man to climb a tall tree, to spy out the country. "Encouraged by his report they continued to follow the precipitous banks of the river. The noise, which had gradually increased, became each instant more terrible, and the swiftness of the current showed that they were near a furious rapid." Presently "they found themselves on the edge of a bare rock which hung over a vast abyss into which two currents of one great river fell with a noise that drowned their exclamations of surprise, and surpassed that of the ocean in a tempest." The "missionaries" narrowly escape being plunged into the abyss by a fall of rock. A description—that is, a sort of a description—of the Falls follows. Among other things, they behold "a large deer struggling against the overpowering suction of the falls . . . but the roar of the cataracts drowned its voice and it was soon precipitated into the boiling abyss."

"The French," concludes the conscientious chronicler, "from the Province of Quebec, may have reached as far before, but Price and his companion believed they were the first who had penetrated to that spot; and when they returned back to their settlements, their description of the unparalleled magnificence of the cataracts, to which Maiook gave the name of Niagara, or the thundering waters, was deemed incredible."

And well it may have been, for the whole yarn is incredible. So far as I have traced it, it was originally contributed to *Fraser's Magazine* by the clever Canadian writer, John Galt. It bears so few earmarks of fiction that no doubt many excellent people, three quarters of a century ago, regarded it as history. But it "isn't so."

Prolific sources of minor error and inaccuracy on the part of many who have written of our regional history, are some of the papers in the collections known as "The Documentary History of the State of New York" and the "Documents relative to the Colonial History of the State of New York." These well-known sources of information are precious—simply invaluable; but they are not always complete, or accurate transcriptions of the original manuscripts; and they need to be used, as any source material does, with discernment. Especially are the Sir William Johnson papers in them full of slips and misstatements, which can usually be detected by the painstaking student. Sir William's innocence of any knowledge of French, and the ingeniousness of his spelling, are responsible for many oft-repeated errors. One instance will illustrate this.

Not long ago I had occasion to review the early history of the Chautauqua and French Creek portages, a part of the old military routes from Lake Erie into the Ohio valley. Of the well-known expedition of 1753, commanded by Marin, I found it stated, in more than one history, that he had a sub-officer, I am not sure of what rank, called "Babeer" or "Barbeer." The story, as usually told, is to the effect that "Babeer" and his detachment of troops, coming on from Montreal in advance of the main expedition, landed at what is now Barcelona Harbor, and began there the construction of a fort, and that the commander-in-chief arriving a little later put a stop to the work, moved the expedition further westward, and opened up the famous portage by way of Presque Isle. There is no great difficulty in getting access to the official records of this expedition; the names of the officers are easily ascertained. They were, for the most part, men conspicuous in the French service in America; but no where in all these sources of trustworthy information can be found the name of this alleged forerunner of the expedition, called "Babeer." The name itself is improbable as a French word, and should have long ago awakened the suspicion of conscientious writers who have told of the exploits of Babeer in the Chautauqua wilderness. If, however, one will take the trouble to consult the "Documentary History of the State of New York," he will find there a certain deposition made by one Stephen Coffen before Col. Johnson (afterwards Sir William), at his home on the Mohawk, in 1754. Coffen was an ignorant soldier, a New Englander, who had been a prisoner among the French for some years. Being at Montreal in the fall of 1752, he was allowed to serve as a soldier under Marin. Deserting from the French service soon after the passage of Marin's troops down the Ohio, he reached the Mohawk and told his story to Johnson. Unable to write, he signed his statement with a cross. The record, therefore, that bears his name was set down either by Johnson or a secretary.

It takes but the slightest familiarity with the names of the French officers of the period to discover how untrustworthy were Coffen's memory and Johnson's spelling. It is a grotesque blending of misinformation, badly spelled. One pauses a moment when he reads of Governor-General "Le Cain" to remember that the officer's name is Du Quesne.

"Presque Isle" becomes "Briske Isle." Every name mentioned by Coffen is distorted. And here we have the source of this mythical "Babeer," who has been so taken for granted by the writers of Chautauqua county histories. Whoever "Babeer" was we may be sure that was not his name, nor was there any officer in the retinue of Marin whose name suggests this form.

The discovery of Chautauqua Lake, like the discovery of Niagara Falls, is still a matter of speculation. Some writers try to show that La Salle discovered the lake, I know not on what evidence. Others have claimed the honor for Céloron, whose name is preserved in the nomenclature of the region. But this is plainly "history that isn't so," for the old records which tell us of his expedition also state that when near the outlet of the lake his forces were shown a path to the high land, a cut-off, I suppose, to avoid the long marsh, by a Frenchman who had been that way before.

This was Dagneaux de la Saussaye, and a little search among the documents of the time discovers that he had passed through the region in the summer of 1743 on a mission to the Chanouanons—i. e., the Shawanees. I do not find in any of the local histories that de Saussaye receives so much as a mention, yet he certainly preceded Céloron by six years, and is the first white man of whom I find official record who can be said to have explored what is now Chautauqua county.

A book could readily be written on the blunders in other books, relating to our region. It would probably add to them, and would be of little service, as ungracious performances usually are. The ordinary kind of misstatement is not "very deadly" to a student who knows the subject at all. Many current errors in our published annals are trivial, many are due to prejudice and the fact that a definite event may be construed variously by different writers—the battle of Lundy's Lane, for instance, which is still being fought—and many are merely amusing. One that I call amusing is the grave statement in William Kirby's "Annals of Niagara" that Lewiston was named for Louis—or, as I believe he spells it, *Lewis* XIV! Shade of Governor Morgan Lewis, what is fame! Mr. Kirby was an excellent gentleman, for many years Collector of Customs at Niagara, Ont. He knew the history of his corner of the world better than any one else, and he rendered a real service to history when he wrote the "Annals of Niagara"; if the work could be overhauled, and its many errors eliminated, its value would be increased.

Another work that the student of our history should know is exceedingly deceptive in its title. That is Ketchum's "Authentic and Comprehensive History of Buffalo," published in two volumes in 1864. Many a reader in quest of Buffalo data has discovered that it really is not a history of Buffalo at all, except in the earliest years, the narrative ending with the burning of the village in 1813. It is an admirable compilation of data relating to the aborigines of Western New York, to events preceding settlement and the earliest years of the town. This is a case of a good book having a title which "isn't so." Probably the author's plan never contemplated a review of events for the half century and more which he did not write about; but if it did he paused on the threshold, like Henry Thomas Buckle, who exhausted himself in writing the two-volume introduction to his "History of Civilization," and never wrote more.

The enquiring student, curious about the history of our region, may run across a book published in Albany in 1841, entitled "A History of the early Adventures of Washington among the Indians of the West," etc. The author was Josiah Priest. If our student knows about Priest, he will be on his guard; if he does not, he will presently be wandering in a veritable maze of "history." One of the characters of this extraordinary narrative, which purports to be "gathered from the Records of that Era," is a mysterious Mingo prophet, Tonnaleuka, otherwise the Laird of Mackintosh, a Scotch outlaw, who tells Washington that through the interests of the Stuarts he procured a commission in the French army:

"In a few years I was sent as lieutenant-colonel of a regiment to Canada. My superior disliking the climate, soon returned to Europe, and I was made Colonel in his place. In this capacity I was stationed for a number of years at a Fort near the Falls of Niagara. Here I had an opportunity of becoming thoroughly acquainted with the manners and customs of the Indians, as well as with many of their languages; and also of greatly improving my fortune by purchasing their furs and transmitting them to Quebec."

Washington is represented as falling in love with this man's daughter. The book is a curio, but the reader who chances upon it must not mistake it for history.

Many of the books relating in whole or part to the Niagara region, which today seem merely amusing and absurd, when first published were no doubt taken seriously enough by their readers, if not by their authors. Such for instance is the anonymous "Travels in North America," published in Dublin in 1824. It is apparently an abridgment of another work, if indeed it is not a manufactured narrative, based on any available works, for the edification of Young Ireland. It relates, soberly enough, the adventures of one George Philips, who visited Niagara apparently in

1816, after having traveled with the Lewis and Clarke exploring expedition to the Pacific, by way of the Missouri and Columbia rivers. The author states, as though it were the simplest thing in the world, that Philips "engaged a canoe and men, and by keeping dexterously in the middle of the stream from Chippeway, reached an island called Goat Island." Having viewed the Falls—of which an amusingly bad cut is given—he and his companion "returned to Chippeway, by keeping their canoe in the middle of the stream"! Lake Erie is described as very deep, while in places "long ranges of steep mountains rise from the very edge of the water." All in all, it's quite a book.

There are many statements in the local guide-books, appropriated by one compiler after another, republished year after year, purporting to be "history," yet utterly without authority or reason. I am not speaking of mere uncertainties or inaccuracies of date; the person who makes no mistakes has not yet been born, and there is very much yet to be learned by all. I criticize only the deliberate inventions which are passed off as truth. Of this class is the much-printed statement that Father Hennepin discovered Niagara Falls from the point known as "Hennepin's View." Of course he may have stood there, or he may not. He passed repeatedly up and down the river bank, but there is no authority for associating him, particularly, with any one spot.

Another fiction, and a silly one, is that which makes La Salle a visitor at the cave in the Devil's Hole. The whole yarn is preposterous, yet it is retold, at intervals, by writers who know better.

Still another incident that is much distorted and embellished, even in pretentious works, is the affair of the Caroline. By some accounts, she was sent blazing over the

Falls, carrying many men down to death. A painstaking study of all available evidence in the case affords proof of the death of but one man, and he was shot on the dock at Schlosser.

There are numerous instances of plagiarism in the literature of our region, and of the appropriation by one writer of the narrative—and experiences—of another. I will not go here into the intricacies of the literary strife that was waged, by all who could share in it, over the exploits of La Salle and his several expeditions. Hennepin, Tonty, Joutel, Cavelier, shared in the contention, to say nothing of the train of commentators to this day. As early as 1750 Peter Kalm felt called upon to correct all Niagara visitors who had preceded him. He found people in Canada calling Father Hennepin *"un grand menteur,"* and added his own repudiation of that worthy. Kalm wanted it understood that he could be relied on: "I like to see things just as they are, and so to relate them." He surely was no plagiarist; but many later writers on the Niagara have been victims of this most widespread literary sin. No one cares, particularly, about such thievery, unless it constitutes a false record—becomes "history that isn't so." An instance of this sort, to which, I think, attention has not been called, is that of Peter Williamson. There are many editions of this wandering Scotchman's book. One before me, printed in Edinburgh in 1768, is entitled: "The Travels of Peter Williamson among the different Nations and Tribes of Savage Indians in America"—and much more, a very prolix inscription. The work purports to contain "a general description of the Falls of Niagara, according to my own observations, during the course of my travels through America, before the late war," that is, the Old French War. Any narrative of observations hereabouts at so early a period would have value and interest; but when I read Williamson, I find that his description is stolen—and rather clumsily stolen—from Kalm's account, written at Albany in 1750. Incidents narrated shortly after his account of Niagara are dated May, 1746, and August, 1748, but there is nothing in the book to fix more definitely his alleged travels in this region. The preface states that the author "was born in Aberdeenshire in the north of Scotland, and was carried off in his infancy from that city, by his own countrymen, and sold as a slave in America; after continuing in this state of slavery for many years he was at last unfortunately taken captive by the savage Indians, in whose hands he remained for some years, and suffered during their hunting expeditions the most severe hardships." The work contains no narrative of these experiences; and I am constrained, in lack of evidence to the contrary, to include much of Williamson's reputed career, especially his alleged Niagara visit, in the category of "history that isn't so."

Most of the early observers at the Falls saw things that were not there. Some of these I have touched on in preceding pages. In looking through Volney's "Views," I note his account of the carcasses of wild boars, found at the foot of the falls. His observation was not disturbed by the fact that the wild boar has never inhabited America.

De Witt Clinton, in his delightful old journal, "Letters on the Natural History and Internal Resources of the State of New York," a volume much more attractive than its title would indicate, quotes from the speech of "a cidevant governor to a great military commander, on the presentation of a sword. . . . In speaking of a nocturnal battle near the cataract of Niagara, he says that it produced a midnight rainbow, whose refulgence outshone the iris of the day."

This is history, though perhaps not so much natural history as unnatural. It belongs in the same class as the eulogium of a country schoolmaster on General Wolfe:

> Great General Wolfe, without any fears,
> Led on his brave grenadiers,
> And what is most miraculous and particular,
> He climbed up rocks that were perpendicular.

Error is everywhere. I pick up a picture post-card from a hotel stand. It is labeled: "Old stone house and barracks where Morgan was imprisoned, Niagara," and it isn't that at all, but a very different building at Fort Niagara. I take a ride on a sight-seeing wagon in Buffalo, and as we pass a certain gray-stone residence the conductor-orator-guide declaims loudly that this house was "General Scott's headquarters in the War of 1812"—and I know of a certainty that the house was built in 1836. As we drive around the Park meadow he calls the attention of the tourists to the large boulder which, he explains, marks a battlefield of the War of 1812! Thus is history made—popular.

If I retreat to the peaceful seclusion of my office in the Historical Building, I have numerous callers who ask to be shown the place where President McKinley stood in that edifice when he was shot! How this last painful and needless error gains currency I cannot guess, but the number of strangers who have been informed to that effect—so they declare—is amazing.

NARRATIVES OF
EIGHTEENTH CENTURY
VISITORS TO NIAGARA

18TH CENTURY VISITORS

IN preceding pages have been given the earliest printed reports concerning Niagara Falls. There are probably no other Seventeenth-century visitors who printed accounts of what they saw here, except Hennepin and La Hontan. The latter's account of Niagara was not printed until 1703. Father Hennepin's first book, the *"Louisiane,"* says much less of the Falls than his later and less trustworthy works. As matter of record I quote from the *"Louisiane,"* first published in 1683:

"On the 6th [December, 1678], St. Nicholas day, we entered the beautiful river Niagara, which no bark had ever yet entered. . . . Four leagues from Lake Frontenac there is an incredible Cataract or Waterfall, which has no equal. The Niagara river near this place is only the eighth of a league wide, but it is very deep in places, and so rapid above the great fall, that it hurries down all the animals which try to cross it, without a single one being able to withstand its current. They plunge down a height of more than five hundred feet, and its fall is composed of two sheets of water and a cascade, with an island sloping down. In the middle these waters foam and boil in a fearful manner. They thunder continually, and when the wind blows in a southerly direction, the noise which they make is heard for from more than fifteen leagues. Four leagues from this cataract or fall, the Niagara river rushes with extraordinary rapidity especially for two leagues into Lake Frontenac. It is during these two leagues that goods are carried. There is a very fine road, very little wood, and almost all prairies mingled with some oaks and firs, on both banks of the river, which are of a height that inspire fear when you look down.

That is Father Hennepin's first description of Niagara Falls. In his subsequent work he increased the height to 600 feet, and elaborated his account in various ways. This later description is the one most often quoted, and need not be included here.

The Baron La Hontan, who saw the Falls in August, 1687, published in 1703 an account which I have given in a preceding paper (p. 291).

During the Eighteenth century, travelers more and more found their way to the Niagara, and more and more descriptions appeared in print. Some of these are among the most interesting records we have, of early days on the Niagara. A few of them are perhaps familiar through much reprinting, but others are unknown except to students who may have made particular research in this subject. As matter of record, therefore, and for the convenience of all, there are brought together in pages following the principal descriptions of the Falls which were written, down to the close of the Eighteenth century. Correction of their many errors is here deemed, for the most part, superfluous.

FROM "THE FOUR KINGS OF CANADA," 1710.

In that curious little book, "The Four Kings of Canada, being a succinct account of the Four Indian Princes lately arriv'd from North America," etc., printed in London in 1710, occurs the following:

"The River of St. Lawrence or Canada, receives in these Parts an Infinite Quantity of fresh Water from the four great Lakes, the Lake Huron, the upper Lake, the Lake of the Illinois, and the Lake Erie or of the Cat, which may properly be call'd little fresh Water Seas. This great Deluge of Water tumbling furiously over the greatest and most dreadful Heap in the World, an infinite Number of Fish take great Delight to spawn here, and as it were suffocate here, because they cannot get over this huge Cataract: So that the Quantity taken here is incredible.

"A Gentleman who was traveling this Part, went to see this Heap, which comes from a River in the North, and falls into a great Basin of Lake Outano [Ontario], big enough to hold a Hundred Men of War, being there he taught the Nations to catch Fish with their Hands, by causing Trees to be cut down in the Spring, and to be roll'd to the Bank of the River, so that he might be upon them without wetting himself; by the Assistance of which he thrust his Arm into the Water up to the Elbow, where he found a prodigious Quantity of Fish of different species, which he laid hold on by the Gills, gently stroking 'em, and when he had taken Fifty or Sixty of 'em at a Time, he use to warm and refresh himself; after this Manner, in a short Time he would catch Fish enough to feed Fifty or Sixty Families."

This account, which puts Niagara well to the fore in the matter of fish stories, would seem to have been drawn from a source quite independent of Hennepin and La Hontan. When it was published the latter was still living—his death occurring in 1715—and Hennepin may have been. In 1710 he would have been but 71 years old, but there is no trace of him later than 1701.

"The Four Kings of Canada" is the first publication I know of, relating to Niagara, after La Hontan. Next in chronological order is the account given by "M. Borassaw," at Albany in 1721, to the Hon. Paul Dudley, who wrote it down and published it. The Frenchman, whose name was probably Borassan or Borassau—it certainly was not as Dudley spelled it—appears to have been a boatman, or possibly a trader. He said he had been at Niagara seven times, and was there in May, 1721, when de Longueuil measured the Falls. His account, as written by Dudley, was printed in many places. I here transcribe it from the *Philosophical Transactions,* Royal Society of London, of 1722:

THE "BORASSAW" NARRATION OF 1721.
WRITTEN BY THE HON. PAUL DUDLEY, F. R. S.

The falls of Niagara are formed by a vast ledge or precipice of solid rock, lying across the whole breadth of the river, a little before it empties itself into, or forms the lake Ontario.

M. Borassaw says, that in spring 1722 [should be 1721], the governor of Canada ordered his own son, with three other officers, to survey the Niagara, and take the exact height of the cataract, which they accordingly did with a stone of half a hundred weight, and a large cod-line, and found it on a perpendicular no more than 26 fathoms— *"vingt et six bras."*

This differs very much from the account Father Hennepin has given to that cataract; for he makes it 100 fathoms, and our modern maps from him, as I suppose, mark it at 600 feet; but I believe Hennepin never measured it, and there is no guessing at such things.

When I objected Hennepin's account of those falls to M. Borassaw, he replied, that accordingly every body had depended on it as right, until the late survey. On further discourse he acknowledged, that below the cataract, for a great way, there were numbers of small ledges or stairs across the river, that lowered it still more and more, till you came to a level; so that if all the descents be put together, he does not know but the difference of the water above the falls and the level below, may come up to Father Hennepin; but the strict and proper cataract on a perpendicular is no more than 26 fathoms, or 156 feet, which yet is a prodigious thing, and what the world I suppose cannot parallel, considering the size of the river, being near a quarter of an English mile broad, and very deep water.

Several other things M. Borassaw set me right in, as to the falls of Niagara. Particularly it has been said, that the cataract makes such a prodigious noise, that people cannot hear each other speak at some miles distances; whereas he affirms, that you may converse together close by it. I have also heard it positively asserted, that the shoot of the river, when it comes to the precipice, was with such force, that men and horse might march under the body of the river without being whet; this also he utterly denies, and says, the water falls in a manner right down.

What he observed farther to me was, that the mist or shower which the falls make, is so extraordinary, as to be seen at five leagues distance, and rise as high as the common clouds. In this *brume* or cloud, when the sun shines, you have always a glorious rainbow. That the river itself, which is there called the river Niagara, is much narrower at the falls than either above or below; and that from below there is no coming nearer the falls by water than about six English miles, the torrent is so rapid, and having such terrible whirlpools.

He confirms Father Hennepin's and Mr. Kelug's [?] account of the large trouts of those lakes, and solemnly affirmed there was one taken lately, that weighed 86 lb. which I am rather inclined to believe, on the general rule, that fish are according to the waters. To confirm which, a very worthy minister affirmed, that he saw a pike taken in Canada river, and carried on a pole between two men, that measured five feet ten inches in length, and proportionably thick.

PIERRE F. X. DE CHARLEVOIX, S. J., 1721.

Father Charlevoix, best known of all the early Jesuit writers on America, twice visited Canada and voyaged down the Mississippi. He came to the Niagara in May, 1721. In the original French edition of his "History of

New France," volume three consists of his "Journal," in the form of a series of letters to the Duchess de Lesdiguieres. Three letters are dated respectively, "Niagara, May 23," "Falls of Niagara, May 26," and "Entrance to Lake Erie, May 27," 1721. In the first English edition of the "Journal," the second Niagara letter is erroneously dated "May 14." In the following extracts I have in the main followed the old English translation, which though now and then quaint in form, is true to the original. A few omissions have also been supplied. So far as I am aware, Charlevoix is the first writer to use the word "horse-shoe" [*"fer à cheval"*] in description of the greater fall.

[NIAGARA, May 23, 1721.]

. . . Now, Madam, we must acknowledge, that nothing but zeal for the public good could possibly induce an officer to remain in such a country as this, than which a wilder and more frightful is not to be seen. On the one side you see just under your feet, and as it were at the bottom of an abyss, a great river, but which in this place is like a torrent by its rapidity, by the whirlpools formed by a thousand rocks, through which it with difficulty finds a passage, and by the foam with which it is always covered; on the other the view is confined by three mountains placed one over the other, and whereof the last hides itself in the clouds. This would have been a very proper scene for the poets to make the Titans attempt to scale the heavens. In a word, on whatever side you turn your eyes, you discover nothing which does not inspire a secret horror.

You have, however, but a very short way to go, to behold a very different prospect. Behind those uncultivated and uninhabitable mountains, you enjoy the sight of a rich country, magnificent forests, beautiful and fruitful hills; you breathe the purest air, under the mildest and most temperate climate imaginable, situated between two lakes the least of which is two hundred and fifty leagues in circuit. . . .

[AT THE FALLS OF NIAGARA, May 26, 1721.]

. . . The officers having departed, I ascended those frightful mountains, in order to visit the famous Fall of Niagara, above which I was to take water; this is a journey of three leagues though formerly five; because the way then lay by the other, that is, the west side of the river, and also because the place for embarking lay full two leagues above the Fall. But there has since been found, on the left, at the distance of half a quarter of a league from this cataract, a creek, where the current is not perceivable, and consequently a place where one may take water without danger. My first care, after my arrival, was to visit the noblest cascade perhaps in the world; but I presently found the Baron de la Hontan had committed such a mistake with respect to its height and figure, as to give grounds to believe he had never seen it.

It is certain, that if you measure its height by that of the three mountains, you are obliged to climb to get at it, it does not come short of what the map of M. Deslisle makes it; that is, six hundred feet, having certainly gone into this paradox, either, on the faith of the Baron de la Hontan or Father Hennepin; but after I arrived at the summit of the third mountain, I observed, that in the space of three leagues, which I had to walk before I came to this fall of water, though you are sometimes obliged to ascend, you must yet descend still more, a circumstance to which travellers seem not to have sufficiently attended. As it is impossible to approach it but on one side only, and consequently to see it, excepting in profile, or sideways; it is no easy matter to measure its height with instruments. It has, however, been attempted by means of a pole tied to a long line, and after many repeated trials, it has been found only one hundred and fifteen, or one hundred and twenty feet high. But it is impossible to be sure that the pole has not been stopt by some projecting rock; for though it was always drawn up wet, as well as the end of the line to which it was tied, this proves nothing at all, as the water which precipitates itself from the mountain, rises very high in foam. For my own part, after having examined it on all sides, where it could be viewed to the greatest advantage, I am inclined to think we cannot allow it less than one hundred and forty, or fifty feet.

As to its figure, it is in the shape of a horseshoe, and is about four hundred paces in circumference; it is divided into two, exactly in the middle, by a very narrow island, half a quarter of a league long. It is true, those two parts very soon unite; that on my side, and which I could only have a side view of, has several branches which project from the body of the cascade, but that which I viewed in front, appeared to me quite entire. The Baron de la Hontan mentions a torrent which comes from the West, but which if this author has not invented it, must certainly fall through some channel on the melting of the snows.

You may easily guess, Madam, that a great way below this Fall, the river still retains strong marks of so violent a shock; accordingly, it becomes only navigable three leagues below, and exactly at the place which M. de Joncaire has chosen for his residence. It should by right be equally unnavigable above it, since the river falls perpendicular the whole space of its breadth. But besides the island, which divides it into two, several rocks which are scattered up and down above it, abate much of the rapidity of the stream; it is notwithstanding so very strong, that ten or twelve Outaways trying to cross over to the island to shun the Iroquoise who were in pursuit of them, were drawn into the precipice, in spite of all their efforts to preserve themselves.

I have heard say that the fish that happen to be entangled in the current, fall dead into the river, and that the Indians of those parts were considerably advantaged by them; but I saw nothing of this sort. I was also told, that the birds that attempted to fly over were sometimes caught in the whirlwind formed, by the violence of the torrent. But I observed quite the contrary, for I saw small birds flying very low, and exactly over the Fall, which yet cleared their passage very well.

This sheet of water falls upon a rock, and there are two reasons which induce me to believe that it has either found, or perhaps in time hollowed out a cavern of considerable depth. The first is, that the noise it makes is very hollow, resembling that of thunder at a distance. You can scarce hear it at M. de Joncaire's, and what you hear in this place, may possibly be only that of the whirlpools caused by the rocks, which fill the bed of the river as far as this. And so much the rather as above the cataract, you do not hear it near so far. The second is, that nothing has ever been seen again that has once fallen over it, not even the wrecks of the canoe of the Outaways, I mentioned just now. Be this as it will, Ovid gives us the description of such another cataract situated according to him in the delightful valley of Tempé. I will not pretend that the country of Niagara is as fine as that, though I believe its cataract much the noblest of the two.

Besides I perceived no mist above it, but from behind, at a distance, one would take it for smoke, and there is no person who would not be deceived with it, if he came in sight of the isle, without having been told before-hand that there was so surprising a cataract in this place.

The soil of the three leagues I had to go afoot to get hither, and which is called the carrying-place of Niagara, seems very indifferent; it is even very ill-wooded, and you cannot walk ten paces without treading on ant-hills, or meeting with rattle-snakes, especially during the heat of the day. . . .

FATHER BONNECAMPS' DESCRIPTION, 1749.

In the summer of 1749, a French expedition headed by Pierre Joseph Céloron, passed up the Niagara, bound for the Ohio. With it was the Jesuit Joseph Pierre de Bonnécamps, hydrographer at the Jesuit college in Quebec. He kept a journal of the expedition, which arrived at the Niagara June 30th. Of the Falls he wrote:

The famous waterfall of Niagara is very nearly equidistant from the two lakes. It is formed by a rock cleft vertically, and is 133 feet, according to my measurement, which I believe to be exact. Its figure is a half-ellipse, divided near the middle by a little island. The width of the fall is perhaps three-eighths of a league. The water falls in foam over the length of the rock, and is received in a large basin, over which hangs a continual mist.

PETER KALM'S ACCOUNT, 1750.

In 1750 there came to the Niagara the eminent Swedish botanist, Peter Kalm, "Professor of Oeconomy in the University of Aobo in Swedish Finland, and Member of the Swedish Royal Academy of Sciences," who wrote a big book about America and left Niagara out. I am not familiar with his work in the original; but in John R. Forster's English translation (Warrington, 1770) I find it stated that "the author, who . . . is still living, has not yet finished this work; . . . the journal of a whole year's traveling, and especially his expedition to the Iroquese, and fort Niagara, are still to come." It does not appear that Professor Kalm ever completed the work as suggested; but at Albany, Sept. 2, 1850, he wrote a long letter to a friend in Philadelphia. If originally written in English, I believe it is the first detailed account of Niagara, not a translation, to appear in that language. It follows herewith:

ALBANY, Sep. 2, 1750.

SIR—After a pretty long journey made in a short time, I am come back to this town. You may remember, that when I took my leave of you, I told you, I would this summer, if time permitted, take a view of Niagara Fall, esteemed one of the greatest curiosities in the World. When I came last year from Quebec, you inquired of me several particulars concerning this fall; and I told you what I heard of it in Canada, from several French gentlemen who had been there: but this was still all hearsay; I could not assure you of the truth of it, because I had not then seen it myself, and so it could not satisfy my own, much less your curiosity. Now, since I have been on the spot, it is in my power to give you a more perfect and satisfactory description of it.

After a fatiguing travel, first on horseback thro' the country of the Six Nations, to Oswego, and from thence in a batteau upon Lake Ontario, I came on the 12th of August in the evening to Niagara fort. The French there seemed much perplexed at my first coming, imagining I was an English officer, who under pretext of seeing Niagara Falls, came with some other view; but as soon as I shew'd them my passports, they chang'd their behaviour, and received me with the greatest civility. Niagara Fall is six French leagues from Niagara Fort. You first go three leagues by water up Niagara river, and then three leagues over the carrying place. As it was late when I arriv'd at the Fort, I could not the same day go to the Fall, but I prepared myself to do it the next morning. The commandant of the Fort, Monsr. Beaujou, invited all the officers and gentlemen there to supper with him. I had read formerly almost all the authors that have wrote any thing about this Fall; and the last year in Canada, had made so many enquiries about it, that I thought I had a pretty good Idea of it; and now at supper, requested the gentlemen to tell me all they knew and thought worth notice relating to it, which they accordingly did.

I observed that in many things they all agreed, in some things they were of different opinions, of all which I took particular notice. When they had told me all they knew, I made several quiries to them concerning what I had read and heard of it, whether such and such a thing was true or not? and had their answers on every circumstance. But as I have found by experience in my other travels, that very few observe nature's works with accuracy, or report the truth precisely, I cannot now be entirely satisfied without seeing with my own eyes whenever 'tis in my power.

Accordingly the next morning, being the 13th of August, at break of day, I set out for the Fall. The commandant had given orders to two of the Officers of the Fort to go with me and shew me every thing, and also sent by them an order to Monsr. Joncaire, who had liv'd ten years by the carrying-place, and knew every thing worth notice of the Fall, better than any other person, to go with me, and shew and tell me whatever he knew. A little before we came to the carrying-place, the water of Niagara River grew so rapid, that four men in a light birch canoe, had much difficulty to get up thither. Canoes can go half a league above the beginning of the carrying-place, tho' they must work against a water extremely rapid; but higher up it is quite impossible, the whole course of the water for two leagues and a half up to the great Fall, being a series of smaller Falls, one under another, in which the greatest canoe or Batteau would in a moment be turn'd upside down.

We went ashore therefore, and walk'd over the carrying-place, having besides the high and steep side of the river, two great hills to ascend one above the other. Here on the carrying-place I saw above 200 Indians, most of them belonging to the Six Nations, busy in carrying packs of furs, chiefly of deer and bear, over the carrying-place. You would be surpris'd to see what abundance of these things are brought every day over this place. An Indian gets 20 pence for every pack he carries over, the distance being three leagues.

Half an hour past 10 in the morning, we came to the great Fall, which I found as follows. To the river (or rather strait), runs here from S. S. E. to N. N. W. and the rocks of the great Fall crosses it, not in a right line, but forming almost the figure of a semicircle or horseshoe. Above the Fall, in the middle of the river is an island, lying also S. S. E. and N. N. W. or parallel with the sides of the river; its length is about 7 or 8 French arpents (an arpent being 180 feet). The lower end of this Island is just at the perpendicular edge of the Fall. On both sides of this island runs all the water that comes from the lakes of Canada, *viz.* Lake Superior, lake Mischigan, lake Huron, and lake Erie, which you know are rather small seas than lakes, and have besides a great many large rivers that empty their water in them, of which the greatest part comes down this Niagara Fall. Before the water comes to this island, it runs but slowly, compar'd with its motion when it approaches the island, where it grows the most rapid water in the World, running with surprizing swiftness before it comes to the Fall; it is quite white, and in many places is thrown high up into the air! The greatest and strongest batteaux would here in a moment be turn'd over and over.

The water that goes down on the west side of the island, is more rapid, in greater abundance, whiter, and seems almost to outdo an arrow in swiftness. When you are at the Fall, and look up the river, you may see, that the river above the Fall is every where exceedingly steep, almost as the side of a hill. When all this water comes to the very Fall, there it throws itself down perpendicular! It is beyond all belief the surprize when you see this! I cannot with words express how amazing it is! You cannot see it without being quite terrified; to behold so vast a quantity of water falling headlong from a surprizing height!

I doubt not but you have a desire to learn the exact height of this great Fall. Father Hennepin supposes it 600 Feet perpendicular; but he has gained little credit in Canada; the name of honour they give him there, is *un grand Menteur,* or The Great Liar; he writes of what he saw in places where he never was. 'Tis true he saw this Fall: but as it is the way of some travellers to magnify everything, so he has done with regard to the fall of Niagara. This humour of travellers, has occasioned me many disappointments in my travels, having seldom been so happy as to find the wonderful things that had been related by others. For my part, who am not fond of the Marvellous, I like to see things just as they are, and so to relate them.

Since Father Hennepin's time, this Fall by all the accounts that have been given of it, has grown less and less; and those who have measur'd it with mathematical instruments find the perpendicular fall of the water to be exactly 137 feet. Monsr. Morandrier, the king's engineer in Canada, assured me, and gave it me also under his hand, that 137 Feet was precisely the height of it; and all the French Gentlemen that were present with me at the Fall, did agree with him, without the least contradiction: it is true, those who have try'd to measure it with a line, find it sometimes 140, sometimes 150 feet, and sometimes more; but the reason is, it cannot that way be measured with any certainty, the water carrying away the Line. When the water is come down to the bottom of the rock of the Fall, it jumps back to a very great height in the air; in other places it is as white as milk or snow; and all in motion like a boiling chaldron.

You may remember, to what a great distance Hennepin says the noise of this great Fall may be heard. All the gentlemen who were with me, agreed, that the farthest one can hear it is 15 leagues, and that very seldom. When the air is quite calm, you can hear it to Niagara Fort; but seldom at other times, because when the wind blows, the waves of Lake Ontario make too much noise there against the Shore. They informed me, that when they hear at the Fort the noise of the Fall, louder than ordinary, they are sure a North East Wind will follow, which never fails: this seems wonderful, as the Fall is South West from the Fort: and one would imagine it to be rather a sign of a contrary wind. Sometimes, 'tis said, the Fall makes a much greater noise than at other times, and this is look'd upon as a certain mark of approaching bad weather, or rain; the Indians here hold it always for a sure sign. When I was there, it did not make an extraordinary great noise: just by the Fall, we could easily hear what each other said, without speaking much louder than common when conversing in other places. I do not know how others have found so great a noise here, perhaps it was at certain times, as above mentioned.

From the Place where the water falls, there rise abundance of vapours, like the greatest and thickest smoke, sometimes more, sometimes less: these vapours rise high in the air when it is calm, but are dispersed by the wind when it blows hard. If you go nigh to this vapour or fog, or if the wind blows it on you, it is so penetrating, that in a few minutes you will be as wet as if you had been under water. I got two young Frenchmen to go down, to bring me from the side of the Fall at the bottom, some of each of the several kinds of herbs, stones and shells they should find there: they returned in a few minutes, and I really thought they had fallen into the water; they were obliged to strip themselves quite naked, and hang their clothes in the sun to dry. When you are on the other East side of the Lake Ontario, a great many leagues from the Fall, you may, every clear and calm morning, see the vapours of the Fall rising in the air; you would think all the woods thereabouts were set on fire by the Indians, so great is the apparent smoak. In the same manner you may see it on the West side of the lake Erie, a great many leagues off.

Several of the French gentlemen told me, that when birds come flying into this fog or smoak of the fall, they fall down and perish in the Water, either because their wings are become wet, or that the noise of the fall astonishes them, and they know not where to go in the Dark: but others were of opinion, that seldom or never any bird perishes in that manner; because, as they all agreed, among the abundance of birds found dead below the fall, there are no other sorts than such as live and swim frequently in the water; as swans, geese, ducks, water-hens, teal, and the like. And very often great flocks of them are seen going to destruction in this manner; they swim in the river above the fall, and so are carried down lower and lower by the water, and as water-fowl commonly take great delight in being carry'd with the stream, so here they indulge themselves in enjoying this pleasure so long, till the swiftness of the water becomes so great, that 'tis no longer possible for them to rise, but they are driven down the precipice, and perish. They are observ'd when they draw nigh the fall, to endeavour with all their might, to take wing and leave the water, but they cannot. In the months of September and October, such abundant quantities of dead waterfowl are found every morning below the Fall, on the shore, that the garrison of the fort for a long time live chiefly upon them; besides the fowl, they find also several sorts of dead fish, also deer, bears, and other animals which have tried to cross the water above the fall; the larger animals are generally found broken to pieces. Just below the fall the water is not rapid, but goes all in circles and whirls like a boiling pot; which however doth not hinder the Indians going upon it in small canoes a fishing; but a little lower begins the smaller fall. When you are above the fall, and look down, your head begins to turn: the French who have been here 100 times, will seldom venture to look down, without at the same time keeping fast hold of some tree with one hand.

It was formerly thought impossible for any body living to come at the Island that is in the middle of the fall: but an accident that happen'd 12 years ago, or thereabouts, made it appear otherwise. The history is this. Two Indians of the Six Nations went out from Niagara fort, to hunt upon an island that is in the middle of the river, or strait, above the great fall, on which there used to be abundance of deer. They took some French brandy with them, from the fort, which they tasted several times as they were going over the carrying-place; and when they were in the canoe, they took now and then a dram, and so went along up the strait towards the Island where they propos'd to hunt, but growing sleepy, they laid themselves down in the canoe, which getting loose drove back with the stream, farther and farther down till it came nigh that island that is in the middle of the fall. Here one of them, awakened by the noise of the fall, cries out to the other, that they were gone! yet they tri'd if possible to save life. This island was nighest, and with much working they got on shore there. At first they were glad; but when they had consider'd every thing, they thought themselves hardly in a better state than if they had gone down the fall, since they had now no other choice, than either to throw themselves down the same, or to perish with hunger. But hard necessity put them on invention. At the lower end of the island the rock is perpendicular, and no water is running there. This island has plenty of wood; they went to work directly and made a ladder or shrouds of the bark of linden tree, (which is very tough and strong) so long till they could with it reach the water below; one end of this bark ladder they tied fast to a great tree that grew at the side of the rock above the fall, and let the other end down to the water. So they went down along their new-invented stairs, and when they came to the bottom in the middle of the fall, they rested a little; and as the water next below the fall is not rapid, as before-mentioned, they threw themselves out into it, thinking to swim on shore. I have said before, that one part of the fall is on one side of the island, the other on the other side. Hence it is, that the waters of the two cataracts running against each other, turn back against the rock that is just under the island. Therefore, hardly had the Indians began to swim, before the waves of the eddy threw them with violence against the rock from whence they came. They tried it several times, but at last grew weary; and being often thrown against the rock they were much brus'd, and the skin of their bodies torn in many places. So they were obliged to climb up their stairs again to the island, not knowing what to do. After some time they perceived Indians on the shore, to whom they cried out. These saw and pity'd them, but gave them little hopes of help; yet they made haste down to the fort, and told the commandant where two of their brethren were. He persuaded them to try all possible means of relieving the two poor Indians; and it was done in this manner. The water that runs on the east side of this island is shallow, especially a little above the island towards the eastern shore. The commandant caused poles to be made and pointed with iron: two

Indians determined to walk to this island by the help of these poles, to save the other poor creatures, or perish themselves. They took leave of all their friends as if they were going to death. Each had two such poles in his hands, to set against the bottom of the stream, to keep them steady. So they went and got to the island, and having given poles to the two poor Indians there, they all returned safely to the main. Those two Indians who in the abovementioned manner were first brought to this island, are yet alive. They were nine days on the island, and almost starved to death.

Now since the way to this island has been found, the Indians go there often to kill deer, which having tried to cross the river above the fall, were driven upon the island by the stream: but if the King of France would give me all Canada, I would not venture to go to this island; and were you to see it, Sir, I am sure you would have the same sentiment.

On the West side of this island are some small islands or rocks of no consequence. The east side of the river is nearly perpendicular, the west side more sloping. In former times a part of the rock at the Fall which is on the west side of the island, hung over in such a manner, that the water which fell perpendicularly from it, left a vacancy below, so that people could go under between the rock and the water, but the prominent part some years since broke off and fell down; so that there is now no possibility of going between the falling water and the rock, as water now runs close to it all the way down.

The breadth of the Fall, as it runs into a semicircle, is reckon'd to be about six Arpents. The island is in the middle of the Fall, and from it to each side is almost the same breadth: the breadth of the island at its lower end is two thirds of an Arpent, or thereabouts. Below the Fall in the holes of the rocks, are great plenty of Eels, which the Indians and French catch with their hands without other means; I sent down two Indians boys, who directly came up with about twenty fine ones.

Every day, when the Sun shines, you see here from 10 o'clock in the morning to 2 in the afternoon, below the Fall, and under you, when you stand at the side over the Fall, a glorious rainbow and sometimes two rainbows, one within the other. I was so happy to be at the Fall on a fine clear day, and it was with great delight I viewed this rainbow, which had almost all the colours you see in a rainbow in the air. The more vapours, the brighter and clearer is the rainbow. I saw it on the East side of the Fall in the bottom under the place where I stood, but above the water. When the wind carries the vapours from that place, the rainbow is gone, but appears again as soon as new vapours come.

From the Fall to the landing above the Fall, where the canoes from Lake Erie put on shore (or from the Fall to the upper end of the carrying-place) is half a mile. Lower the canoes dare not come, lest they should be obliged to try the fate of the two Indians, and perhaps with less success.

They have often found below the Fall pieces of human bodies, perhaps drunken Indians, that have unhappily came down the Fall. I was told at Oswego, that in October, or thereabouts, such plenty of feathers are to be found here below the Fall, that a man in a day's time can gather enough of them for several beds, which feathers they said came off the birds kill'd at the Fall. I ask'd the French, if this was true? They told me they had never seen any such thing; but that if the feathers were picked off the dead birds, they might be such a quantity. The French told me, they had often thrown whole trees into the water above, to see them tumble down the Fall. They went down with surprising swiftness, but could never be seen afterwards; whence it was thought there was a bottomless deep or abyss just under the Fall. I am also of Opinion, that there must be a vast deep here; yet I think if they had watched very well, they might have found the trees at some distance below the Fall. The rock of the Fall consists of a grey limestone.

Here you have, Sir, a short but exact description of this famous Niagara cataract; you may depend on the truth of what I write. You must excuse me if you find in my account, no extravagant wonders. I cannot make nature otherwise than I find it. I had rather it should be said of me in time to come, that I related things as they were, and that all is found to agree with my description; than to be esteem'd a false Relater. I have seen some other things in this my journey, an account of which I know would gratify your curiosity; but time at present will not permit me to write more, and I hope shortly to see you. I am &c.,

PETER KALM.

THE ABBE PIQUET IN 1751.

Peter Kalm was a thorough naturalist and a good observer. In strong contrast is the next visitor I am able to note—the Sulpitian priest, the Abbé François Picquet, who came to the Niagara, from his mission near the present Ogdensburg, in 1751. Of Niagara he wrote the following extraordinary passage:

"This cascade is as marvelous for its height, and the quantity of water which falls there, as for the diversity of its falls, which are in the number of six principal ones separated by a little isle which puts three to the north and three to the south; they have a regular symetry and an astonishing effect."

ADVENTURES OF M. BONNEFONS, 1753.

A narrative of American travel and adventure very little known, and I believe unpublished as yet in English, is the *"Voyage au Canada dans le Nord de l'Amérique Septentrionale fait depuis l'an 1751 à 1761."* The original manuscript, written in journal form during the decade 1751 to 1761, was at last accounts in the possession of the Marquis de Bassano, in Paris. The National Library of France possesses a manuscript copy of it. In 1887 it was printed, in French, at Quebec, with some editing by the very capable hand of the Abbé H. R. Casgrain. The only acknowledgment of authorship on the original manuscript is the initials "J. C. B." which the Abbé Casgrain ascertains, with probable accuracy, to stand for J. C. Bonnefons, who held various posts in the French military service in America, and who became secretary to Capt. Pouchot, the last French defender of Fort Niagara. The whole journal is full of interest; but I translate from it only a few paragraphs relating to M. Bonnefons' adventures at Niagara Falls in 1753. A few errors will be corrected at the close of the quotation:

Fort Niagara, situated on the high ground and at the south of Lake Ontario, was originally named Denonville. It stands on an elevated spot which is overlooked by mountains at the west bordering a strait three leagues in length, which bears the name of the Niagara river. This fort, built in 1687, was palisaded. It was rebuilt and fortified in 1763. We find it built partly of stone and partly of wood, well fortified on the land side and surrounded with ditches, with bastions supplied with eighteen pieces of cannon, a drawbridge and eighty men in the garrison.

Opposite this fort, at the north and nearly at the end of Lake Ontario, is a great bay, named Toronto, since called by the English, York Bay. On the shore of this bay, there had been built by order of the Governor Joncquiere a fort named Toronto, which has since been destroyed as useless.

The next day, April 12th, we went on by land. From Fort Niagara we ascended the three mountains which are at the west of the fort and on the top of each of which we found a level space formed of flat rock, very even, which makes a resting place for travelers who pass there. It is about two leagues from the bottom to the top of the mountains. When we had reached the top we had to rest, after which we continued to march. At a quarter of a league to the north of the last mountain is the famous fall of Niagara, the noise of which may be heard nearly three leagues. At the place to the south of where we were was a little station, newly established, for the building of batteaux and canoes needed for the navigation of Lake Erie. This station was named Toronto, the English gave to it that of Scuyler or Sckuiler. At the time of our passage there was there a garrison of forty men, Canadians, all boat carpenters. We rested there three days, during which they loaded the provisions, ammunition and goods which we had to take with us to the upper end of Lake Erie.

The curiosity permitted to travelers made me wish to visit the Niagara fall, which I had heard spoken of as a marvelous curiosity. I was one of three to go there. I examined this astonishing cataract, which has the form of a crescent, a quarter of a league in extent. They give to it the height, according to common report, of 180 feet. It is the discharge of Lake Erie, and receives its waters, which it throws into the strait or river of Niagara, which then empties into Lake Ontario near Fort Niagara.

The approaches to this fall appear inaccessible, especially on the south side where we were, and present from both sides a rock covered with bushes, which grow naturally in the crevices. It is impossible when near it to make speaking heard, unless very near to the ears. After having well examined this fall from above, I proposed to the two persons who had accompanied me to go down below. They opposed the difficulty of getting there, there being neither road, nor path, nor security, and that the undertaking was perilous and rash to go there by the bushes, which appeared too weak to sustain us, or by the roots which were not strong, having only hold in the joints of the rock. These reasons, all of force as it appeared to me, did not prevent me from persisting in my curiosity. I resolved then to expose myself alone and presently I began to descend with the intention of making sure of the branches which I encountered on my way; descending backwards, so that I would not let go one after another, until I had seized others of the same firmness.

I was about an hour in getting down, not without commending myself to Providence, for I perceived the rashness of my undertaking, but I had to finish as much from pride as from curiosity. Finally, I came to the bottom, at about twenty toises from the foot of the fall, which even at that distance, did not prevent me from being drenched by the rain-like spray which the fall made. I advanced still nearer. I passed over a fine shingle of flat rock, which led me under the sheet of falling water. It was then that I was very much more drenched and felt the trembling of the rocks caused by the fall of water, which made me hesitate whether I ought to go on or retreat. However, reflecting that this trembling must be the same always, I resolved to go forward, and after having made thirty steps more I found myself in a sort of cavern, formed in the rocks, in the midst of which ran the sheets of water from crevices at several points, which made cascades, agreeable and amusing enough if the rain caused by the fall had permitted me to stay there a little time. I seemed in this place to be in the midst of the cataract. The noise and the trembling were very great. That did not prevent me from examining the cavern, which appeared of a length of six toises by about twenty feet in height. Its depth was scarcely more than fifteen feet. I would have passed it, but was unable to go further because of large clefts which I was unable to cross. I had to retrace my steps. All shivering with cold, and drenched, I hastened to take again the road by which I had descended. I climbed up the bushes quicker than I had descended them. Arrived on top, I found the two people with whom I had come. They wished to interrogate me. This was futile. I was deaf and was not able to hear them. Cold and hunger forced me to hasten to Toronto, where, being arrived, I at once changed my clothes, after which I ate.

It was not until two hours afterwards that the deafness left me and I was able to give an account of what I had seen. I have since questioned several travelers to learn if they had knowledge of any one who had descended this fall. They had heard no one tell of it. That does not seem extraordinary to me, knowing that the Canadians are so little curious that they would not deign to turn aside from their route for something worthy of report. This indifference on their part does not however give me pretence of being the only one who may have risked himself in this perilous visit, nor that there will not be found in days to come others as curious as I. But if that happens, those who will have the enterprise will be able to confirm what I report to have seen.

It is common report in this country that a native Iroquois, finding himself with his canoe drawn into the current from above, and not being able to draw out of the force of it, wrapped himself in his blanket, glided along in his canoe, and abandoned himself to the current, which quickly precipitated him over the fall, where he was swallowed up with his canoe without reappearing. I have seen the fall of a tree, drawn down by the current, which did not again appear; from which I have concluded that there is a gulf where everything that falls from above is swallowed up.

About twenty feet above this fall is a little island, formed of rock, some fifteen toises in length, by 10 or 12 feet in width, overgrown with bushes, with one single tree in the midst. The water of Lake Erie, which rushes around it and throws itself into the fall, is very rapid and glides over a shelf of flat rock at a depth of four or five feet, especially on the side to the south, where I examined it.

One finds at the foot of the fall, along the river Niagara, a great many dead fish. Travelers pretend that these fish come from Lake Erie. They find they have become drawn down into the fall by the rapidity of the water. I have given to this matter a reflection which seems to me just. It is that they first ascend rather than descend, and that coming from Lake Ontario, ascending near to the fall, they are there killed, afterward drawn down by the current which throws them on the banks, where one often finds them only stunned. Now if they came from Lake Erie they would be killed and, what is more, swallowed up in the fall.

It is said also that birds which fly over the fall are drawn into it in spite of themselves, by the force of the air. I am not sure of this fact, which, however, is not lacking in probability, since there is often seen there a rainbow which seems strongly to attract the birds who direct their flight into it, where they become confused and drenched, lacking strength to ascend. And it may perhaps be only birds of passage, for those which inhabit the neighborhood are so accustomed to the rainbow and to the noise of the fall that they know how to preserve themselves, since they are seldom seen there, although there are a great many of them in this vicinity.

The place called Toronto is not, except in the first allusion, the present Toronto, but the old landing-place above the Falls, long known as Schlosser. It was no doubt this last name that Bonnefons aimed at when he wrote *"Scuyler ou Sckuiler."* The early French writers made as bad a mess of English names—or in this case of a German—as the English did of French names. One has but to look at Sir William Johnson's attempts at French names to see how bad that could be. I have used the old French word *"toise,"* which occurs in Bonnefons' journal; it could be translated "fathom," or six feet. The "little island" described by M. Bonnefons was no doubt that afterwards named Gull island; numerous early visitors speak of it, Tom Moore among others, in 1804. It disappeared not many years later.

DIARY OF RALPH IZARD, 1765.

The following is a portion of a diary, ascribed to Ralph Izard of South Carolina; it was published anonymously in New York in 1846, it is said by his grand-daughter, Anna Izard Deal. The writer was born in Charleston in 1742, and fell heir to large property, both in land and slaves. He was educated in England; returning to America he married a niece of Lt. Gov. De Lancey. It was apparently before his marriage that he made the journey to Niagara described in his journal. In 1771 he went to England, residing in London, and, after the outbreak of war with the American colonies, in Paris. He returned to America in 1780, became devoted to the patriot cause, and pledged his estate as security to the Government, when Congress was trying to arrange for the purchase of ships of war in Europe. In 1782 he was a delegate to the Continental Congress, and from 1789 to 1795, United States Senator from South Carolina, and a part of the time president *pro tem* of the Senate. He stood high in the esteem of Washington, and was a loyal and active patriot; he was, however, says a biographer, "violent in his temper and practically useless as a diplomatist." He died at South Bay, near Charleston, May 30, 1804. The following extract from his diary preserves some of the peculiarities of the original:

Monday, 24th June, 1765. Went with my three companions on board a sloop for Albany—a very hot day, with the wind at south. After sailing about fifty miles through a very rocky and mountainous country, the wind came about contrary and we anchored. *Friday, 28th.* Arrived at Albany, one hundred and sixty miles from New York. Albany is a dirty, ill-built Dutch town, of about three hundred houses; stands upon Hudson's River. Dined at Schuyler's. *July 2d.* Left Albany in a wagon, came to Schenectady. Lay at Sir William Johnson's; he is superintendent for Indian affairs in the northern district. Breakfasted at Fort Johnson, where Sir William's son lives, eighteen miles from Schenectady; good land all the way thither. Dined with Sir William at Johnson Hall. Extraordinary good land about his house. The office of superintendent very troublesome. Sir William continually plagued with Indians about him, generally from three hundred to nine hundred in number—spoil his garden and keep his house always dirty. *7th.* Left Sir William's; lay at Nicholas Failings, a very civil Dutchman, who seemed glad to give us whatever he had in his house; it is forty-two miles from Schenectady. *8th.* Got to Nicholas Harkimer's, sixteen miles from Failings. *9th.* Fort Harkimer, eight miles. The land about it belongs to old Harkimer, excellent land, settled by Germans. During the war this fort was built for the protection of the neighborhood from the attacks of the Six Nation Indians, who live round about it. *10th.* Discharged our wagon; went on board a batteau; hunted and rowed up the Mohawk River against the stream which, on account of the rapidity of the current, is very hard work for the poor soldiers. Encamped on the banks of the river, about nine miles from Harkimer's.

The inconveniences attending a married subaltern, strongly appear in this tour; what with the sickness of their wives, the squealing of their children, and the smallness of their pay I think the gentlemen discover no uncommon share of philosophy, in keeping themselves from running mad. Officers and soldiers, with their wives and children, legitimate and illegitimate, make altogether a pretty compound oglio, which does not tend towards showing military matrimony off to any great advantage.

Friday 11th. Got to Fort Schuyler, fifteen miles from our last night's encampment. A little block-house, built during the late war, not capable of containing above six or eight people.

Saturday 12th. Had a disagreeable ride twenty-two miles through a thick wood, with a bad path, to Fort Stanwix built in the year 1759 by General Stanwix. Lieutenant Allan Grant commanded there.

Monday 14th. Went on horseback by the side of Woodcreek, twenty miles to the royal block-house, a kind of wooden castle; proof against any Indian attacks. It is now abandoned by the troops, and a settler lives there, who keeps rum, milk, rackoons, etc., which though nothing of the most elegant, is comfortable to strangers passing that way.

This block-house is situated on the east end of the Oneida Lake, and is surrounded by the Oneida Indians, one of the Six Nations. Some of our batteaux not being come up, we stayed next day at the block house.

16th. Embarked and rowed to the west end of the lake which is twenty-eight miles, to Fort Brewington, a small stockade, built last war. The Oneida Lake is twenty miles broad from north to south.

17th. Rowed down Oswego River to the Onondaga Falls, thirty-nine miles. These falls, are so rapid, that the batteaux were all drawn out of the water, and rolled twenty yards, upon logs, made for that purpose below the Falls, where we encamped.

18th. Arrived at Fort Ontario (commanded by Captain Lieut. Jonathan Rogers of the Seventeenth), situated on the lake of that name, near a point formed by the lake and Oswego river. Fort Ontario is of wood, has five bastions, built in 1759.

Fort Oswego, which was taken by the French, is on the opposite side of the river, within sight of this Fort.

Pondiach, the famous Ottawa chief, with fifty head men of the neighboring Indians, were arrived here to meet Sir William Johnson, about matters of consequence.

21st. Sir William arrived.

22d. At two o'clock in the morning, left Fort Ontario, encamped on the banks of Lake Ontario, about thirty miles from the Fort.

23d. Proceeded and encamped. *24th.* Arrived late in the evening at Niagara Fort, one hundred and seventy miles from Fort Ontario. Captain Thomas Norris, of the Seventeenth regiment, commanded here. Many civilities received from him and the officers of the regiment.

26th. Rode to Fort Schlosser, about fifteen miles from Niagara, which is situated on Niagara River, about two miles above the famous Falls.

Mr. Pfister, a German half-pay lieutenant of the Royal Americans, lives at Fort Schlosser. He has made a contract with General Gage, commander-in-chief, to carry all stores, batteaux, etc., belonging to the army, in wagons over land, about seven miles, the Falls of Niagara making the river of that name so rapid both above and below them, that it is absolutely necessary for every thing going towards Lake Erie, to be carried that distance by land. Every batteau, besides those belonging to the army, pays him £10, New-York currency, and upwards, according to their size.

Batteaux and all heavy baggage are raised to the top of an high hill on the river, by means of a capstan.

From Fort Schlosser we went to see the Falls, which are two amazing cataracts, divided by an island in the river. We were inclined to go down a steep rock and view the Falls from the bottom, but having no rope with us to fasten to a tree above, the dangerous appearance of the precipice deterred us.

A few days after, we crossed the river from Niagara Fort and rode to the Falls, which appeared much higher and more beautiful than from the opposite side.

We had got a rope, and resolved by its assistance to go to the bottom of the Falls; but some accident happening to the horse of the man who had charge of the rope, he was obliged to stop on the road, and endeavoring to overtake us, he lost his way; so we should have been a second time disappointed of the pleasure of seeing the Falls from the bottom had we not resolved to go down at all events, without a rope. Before this resolution could be executed, it was necessary to find out a proper place from which we might make an attempt with some probability of success.

This was no easy matter; and we examined the banks of the river for at least an hour and a half before any such place could be found. Nothing but the bare face of a rock was to be seen. At last an opening appeared between some trees and bushes, which, though dangerous to go down, seemed the most likely place for our purpose of any we had seen. A council was now held, whether an attempt should be made there. We all seemed pretty well agreed, that if any one of us would jump down a smooth perpendicular rock, about twenty feet in height, when he got to the bottom it was likely he might find a place where we might descend lower with ease. Nothing was now wanting but a mouse hardy enough to tie the bell about the cat's neck. At last one of the company, after having made one or two fruitless attempts, fixed a forked pole to the branch of a tree that hung over the rock, and by that means let himself down to the bottom. The fork of the pole broke as he was going down, and I think it is a wonder he did not break his neck.

After looking about him some time, he found some notched logs, not twenty yards from the place where he had risked breaking his bones, that served as a ladder, by which the whole company went down easily to the place where he was.

We then scrambled down, holding by stumps and roots, and tufts of grass, to the bottom, and a terrible piece of work we had before we got there. Our labor, however, was in a great measure recompensed by a sight of the Falls, which appear much higher and much more beautiful than from above, on either side. We went so near, as to be wet through with the spray. After getting to the bottom of the precipice our anxiety to be near the Falls was so great, that we forgot to mark the place where we came down; and so, after our curiosity was satisfied with looking, we were obliged to wander up and down for three hours, and scramble over many dangerous places, before we could find our way. The night approaching, gave us a comfortable prospect of staying there till morning; and the appearance of wolves' tracks in many places added much to our pleasant situation. We were informed that those animals frequently travelled about that place, in companies of about twenty or thirty at a time, and were so fierce as to attack men even in the middle of the day. As we had nothing with us to defend ourselves, nor flint and steel to make a fire, I think the odds were about five to four that no part of us except our bones would have ever got to the top of the hill, undigested, if we had not luckily found our way.

Upon the whole, our jaunt was difficult and dangerous,

and although a sight of the Falls from below affords great pleasure, yet it is not adequate to the trouble and hazard necessary to the obtaining it.

The Falls of Niagara have been measured several times by a line, let down from a rock near the top of the Falls. From the best accounts I could get, I think they are about one hundred and forty feet perpendicular. They are extremely grand, and are well worth seeing.

During our stay in this part of the world, we went to Fort Erie, which is situated on the mouth of the Lake of that name. Lake Erie is about three hundred miles long and about one hundred and twenty broad.

At the north-west corner of Lake Erie is Detroit on the Straits between that Lake and Lake Huron; eighteen miles up these Straits is Fort Pontchartrain.

Niagara seems to be the key of all our northern possessions in America; yet so fond are the Ministry of the appearance of economy that this Fort, for want of a trifling annual expense, is suffered to go to ruin. The works are built of turf; they are very extensive and very much out of repair. The commanding officer assured me, that if the Fort was attacked it must fall, as he did not think it tenable. There is indeed in the Fort a large stone house, ninety by forty-five feet, which is proof against any Indian attacks, even though they were in possession of the Fort, yet if there were three or four Frenchmen, with these Indians, who could show them the use of the cannon in the Fort, the house would soon be levelled to the ground. This large house was built by the French, under the pretence of its being a trading-house, the Indians refusing then to permit them to build a fort. Soon after the house was built, they raised a stockade about it, and by degrees constructed the regular fortification, which is now seen here.

The officers' fresh provisions were entirely out, and they had not a drop of wine; we luckily had a little which we brought up with us.

When we first arrived we were told that the schooner that carries provisions between Niagara and Oswegachy, would certainly arrive in two or three days; we waited with the utmost expectation for her, but she did not appear until Saturday, 16th August, when to our great joy she arrived.

The diary continues with an account of the return journey, down the St. Lawrence to Quebec, back to Montreal, thence through Lake Champlain to Albany, and by river sloop to New York.

A few peculiarities in the preceding journal may be noted. "Harkimer" is a much-used early form for the family name now usually written "Herkimer." "Pondiach" is a permissible spelling for "Pontiac"; but "Fort Brewington" is an error for "Fort Brewerton." Other minor slips do not call for correction.

JONATHAN CARVER, 1766.

Jonathan Carver passed this way in 1766 and observed "those remarkable Falls which are esteemed one of the most extraordinary productions of nature at present known"! But, he adds, "As these have been visited by so many travelers, and so frequently described, I shall omit giving a particular description of them." If that had to be said in 1766, what would Carver think of the cataracts of description which have been poured out in the last century and a half?

ST. JOHN DE CRÈVECOEUR, 1785.

To the researches of Mr. O. H. Marshall we are indebted for one of the most important of the early narratives of travel in the Niagara region. It is a letter written in 1785 by Hector St. John de Crèvecoeur to his young son Alexander, in France. A copy of it, and of an accompanying map, were given to Mr. Marshall, some thirty odd years ago, by a grandson of the writer, Count Robert de Crèvecoeur, at that time the head of the family in France. Mr. Marshall sent a translation of the document, with the map, to the *Magazine of American History,* in which they were printed, October, 1878. I am not aware of any other publication of this very interesting and useful narrative, which amply merits inclusion in the present collection.

Hector St. John de Crèvecoeur, usually called, it appears, at least during his American sojourn, Mr. St. John, was born, of a distinguished French family, at Caen in Normandy in 1731. He was educated in England and in 1754 came to America, where he married, and for some years was settled as an agriculturist. I quote from a sketch of him by Mr. Marshall:

"In 1780 he was arrested by the British as a spy and imprisoned for three months. Released through the mediation of a friend who became security for his neutrality, he returned to his paternal home in Normandy. On the ratification of peace in 1782 between the United States and Great Britain, he was appointed French Consul-General for New York, New Jersey and Connecticut. On his arrival at New York he found his property burnt, his wife dead and his children in the hands of a stranger. A Mr. Fellows of Boston, having learned that Mr. St. John had befriended some American sailors wrecked on the coast of Normandy, went over three hundred miles to the relief of his children and took charge of them in their father's absence.

"Mr. St. John remained in America until 1793, during which time he traded extensively among the western Indians. He visited an Onondaga council in 1789, where he was received as an adopted son of the Oneidas under the name of *Kayo.* He was also present at an Indian treaty held at Fort Stanwix, now Rome. He had a daughter who was married to an attaché of the Consular office by the name of Otto, who rose to high diplomatic rank in the

French service, even to the embassy to England for a short time."

Crèvecoeur was the author of two curious and interesting works. One, "Letters from an American Farmer," was written and first published in English. There are London editions of 1782 and 1783. The author subsequently enlarged it and translated it into French, Paris editions appearing in 1784 and 1787. "In it," writes Mr. Marshall, "he paints in glowing colors the attractions of rural life in America. His graphic descriptions drew many an emigrant from Europe to our shores, to find disappointment in the hardships and privations of a new country. General Washington briefly characterizes the book as 'a work, though founded in fact, embellished in some instances with rather too flattering circumstances'."

His other work, written in French, is entitled *"Voyage dans la Haute Pensylvanie, et dans l'Etat de New York."* It was published, three volumes, in Paris, 1801. It purports to have been translated from an English manuscript, rescued from an American vessel wrecked at the mouth of the Elbe. This gave the author an excuse for disconnected writing, under pretense that portions of the original manuscript were lost. He describes his travels in America and his intercourse with the Indians. Many pages are devoted to the Niagara region, but they are so embellished with incidents apparently the invention of the author, that one can only regard them as fiction, rather than as trustworthy history. The letter to his son, however, written after his excursion to Niagara in July, 1785, is indubitably trustworthy, and his map is unequaled, in that period, for accuracy and useful data.

Crèvecoeur corresponded with Washington and with Franklin. In 1787 he accompanied the latter to Lancaster,

Pa., when Franklin laid the corner-stone of the college that bears his name. He spent his last years in France, dying at Sarcelles, near Paris, in 1813, aged 82 years.

In the account that follows, there are numerous references, by letters, to places on the map, marked to correspond. "The gentleman of the name of Hambleton" was probably Robert Hamilton, the founder of Queenston, which is the "Landing" or "landing place" of Crèvecoeur's letter. The allusion to "surrounding mountains" is singular. Early travelers called the Lewiston heights "mountains," but it was an oddly perverse memory which made mountains visible at the Falls.

Having no access to the original manuscript, I have had to follow Mr. Marshall's translation, which has some obvious slips, as for instance where two falls, each a quarter of a mile, are said to make in all a mile; probably the first-mentioned should read "three quarters." Further explanation will be found in connection with the map, at the end of the letter.

It was in the month of July, 1785, my friend Mr. Hunter and I arrived at the Fort of Niagara, after a long and painful voyage up the river St. Laurence, the particulars of which being foreign to my present subject, I will therefore proceed to the immediate description of the wonderful Cataract of Niagara, which of its kind, is the greatest phenomenon in nature.

Early in the morning of July the 12th, a gentleman of the name of Hambleton to whom we had been introduced, called upon us with horses to accompany him to Fort Slausser, "A," near which place the falls are situated. Our route was upon the banks of the river which takes its name from the Cataract and is generally one quarter to one half a mile wide, the current extremely rapid, but being deep water for about 9 miles, is navigable with a strong northerly wind to "B." Here the rapids begin and whose fury and violence increases for 9 miles more, which bring you to the head of the river "C."

From the landing place, as it is called (because the boats discharge their loading) we found the banks became more steep, and we continued to ascend them until we arrived at Mr. Stedman's house "D" who forms this place of Government and has the exclusive right of transporting the stores and merchandise from Lake Ontario to Lake Erie. The men were received by the gentleman with the greatest hospitality, who amused us for the remaining part of the day with various details of the incidents which had occurred during his residence here. Having concerted every thing for our Expedition to the Falls, we retired to our rooms.

July 13. We arose before the Sun, and in company with several gentlemen of the Army, began our walk to the river Erie, which is here some miles over and interspersed with a number of beautiful small islands, covered with forest trees.

We pursued the course of the river for nearly two miles, our Expectations were kept awake by the distant sound of the Fall, which became louder as we approached it. About a mile before you arrive at the Cataract, "E," the rapids commence, and which of themselves, in any other part of the world would be thought superior to anything of the kind. You distinguish them best from a sawmill, "F," which projects from the shore. These rapids are formed by a continuous chain of craggy rocks of various heights and the descent below the bed of the river being great, the vast body of water which comes from the upper lakes and which are discharged by this river, force themselves over these rocks, with inconceivable fury and rapidity, producing billows of white foam which for magnitude, can only find a companion in the agitation of the Atlantic Ocean in a gale of wind.

We continued our route through a wood until we came in view of this tremendous Cataract; but where shall I find language to convey even an idea of the grandeur of the Scene? When the period of astonishment was over, and the mind at liberty to investigate each part of these varied beauties, we found a very ample field for observation.

The most sublime and elevated object was a column of spray or vapor, that rises from the basin "C" into which the waters are hurled, the weight and elasticity of which make it rebound at least one half the height of the fall. The upper particles being light form into a thin vapor, which appears like a cloud. The weather was remarkably serene, not a breath of air nor a cloud to be seen. The sun rose with peculiar lustre, and as the night clouds were dissipated then succeeded a clear Azure sky. The rays of the sun gilded the tops of the surrounding mountains, and at length, in oblique angles, struck the cloud I have mentioned. It was instantly vivified by the colors of the rainbow, three of which were visible at once. One as it were under our feet upon the surface of the basin below, was at 180 feet. The splendor of those objects was truly beautiful, and lasted some time until the sun rising in the horizon, from its attracting influence, left only a light cloud which upon many occasions has been seen at the distance of 50 to 60 miles.

Our attention was now taken up with the general appearance and shape of the Cataract, which, from the situation we were in, appeared an irregular curve. We were standing upon a rising ground on the Eastern Shore, and within a few yards of the lesser fall, for it is so distinguished from another which is separated from this by an island, and which conceals a great part of the large fall, and can only be seen to advantage on the opposite side.

I shall here confine myself to the small fall, which is near one quarter of a mile wide; this vast body of water all in a foam, is precipitated 150 feet perpendicular, with a noise like thunder. I shall reserve the most minute and descriptive part until I arrive on the Western Shore, but before I leave this, I must mention the perilous and dangerous descent we made. We had provided a strong rope which we attached to the trunk of a large tree about 40 or 50 yards from the edge of the little fall. The rocks are nearly perpendicular, from the fissures of which grew a number of shrubs and plants, which served to fix our feet upon whilst we held firm by our hands on the rope. In this manner we descended nearly 150 feet, not without having experienced the greatest bodily fatigue, but also some fearful apprehensions. What will not curiosity stimulate us to encounter, for certainly there was more danger than pleasure or advantage.

However this is considered as a part of a traveler's duty, and being come so far, we were determined not to be excelled in spirit or variety of attempt. We approached the falling waters until we were completely wet. We rested ourselves upon a rock and from thence we could see these tumultuous waters which seemed to threaten us with instant death, but before they could arrive to us, they were diverted from us by a ledge of rocks which conveyed them into the immense vortex below, for we were still elevated above the bed of the river. We had now to return by the way we came, which we effected without any material injury, except some bruises which could not be avoided. We had been several hours on this Expedition, and returned to Mr. Stedman's where we ate our breakfast with keen appetites, which were whetted by the feast of mental gratification we had just been enjoying.

We had the pleasure of an introduction to Capt. Jones, commanding officer of this Post, whose obliging communications and very polite attention, I shall ever recollect with gratitude. We were desirous of crossing the river Erie to the opposite shore, where we might see the Cataract in the best situation. The general route is to return to the landing place upon the river Niagara "B," pass the river and proceed by a road through the thick woods until you arrive at the falls. We were saved this troublesome route by Mr. Jones offering us one of the Military Batteaux, with six soldiers, to put us and our horses over. After expressing our obligation to him for his convenient offer, which we accepted, we took our leaves of the friends we had met with. The river here is about three miles wide, the waters very deep, which conceals in some measure the rapidity of the current, which is so great that we were obliged to pole up the river close in shore for near two miles. Our men then took to their oars and with incredible labor arrived at the other side and landed in Chippeway Creek "I." This passage is extremely awful, for many accidents have happened from the breaking of an oar and the current running at the rate of six miles an hour, it requires great exertion to prevent being hurried along with it; and this is the reason they ascend the river so high, for Chippewa Creek is even lower down than Fort Slausser. The terror is increased by a full view of the rapids I have described, and the spray and cloud within two or three miles. An accident such as I have mentioned would expose persons to be driven by the current into the rapids, where you must inevitably perish.

We however had this only in idea, for we were safely landed upon a beautiful plantation occupied by Mr. Birch, a gentleman from London, but who from a long residence in the State of New York and attached to the British Government, came under the description of a Loyalist. He had the lands granted him which now seem to repay his labors and difficulties, with the greatest abundance of every thing useful; we were entertained by him with great hospitality and we found him a very sensible, well informed character, his conversation pleasing and instructive, and his communications very novel, which some day I may take an opportunity of imparting. This gentleman directed us how to proceed in a choice of situation and objects, and we derived considerable advantage from it. We pursued our route upon some elevated ground covered with large forest trees, through which we now and then caught a glimpse of the river. One station we took gave us one of the most beautiful views I had ever seen. We arrived at the house of Mr. Ellsworth, a Loyalist, "K," who is settled upon a fine plot of land which is cultivated to the very edge of the Falls "L," and which with the river and extensive prospect is plainly seen and commanded from his house. We induced him to act as a guide, and having put ourselves under his direction, he conducted us to a shelve of rocks which are upon a level of the river Erie, "M." Upon one of those we took our stand, and how shall I attempt to describe the scene before me! The bare recollection seems to deny my pen expression of the influence of the mind; in vain the ideas form and seek expression. They multiply upon each other so quick that even now I require reflection to arrange them.

The view of this cataract from the Eastern shore seems only preparative for that on the west side, where we now stood. I shall begin with observing, that you command here every drop of water, since there is not a curve or indented line but may be seen. We were within 30 or 40 yards of the great fall, the waters of which force themselves over these great rocks, and occasionally two small falls, the waters of which washed our feet. The great fall is in the shape of a horse-shoe, and is about a quarter mile broad, its descent at least 175 feet. The vast bodies of water which are discharged here, are more than the ingenuity of man can ascertain. To form a competent idea, we must trace them to their sources, which are derived from those great inland seas which are distinguished as lakes and which in order of magnitude are:

The Lake of the Woods which is of no fixed size.
The two chains of Lakes, which are small.

Lake Superior	is	350	miles long,	250	miles broad.	
Lake Michigan	"	290	"	"	60	" "
Lake Huron	"	280	"	"	180	" "
Lake Erie	"	330	"	"	75	" "
Lake Ontario	"	190	"	"	70	" "

These lakes have all a communication with each other, and their collected waters, except Lake Ontario, are precipitated over the falls of Niagara with a force and weight inconceivably great. It rises again at least 80 feet and produces a spray, which when the wind blows is like a shower of rain and is felt at some 100 yards distance. The vapor and cloud are similar to what we observed on the

East side, only here we observed four distinct rainbows at once.

The waters in the center of the great fall appear of a fine green color. On each side of the crescent the waters are in a white foam, the contrast of which has a very beautiful effect.

At the extremity of the crescent a right line runs for 100 yards over which the water flows. You then come to an island covered with trees and shrubs, whose foliage and situation have a very happy effect amidst the turbulent scene around. The breadth of it may be near a quarter of a mile when the lesser fall continues for about a quarter more, making in all a mile. The appearance of the whole is level, and the island enables you to see the ledge of rocks which form the base over which it runs, being like a wall, the sides of which are so smooth that you might think it proceeded from the chisel rather than from the hand of nature. The waters fall as it were into a large basin, which from the fermentation of the water may be justly compared to an immense caldron of boiling water, every part of which is only increased by the magnitude of the object. This immense basin appears land-locked from this station and the turn of the river is so quick and the body of the water so great, seeking a bent [vent?], that it causes an amazing whirlpool, which would swallow up the largest vessels. The basin is surrounded, except the outlet, by high steep craggy rocks, covered with trees of various sorts, and which are from 150 to 200 feet above the level of the water. Objects below are very minute. The rock we were upon, bends over at least 20 or 30 feet, and to look down makes you giddy, particularly from the agitation of your feelings.

Our attention had been so much taken up with the cataract, that we could think and see nothing else for some time, but when we raised our eyes to make a more general survey, I was at once transported and astonished with the variety of natural scenery and beauty, that had been overlooked in the contemplation of a more sublime and uncommon object than is to be found in any other part of the world; we were relieved from this by one of the most varied prospects I had ever beheld. First you see the rapids sweeping with inconceivable force and in different courses round the several islands which are interspersed in the river, which from its breadth and great extent appears like a lake. At some miles distant appears, on the opposite shore, Fort Slausser, Mr. Stedman's house and his plantations, and if you pursue the scenery around, you are lost in the immeasurable extent. The back grounds at a great distance are terminated by a chain of high mountains, which lose themselves in the clouds and are bounded by the horizon.

Having dwelt with pleasure and delight upon the objects before us, which my eyes run over a thousand times and with which the mind could never be fatigued, we were at length admonished by our conductor that we had no time to spare, if we meant to complete our tour, and satisfy our curiosity. We followed him upon the bank or ledge of rocks for a short mile, in which walk we had many striking views of the falls, altering their appearance as we saw them from projecting points. We arrived at a break in the rock, "N," which serves as the only admittance or path to descend to the river. This we pursued for some distance down to a very steep bank, and were obliged to hold by the roots of trees and shrubs that surrounded us. We came to a large tree which stands alone, "O," and upon the back of which were carved a number of names of different persons who had been here. Being fatigued we rested here some little time, and amused ourselves by adding ours to the number. We now continued our route until we came to a large rock the sides of which are perpendicular and near 30 feet high. We were obliged to make use of an Indian ladder, which is simply two straight trees in which, with their tomahawks or hatchets they cut notches at 12 or 15 inches from each other. In these notches you put your feet and by this means we got to the bottom. We now found our route more difficult, being obliged to change our course in different directions, according as we thought it could accelerate our passage; sometimes we crept on all fours for many yards together, passing through holes in the rocks, which would scarce admit our bodies. At other times we absolutely passed under the roots of trees which had been hollowed by the savages who have made this Indian path in order to amuse themselves with fishing, which is a very favorite amusement. At some seasons fishes are found here in great plenty, and then many hundred savages frequent it.

We had now been near an hour in descending and but a very small part of our difficulty overcome. We were arrived upon a broken shelve of rocks which had fallen from above in the spring of the year when the ice began to thaw, the rocks being loosened. It is from the expansion of the fissures which have snow and water in them during the winter, and melting in the spring of the year, that this effect is produced. There have been instances of persons losing their lives or being lamed from the falling of these pieces, some of which would weigh many tons. At this period of the year there was little danger. We were nearly a mile and a half from the foot of the cataract, and the whole way back was strewed with these broken pieces of stone, and owing to the great declivity to the river we were in fear of falling in, as the stones sometimes gave away, and the only way to save ourselves was by lying down, by which we frequently were hurt. The pending rocks above us added much to the horrors of our situation, for knowing those under our feet had fallen at different periods, we could not divest ourselves of apprehension. However we encouraged each other with the idea of surmounting the same difficulties which others had done before us. We came at last to the two small falls which I have mentioned before. Being excessively fatigued and warm we sat down some time to refresh ourselves, and prepare for advancing. Here we undressed and in our boots and trousers began the most hazardous expedition I was ever engaged in.

After climbing over several very high and craggy rocks,

we came to the first of the small falls, under which we passed without much inconvenience, though the pressure of the water was so great from the height it fell, that I can only compare it to a violent storm of hail, but when we came to the second through which our guide with difficulty passed, I felt no inclination to proceed. Our guide returned to encourage us, and upon my hands and feet I followed him, expecting each moment to sink under the weight of water, but I began to find it less disagreeable as I advanced, and I was soon relieved by enjoying the open air, which now I breathed with pleasing avidity. Here we reposed a little. My friend Hunter was entirely spent; I repented his coming, for fear of some accident, and indeed had endeavored to dissuade him from this perilous excursion, but he could not bear being left behind.

We now were recovered in some degree, and proceeded toward the great fall, and here I may say with propriety, that the most awful scene was now before me that we had yet seen. Our difficulties and dangers as well as our gratifications, had been progressive and this was the height of our ambitious pursuit. I have before remarked that the waters run over the shelve of rocks, that in many places pend over their base. The great force with which they are precipitated, gives them an horizontal direction, so that at the bottom where we stood, it left an opening between the water and rocks. It was here we entered by slow and cautious steps. It soon became dark, which proves the immense body of water there must be betwixt us and the light, for we all know we can see a great depth in the river, and here I should imagine the light would assist in rendering it more transparent, but we found it opaque or dark. We had proceeded about 15 or 20 yards, when we found it so very sultry that we might be said to be in a fumigating bath. We hastened out of this dreary place, and once more congratulating each other upon our safety, and in seeing the sun whose beams seem to shine with peculiar lustre, from the pleasure and gaiety it diffused over our trembling senses. I found here ample subject for reflection. I admired this cataract as one of the great efforts of a Providence, showing the omnipotence of a Supreme Being, for it certainly is one of the most sublime and terrific objects in nature, at once impressing the mind with reverence and admiration. It has often been matter of surprise to me that men do not pursue the study of nature more. Its works are possessed with every requisite to gratify the senses, and our feelings are harmonized into placid contemplation. Where is there in being one who could refuse his cheerful matin praise when he rises from his pillow after the refreshing slumbers of the night and beholds that grand luminary, the sun, vivifying every object; there is not a tree or a shrub but seems to welcome the return of day. If we indulge in a contemplative walk, what an immense variety presents itself to our notice. We may learn the most useful lessons of moral duties from every surrounding object. The progressive rise of every plant and flower, teaches us the gradation of man from infancy. Their decay informs us of the instability of human nature, and indicates the dissolution of time and the whole of the animated universe. How preferable are these innocent contemplative reflections, to the hurry and bustle of a licentious world, where our sensibilities are alarmed with the sight of men preying upon men, and degrading the finest and noblest works of God-man, below the level of the brute creation. The awful majesty and craggy appearance of the great and stupendous works which are on both sides of the river, form a kind of impenetrable barrier for many miles, except the winding path by which we descended, seemingly made by the hand of nature to admit prying man into every one of its secrets.

Here also is to be found a Phenomenon of which kind there can be seen no other, that is an eternal or never ceasing shower, the influence of which is felt to a great distance. I mean the spray of the clouds which is occasioned by the concussion of the water; the rainbows are ever visible where the God of day, bright Phoebus, makes his daily course and diffuses his genial rays.

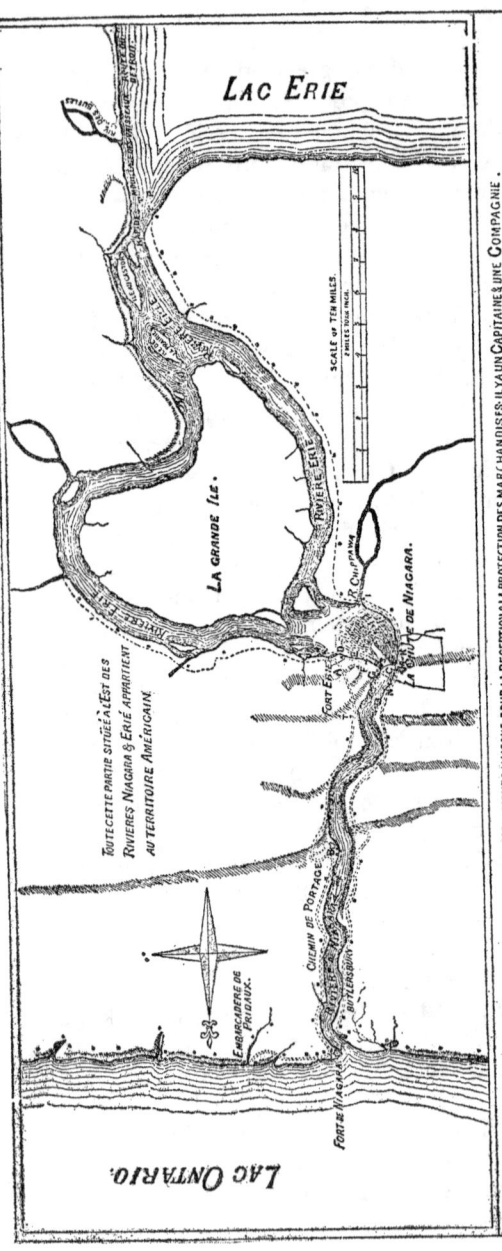

Crèvecoeur's Map of the Niagara. See "Notes," etc., p. 361.

NOTES ON THE MAP.

The map is here reproduced except a marginal inscription in French, in effect as follows: "Plan of the communication between Lakes Erie and Ontario, towards the middle of which is found the Fall of Niagara, the greatest known, as much for its height, estimated to be 160 feet, as for the immense volume of the waters there precipitated. Addressed to M. Ally [Alexander] St. John by his affectionate father; drawn to help the description of this cataract which he sends to him."

The upper river is here called "Erie"—sometimes more properly "Erié." The early writers more often called it the St. Lawrence. The key to the letters, given on the map in French, is as follows:

A. Fort Erie, spot surrounded with palisades, in which are built several houses for the reception and protection of goods. There are here a captain and company. [This was Fort Schlosser.]
B. Wharf, consisting of two quays and three large storehouses, surrounded by palisades.
C. Foot of the fall; group [of rocks] more than 200 feet in diameter, where the water churns about before escaping.
D. House of Mr. Stedman, a little distance from the river, where we slept the first night.
E. Beginning of the rapids and head of the rocks.
F. Saw mill on a point, belonging to Mr. Stedman.
G. Site whence we viewed the west branch of the fall, estimated to be 800 feet wide, and from which we descended to the edge of the great group.
I. Plantation where we landed after crossing the river.
K. Plantation belonging to Mr. Elsworth, who served us as guide.
L. West branch of the fall, estimated to be at least 1700 feet in width.
M. Isolated rock surrounded with water, from which we studied the great fall.
N. Place where we descended to the water's edge.
O. Great larch tree on which we wrote our names.
P. Anchorage for vessels which come from Detroit and Mackinac, the first distant [..] miles and the second [..] miles.
S. Isle in the midst which divides the great cataract in two, 900 feet wide by about 1000 to 3400 feet long.

[The English "Scale of ten Miles" on the map was probably added by Mr. Marshall.]

I found here a kind of calcareous earth, which is called Surf stone. It certainly derives its formation from some hidden cause proceeding from the agitation of the waters which imbibe certain cohesive particles, but I am not sufficiently acquainted with chemistry to analyze its peculiar properties.

It is dissolvable in water though formed by it, but it acquires its solidity by being thrown upon its shores and exposed to the sun and air. It seems to have many of the qualities of soap but less greasy. It may be melted by heat, but when cold becomes a solid mass again. When found it has the appearance of Derbyshire Spar or marble, is quite white but much lighter. I saw nothing else curious here. There are great numbers of snakes amongst the rocks, particularly the rattlesnake, which delights in these retired and gloomy places. We found an Indian of the Messasauga nation fishing at the mouth of the Basin. We exchanged some friendly signs and took our leaves. We could have wished for a balloon to have ascended at once, but we were obliged to toil the same way back, in which we were often constrained to repose upon the ground. We at length arrived upon the summit, and who can speak the pleasure we received from our safe return. We had been six hours and upwards descending and ascending.

Our friend Mr. Hambleton had been under some fears for us and welcomed us back. He had prepared us a homely but wholesome repast at Ellsworth's house, which we ate voraciously. The night was advancing and we wished to return to Niagara that evening. We mounted our horses and after riding some miles in the woods, we came to a fine cultivated country interspersed with good farms. Government lately has given every possible assistance to these new settlers. After a ride of 18 miles we arrived at Butlersburg, so called from Col. Butler, who had barracks for his Corps of Loyalists and another for the savages. There are several good buildings here and an appearance of civilization. We had only to cross Niagara river and found ourselves once more in that hospitable garrison. The commanding officer, Major Campbell, to whom we had brought letters of introduction, had shown us great attentions, and continued them during our stay there. I saw very little worth remarking at Niagara Fort. The garrison consisted of 400 soldiers. The fortifications are defensible. The fort is built upon an elevated point of land which commands the entrance of the river from Lake Ontario, which is seen to great advantage.

CAPTAIN ENYS' VISIT IN 1787.

The original manuscript of the following journal is in the Dominion Archives at Ottawa. It was in the possession of a son of Captain Enys, the writer, who a number of years ago emigrated to New Zealand. At the Centennial Exposition in Philadelphia, in 1876, Dr. Selwyn, then Director of the Canadian Geological Survey, met Mr. Enys, who in the course of conversation respecting the changes that had taken place at Niagara Falls, mentioned that at his home in New Zealand he had his father's manuscript journal of his visit to Niagara in 1787. On Mr. Enys' return to New Zealand he sent the manuscript to Dr. Selwyn, who transferred it to the Archives Branch. The late Douglas Brymner, then archivist, printed it in his report for 1886. This was, it is believed, its only publication. The sketch is reproduced from a drawing preserved with the manuscript.

1787, July 18th.—From hence to Fort Slosser is about a mile & a half or two miles on a perfectly straight and good road, at which place we at length arrived, after being four hours on the road from Niagara, which is only fourteen miles. On our arrival we found dinner over but we soon got a mutton chop, which we had no sooner swallowed than we all set out to see the Falls taking Mr. Hamilton of the 53d

Regiment for our guide, who having commanded Fort Slosser for some time knew his way.

After passing through some fields and a small piece of wood, we came to the river side at an old saw-mill, about a quarter of a mile from the brink of the Falls. This view alone is worth going many miles to see. The current, which is very strong more than three miles above the Falls, is here increased by many causes, for the river which grows naturally narrower as it approaches the brink of the cataract, is here divided by a large island in the middle; it also begins to be shallow and rocky, so that from hence quite down to the brink of the Falls the water is in a continual foam and has in many parts of the distance Falls which would be much talked of were they in any other situations, which may be easily conceived from the perpendicular height which the water falls in the course of this quarter of a mile previous to its reaching the brink of the cataract, which is at least sixty feet; this many seem to think should be added to the perpendicular height of the Falls; whether it should or no I shall not presume to determine.

I already find my pen, or at least my ideas, inadequate to give any account of what is now before me, as it is not only the water which is beautiful but the island also is covered with noble trees down quite to the edge of the water; to this we must add the many small islands which have been severed from time to time from the larger one by the force of the current, and which still partake of their parent's verdure and beauty. It was with difficulty we could prevail on ourselves to leave the place, even tho' we knew we were to go to parts infinitely more beautiful. We at length, however, struck again into the wood and, passing down its skirts, Mr. H. brought us out a few yards below the Fall. Here I for one sat down for some time in silent admiration and astonishment, at a sight which I am fully persuaded no pen or pencil can ever convey across the sea. In our present situation we were too near to the highest part of the Fall, which in a kind of a sketch or plan I have annexed is marked 1, to enjoy its full beauty, but we had a tolerable good view of the great, or as it is generally called, the Horseshoe Fall, which is here marked 4, 5, 6. To give any adequate idea of the astonishing variety which here crowds upon your mind is impossible, and it may be well said to be the real sublime and beautiful conveyed in the language of nature, infinitely more strong than the united eloquence of Pitt, Fox and Burke, even if we give them the assistance of Loutherbourg to help them.

CAPT. ENYS' SKETCH OF THE FALLS.

As the water during its fall from different parts meeting the rays of the sun in different directions takes an infinite number of different colours and shades; to this we must add the numberless beautiful breaks in the water; the delightful verdure which covers the islands and neighbouring shores; the beauty of the most noble rapid which can be conceived, before it ever reaches the brink of the precipice; the astonishing column of spray which rises from the great Fall; the thundering noise which the whole makes by its fall on the heap of stones below, from whence it runs, no longer like water but absolutely in such a state of foam as to appear like a perfect river of milk, for about 100 or 150 yards, after which it resumes its natural state again, although it is still carried away by means of a strong rapid. To all this I must add the lofty banks which surround the basin into which the water falls, the tops of which are covered with noble trees quite close to the edge of these cliffs. Hence I could not help remarking to Mr. Humphry that before my arrival I expected to have been disappointed, from having my ideas raised too high by hearing so many people join in their praise, but that I was sure from this view alone no one can say too much of it.

Here some of our party wished to go down to the bottom, a thing very seldom done on this side, as well from the difficulty of the descent as that when down your view is by no means so good as on the opposite side. It was however agreed upon to make the attempt, preparatory to which Mr. Hamilton made us all take off our shoes, as in many places it is so very slippery it would have been more dangerous to attempt with them on. Our party now consisted of Mr. H. our guide, Mr. Douglas of the 65th and Mr. Brunton of the same Regiment, myself, and last of all Mr. Humphry. We all with great difficulty got down about one third part of the way. But when I saw the path by which I was to descend further I gave it up, telling Mr. Humphry that if he choose to go further I would get out of his way, which I accordingly did and he descended as low as I had done where like me he gave up the point. The other three gentlemen completed their design and on their return very candidly allowed, although they were well pleased with what they had done, now it was over, they would by no means attempt it again until ropes or something more secure were placed in the most dangerous parts, as in some of the steepest parts they were obliged to let themselves down by means of twisted stick, in the manner of the faggot band, which was tied to an old stump above, which stick had been then in use for three years. Mr. H. indeed went further and acknowledged that on reflection when at the bottom he entertained some doubts their being able to reascend. However, they all got up safe with no other loss than the feet of their stockings, which were perfectly worn out.

We next went back a few yards to the brink of the Falls and found to my surprise that we could not only approach close to the top of the Falls, but that the water was nearly on a level with the flat rock on which we stood (marked 1,) that I could without the least danger stoop and take up the water with my hand after it had fallen over the precipice. The view which we have here straight over the Falls is very fine, but not so grand as the one we had before left, except that we saw the pillar of spray to greater advantage, as the Fall from whence it proceeded appeared less in this direction than the former. I do not know how long we should have stood looking at the scene before us, if the setting of the sun had not reminded us that it was time to return, on which we began to retreat. After we had returned more than a mile, on looking back from a little eminence we could see the spray of the Fall rising to an immense height above the surrounding woods, like the large column of smoke which ascends from any large building on fire, but not of so dark a colour.

Having gone a little further we came to the house of Mr. Philip Stedman where we passed an agreeable hour in company with him and his niece. As Mr. Humphry and myself had no business at the Fort, we staid a short time after the rest of the party, and were at last going in quest of our supper without any hopes of seeing any of the Fall for the night. Notwithstanding it was the very middle of summer and the day had been extremely hot, the night was very cold, so that we had run a good deal of the way, when stopping just before the Fort gate we saw the most beautiful as well as strange appearance, that can be well conceived. It was the moon which was now just setting behind the spray of the Falls; it appeared to rise to a very uncommon height in likeness of a very dark column, but the thinner part of the spray which admitted the light through it, gave all the edge of the column a luminous appearance which looked more like a pillar fringed round with fire, than anything I can compare it to. Not wishing to keep the sight to ourselves we ran to call the rest whom we found collected round a large fire from which we could with great difficulty draw them, as they supposed it was only a story made for the purpose of drawing them from their seats by the fire, that we might ourselves get possession of them, by which means they were not out until the moon was very near gone, when from what they saw they sincerely lamented they had been so tenacious of their seats.

This over we all returned to the Fort and after a hearty supper we returned to Mr. Stedman's again to bed and slept very sound until past 7 o'clock next morning (19th), at which time from the orders which had been given to the servants over night, I was in hopes our chair and horses were on the other side of the water; in this I was again disappointed. I next hastened to the Fort with all expedition, where I found both officers and men still in bed, from whence they were soon roused and a boat and party of men got to put the chair and horses over, which we soon sent off with orders to land them on the north side of the Chipaway Creek, whilst we, having procured Mr. Stedman's light boat, remained behind to breakfast.

Breakfast being finished, we left Mr. Brunton alone at his new Government, about ten in the forenoon, and after having rowed up a mile or more under the East shore, we crossed a very large island that lies in the middle, which having gained we rowed up under its western bank for a considerable distance before we ventured to cross to the western side of the river. At length we made our crossing and landed about four miles from the Falls, at a farm of Mr. Stedman's; here Mr. Hamilton left us and striking to the left went to Fort Erie, whilst the rest of us taking the right-hand road after a walk of two miles came to Chipaway Creek where we found our horses at the house of Mr. Birch, one of the principal people in the settlement. As the squire was not at home, we were glad to wave the ceremony of a visit, so as soon as our cavalry were ready we set out toward the Falls. About another mile brought us to the head of the rapid, and a short way further we came to a mill Mr. Birch has lately built; it appears to me a very elegant piece of workmanship, and is to be both a grist and saw mill, but I am very much afraid from the rapids above it he will find it difficult, if not dangerous, to bring down boats and rafts to it, although the man who superintends it says he thinks it may be done with ease when they become better acquainted with the currents.

About 100 yards below the mill, from a point that

projects a little, we had a most delightful view of the whole rapid, which is near a mile in length and I should think three times as broad as that on the east side; the numerous falls are large in proportion, which of course renders it infinitely more grand than the one we had seen the evening before, but still it wanted those beautiful little islands with which the smaller one is adorned. In the course of this long rapid I conceive the perpendicular fall of the water is not less than 100 feet before it reaches the brink of the Fall, and so full is it of rocks and cascades that I conceive it utterly impossible that any boat can ever get down to the Fall without being overset; indeed some of the 29th Regiment whilst in these parts sent down an old boat for the purpose of seeing it go over the Fall. They went themselves below the Falls to look out for it, whilst they left men on the different points to make signals when it passed them, but some of those near the Fall nor the Gentlemen at the bottom never saw any thing more of it.

As the day was now advancing, we could not stay so long here as I could have wished for fear of being stinted in time at the Fall itself, for which we now set off, and very soon reached the nearest house to it and got permission from Mr. Elsworth the owner to put our horses in his stable; but all the family being busy carrying their corn we could get no one to go with us. However, as Mr. Humphry had been here before, he undertook to guide us, and we accordingly set out under his directions. Not far from the house we came to the edge of a very steep bank, which we descended through a very deep ravine or gully, not without some dread of rattlesnakes, for whose habitation this place seemed particularly suited, and the pass being so very narrow and full of stones and stumps, that had any such thing been there it would be difficult to avoid it. After going some distance we got to the bottom of this nasty place and found ourselves again on level ground, which took us to the brink of the Fall at a place from its appearance called the Table rock, over a part of which the water rolls. This being the nearest part to the Great Fall, you are of course almost stunned with its noise and perfectly wet with the continual mist arising from the bottom, in form of a pillar, which having gained a sufficient height is separated by the wind and falls like small rain or mist. From hence we had a much better view of the Falls than that which we had the preceding evening, but like that we were too near the object to see it to perfection. I am told many people think this is the best view in which you can place the Fall, but I rather think it can only be such as have never given themselves the trouble to search for any other. Here, they say, you can likewise dip up the water after it has passed the brink of the precipice. However true this may be, it is not so perfectly so as on the opposite side, as here it is only a small branch of the Fall you approach; on the other side it is actually the main body of water itself, as may be seen in the little sketch of the top of the Fall before given; the former or Fort Slosser side being marked 1 in the plan; I am now speaking of 8. The Table Rock is a very large flat rock projecting from the bank and overhanging its base very much, by which means it forms one of the best modes of determining the height of the Fall, being exactly upon the same level and projecting so much that a line let down from its summit will drop very nearly at the water's edge at the bottom. But whatever methods may have been taken to ascertain its height, that of both sides is very well determined, being agreed by all hands to be 170 feet on the east, or Fort Slosser side, whilst from the Table Rock it is only 140, but this 30 feet if it is taken from the perpendicular of the Fall adds to the noble rapid that is above it.

Having staid a long while we at length set off from hence, hoping to find a way to a point not many hundred yards below where we now were, without returning to the top of the bank again; in this, however, we were disappointed, finding the brake too thick and the ground too swampy to admit of our passage, although I hear there is a possibility of going to those who are acquainted with the place. This was not our case, so we were obliged to ascend the gully by which we came, at the top of which we turned off to the right and soon found a path leading to another gully of the same kind, through which we a second time descended the bank. Having got down to the level ground, we could find no kind of path; we therefore marked the trees as we went, thinking they might serve us as a guide on our return. Thus, guided by the noise of the Falls more than by any thing else, we soon came to the brink of the clift and striking off a little to our left found the place we were in search of, and which I believe is now called Painter's Point, from a man of that name in whose ground it is. Here we found a spot which had been in some measure cleared (by Lieutenant Tinling of the 29th when he was acting Engineer at Niagara) on purpose to give you a good view of the whole of this grand object at once, and it most certainly is the best view of any on a level with the Fall, as here every part is by far more equidistant than in any other point you can look at it from. From hence you look directly against the island which is in the centre, having the Great Fall to the right and the smaller one to the left; from this place you have also a better view of a small Fall on the east side of Goat Island which is called the Montmorrency Fall, and which is said to disembogue more water in the course of a year than the famous fall of that name near Quebec, which perhaps it may, but I do not think it is so broad as that Fall. Perhaps its very diminutive appearance here may be only occasioned by its being placed in the midst of such astonishing large ones, as the nearest computation that has ever been made allows the breadth of the Fall from one side to the other to be 1,300 yards, including all the turns which there are in the summit and the island in the centre; which last may be something more than 100 yards broad.

I could willingly have staid here much longer than we did, but having determined to go down to the bottom we were obliged to hasten towards the place where you descend. This place lies some yards to the left of Painter's Point, from which you pass all the way on the brink of the precipice, nor is it easy to find the opening unless you are acquainted with it, as you pass round a small bush where you find some stumps and roots which assist you for the first three or four yards of a very steep bank, when you come to a place quite perpendicular for perhaps about twelve feet. Here they have put what they call Indian-ladders, which is no more than a tree about a foot in diameter with notches cut in its sides that is placed rather slantwise to answer the purpose of going down. Not far after you pass the first of these ladders, you come to a second, not quite so long, after which you descend through a very steep gully full of rocks and stumps, most part of the way being assisted by the branches of the neighboring trees. It surprised me to find that the descent was so easy to what I had always been led to think it, which I conceive proceeds from many who have never tried it but speak from hearsay; indeed I am fully persuaded that many who say they have been at the bottom never have been there, as they are frequently betrayed by the erroneous accounts they give of the lower region, which in fact is, I believe, visited by but few.

Once arrived at the bottom, you receive ample reward for the pains the descent has occasioned you. If this noble scene inspire you with awe when above, it may be easily conceived how much it must be augmented when you get to the bottom, absolutely into the very basin whence all this sheet of water falls. You are no sooner clear of the wood than you have a full and complete view of all the magnificent scene, in which all the various shades which the water receives in its fall, either from the projecting rocks or from the intersection of the rays of the sun, appear to the greatest of all possible advantage; besides which you here see nothing of the rapid above, your prospect being confined to the perpendicular fall and the basin which receives it, but then that fall appears to much greater advantage and much higher than it does from any of the views above.

Having sat down a few minutes to rest after our descent and drank a glass or two of wine, we proceeded to get as near the Fall as we conveniently could. This is by far the most difficult and I may add, dangerous part of the day's journey. The distance from hence to the fall, is very considerable and you have no kind of road, the way lying along the beach, which is formed of large stones which have from time to time fallen from the high clifts which overhang most part of the way. These rocks lie just as they happen to have fallen, so that sometimes you are obliged to climb over them, at others to creep under them, whilst they seem to threaten your destruction every step you take; many of them appear as if they would fall every moment, being only ballanced on a point, others seem to have no other support than trees which have fallen at the same time with themselves, which appear very slight supporters for such immense masses of stone; then as the apertures among these rocks are not large enough to admit of your walking through, you are obliged to creep through them on your hands and knees, or slide through them on your back, every moment in danger of meeting with either a water or a rattle snake, for both of which this place is very remarkable, particularly the latter, and the very best part of the road lies over a parcel of large round stones that slide under your feet. Notwithstanding all these dangers, such is the beauty of the surrounding prospect and such the pleasing kind of awe which I felt at the time, that it never once struck my mind that I was in the least danger until the whole was over and we had got back again to the entrance of the wood.

But to return to my tale. Having scrambled over these rocks until we got pretty near the Fall, we found the spray begin to fall like hard rain. Here Mr. Humphry stopped, but Mr. Douglas and myself went on until we got within about twenty yards of the Falls. Here we were in some doubt whether or no we should strip and go as far as we could under the Fall; this we however at length rejected, as we never found any one pretends to have gone further than under the first small shoot, which we thought unworthy the trouble of undressing for. There are reports of people that have gone under the great shoot but who they were I could not learn, although I have examined several who asserted they had been under the Falls of Niagara, yet, when questioned closely upon the subject, it appeared to have been only the small spout they had been under. Yet I by no means mean to assert there is not that kind of cavity betwixt the under part of the rock and the fall itself, that would admit of a man going under for some distance. On the contrary from the Table Rock being so very much undermined near its base, I conceive it to be highly probable the rock over which the Fall rolls is the same, but as the falling of the spray is so very thick and troublesome as to prevent your seeing and almost to prevent your breathing even where we were, I do not conceive it is possible for a man to exist under the great shoot itself.

However, we did not advance thus far without finding something which had so far as I could find never been spoken of before. Within a few yards of the place we turned round, I could perceive a very strong smell of sulphur, which I remarked to Mr. Douglas and on further examination we perceived a small rill which descended from the rocks above and all the stones over which it passed seemed covered with a whitish kind of slime. This induced me to taste the water, which I found to be exactly the same as the water at Harrowgate, in Yorkshire. Mr. Douglas also tasted of the same water and directly exclaimed, "it is just like the washings of a gun barrel," although he declares he had never heard the Harrowgate water compared to that mixture.

Having staid here for some time contemplating the grandeur of the object before us, our time passed away insensibly until we found by our watches that it was high time we should turn our backs upon the scene from which we had received so much delight. On our return we employed ourselves in picking up a kind of stone which is said to be the spray of the Fall petrified, but whether it is or no, I will not pretend to determine; this much I can say, that it grows or forms itself in cavities in the clift about half way to the top, from whence it falls from time to time; its composition is a good deal like a piece of white marble which has been burnt in the fire, so that it may be pulverized with ease. Whatever may be its composition, it does not appear that it will bear to be exposed to the air, as some pieces which seem to have fallen longer than the rest are quite soft, while such as have lately fallen are of a much harder nature.

Having again made our way back to the edge of the wood where we were to reascend, we sat down to take some refreshment, very well satisfied to have seen everything worth our notice except the rainbow, which very often forms itself in the spray. During the time we were lamenting the loss of this object, it made its appearance in a most perfect state across the highest part of the Fall, which made our sight of this place as complete as possible.

We now began our ascent and after again visiting Painter's Point, in our way we came to the place where we had marked the trees; we found one or two of the first but had done it so very ill that we could not trace our way back by them. We therefore struck into the wood and endeavoured to keep the sound of the Falls directly behind us, by which means we found our way by a much nearer route than the one we had descended, from which we again soon reached the house we had left our horses at, after an absence of five hours and a half, from which time we had been employed walking about the place.

It may not be improper here to take notice of an opinion which is held by some people of this place, who seem to think the original situation of the Falls was at the landing which as before observed is seven miles from where they now are, and that through a series of years the water has worn away the channel that distance. Among those who favour this opinion is a Mr. Hamilton, a merchant at Niagara and a man of very good understanding, who says also that he has examined the face of the adjacent country, which has confirmed his opinion, and in particular conceives the place which has before been taken notice of by the name of the Lion's Den, to have been made by a channel of the river formerly passing through it. How far this may be true I do not know; I did not hear this opinion until after I had seen the place, at which time no such idea ever entered my head. The principal reasons they seem to give for this opinion are two: First, from the abrupt rise of the bank of the river at the Landing, which from being of a moderate height and almost every where accessible from the water's edge, they became at once very high and perpendicular clifts; at the same time the river becomes much more narrow and rapid than before. The second reason seems to have more reason in it, and is, that according to their language the Falls have altered their position or retreated since the memory of men. Having made all the inquiries I could concerning this movement, I found that about twenty years since, there was a projecting rock at the end of the centre island which had fallen and seems to be the only ground work for this strong contested opinion. One thing I must grant, that it is possible that in a very long series of years they may alter a little and for this reason: the spray rising from the bottom continually striking against the clifts wears it away and forms a kind of cavity over which a large rock projects, as the Table Rock already mentioned, which, when it becomes so undermined that it is not able to sustain the weight of water which overflows it in great floods, must naturally fall. How long it may take the water to excavate its clifts in this manner I cannot determine; all I can say is, the place where the rock fell twenty years ago does not yet appear to be the least worn by its influence, nor does any one pretend to remember the Table Rock any other than it now is, projecting very far over its base. By which I conceive we may fairly conclude it will take many centuries to bring about this revolution, which when done only alters one small part of the Fall for a yard or two. At that rate, how long it would have taken to have retreated from the landing I shall leave to those who pretend from such causes to ascertain the age of our terrestrial globe. But even if we should for a moment grant the possibility of their favourite maxim, what is become of the immense quantity of stone, which must from time to time have fallen during its movement. This seems to me to be a question none can answer, certain a great quantity of stone must have been in a channel above seven miles long and from a half to a whole mile broad, and from seventy to eighty feet deep. Had it fallen in such quantities as it is natural to suppose it is very strange the fall should keep its present perpendicular form; it is by far more natural to think had this been the case that these immense rocks, reposing where they fell, would have altered the Fall from a perpendicular to a strong rapid. But say the advocators for this opinion, the force of the water has driven them away from its foot. This may also be true in a small measure, for where it is, the rocky part of the river would not break off so abruptly just at the same place where the mountain ends, which is at present the case, for not more than two hundred yards from the end of this rocky rapid part which is the spot they say the Fall originally occupied, the River expands itself and becomes deep, muddy and tranquil, which course it continues for about 9 miles by the water to the mouth, the outside of which is encumbered with a bar of sand.

I also when at the Fall observed another circumstance which seems to be against their having been once so far down the river. Below the present situation of them is a circle of more than a quarter perhaps a mile or more in diameter whilst the outlet is not so wide. I conceive this part has been widened by the same means the Falls have retired, as when you get beyond the influence of the spray the river assumes its natural breadth. Speaking to Mr. Birch, who lives at the mouth of the Chipaway Creek, he said he had perceived a regular flux and reflux in the Creek, resembling the tide of the Sea. Mr. Hamilton who I have before mentioned, says it is not a regular flux or reflux at all, but that occasionally the current runs up instead of down, and what appears at first more extraordinary is, that the Creek has its source to the West and runs to the Eastward yet it is a Westerly or a wind directly down the Creek which occasions the Current to run up it to the Westward.

This he accounted for in some measure to my satisfaction. It is well known that Lake Erie is to the Westward of this place in which a Westerly wind has great powers and driving its waters into this outlet meets with no resistance until it comes to the Falls where not being able to empty itself so fast as it comes from the Lake it causes the waters above the rapids to rise. Now this Creek being a dead swampy Creek, just above the rapid, some of the repulsed water forces itself into it and counteracting its own current favours one of the contrary way.

JAMES SHARAN IN 1787.

An exceedingly rare book is "The Adventures of James Sharan: compiled from the Journal, written during his voyages and travels in the Four Quarters of the Globe." A neat little demi-octavo of 240 pages, it was printed at Baltimore in 1808. "The publication," says the preface, "owes its appearance from the press, to the solicitations of a great number of respectable persons in the neighborhood in which the author resides," which, the reader presently learns, was Charleston, S. C.

According to this narrative, James Sharan was born in Liverpool in 1762; was stolen, when a lad of ten, by a press-gang, and carried off to sea on board the Princess. They fought with a pirate, and after a desperate battle, in which twenty-five of the Princess crew were killed, the pirate was taken, and towed into Plymouth, Eng. In August, 1772, having refitted, they sailed again. Many adventures follow, but there is a break in the journal from 1772 to 1777, when we find the author embarked on another cruise. The next year he was injured in an engagement and left in a New York hospital. When recovered, he forsook the sea, went to Philadelphia and wandered inland. Then follows an interesting account of his life, first as an apprentice wheelwright, then as an itinerant trader. He prospered, and made various voyages to Europe, on one of which he narrowly escaped drowning. He carried furs to Scotland, and brought back Irish linens. A venture in tobacco paid well. In the spring of 1787, being at New Orleans, "I resolved," he says, "to penetrate into the United States by a course up the river Mississippi, and endeavor to find my way through the forests and Indian tribes, until I had seen that wonder, the Falls of Niagara." He had experiences with the Spanish, the French, and various Indian tribes. "I pursued my way through the North Western Territory, and after the lapse of several weeks, came to a settlement of Americans near the Lakes. I had during my journey met with several tribes of Indians, and a considerable number of traders, by whom I was supplied, and received every direction to reach the object of my desire, the Falls of Niagara."

The absence of dates and precise data, gives a dubious quality to Sharan's pages. If we take his word for it, it was, apparently, in the summer or autumn of 1787, or perhaps later, when he reached Niagara, of which he gives the following account:

The waterfall of Niagara, by far the greatest in the world hitherto discovered, is about ten miles from the fort of the same name. The course of the river is from S. S. E. to N. N. W. and the rock of the fall forms a kind of figure like a hollow circle or horse shoe. Above the fall in the middle of the river, is an island about 300 yards long; the lower end of which is just at the edge of the fall. Before the water comes to this island, it runs but slowly compared with its motion afterwards, when it grows extremely rapid, running with surprising swiftness before it comes to the fall. It is perfectly white, and in several places is thrown high up into the air. The water that runs down on the west side is in greater abundance, and whiter than that on the opposite side; and seems almost to outfly an arrow in swiftness. When a person is at the fall and looks up the river, he may perceive that the water is every where exceedingly steep, almost like the side of a hill; but on looking at the fall itself, the astonishment it occasions is impossible to be described.

The height of the fall is exactly 137 feet; and when the water is come to the bottom, it flies back to a great height in the air. The noise may sometimes be heard at the great distance of forty miles. The peculiar strength of the sound which is sometimes heard, is an infallible prognostic of rough or rainy weather.

From the place where the water falls there arises a prodigious vapour, like a thick smoke, insomuch that when viewed at a distance, a stranger might suppose, that the nations [natives?] had set the forests on fire. These vapours rise very high in the air when it is calm, but are dispersed by the wind when it blows hard. If any person go into this vapour, or if the wind blow it on him, it is so penetrating that in a few moments, he will be as wet as if he had been emersed in water.

Some persons are of opinion, that when birds happen to fly into the smoke of the fall, they immediately drop down and perish in the water; either because their wings become wet, or that the tremendous noise of the fall astonishes and confounds them: but others think that this opinion is merely fancy; because among the great number of birds found dead about the fall, there are no other sorts than such as mostly live in the water, swans, geese, ducks, teal, &c. Great flocks of these animals are often seen going to destruction in the following manner: They swim in the river above the fall, and so are carried down lower and lower by the water; and as water fowl are commonly pleased with being carried by the stream, they indulge themselves in this pleasure, till the rapidity of the water, renders it impossible for them to rise, and they are consequently hurried down the precipice.

In the months of September and October, such prodigious quantities of dead water fowl are found every morning below the fall, that they afford ample subsistence for the garrison at the fort. Here are also frequently found the bodies of deer, bears, and other animals which have attempted to cross the water above the fall.

A variety of melancholy instances of persons having lost their lives in this fall, is recorded, but few are more affecting than the following, which is related by a traveller, who explored the cataract.

"An unfortunate Indian was reposing in a state of inebriety in his canoe, which was properly secured at the distance of some miles above the cataracts, while his wife sat on the shore to watch his slumbers. After some time, a sailor from one of the vessels on the lake, arrived at the spot, and took some indecent liberties with the Indian female. The woman naturally attempted to rouse her husband, but before she could effect her design, the brutal mariner, cut the cord of the canoe and set it adrift. The little vessel glided down the stream, and in the space of a few minutes it was seen to enter the rapids.

"The Indian, awakened by the violent motion of the waves, started up, and on perceiving his perilous situation, he grasped his paddle with a look of inexpressible horror; but finding it absolutely impossible to stem the force of the current, he calmly wrapped himself up in his blanket and resumed his former position at the bottom of the canoe. In the space of a few moments, he was hurried down the precipice and was never discovered more."

The following instance of magnanimity and heroism in an attempt to save human life deserves insertion here; not only as a proof that those whom we call savages, possess the most tender feelings of our nature, but also as it may excite a blush in the cheek of many selfish, brutal, hard-hearted persons who call themselves civilized Christians.

There is an island in the middle of the fall which was formerly supposed inaccessible; but an accident that happened about sixty years ago made it appear otherwise.

Two Indians went out from Fort Niagara to hunt upon an island that is situated in the middle of the river above the great fall, which was then stocked with abundance of deer; but having indulged too freely in the use of some French brandy, they fell asleep, and their canoe drove back with the stream until it approached that island which is in the middle of the fall. Here they were awakened by the noise of the cataract, and began to give themselves over as lost, but after some vigorous exertions, they effected a landing upon the island. At first they exulted in the idea of their escape; but upon cool reflection they found themselves hardly in a better state than if they had gone down the fall, since they had no other alternative than either to throw themselves down the same, or to perish with hunger. After some time, however, hard necessity put them on invention; and as they found plenty of wood on the island, they made a ladder of the bark of the lind tree, in order to reach the water below; one end of this ladder they fastened to a large tree that grew on the side of a rock above the fall and let the other end to the water. By this contrivance they descended to the bottom in the middle of the fall; and then threw themselves out into the water, thinking to swim on shore. Scarcely, however, had they begun to swim, before they were thrown back with violence against the rock from which they came, and after several fruitless attempts they were compelled to re-ascend to the island. After some time they discovered Indians on the shore, who appeared to pity their misfortune, but gave them little hope of assistance. These ran to inform the commandant of the fort of the situation of their friends and he soon projected the means of their deliverance in the following manner.

The water that runs on the east side of the island is shallow, especially toward the shore. The commandant, therefore, caused some poles to be made and pointed with iron, and by the help of these, two Indians offered to walk to the island to save their unfortunate brethren or to perish in the attempt. Each had two such poles in his hands, to set to the bottom of the stream in order to keep him steady;

in this manner they safely reached the island, and brought away the poor creatures, who were almost perishing for want of food.

On the west side of this island, are some small rocks; and in former times a part of the rock at this side of the fall hung over in such a manner, that the water which fell perpendicularly from it left a vacancy below, so that people could go under between the rock and the water; but some years ago, the prominent part broke off and fell down. The breadth of the fall as it runs in a semi-circle is about three hundred feet. [!]

Every day when the sun shines, from ten o'clock in the morning till two in the afternoon may be seen, below the fall, the similitude of a beautiful rainbow, and sometimes two; within one another. The brightness and clearness of this phenomenon depends on the quantity of vapour that results from the spray of the cataract; for when the wind drives the vapours away the rainbow disappears; but as soon as new vapours come, it resumes its former appearance. The rock of the fall consists of a grey lime stone.

It is hardly necessary to correct any statements in the foregoing. Many of them seem based on what earlier travelers had published, Peter Kalm in particular, rather than on Sharan's own observation. He says that from Niagara he "traveled through the Gennessee country to Albany," and so on to New York, but all with a suspicious absence of dates. The next date in the narrative is February 17, 1789, when he reached his home at Charleston, "having traveled during my absence more than 10,000 miles, principally on foot, and alone, and having been from home nearly twenty-two months."

His subsequent travels took him to Africa, where he had experiences recalling those of Mungo Park among the Moors; to China, and elsewhere, a most adventurous and varied career.

ANDREW ELLICOTT, 1789.

The following description of the Falls of Niagara is from a letter by Andrew Ellicott to Dr. Benjamin Rush, dated "Niagara, Dec. 10, 1789." It is here taken from the *Massachusetts Magazine* of July, 1790. It appeared in several other publications, in the United States and Europe, at about that time.

NIAGARA, Dec. 10, 1789.

DEAR SIR—Among the many natural curiosities which this country affords, the Cataract of Niagara is infinitely the greatest. In order to have a tolerable idea of this stupendous fall of water, it will be necessary to conceive that part of the country in which Lake Erie is situated, to be elevated above that which contains Lake Ontario about three hundred feet. The slope which separates the upper and lower country is generally very steep, and in many places almost perpendicular. It is formed by horizontal strata of stone, great part of which is what we commonly call limestone. The slope may be traced from the north side of Lake Ontario, near the Bay of Toronto, round the west end of the Lake; thence its direction is generally east, between Lake Ontario and Lake Erie—it crosses the strait of Niagara and the Cheneseco river, after which it becomes lost in the country towards the Seneca Lake. It is to this slope that our country is indebted, both for the Cataract of Niagara and the great Falls of the Cheneseco.

The Cataract of Niagara was formerly down at the northern side of the slope, near to that place which is now known by the name of the Landing; but from the great length of time, added to the great quantity of water, and distance which it falls, the solid stone is worn away for about seven miles up towards Lake Erie, and a chasm is formed, which no person can approach without horror.—Down this chasm the water rushes with a most astonishing velocity, after it makes the great pitch. In going up the road near this chasm, the fancy is constantly engaged in the contemplation of the most romantic and awful prospects imaginable, till, at length, the eye catches the Falls:—the imagination is instantly arrested, and you admire in silence! The river is about one hundred and thirty-five poles wide at the Falls, and the perpendicular pitch one hundred and fifty feet. The fall of this vast body of water produces a sound which is frequently heard at a distance of twenty miles, and a sensible tremulous motion in the earth for some poles round. A heavy fog, or cloud, is constantly ascending from the Falls, in which rainbows may always be seen when the sun shines. This fog, or spray, in the winter season, falls upon the neighboring trees, where it congeals, and produces a most beautiful crystalline appearance. This remark is equally applicable to the Falls of Cheneseco.

The difficulty which would attend levelling the rapids in the chasm, prevented my attempting it; but I conjectured the water must descend at least sixty-five feet. The perpendicular pitch at the Cataract is one hundred and fifty feet; to these add fifty-eight feet, which the water falls in the last half mile, immediately above the Falls, and we have two hundred and seventy-three feet, which the water falls in the distance of about seven miles and an half. If either ducks or geese inadvertently alight in the rapids above the great Cataract, they are incapable of getting on the wing again, and are instantly hurried on to destruction.

There is one appearance at this Cataract worthy of some attention, and which I do not remember to have seen noted by any writer. Just below the great pitch, the water and foam may be seen puffed up in spherical figures, nearly as large as common cocks of hay; they burst at the top, and project a column of spray to a prodigious height; they then subside, and are succeeded by others, which burst in like manner. This appearance is most conspicuous about half way between the island that divides the Falls and the west side of the strait, where the largest column of water descends.   I am, &c.,

ANDREW ELLICOTT.

This description was widely printed. It appeared in the *Columbian Magazine* for June, 1790. It was printed in the

Massachusetts Magazine, July, 1790. On being reprinted in the *European Magazine,* October, 1793, the editor added this comment: "It is said by those who have visited this stupendous Cataract, that the descent into the chasm is exceedingly difficult, because of the great height of the banks. A person having descended, however, may go up to the bottom of the Falls, and take shelter behind the torrent, between the falling water and the precipice, where there is a space sufficient to contain a number of people in perfect safety, and where conversation may be carried on without much interruption from the noise, which is less here than at a considerable distance. This is not unworthy the attention of the philosophic reader."

PATRICK CAMPBELL, 1791.

Patrick Campbell, who traveled through Canada and the region of the Lower Lakes in 1791-2, sojourned for some time on the Niagara. The pages of his exceedingly rare book ("Travels in the interior inhabited parts of North America," etc., Edinburgh, 1793), afford many data for our local history, but little by way of description. He prints Ellicott's figures of the height of the falls, and adds the following note:

A description of these tremendous Falls has been so often attempted by preceding travellers, without giving the least idea adequate to the grandeur of the scene, that, lest I split on the same rock, I will not essay it here; I shall therefore only remark, that there is an island of a mile or two long, and about a quarter broad, which divides the stream about two-thirds over. This island is clad with poor spruce pine, and so overrun with Rattlesnakes, that it was dangerous for any person to walk through it, until a parcel of Swine were put in, which nearly rooted them out. Hogs are so fond of Snakes, that if once they get a hold, should they be so hard bitten by a strong Rattlesnake as to make them squeel, which sometimes happens, yet they hold fast until the Snake is devoured. It is said a Hog sometimes swells when severely bitten by a Rattlesnake, but that a crevice bursts open between the hoofs, through which the venom is discharged, the swelling subsides, and the Hog soon becomes as well as formerly.

DUNCAN INGRAHAM IN 1792.

The following narrative, entitled "Extract from a Letter from a Gentleman upon his return from Niagara," dated August 8, 1792, was printed in the *Collections* of the Massachusetts Historical Society for 1792. The author is said to be Duncan Ingraham—possibly an ancestor of the distinguished naval officer of that name.

I am just returned from Niagara, about 560 miles west of Boston. I went first to Albany, from thence to Schenectada, about sixteen miles; this had been a very considerable place of trade, but is now falling to decay: It was supported by the Indian traders; but this business is so arrested by traders far in the country, that very little of it reaches so far down; it stands upon the Mohawk river, about 9 miles above the Falls, called the Cohoes; but this I take to be the Indian name for the falls: Its chief business is to receive the merchandize from Albany, and put it into batteaux, to go up the river, and forward to Albany such produce of the back country as is sent to market. After leaving Schenectada, I travelled over a most beautiful country of eighty miles to Fort Schuyler, where I forded the Mohawk: This extent was the scene of British and Savage cruelty, during the late war, and they did not cease, while any thing remained to destroy. What a contrast now! every house and barn rebuilt, the pastures crowded with cattle, sheep, etc., and the lap of Ceres full. Most of the land on each side of the Mohawk river, is a rich flat, highly cultivated with every species of grain, the land on each side the flats, rising in agreeable slopes; this, added to the view of a fine river passing through the whole, gives the beholder the most pleasing sensations imaginable.

I passed next through Whitestown. It would appear to you, my friend, on hearing the relation of events in the western country, that the whole was fable; and if you were placed in Whitestown, or Clinton, ten miles west from Fort Schuyler, and see the progress of improvement, you would believe it enchanted ground. You would there view an extensive well built town, surrounded by highly cultivated fields, which spot in the year 1783 was the "haunt of tribes" and the hiding place of wolves, now a flourishing happy situation, containing about six thousand people. Clinton stands a little south of Whitestown, and is a very large thriving town. After passing Clinton, there are no inhabitants upon the road, until you reach Oneida, an Indian town, the first of the Six Nations; it contains about five hundred and fifty inhabitants; here I slept, and found the natives very friendly. The next day I went to Onondaga, leaving the Oneida lake on the right, and the Onondaga lake on the left, each a few miles distant. I slept at Onondaga, at the house of a Mr. —— who is employed in boiling down the waters of the salt springs, which are about 7 miles north of his house, for supplying the country with salt—he told me that he made about fifty bushels per week, which he sold at five shillings per bushel, but that any quantity may be made, and at a less price; these springs are in the State reservation, and are a wonderful benefit to the country, every part of which is so united by lakes and rivers as to render the supply of this bulky and necessary article very easy. Independent of our own settlements we can supply the British in the whole of Upper Canada. Thirty-five miles from this place I struck the Cayuga Lake. The road is tolerable for a new country; the land excellent, and very heavy timbered. There are but three houses upon this road. This lake is from about thirty-five to forty miles long, about two miles wide, and abounds with salmon, bass, catfish, eels, and many other kinds of fish. This lake empties itself into what is called Three Rivers, joining the waters of the Oneida Lake, and then proceeds by Oswego into Ontario. On each side the Cayuga Lake is a ferry house and good attendance given.

Twelve miles west of the Cayuga I struck the Canada Saga lake—no inhabitant upon this road—this lake is the handsomest piece of water I ever beheld; its length and breadth nearly that of Cayuga, into which it empties. Upon a pretty slope, on the new part of this lake, stands a town, called Geneva; it has a fine effect from the opposite shore, but disappoints you when you arrive at it. It consists of about twenty log houses, three or four frame buildings, and as many idle persons as can live in them. Eighteen miles lower, on the same side of this lake stands the Friend's Settlement, founded by Jemima Wilkinson; there are eighty families in it, each has a fine farm, and are quiet, moral, industrious people. There is a road from the Friend's Settlement nearly completed, across the country, to Genesee river, forty-five miles. I went from Geneva to Canadaqua, sixteen miles, crossing the outlet of Canadaqua lake, just as I entered the town. This is a settlement made by Mr. Phelps, and promises to be a very flourishing one; there are now about thirty houses situated on a pleasant slope from the lake, and the adjacent farms are very thriving. The Indians are settled on all the reservations made by this State, and are to be met with at every settlement of whites, in quest of rum!

From Canadaqua I travelled about twenty-six miles through a fine country, with many settlements forming; this brought me to Genesee river. On this river a great many farms are laying out; sixty-five miles from its mouth is a town marked by the name of Williamsburg, and will in all probability be a place of much trade; in the present situation of things it is remote, when considered in a commercial point of view; but should the fort of Oswego be given up, and the lock navigation be completed, there will not be a carrying place between New-York and Williamsburg. The present carrying places are as follow, viz: Albany to Schenectada, sixteen miles—the Little Falls, on the Mohawk river, two miles—from the head of the Mohawk to Wood Creek, one mile—Oswego Falls, two miles—Genesee Falls, two miles. Thus you see there is only twenty-three miles to cut and lock, in order to carry commerce by water, through an extent of country capable of maintaining several millions of people. The famous Genesee flats lie on the borders of Genesee river; they are about twenty miles in length, and about four miles wide; the soil is remarkably rich, quite clear of trees, and producing grass near ten feet high. I estimate these flats to be well worth 200,000 £. as they now lie. They are mostly the property of the Indians. Taking a view of this country altogether, I do not know such an extent of ground so good. Cultivation is easy, and the land is grateful. The progress of settlement is so rapid, that you and myself may very probably see the day when we can apply these lines to the Genesee country,

> "Here happy millions their own lands possess,
> No tyrant awes them, nor no lords oppress."

Many times did I break out in an enthusiastic frenzy, anticipating the probable situation of this wilderness twenty years hence. All that reason can ask, may be obtained by the industrious hand; the only danger to be feared is, that luxuries will flow too cheap.

After I had reached the Genesee river, curiosity led me on to Niagara, ninety miles—not one house or white man the whole way. The only direction I had was an Indian path, which sometimes was doubtful. The first day I rode fifty miles, through swarms of musquetoes, gnats, &c. beyond all description. At eight o'clock in the evening I reached an Indian town, called Tonnoraunto—it contains many hundreds of the savages, who live in very tolerable houses, which they make of timber and cover with bark. By signs I made them understand me, and for a little money they cut me limbs and bushes sufficient to erect a booth, under which I slept very quietly, on the grass.

The next day I pursued my journey, nine miles of which lay through a very deep swamp; with some difficulty I got through, and about sun-down arrived at the fort of Niagara: Here the centinel inquired from whence we came; upon his being told, he called the sergeant of the day, who escorted us to the captain of the guard, he asked our names (a Mr. ——, of ——, was with me), and said he supposed we came upon our private business, &c.—he sent us to the commandant who entered our names, and offered us a pass to go over to the British side, which we accepted. Quite fatigued, we were happy to find a tavern, and something to eat; a few hours' sleep brought me again to myself. This fort is now garrisoned by the 5th regiment, commanded formerly by Earl Piercey, and had the honour of dancing yankee doodle on the plains of Cambridge, 19th April, 1775. The commander of the fort is a Col. Smith. The day after our arrival we crossed the river Erie to the town of Niagara where probably the British fort will be built, when the present one is given up. We met Col. B[utler]. This is the man who did so much execution in the late war with the Indians, upon the Mohawk river, Schohary and Cherry Valley. We found him holding a council with a body of the chiefs who were at Philadelphia in April last, informing him what they had done there. A Mr. Johnson, some relation of the famous Sir John Johnson, interpreter to the Indians, was also present; and I have no doubt remaining but they effaced every favourable impression made on their minds by presents from Congress. I see enough to convince me of the absurdity of our endeavours to hold the savages by presents, while the British are situated at Detroit, Niagara, &c. They have all their clothing, cooking utensils, ammunition, &c. served almost as regularly as the troops on garrison; if they want provisions they get it free.

Those tribes called the Six Nations we are at peace with and take much pains to cultivate a good understanding, but we deceive ourselves. The old men, the women, and the children remain at home inactive while all the young warriors join the fighting powers against us—this is all they could do, if we were at open war with them. An Indian becomes a miserable being when deprived of his hunting-ground, and surrounded with cellars of rum or whisky. The whole Six Nations live on grounds called the State Reservations, and are intermediate spaces settled on both sides by white people; this has a tendency to drive off the game, and if by chance they kill a bear, or a deer, his skin goes at once for rum; in this way they are become poor enervated creatures. They cannot keep together a great while, and I expect they will quit all this part of the country, and retire over the lakes Ontario and Erie. Their whole number is about 6000, of which 1000 are warriors—how contemptible compared with their former greatness! The leading men of these Six Nations, or what they call Chiefs, were on the road with me going to Buffaloe Creek, to hold a council; their object I was informed was to use their influence with the hostile tribes to make a peace. This will have no effect! Power is the influence with Indians; this alone will give us peace. I see some of the Indians who fought the battle at the Miami; and by an interpreter received a very tolerable account of the action; they were of opinion that our troops did not do their duty.

Col. B. told me that the only way to make a peace with the Indians was to apply to Lord Dorchester, or the commander in chief at Quebec, and let him appoint some of the Commanders of the garrisons, say Detroit, Niagara, &c. to meet on the part of the British, to draw a line that shall be deemed right and reasonable between the Americans and Indians, and have the treaty guaranteed to the Indians by the British. I spurned at the idea, and told Col. Butler, that it was my wish, whenever Americans became so contemptible, that the whole country might be annihilated.

I visited the great curiosity, the falls, and must refer you to Mr. Ellicott's account of them in the *Columbian Magazine* for June, 1790.

I cannot help being of opinion that Indians (or what are called Redmen) never were intended to live in a state of civil society. There never was, I believe, an instance of an Indian forsaking his habits and savage manners, any more than a bear his ferocity.

The Rev. Mr. Kirkland, who acts as missionary among the Oneidas, has taken all the pains that a man can take, but his whole flock are Indians still, and like the bear which you can muffle and lead out to dance to the sound of musick, becomes again a bear when his muffler is removed and the musick ceases. The Indians will attend publick worship and sing extremely well, following Mr. Kirkland's notes; but whenever the service is over, they wrap themselves in their blankets, and either stand like cattle on the sunny side of a house, or lie before a fire. This is their mode of passing life: even the bold energy of their forefathers, which was conspicuous in the chace, is unstrung in their descendants, and instead of sliding to the grave "like a shock of corn in its full ear" they become ripe for it in youth, and often find it by the most disgraceful means.

BENJAMIN SMITH BARTON, 1798.

Benjamin Smith Barton, professor of Materia Medica, Natural History and Botany in the University of Pennsylvania, visited Niagara Falls in 1798. He published the following account in the Philadelphia *Medical and Physical Journal* in 1804. His pseudo-scientific observations on the recession of the falls, feeble at best, were controverted by Felix Robertson of Tennessee, in a letter to the editor of the *Journal*, dated Philadelphia, Feb. 9, 1805.

The falls are formed by a general descent of the country between Lake Erie and Lake Ontario of about 300 feet, the slope of which is generally very steep, and, in many places, almost perpendicular. This general description of the country is observable for about 100 miles to the east and above 200 miles to the west, or rather northwest, of the falls.

The slope is formed by horizontal strata of stone, a great part of which is limestone. At Fort Erie, which is 20 miles above the cataract, the current is sometimes so strong that it is impossible to cross the river in the ferry-boat. Proceeding downwards, the rapidity of the stream increases. It may, however, generally be crossed by hard rowing in a boat opposite to the mouth of Chippewa Creek. As we rowed along the St. Lawrence, from Fort Erie on the Canadian side, we heard the sound of the falls at a distance of ten miles, the wind was northeast and the weather clear. Had it been northwest, we should have heard it at a much greater distance. In heavy weather, and with a fair wind, the sound is sometimes heard 40 or 50 miles.

The rapids, or first falls, begin about one-half mile above the great cataract. In one instance has a man been saved who had been carried down to them. His canoe was overturned, he retained his fast hold of it, and it very providentially fastened itself to the uppermost rock. Some people on shore, seeing this, ventured to his assistance and saved his life at the risk of their own.

As we approached the falls the first time, the sun was low in the west, which gave us an opportunity of viewing the beautiful rainbow which is occasioned by the refraction of his rays on the cloud or fog that is perpetually arising from them. We afterwards found that the whole phenomenon is never viewed to so much advantage from the Canada side as on a clear evening. The vast fog ascending from the grand cataract being in constant agitation, appears like the steam of an immense boiling caldron. In summer it moistens the neighboring meadows, and in winter, falling upon the trees, it congeals and produces a most beautiful crystaline appearance. The view of this fog at a distance, which, when the cause of it is known is in itself a singular phenomenon, fills the mind with awful expectation, which on a nearer approach can never end in disappointment.

The first sight of the falls arrests the senses in silent admiration. Their various hues arising from the depth; the descent and the agitation of the water and the reflection of the sunbeams upon them; their great height; their position between lofty rocks and their roaring noise, altogether render them an unparalleled display of Nature's grandeur. But what chiefly distinguishes them and gives them a majesty incomparably superior to anything of the kind in the known world, is the vast body of water which they precipitate into an immense abyss.

The St. Lawrence is one of the greatest rivers of America. It is very deep and about 742 yards wide at the Falls. The perpendicular descent there is about 140 feet down to the level of the water below. How far the water rushes downward still further within the chasm underneath is uncertain. It falls 58 feet within the last few miles above the falls, which adds to the force and velocity of the cataract. The sound occasioned by the great and precipitate fall of such a vast body of water has the most grand effect that can be conceived. It far exceeds in solemnity any other sounds produced by the operation of nature. It is only at the falls that the force of that figure made use of in the book of Revelation can be fully felt: "I heard a voice as the voice of many waters." And what did that voice say? It proclaimed aloud as if all Heaven spoke "Hallelujah, Hallalujah, for the Lord God Omnipotent reigneth." This is the language that has been thundered for ages from the Falls of Niagara.

Every hour of the day and every change of the weather varies the scenery of this romantic, this magnificent display of the wonders of Nature, comparable with which every attempt of art to produce the sublime sinks into utter insignificance. The first day that we spent there, the weather was clear, the next day it became cloudy and rained a little. As we were desirous to enjoy the prospect before us from every possible point of view, we went down the high bank below the cataract into the immense chasm below, from thence walked, or rather climbed, along the rocks so near the cataract till it appeared ready to overwhelm us.

The descent though steep is not dangerous. General Simcoe, the late Governor of the Province, caused a ladder to be fixed in the most perpendicular part of it, which is so safe that his lady ventured to go down it. Below the air is, in some places, strongly tainted with the smell of dead fish, which lie in great numbers on the beach. Every creature that swims down the rapids is instantly hurried to destruction. We had seen a loon a little above them, which was unknowingly approaching swiftly to its ruin. Even birds which fly above them are frequently impelled downwards by the strong current of air, as their shattered fragments among the rocks do attest. Perhaps these were the fragments of water fowl, in which case the above remark is incorrect.

When the river is low, it is easy to walk up to the foot of the falls; but when high, one has to climb over rocks and piles of large loose stones for nearly half a mile. This last was the case when we were there. In many places the impending mass of stone seemed ready to fall upon us. It is known that the falls are divided into the greater and lesser fall by means of a lofty island between them. At the place of descent we were nearly opposite to the lesser fall, the water of which rushes down in a direction nearly parallel with the beach we walked along. They are again divided into two very unequal falls, the least of which probably discharges more water than the great fall of the Rhine in Switzerland, which is the most famous waterfall in Europe.

We now approached the great fall, which discharges at least four times as much water as the two lesser ones together. It is nearly in the form of a horseshoe. We observed below, what is imperceptible above, that the fall is not throughout the same pitch. In the hollow of it, where the greatest body of water descends, the rocks seem to be considerably worn away. We cannot however subscribe to the opinion that the cataract was formerly at the northern side of the slope near the landing, and that from the great length of time, the quantity of water and the distance which it falls, the solid stone is worn away for about 9 miles up the river towards Lake Erie.

This notion seems extravagant. The island which separates the fall, is solid rock and so high that the river can never have run over it. Its bank towards the falls runs in the direction with them and at the same time does not project beyond them, as would surely be the case if the whole body of rocks, from which the water descends, was fast wearing away. The situation and appearance of the falls is exactly the same as described and delineated by the French artist 160 years ago; besides, according to the laws of motion, the principal pressure of the water here must be in the direction in which it moves, and consequently not against the rocks it merely flows over and where it meets with no opposition. There is less probability of the bottom wearing away here than in any other river of equal depth where there are no such falls; for where the current is so very strong the pressure downwards must thereby be very considerably diminished, and for the same reason the water being ejected far beyond the precipice acts with little force against its edge. How, then, can it wear or bear it away for miles even in the greatest length of time? If the solid stone at the falls had been carried away, at so monstrous a rate as is supposed by some, it might be expected that the rapids would in length of time become smooth or vary their appearance, which has not been observed to be the case.

That the perpetual descent of such a vast body of water has produced an immense chasm below is more than probable, and that where the greatest quantity of it falls, the surface of the rocks may in great length of time have become more hollow is very credible; but it appears difficult for us to conceive that in any one period an immense bed of rock should have been so completely worn away for 9 miles that no vestige should be left of them and the falls exhibit at length their present appearance. An old Indian told us that many years since a grey-headed Chippewa had said to him: "The white people believe that the falls were once down at the landing. It is not true. They were always where they are now. So we have heard from our forefathers." We are led thereby to conclude that the Niagara Falls received their present singular position at . . . [*so in original, meaning, perhaps, Creation.*]

It is generally supposed because the assertion has frequently appeared in print that it is possible to go behind the descending column of water at the Falls and to remain there in perfect safety. Conversation, it has been said, may be held there without interruption from the noise, which is less there than at a considerable distance. People who live near the spot have daily to contradict these fables. They have themselves been repeatedly as far as possible under the falls and are in the habit of conducting strangers there. Their information is, therefore, to be relied on.

Under the Table Rock, as it is called, from a part of which the water descends, there is, it is true, space sufficient to contain a great number of people in perfect safety. But how should they get there? Were they to attempt to enter the cavity behind the fall, the very current of air (as the guides say) even were the stream of water not to touch them, would deprive them of life. The truth is, it is possible to go under, that is, below the falls, as we did, but not to go behind them.

The motion of the water below the cataract is, as may be supposed, extremely wild and irregular, and it remains so down to the landing. As far as the fog extends, it is impossible to judge of the state of the atmosphere with respect to heat and cold. In summer it cools it and in winter renders it milder. The surrounding country on the Canada side is very delightful, affording charming situations for pleasure grounds from whence the falls might be viewed to advantage. On this account, as well as for the sake of trade, the land here will probably, at some future period, sell for a very high price. It is at present, 1798, valued at £10 an acre.

CHARLES WILLIAMSON, 1799.

This well-known pioneer of the Genesee Valley wrote the following brief description of Niagara in 1799.

Should curiosity induce you to visit the Falls of Niagara, you will proceed from Geneva by the State Road, to the Genesee River, which you will cross at New Hartford, west of which you will find the country settled for about twelve miles; but after that, for about sixty-five miles, to Niagara River, the country still remains a wilderness. This road was used so much last year by people on business, or by those whom curiosity had led to visit the Falls of Niagara, that a station was fixed at the Big Plains to shelter travelers. At this place there are two roads that lead to Niagara River; the south road goes by Buffalo Creek, the other by Tonawandoe Village to Queen's Town Landing.

The road to Buffalo Creek is more used both because it is better and because it commands a view of Lake Erie; and the road from this to the falls is along the banks of Niagara River, a very interesting ride. The river is in no place less than a mile over, and the picture is enlivened by a variety of landscapes. Niagara River is the only outlet of Lake Superior, and all these immense lakes that afford from the falls an uninterrupted navigation of near two thousand miles to the westward. As you approach Chippaway, a military station two miles above the falls, the rapidity of the river increases, bounding to a great height when it meets with resistance from the inequality of the surface; and this vast body of water at last washes over a precipice of one hundred and seventy feet. The falls can be viewed from several different places; but they are seen to most advantage below. You can, with safety, approach the very edge of the fall, and may even go some distance between the sheet of falling water and the precipice; but this experiment requires caution; the footing is unequal and slippery; and blasts of condensed air rush out with such violence as to deprive you for some moments, of the power of breathing. From the falls to Queenstown, the nearest place to which shipping approach the falls, the roar is confined within a chasm in the rocks, one hundred and fifty feet deep, and to all appearance cut by the force of the water.

Among other Eighteenth century accounts, far better known, are the descriptive pages in the well-known works of Isaac Weld (1796) and the Duke Rochefoucault Liancourt (1795). Their books are in many libraries. John Cosens Ogden, who was on the Niagara in 1794, makes many useful notes in his "Tour," but does not indulge in description. An earlier writer of wide fame was Major Robert Rogers, who passed up the Niagara in October, 1760. In his "Concise Account of North America" (London, 1765), he gives a description of Niagara Falls; but his book is not so rare as to make advisable the reprinting of his pages. Much of the greatest importance was written about Niagara, and from the vicinity of Niagara, during and after the campaign of 1759; as for instance the letters of Charles Lee, afterwards Washington's major-general of treasonable fame; but these really belong to a different phase of our regional history.

Numerous accounts of Niagara may be found in Eighteenth-century compilations of travels, but they are either taken bodily from one or another of the accounts here given—usually from Hennepin, La Hontan, Kalm or Ellicott—or they are based on those narratives, and rewritten by book-makers who never saw the Falls.

The foregoing collection of rare and little-known narratives of personal experience at Niagara well shows the gradual acquisition of correct information, and the difficulties under which it was gathered, prior to the era of good roads and means of travel, of bridges and stairs and hotels. Niagara, even to the close of the Eighteenth century, was a Niagara of the wilderness.

APPENDIX

PROCEEDINGS

OF THE

BUFFALO HISTORICAL SOCIETY

1911

OFFICERS OF THE
BUFFALO HISTORICAL SOCIETY
1911

HONORARY PRESIDENT . . . . ANDREW LANGDON
PRESIDENT . . . . HON. HENRY W. HILL
VICE-PRESIDENT . . . . CHARLES R. WILSON
SECRETARY-TREASURER . . . . FRANK H. SEVERANCE

BOARD OF MANAGERS

Term expiring January, 1912.

ALBERT H. BRIGGS, M. D.,   LEE H. SMITH, M. D.,
R. R. HEFFORD,   WILLIS O. CHAPIN,
LORAN L. LEWIS, JR.

Term expiring January, 1913.

ROBERT W. DAY,   HENRY A. RICHMOND,
HUGH KENNEDY,   CHARLES W. GOODYEAR,*
G. BARRETT RICH.

Term expiring January, 1914.

HON. HENRY W. HILL,   HENRY R. HOWLAND,
J. N. LARNED,   CHARLES R. WILSON,
J. J. MCWILLIAMS.

Term expiring January, 1915.

ANDREW LANGDON,   JAMES SWEENEY,
FRANK H. SEVERANCE,   GEORGE A. STRINGER,
OGDEN P. LETCHWORTH.†

The Mayor of Buffalo, the Corporation Counsel, the Comptroller, Superintendent of Education, President of the Board of Park Commissioners, and President of the Common Council, are also *ex-officio* members of the Board of Managers of the Buffalo Historical Society.

---

*Died, April 16, 1911.
† Resigned.

LIST OF THE
PRESIDENTS OF THE SOCIETY

FROM ITS ORGANIZATION TO THE PRESENT TIME.

---

*MILLARD FILLMORE, ... 1862 to 1867
*HENRY W. ROGERS, ... 1868
*REV. ALBERT T. CHESTER, D. D., ... 1869
*ORSAMUS H. MARSHALL, ... 1870
*HON. NATHAN K. HALL, ... 1871
*WILLIAM H. GREENE, ... 1872
*ORLANDO ALLEN, ... 1873
*OLIVER G. STEELE, ... 1874
*HON. JAMES SHELDON, ... 1875 and 1886
*WILLIAM C. BRYANT, ... 1876
*CAPT. E. P. DORR, ... 1877
*HON. WILLIAM P. LETCHWORTH, ... 1878
WILLIAM H. H. NEWMAN, ... 1879 and 1885
*HON. ELIAS S. HAWLEY, ... 1880
*HON. JAMES M. SMITH, ... 1881
*WILLIAM HODGE, ... 1882
*WILLIAM DANA FOBES, ... 1883 and 1884
*EMMOR HAINES, ... 1887
*JAMES TILLINGHAST, ... 1888
*WILLIAM K. ALLEN, ... 1889
*GEORGE S. HAZARD, ... 1890 and 1892
*JOSEPH C. GREENE, M. D., ... 1891
*JULIUS H. DAWES, ... 1893
ANDREW LANGDON, ... 1894 to 1909
HON. HENRY W. HILL, ... 1910 and 1911

* Deceased.

APPENDIX

PROCEEDINGS OF THE
BUFFALO HISTORICAL SOCIETY

FORTY-NINTH ANNUAL MEETING.

The forty-ninth annual meeting of the Buffalo Historical Society was held at the Historical Building, Tuesday evening, January 10, 1911. President Henry W. Hill presided; in the absence of the secretary, Mr. George A. Stringer was made secretary pro tem. The minutes of the last annual meeting were read; reports of officers submitted; and Messrs. Andrew Langdon, O. P. Letchworth, Frank H. Severance, George A. Stringer and James Sweeney were reëlected as members of the Board of Managers for the ensuing four years. President Hill delivered the annual address of the president, as follows:

THE PRESIDENT'S ADDRESS.

Members of the Buffalo Historical Society, Ladies and Gentlemen: The Board of Managers of the Buffalo Historical Society with pleasure bid you welcome to this forty-ninth annual meeting and to assure you that they deeply appreciate your continued interest in its welfare and participation in its activities.

From its organization in 1862, it has been supported by many of Buffalo's distinguished citizens and finally established on a permanent basis through the liberality of the taxpayers of this city. In this respect it occupies a unique position among the historical societies of the country, for there are few that are so sustained. In return, however, its doors are kept open to the public and its archives and collections are daily consulted by the teachers, students and citizens of Buffalo as well as by writers of this and other states, interested in historical research. Inquiries come frequently from within and without the state for information in relation to genealogies and other matters of an historical nature, that can be found nowhere else so readily as in the archives of this society. We have a large and valuable collection, which is being yearly increased, of books, pamphlets, papers, manuscripts, letters, coins, portraits, Indian relics and other original data relating to the people and institutions of Western New York and especially of the city of Buffalo. For several years this Society has maintained a course of popular lectures free to the public, which have brought it into popular favor with all classes of our citizens. These have included historical, biographical, patriotic and educational subjects, several of which were prepared and given by our secretary, Frank H. Severance; and others were given by professional men and others well qualified to speak on their respective subjects. These weekly afternoon lectures have been attended by hundreds of our citizens, including a large number of young people interested in such matters. It has also maintained a formal course of lectures, open to the members of the Society. The year's entertainments have included the following:

Jan. 20. "An Evening with Dickens," by E. E. Williamson, Toronto.
Feb. 6. "Forts on the Niagara Frontier," by Hon. Peter A. Porter.
Feb. 13. "Lincoln." Address by Rev. John W. Ross.
Feb. 20. "Western New York in the Days of Washington," by Frank H. Severance.
Feb. 24. "Emerson and His Friends at Concord," by Mrs. Mary K. Babbitt, Concord, Mass.
Feb. 27. "The Story of Seneca Park, the old Indian burial ground at South Buffalo," by Frank H. Severance.
Mar. 13. "The City of Buffalo," by John Sayles.
Mar. 20. "The Career of General Philip Sheridan," by James Harmon.
Mar. 27. "The First Easter Observance on the Niagara," by Frank H. Severance.
Mar. 28. Illustrated lecture on "Arabia," by Dr. Edgar J. Banks, New York City.
May 8. "Some Facts about Father Hennepin," by Frank H. Severance.
May 31 - June 2. Meetings of the American Association of Museums.
Jun. 6. "The Story of Hingham Plantation," by Rev. Louis C. Cornish, Hingham, Mass.
Oct. 25. Illustrated lecture, "The League of the Five Nations," by Arthur C. Parker, New York State Archaeologist.
Nov. 10. "The Governors of New York," by Hon. Charles Z. Lincoln.

Nov. 17. Illustrated lecture, "Holidaying in Picturesque Brittany," by Frank Yeigh, Toronto.
Dec. 12. Illustrated lecture, "The Evolution of our Flag," by Charles Wm. Burrows, Cleveland, O.

These indicate to some extent the scope and popularity of entertainments offered our members during the past year. Others fully as entertaining are to follow. All these free, as well as the formal lectures, together with its Publications, of which I shall speak later, have given the Buffalo Historical Society a unique position in the intellectual life of this city. It may be said that its sphere of usefulness is somewhat extended beyond that contemplated by its founders, but we confidently believe, it is being better understood and that it is steadily growing in popular favor, if we may judge from the attendance at the public exercises and the number of the Society's daily visitors.

The original Certificate of Incorporation, filed in the office of the Secretary of State on January 10, 1863, defined its purposes to be "to discover, procure and preserve whatever may relate to the history of Western New York in general and the City of Buffalo in particular, and to gather statistics of the commerce, manufactures and business of the lake region, and those portions of the West, that are intimately connected with the interests of Buffalo."

In the federal, state and other reports annually received and catalogued in our library may be found the statistical information of the commerce, manufactures and business of the lake region, so that it is no longer necessary to make special compilation of those data, although it is important to see to it that all such reports are securely deposited in the library, as is now being done and as has been done since we came into possession of this spacious building.

If we have enlarged the domain of this Society, still we have faithfully adhered to the objects for which it was founded, as hereinbefore stated, and as somewhat elaborated by the Honorable Millard Fillmore in his first inaugural address as the first president of this Society, at the American Hotel in this city, on July 1, 1862. He said: "Its object is not to teach but to preserve history. And it is certainly a grateful task to commemorate the virtues of those who have built up this city and its noble institutions and to be sure that their names are not forgotten. . . . Now is the time to photograph their character in all lineaments of active life, that the generations who shall come after us may see them as we have seen them, and be stimulated to emulate their virtues and if possible rival their enterprise." In conclusion, he said: "Finally, let this institution be the grand repository of everything collected to throw light on our history. Books, newspapers, letters, pamphlets, maps, medals and relics of every description should be deposited here, and let our citizens unite heart and hand in building up this Society, which, while it does justice to the dead, reflects honor upon the living."

The prominent part taken by this Society on its own initiative and in coöperation with such other organizations as the Niagara Frontier Landmarks Association and the Historic Sites Commission in discovering and marking historic places in Western New York and in preserving a record of the important events occurring in connection therewith is in fulfillment of the declared purposes that led to the foundation of this Society. Its large and varied historical collections have been made also in fulfillment of its purposes by its friends, including many large donors and the successive boards of managers, who have administered its affairs from its organization. President Fillmore's advice that it be a repository of everything that might throw light on our history has been very generously followed. In this connection, and bearing in mind the statement of President Fillmore as to the functions of this Society that "while it does justice to the dead, reflects honor upon the living," I may be permitted to digress from the current of my remarks long enough to say a few words in justice to two of our members, viz., Mr. Langdon and Mr. Severance, both of whom are absent tonight. Mr. Andrew Langdon was president of this Society for sixteen consecutive years, from 1894 to 1909, inclusive, a period equalling those of President Fillmore, who presided over the Society for five years, from 1862 to 1867, and Hon. James Sheldon, who presided over it for eleven years, from 1875 to 1886, inclusive, the two other longest terms of any of its twenty-five presidents. But length of service is not alone the measure of his contributions to this Society. As chairman of the building committee he brought about the aggregation of three funds that made it possible to build this beautiful building designed by the architect, Mr. George Cary of Buffalo, of marble rather than of brick—after the manner of Augustus, of whom it has been said *"Urbem lateritiam invenit, marmoriam reliquit."* Mr. Langdon was the donor of the beautiful solid bronze gates, designed by the sculptor R. Hinton Perry and embellished with female figures representing Ethnology, History, Science and Art. He presented to this Society the two fifteenth century Medicean bronze candelabra that adorn and at night light the northwesterly entrance of this building. He also presented to the Society the Washington bust of Carrara marble, the work of the Florentine sculptor Pugi; and the antique bust of the Roman Emperor Nero. He presented to the city the bronze replica of the superb statue of David by Michael Angelo within view from the portico of this building. He was the chairman of the committee that secured for us the Julius H. Francis collection and the Lincoln statue, the work of the sculptor, Charles H. Niehaus. His gifts have been many and his interest in this Society has been untiring. Much pertaining to this Society is due to his keen appreciation of the ideals in architecture, sculpture, painting and landscape gardening, for it will be remembered that he was for years one of our efficient Park Commissioners. In addition to all these and what is quite as important, is that during his long service as president of this Society, he devoted his time unsparingly to its interests and the extension of its usefulness to the people of this city. His name will ever be associated with that of President Fillmore as one of the Society's most helpful friends and most liberal benefactors.

[President Hill here spoke appreciatively of the work of the Secretary, who had been granted a needed leave of absence.]

The founders of this Society, appreciating Buffalo's commercial importance at the foot of the Great Lakes, whose annual waterborne tonnage exceeds that of all the Atlantic seaports, laid emphasis upon the compilation and preservation of statistics relating to that subject. The summary of the tonnage of the port of Buffalo for 1910 was as follows:

Vessels Entered.	No.	Tonnage.
Coastwise	2,874	6,615,912
American vessels in foreign trade	765	507,741
Foreign vessels in foreign trade	76	53,186
Totals	3,715	7,176,839

Vessels Cleared.	No.	Tonnage.
Coastwise	2,992	6,989,116
American vessels in foreign trade	699	334,012
Foreign vessels in foreign trade	62	46,534
Totals	3,753	7,369,662

The total grain receipts, including flour in its equivalent of grain and flaxseed, were 138,229,075 bushels. The receipts of iron ore were less than in 1909, but of pig iron greater by 51,000 tons. The lumber imports were 177,136,000 feet at Buffalo and the Tonawandas. The total shipments were of coal 3,639,368 tons, of cement 2,895,510 barrels, of salt 469,509 barrels, of sugar 1,179,070 pounds. The total tonnage received on the Erie canal was 649,471 tons, valued at $18,542,775, and the total shipments by the Erie canal were 885,235 tons, valued at $16,912,769.

The total tonnage of the port of Buffalo for the year 1910 cannot now be given, but it was somewhat smaller than it was in 1909, owing to inactivity of lake commerce during the summer months.

The arrival and departure of vessels by lake and canal and the tonnage handled at the port of Buffalo, as compiled by Mr. George E. Pierce, were as follows:

Year	Lake		Canal	
	Number	Tons	Number	Tons
1903	8,727	11,586,719	6,974	1,324,216
1904	7,375	10,783,980	5,132	988,725
1905	7,950	12,090,153	4,902	985,861
1906	8,294	13,876,759	5,666	1,769,919
1907	8,205	14,578,233	5,014	1,942,455
1908	6,191	12,003,968	4,482	1,621,527
1909	6,659	14,145,013	4,230	1,568,615

The total tonnage of the port of Buffalo during the season of navigation in 1909, was 15,713,628 tons and exceeded the tonnage of any other port on the Great Lakes, except that of the port of Duluth, which is principally a shipping port of iron ore and grain, whereas Buffalo is both a shipping and receiving port for various classes of freights. Duluth at the upper end and Buffalo at the lower end of the Great Lakes in 1909, had the largest tonnage of any fresh-water ports in the world, and they are likely to maintain that commercial rank for years to come.

The founders of this Society wisely inserted. therefore, in its charter a provision that record be kept of the commerce of the Lake region, which for three-fourths of a century has been the principal business of the people of Buffalo and has made it one of the large inland ports of the world.

The commerce of the Great Lakes has been largely promoted by the Erie canal, extending from Buffalo to the Hudson river, thereby affording water inter-communication between these vast commerce-bearing natural bodies of water. Intimately associated historically with the growth of Buffalo, therefore, are the waterways of this state, the story of whose construction, enlargement and utilization was thought worthy of preservation and is told in the three latest volumes of the Society's Publications. Some of the contributors to these volumes were active participants in enlarging upon the policy, that had its inception in the Colonial era and its conclusion in the construction of the Barge canal system now in progress. These Publications have had a wide sale and form an important part of the history of Buffalo as well as of the State of New York.

BUFFALO HISTORICAL SOCIETY. 411

We still have many unpublished manuscripts, that may, in our future publications, be given to the world. These will bring this Society into still closer relation with the historical societies of the state and nation, of which there are many now crowding forward in their several fields of original investigation. Among such may be mentioned the New York State Historical Association, presided over by our former esteemed townsman and former State Comptroller, the Honorable James A. Roberts. The annual proceedings of that organization are being published in book form and thus adding materially to the wealth of Americana relating to the discovery, conquest, settlement, and institutions of the domain of New York. That organization is doing important work. Its tour of Lake Champlain last fall and the scholarly papers and addresses of its distinguished guests on that occasion will be read with interest by all students of the history of the Champlain valley. Our secretary, Mr. Severance, had part in that tour of the lake and of inspection of its historic forts, of which he has made report.

During the year 1909, two great historic celebrations were held in this state. There were the Lake Champlain Tercentenary celebration, from July 4th to July 9th, and the Hudson-Fulton celebration, from September 25th to October 9th. The State made liberal appropriations for both these celebrations and the Federal Government made an appropriation and formally participated in the former. In the Lake Champlain Tercentenary celebration the Federal Government was represented by President William H. Taft and its Secretary of War, the Honorable Jacob M. Dickinson. The Republic of France was represented by its Ambassador, the Hon. J. J. Jusserand; the Kingdom of Great Britain, by its Ambassador, the Right Honorable James Bryce; the Dominion of Canada, by its Postmaster-General, Rudolphe Lemieux; the Province of Quebec by its Premier, Sir Lomer Gouin; and the states of New York and Vermont by their respective Governors and other officials, and many distinguished citizens.

The Hudson-Fulton celebration was largely the work of the enterprising and patriotic citizens of New York City, who threw open the gates of the metropolis to the distinguished official guests of many foreign nations. The official reports of the two commissions having these historical celebrations in charge, are now in press and will be read with deep interest by students of the history of this state.

As secretary of the New York-Lake Champlain Tercentenary Commission, and by the authority of that commission, I prepared the literary programme of exercises that were given in the State of

New York, which comprised historical and other addresses, poems and Indian pageants at Crown Point, Ticonderoga and Plattsburgh. The Vermont-Lake Champlain Commission had similar exercises at Burlington and Isle la Motte. All the addresses and poems are included in full in the Report of the New York - Lake Champlain Tercentenary Commission, and the Report of the Vermont Commission includes all addresses and poems at Burlington and Isle la Motte and something of the local exercises at Vergennes, Swanton and at other places in Vermont.

The Vermont Commissioners in their official report say that the "Tercentenary has permanently enriched American literature in the notable addresses and poems prepared for the occasion. It has added largely to our knowledge of early history of this region, which we inhabit. It has increased our pride in the land we love, and has heightened our patriotism." The press of the country quite generally published reports of the exercises and in many instances gave copious excerpts of the addresses and poems.

The Hudson-Fulton celebration was conducted on a much larger scale than the Lake Champlain celebration, but after entirely different plans. The growth and prestige of the emporium of the Western Hemisphere could not well be more forcefully and brilliantly represented than it was on that occasion to the guests from many nations, who came to do honor to New York. The history of the entire period, from the discovery of the Hudson to the building of the last great bridge over the East river and the great subway from the Bronx to Brooklyn, was fittingly reproduced in historic and naval parades, aquatic pageants, electric displays, musical festivals, dramatic exhibitions and literary exercises of great variety and brilliancy. These will be fully described and as far as possible reproduced in the final report of that commission, now in press. The foreign guests were amazed that such a city, with world-wide commercial relations, had arisen, as it were, like Aphrodite from the foam of the sea, in the short period of time elapsing since Henry Hudson sailed the Half-Moon up the Hudson in September, 1609. Our vice-president, Mr. Charles R. Wilson, was on the board of directors of the Hudson-Fulton commission.

In both these historical celebrations prominence was given to "pageantry," which Percy Mackay defines as "poetry for the masses." In the Indian pageants at Lake Champlain, under the direction of L. O. Armstrong of Montreal, were 150 descendants of the native tribes occupying the Champlain valley, and in the drama founded on such records as are extant and available, there enacted, was a representation of the battle of Champlain with the Iroquois; and the formation of the Iroquois Confederacy. No one who was fortunate enough to witness the pageants of the Quebec Tercentenary, under the direction of that Oxford scholar and successful pageant director, Frank Lascelles of London, failed to appreciate that the realistic presentation in the open air on the Heights of Abraham, of the great events of Canadian history and of the Court of Henry IV of France, made a deep and lasting impression on the thousands in attendance.

Pageantry has thus been employed ever since "The Canterbury Pilgrims," as one of the most effective means of impressing historical facts upon the masses, who may not take the time to read, or possess the imagination to be stirred, if they were to read, the record of a nation unillustrated and entirely divorced from dramatic art.

On January 25, 1910, I introduced a concurrent resolution in the State Senate, authorizing the appointment by the Governor of a commission to confer with similar commissions of Ohio, Pennsylvania, Michigan, Illinois and Wisconsin in relation to the Centennial celebration of the victory of Commodore Oliver Hazard Perry on Lake Erie, September 10, 1813. The resolution passed the Senate and Assembly and the Governor appointed as members of that Commission Messrs. Ogden P. Letchworth and George D. Emerson of Buffalo, both prominent members of the Buffalo Historical Society, and Col. John T. Mott of Oswego, Dr. Clinton Bradford Herrick of Troy and Henry Harmon Noble of Essex, N. Y. The states of Kentucky and Rhode Island have also appointed commissioners, and Indiana and Minnesota are expected to appoint others, soon.

On September 10, 1910, a meeting was held of the commissioners of the eight states at Put-in-Bay, Ohio, at which articles of association were adopted, the first section of which reads as follows:

"This association shall be known as the Inter-State Board of the Perry's Victory Centennial Commissioners, organized for the purpose of promoting the historical, educational, naval and military celebration and the erection of the proposed Perry memorial at Put-in-Bay, Ohio, in the year 1913, in honor of the one hundredth anniversary of the battle of Lake Erie and of the Northwestern campaign of General William Henry Harrison in the War of 1812, which terminated in the battle of the Thames, October 5, 1813."

In that organization Mr. Letchworth was chosen vice-president for the State of New York.

The New York Commission organized on November 2, 1910, at Albany, by electing Mr. Letchworth chairman and Mr. Emerson secretary. Application has been made to Congress for an appropriation for the erection of a memorial at Put-in-Bay Island, and the Committee on Industrial Arts and Expositions has reported favorably thereon.

It is possible that the Perry Centennial Celebration may also include a review of the commerce of the Great Lakes, which has ever been and still is the chief contributing agency in the building up of Buffalo. Should that be done, the people of the city and of Western New York might very properly actively participate in that celebration.

Although the Buffalo Historical Society was not formally identified with either the Lake Champlain or with the Hudson-Fulton Tercentenary Commissions, still our members have held prominent official positions on those commissions, and were, therefore, to a certain extent charged with the responsibility of the conduct of those celebrations. That relation has necessarily brought this Society into close touch with these two most notable historical celebrations which have ever occurred in this State, and which, therefore, I have considered worthy of special mention on this occasion.

These have extended the work of some of us into wider fields of historical research during the two years past, but, as may be seen from the present report of our secretary, that has been done without encroaching upon the work of the Society within its own more limited domain of discovering and preserving whatever relates to local history.

In closing the work for the year, we sincerely deplore the loss of eleven of our esteemed members, whose deaths are chronicled in the secretary's report. We have gained, however, twenty-eight new members during the year and our present membership includes 124 life members and 572 annual members, a total of 696 members in a city with a population of 423,715 inhabitants. Evidently there are many in this city who are not availing themselves of the privileges and benefits of this Society, which is generally recognized as the leading literary institution of Buffalo. For its members is maintained a formal course of lectures, and its annual Publications are presented to them without other charge than their annual dues. In many ways its silent appeal is more eloquent than words. Let us have more members, that we may extend its sphere of usefulness to Buffalonians, whose family records it is founded to preserve and whose history it is ordained to perpetuate.

In conclusion I wish to express to my colleagues of the board of managers, including the city officials, who are ex-officio members, my grateful appreciation of their timely counsel and friendly coöperation in the administration of the affairs of this Society during the past year. They have spared no efforts at whatever personal loss of time to promote its welfare and are entitled to the gratitude of its friends as well as of the people of Buffalo.

THE SECRETARY'S REPORT.

Mr. Stringer read the following, which had been prepared by the Secretary:

Mr. President, Members of the Buffalo Historical Society: I respectfully submit the following notes on the work of the year:

Building. After the extensive construction work of 1909, we have not been called upon to do much in the way of repairs or betterments on the building. A needed extension of the heating system has been made by installing at the east end of the library a four-column radiator. This is expected to make that room comfortable for visitors in severe weather. Heretofore it has often been found impossible to warm.

During the summer a thorough overhauling of the roof was made under the supervision of Mr. Jones, our engineer. Some slight repairs of tiling and metal work were all that we found needed.

The tract of land at the north of the building, during the year, has been opened up for residence purposes. Streets have been laid out and paved, and sewer, water and gas mains installed. This work cut off the temporary sewer running from this building north and connecting with the city sewer at Elmwood and Amherst streets. There being no city sewer with which we could connect, application was made to the Nye Improvement Company for permission to sewer into their system. This was courteously granted, so that we now have a much better provision for this need than ever before.

During the year we have continued the so-called Still Alarm electrical installation as protection against burglary. Even when the device as installed is in perfect working order, it is not, in the judgment of the secretary, a very efficient protection. Frequently it has been out of order and often, no doubt in spite of the best efforts or intentions of the company, it has been left out of order for days after we have reported it. To rely for protection in this respect upon a device so uncertain, seems to your secretary most unwise. The alternative is either to employ a night watchman—a system which, in the judgment of the board, has heretofore been thought to have many drawbacks—or to further protect the windows with iron gratings. If the eight or ten most readily accessible windows on the main floor were thus protected, the building would in all probability be secure, as only the most determined burglar with ladders and elaborate outfit could gain entrance. As it is now, some of these windows, opening directly on the south porch, present an easy means of ingress to anyone armed with a glass-cutter. It may be objected that to protect these windows with iron gratings is to give to a beautiful structure the appearance of a jail. In reply to this, it may be said that the same objection was raised before the iron gratings were placed on the basement windows, but that since they were put on there is no jail-like appearance. It is possible to combine beauty of design with utility in such work; and although we all desire to preserve the attractiveness of the exterior of this building, we must recognize the fact that a greater desire is to protect its contents. Such barring of windows is most common in museum buildings the world over. The need for that kind of protection exists here. So far as cost is concerned, a few years of more or less uncertain and inefficient so-called burglar alarm service, would cost quite as much as permanent protection of the building by suitable gratings.

It is probable that early the coming year, say at the usual time of spring housecleaning, it will be necessary to paint or kalsomine the basement walls, at least in such portions as have become soiled and marred by the passing of many hands. So far as can now be foreseen, there is no urgent call for any other work on the building.

The retaining wall at the side of the area-way on the east end of the building, is gradually settling out of the perpendicular and before many years will have to be relaid, but, apparently, it will not need our attention this year.

Library. There have been added to the library by gift and purchase 890 volumes, making the number of catalogued volumes in the general collection 19,847. The Lord library and the Marshall collection continue unchanged. Mrs. A. A. Andrews has continued, as heretofore, to give most of her time to the library work. As opportunity permits, our card catalogue is being much extended, not only by the new accessions, but by the making of many entries of cross reference and other data which make it of greater use to the people who come to us for assistance. In this connection may be mentioned the listing of the Society's manuscripts, which was accomplished during the year. A report of that work and rough list of the manuscripts were contained in volume Fourteen of our Publications. There has also been made a card catalogue of the manuscripts, by the aid of which this unprinted material is made as available as are the classified books. Fifty copies of the printed list of manuscripts were distributed, chiefly among other historical societies, for the purpose of informing them of what we have, of extending help to those who may care to use our manuscripts, and in the hope of stimulating like work on the part of our sister societies.

Among the donors of books to our library during the year, precedence should be given to the Hon. T. Guilford Smith. He has not only added to our shelves some scores of works, both genealogical and historical, but has made this institution one of the three American libraries to have a copy of his great genealogical compilation, "The Making of Smith." This is a three-volume folio work, for the most part typewritten, with hundreds of maps, portraits, views, and other illustrative material, all bearing on the history of the families to which he belongs.

Other donors of books include William A. Galpin, Mrs. J. H. Jewett of Canandaigua, J. N. Larned, Frederick W. Danforth, Madison C. Peters, Brooklyn, N. Y.; William H. Walker, M. F. Elliott, New York City; H. T. Green, Walter L. Brown, John Debar, Cincinnati; Dr. S. A. Freemen, Mrs. James W. Ward, Mrs. George Fuller Tuttle, Plattsburgh; Hon. George Clinton, Mrs. Robert A. Bethune, Mr. Slason Thompson, Chicago; Mrs. Wm. D. Doherty, Mrs. Julia F. Snow, and Mr. James A. Ellis, representing the Lewis Historical Publishing Company.

The enlargement of the newspaper collection is a matter dear to the secretary's heart, believing as he does that no department of our library presents more valuable material for the student of our regional history. The room fitted up a few years ago for the bound newspaper files, is rapidly filling up and although we are binding only the more important of the local papers, yet the yearly addition is such that before long more room will be needed if these files are to be continued. We have on hand a large number of duplicate files which the Society might well exchange or even send as a gift outright to institutions which would pay the freight on them. We are, as opportunity offers, filling in the gaps of the earlier papers. A most fortunate find came the past summer, when a gentleman of Black Rock, Mr. George Morrissey, turned over to us a quantity of unbound papers, including long runs of early Buffalo and Black Rock issues. Although none of these is complete as a file, all of them are well worth caring for and binding. They extend from about 1820 to 1840.

Even more noteworthy was the gift of Mr. J. G. Shuler, of a complete file of the Buffalo *Freie Presse*, from its establishment in 1872 to date. As this was a paper not heretofore represented in our collection, the gift of a complete file was most welcome.

Museum. The Society's museums have been much improved during the year. As we rarely buy anything for these collections except the cases to hold the articles given us, it will be seen that the growth of the museum, both in number of specimens and in historic value, depends on the interest taken in it by our friends.

Fortunately several friends have made notable and worthy additions during the past year. In the Indian Department, the collection of Mr. Dilworth M. Silver and that of Dr. A. L. Benedict, the latter merely deposited with us, have both been enlarged and much improved. We have added to the Indian articles by purchase the tomahawk-pipe formerly owned by Chief Strong, prominent in the early councils of the Seneca Nation.

Among the miscellaneous articles received for the museum, one of more than ordinary interest should be mentioned: a saddle of the Mexican War period, handsomely inlaid, with ornamentation in carved leather. This is loaned by Mrs. Albert J. Barnard. Two large frames of Masonic badges from the estate of William H. Kirkholder; numerous articles of antiquarian interest, including old-time surgical instruments, from Mrs. F. H. James; and others of equal interest, were received. A full record of all donations is kept by this society.

To our portrait collection, several notable additions have been made. They include portraits of Samuel M. Welch, the gift of Deshler Welch; Stephen C. Clarke and Mr. and Mrs. E. H. Dutton, the gift of Mrs. S. C. Clarke; Mr. Frank H. Goodyear, from Mrs. Goodyear; Hon. David S. Bennett and Miss Charlotte Mulligan, a gift of Mrs. Albert H. Chester of New Brunswick, N. J.; Hon. Franklin A. Alberger, Mayor of Buffalo in 1860-61, a gift of his brother, Col. M. A. Alberger, of Hamburg, N. Y.; Patrick Reily, the gift of his daughter, Miss Emma Reily. One portrait of especial historical interest is that of Mrs. Mary Harris, who came to Buffalo from Hartford, Conn., in 1809, and in 1814 was married to Captain A. C. P. Harris, at Harris Hill. Mr. and Mrs. Harris for many years were active and influential residents of this county, Mrs. Harris dying in 1880. The portrait is a gift of her daughter, Mrs. Sophia Atkins, now a venerable lady of this city. Very welcome too is an oil portrait of Michener Cadwallader, the first comptroller of the city of Buffalo, painted by Le Clear. It is one of the most artistic portraits in our collection. It comes to us from the estate of Miss Juniata Stafford of Chicago. A portrait designed for our collection, though not yet placed here, is a full length life size study of Commander Charles A. Orr, ultimately to be presented to this Society by Chapin Post, G. A. R., of this city.

To Mr. William A. Galpin is due a word of special recognition for the interest he has taken in the improvement of our museum. His gifts to it during the year have been many. Among numerous rare and valuable steel engravings which he has added to our collection, are a most interesting group relating to Washington, among them some of the rarest and most prized of the early plates. He has also given us a number of valuable engravings of Lincoln, of Grant and other subjects. Among the articles of antiquarian interest should be mentioned some score or more of curious and artistic clocks, also a donation from Mr. Galpin. He has also given us an instructive exhibit of old pewter and miscellaneous articles, most of them dating back to Colonial days. Appreciated quite as much as are his gifts, is his spirit of interest in the institution and eagerness to help it as he can.

DEATHS IN 1910.

The year's death roll from our membership is as follows:

Apr. 7. S. DOUGLAS CORNELL . . . . . . Resident member
Jun. 16. JAMES MOONEY . . . . Resident member
Jul. 22. EMIL MACHWIRTH . . . . Life member
Aug. 15. WILLIS H. MEADS . . . . Resident member
Aug. 19. HON. JACOB STERN . . . . Resident member
Sep. 24. D. A. A. NICHOLS, Westfield, N. Y. Corresponding member
Oct. 13. HENRY S. SILL . . . . Resident member
Nov. 12. MISS LUCY S. LORD . . . . Resident member
Dec. 1. HON. WILLIAM P. LETCHWORTH . Life member
Dec. 18. HON. HENRY F. ALLEN . . . . . Resident member
Dec. 18. GEN. WILLIAM BULL . . . . . . Resident member

Conventions. In June, the Society shared with other Buffalo institutions in entertaining the American Association of Museums. In October the Society was represented by its secretary at the annual meeting of the New York State Historical Association on Lake Champlain. We have also been represented in the conferences regarding the proposed Centennial Peace Jubilee on the Niagara Frontier in 1915.

Historic Sites Commission. In February, 1910, the Society received a communication from Prof. Charles H. Haskins of Harvard University, Secretary of the Council, the governing body of the American Historical Association, appointing the Secretary of the Buffalo Historical Society one of a committee of five for establishing an Historical Sites Commission "to serve as a central coördinating body in the work of marking and commemorating historical sites and buildings throughout the United States." The committee as constituted represented the following institutions: State College, Pa., by its president, Edwin Erle Sparks, who is chairman of the committee; University of Washington, Seattle, represented by Prof. Edmond S. Meany; Western Reserve University, Cleveland, Ohio, Prof. Henry Eldridge Bourne; Wisconsin State Historical Society, Madison, Dr. Reuben Gold Thwaites; and the Buffalo Historical Society, Frank H. Severance. The entire territory of the United States was apportioned among the members of this committee, and to the Buffalo Historical Society was allotted New England, New Jersey and New York, the requirements being that reports should be made on all historic sites which have been marked by monument, tablet or otherwise, with mention of other sites not yet marked, but deemed worthy of commemoration. The Secretary has devoted considerable time to the collection of data in his field and preparation of a report. This report, however, cannot be regarded as final, nor the survey of the field thus far made as thorough. The committee will, no doubt, be continued another year, though it is to be hoped, with an enlarged representation. The outcome of this work will probably be a most comprehensive report on the subject as stated, covering the whole country and making when published a substantial and valuable volume. Your secretary regards it as matter for gratification that the Buffalo Historical Society was given a part in this work.

Publications. Volume Thirteen of the Society's Publications was completed in December, 1909, but much of its distribution and practically all of its sale to purchasing libraries and other institutions came in the year 1910. By July a succeeding volume was completed, its distribution being postponed until September. We have, therefore, virtually sent out two volumes within the past year. They have been very well received, and although for the most part ignored by the local press, they have had truly critical, and usually commendatory, notice in papers of other cities, and especially in the historical journals and reviews of a national character. With each succeeding volume of our series, our standing order list makes some gain. Although we have not yet reached the point where the sales of any volume equal the cost of publication, yet they are a substantial income towards that end, and warrant the belief that the time is not distant when a volume of our Publications, if devoted to topics of general interest, will find a sale sufficient to offset the cost of publication.

Your Secretary believes that this character can be given to our volumes without loss of the local interest which may be demanded by our members. It should be borne in mind that a large part of each edition is distributed free to the paying members of the Society.

Other Work. Besides the preparation of these volumes and of the report on historic sites already mentioned, one other task has taken no little of the Secretary's time. At the request of President Henry W. Hill, who as Secretary of the Lake Champlain Tercentenary Commission for New York State, was charged with the preparation of the official report of that celebration, your secretary has given assistance in the preparation of this report for the printer. Although our institution had no official connection with that work, our share in it may be regarded as a part of the general effort to make the Buffalo Historical Society useful in any legitimate field.

Our institution is naturally interested in the improvement of the grounds adjoining the park on the north and immediately in front of the Historical Building. The owners of that tract, in laying out Nottingham Terrace, a new street to run easterly from Elmwood avenue, bordering on the park line, have left an irregular triangle of land on the park side of the street at its junction with Elmwood avenue. The Society has asked the owners to donate this triangular plot to the city that it may be added to the park system. We have also asked of the Park Commissioners, in case such donation is made, that they so improve it that a finer and more convenient entrance from the street to the Historical Building may be laid out.

Your Secretary makes these notes on the eve of his departure on a leave of absence, very considerately granted by the Board of Managers. Because of this absence and for other reasons, one feature of the work which for a few years past has been carried on with varying success, the free Sunday afternoon talks, for the present, will be omitted. It is the purpose, however, of the Secretary not to discontinue any phase of the work which brings results or for which there seems to be any public demand, and he goes away for a needed rest with the firm purpose of taking up, on his return, whatever work may be suggested which will contribute to the satisfaction of the community or the prosperity of the Society.

The Society is limited in its expenditures for entertainments, but if to the evening lectures we can add a course of talks on home history or any other topic, by the Secretary or others whose services may be had without cost, such work will cheerfully be undertaken.

In 1912 occurs the 50th anniversary of the founding of this Society. It is the purpose of our Board of Managers to mark this semi-centennial with some fitting observance, for which we bespeak the coöperation and interest of all our members.

FRANK H. SEVERANCE,
Secretary.

ANNUAL MEETING.

The annual meeting of the Board of Managers for the election of officers, was held, according to law, on Thursday, January 12, 1911. The officers of 1910 were reëlected, the voting being by ballot, as follows: President, Henry W. Hill; vice-president, Charles R. Wilson; secretary-treasurer, Frank H. Severance.

In Memoriam

WILLIAM PRYOR LETCHWORTH

THE BOARD OF MANAGERS OF THE BUFFALO HISTORICAL SOCIETY DIRECTS THE FOLLOWING TRIBUTE ENTERED UPON ITS MINUTES:

IN THE DEATH OF WILLIAM PRYOR LETCHWORTH, WHICH OCCURRED AT GLEN IRIS, DECEMBER 1, 1910, THIS SOCIETY HAS LOST ONE OF ITS OLDEST AND MOST FAITHFUL MEMBERS AND FRIENDS.

IN 1878 HE WAS ITS PRESIDENT, AND HIS INTEREST IN ITS WELFARE HAS ALWAYS BEEN UNFAILING. THE REAL WORK OF HIS LIFE BEGAN WHEN, RELEASED FROM THE RESPONSIBILITIES AND CARES OF ACTIVE BUSINESS, HE WAS ENABLED TO DEVOTE HIS THOUGHT AND ENERGIES TO THE WORK OF THE STATE AND THE NATION IN BEHALF OF DEPENDENT AND SUFFERING HUMANITY.

AS A MEMBER OF THE NEW YORK STATE BOARD OF CHARITIES FOR MORE THAN A QUARTER OF A CENTURY, AS ITS PRESIDENT FOR MANY YEARS, AS A PROMINENT MOVER IN STATE AND NATIONAL ORGANIZATIONS, AND ALWAYS AS A GENEROUS PHILANTHROPIST, HIS HUMANITARIAN LABORS WERE MOST FRUITFUL. ESPECIALLY WERE THEY FELT IN THAT WHICH HE ACCOMPLISHED ON BEHALF OF DEPENDENT CHILDREN, IN HIS INVESTIGATIONS AND PUBLISHED WRITINGS REGARDING THE PROPER CARE OF THE INSANE, THE CARE AND TREATMENT OF EPILEPTICS, AND IN THE IMPORTANT RESULTS WHICH HAVE EMANATED THEREFROM.

HIS MOST GENEROUS GIFT TO THE STATE OF NEW YORK OF HIS LARGE ESTATE WITH ITS PICTURESQUE SURROUNDINGS AS A PUBLIC PARK HAS ENDEARED HIS MEMORY TO THE PEOPLE OF THIS COMMONWEALTH. WE, WHO HAVE BEEN HIS FRIENDS AND ASSOCIATES, HOLD IT IN AFFECTIONATE REMEMBRANCE.

INDEX

INDEX

"A British Subject," *pseud.*, 36.
Abbott, Francis, "the hermit of Niagara," 40, 86, 196.
Abbott, Jacob, 86.
Abbott, John S. C., his life of La Salle, 298.
Abdy, E. S., 41.
Aberdeenshire, 310.
Ackermann, R., London publisher, 130.
Adam, —, artist, 134.
Adams, John, 263.
Agassiz, Louis, 202.
"Age (The) of Wire," 259.
Aiken, *Rev.* Solomon, of Dracutt, 272.
Albany Institute, *Proceedings*, 184.
Alexander, *Capt.*, J. E., 40.
Allen, Z., 189.
Almy, Frederick, 195.
American Ass'n for the Advancement of Science, its 3d meeting in Buffalo, 188.
American Philosophical Society, *Proceedings*, 177, 178.
American Revolution, service of Lord Edward Fitzgerald, 218, 235.
Ampere, J. J., 57.
Allen, *Hon.* Lewis F., 191; his historic house, 242.
Allston, Joseph, 171.
Anderson, A., early American engraver, 32.
Archer, —, engraver, 127.
Arfwedson, C. D., 41; comments on Niagara in art, 157.
Argyll, *Duke of*, 201, 202.
"Ariadne of Naxos," painting by Vanderlyn, 163, 170.
Arnold, *Sir* Edwin, 68.
Audubon, John James, 197-201.

"Babeer" ("Barbeer"), [? Baby], 303-305.
Baird, Robt., 55.
Bakewell, Robt., 183, 185, 186.
Bakewell, Robt., *Jr.*, 186.
Barcelona harbor, N. Y., 303.
Barlow, W. H., 177.
Barr, Robt., 93.
Bartlett, Chas. M., 212, 213.
Bartlett, W. H., 134-137.
Barton, *Dr.* Benj. Smith, 177; acct. of his Niagara visit, 1798, 393-398.
Bartram, John, 204.
Bassano, *Marquis de*, 334.
Bates, Joshua, 141.
Bauer, W. C., 147.
Baxter, W. E., 58.
Baynes, T. M., 132.

Beard, Jas. H., 148.
Beard, Wm. H., 148.
Beardsley, Levi, 29.
Beaujou, *Mons.*, 325.
Beck, Raphael, 148.
Bédiér, M. Joseph, critical study of Chateaubriand's American travels, 106-107.
Beecher, Harriet, 72.
Bennett, W. J., 132.
Bernhard, *Duke of* Saxe-Weimar Eisenach, 34.
Bianchi, Alberto G., 68.
Biart, Lucien, 62.
Bigelow, Timothy, 27.
Bigsby, *Dr.* John, 188.
Bigot, Chas., 68.
Birch, Wm. Russell, 156.
Birch, —, a Loyalist near Chippewa, Can., 1785, 353; his house and mill in 1787, 368; notes tide-like action at Chippewa creek, 377.
Bird, Jas., 86.
Bird, *Col.* Wm. A., his house in Buffalo, 242.
Bissell, Wilson S., 248.
Blackwell, E. R., 189.
Blanchard, Amy E., 85.
Blaney, *Capt.* Wm. Newnham, 33.
Blouet, —, 132.
Bodham-Whetham, J. W., 66.
Bodmer, *M.* Chas., 134.
Bonaparte, Charles Lucien, 197.
Bonfils, —, artist's signature, 128.
Bonnécamps, *Rev.* Joseph Pierre de, 20, 176; his account of Niagara falls, 323, 324.
Bonnefons, J. C., 20; adventures at Niagara, 334-339.
Bonnycastle, *Sir* Richard H., 49.
"Borassaw, M." (? Borassan or Borassau), 317; his account of Niagara, 318, 319.
Bornet, John, 148.
Boston Museum of Fine Arts, 156.
Bouchette, Joseph, 41.
Bowles, Samuel, 75.
Boyd, —, commanding at Ft. Erie, 1789, 229.
Brant, Jos., travels with Lord Edward Fitzgerald, 220, 221, 227.
Brébeuf, *Rev.* Jean de, 11.
Bremer, Fredericka, 55, 208.
Brewer, Wm. H., 189.
Brewer, —, his panoramas, 153, 154.
Brisbane, James, visits site of Buffalo, in 1789, 229, 232.
"Briske Isle" (Presqu' Isle), 305.

INDEX.

Bristol, Eng., 4.
Brock's (*Gen.*) monument, Queenston, Can., 287.
Brooks, *Rev.* Chas., 277; letter to, from Harriet Martineau, 284.
Brown, Geo. Loring, 156.
Brown, Jas. Francis, 149.
Brûlé, Etienne, 5.
Brunton, —, of the 65th regt., with Capt. Enys at Niagara, 1787, 366, 368.
Bryant, Wm. Cullen, 54.
Bryant & Gay's "History of the U. S." on the building-place of the Griffon, 298.
Brymner, Douglas, 363.
Buckingham, J. S., 49.
Buckle, Henry Thomas, 306.
Buffalo (Buffaloe, New Amsterdam), in 1802, 168; visit of Lord Edward Fitzgerald and Ann Powell in 1789, 229-234.
Buffalo, Albright Art Gallery, 156.
Buffalo Female Seminary, 190.
Buffalo, Forest Lawn cemetery, 240.
Buffalo, Franklin-st. cemetery, 240.
"Buffalo, Historical associations of," 237-252.
Buffalo Historical Society, given use of Vanderlyn Mss., 164; has original subscription list for Niagara power fund, 214; reburies remains of Red Jacket and other chiefs, 239; proceedings, 49th an. meeting, 405-422.
Buffalo, Indian Church avenue, 239.
Buffalo, Indian Mission church, 239.
Buffalo, "Old Indian cemetery," 239.
Buffalo creek, 218, 234, 238; council houses on, 239; first white settlement on, 241; road to in 1799, 399.
Bull, Ole, visits Niagara, 192; his musical composition, "Niagara," 192; interpreted by N. P. Willis, 193; by Lydia Maria Child, 193-195.
Burden, —, settler near Niagara Falls in 1802, 168.
Burford, Robt., his panorama of Niagara, 152, 153.
Burlington Bay (Ont.), volcano at, 295.
Burr, *Col.* Aaron, relations with John Vanderlyn, 159-163; portrait by Vanderlyn, 163.
Burr, Theodosia (Mrs. Jos. Allston), portrait of, by Vanderlyn, 163.
Busch, Moritz, 57.
Bustamente y Campuzano, *Don* Juan, 67.
Butler, Frances Anne ("Fanny Kemble"), 42, 43.
Butler, *Col.* John, 362.
Butler, *Capt.* W. F., 62.
Butlersburg (Butlersbury), 362.
Büttner, *Dr.* J. G., 46.
Buttre, J. C., 137.

Cabanel, A., 155.
Cabot, J. Elliot, 202.
Cadillac, Antoine de la Mothe, 81.

Calhoun, John C., portrait by Vanderlyn, 171.
Callington, W. R., 127.
Cameron, P. Calderon, 150.
Cameron, Peter, 212.
Campbell, Patrick, 23; at Niagara, 386, 387.
Campbell, *Maj.* —, commands at Ft. Niagara, 1785, 363.
Canadaqua (Canandaigua), 389.
Canandaigua in 1802, 166.
Carlisle, *Earl of*, 50; letter to, from W. H. Prescott, 141-143.
"Caroline," affair of the, 308, 309.
Carlyle, Thos., 293.
Carus, Paul, 88.
Carus-Wilson, Chas. A., 206.
Carver, Jonathan, 23; at Niagara falls, in 1766, 346.
Casgrain, *Abbé* H. R., 335.
Cass, *Gov.* Lewis, on the building-place of the Griffon, 298.
Casson, Dollier de, 12.
Cat nation, see Erieehronons.
Catherwood, Mary Hartwell, 81.
Catlin, George, 211.
Cavagnal, *Marquis de la*, 20, 175.
Cavelier, Jean, 309.
Cayuga Bridge, N. Y., 166.
Cayuga lake, 388, 389.
Cazenovia creek, 238.
Céloron, Pierre Joseph, 305, 323.
Chambers, Wm., 58.
Champlain, Samuel de, his "*Des Sauvages*" the beginning of Niagara literature, 4; its value, 5; cited, 10, 16, 294.
Channing, Wm. Ellery, 271.
Chanouanons (Shawanees), 305.
Charleston, S. C., 235.
Charlevoix, *Rev.* Pierre F. X. de, 16; his Niagara letters, 319-323; first writer to designate the "Horseshoe" fall, 320.
Chase, Wm. M., 150.
Chateaubriand, François Auguste, *vicomte de*, 94; "A Dreamer at Niagara, 97-111.
Chaumonot, *Rev.* Pierre Joseph Marie, 11.
Chautauqua county, N. Y., first exploration, 305.
Chautauqua lake, 5; question of its discovery, 305.
Chautauqua portage, 303.
Chauvignerie, *Ensign de la*, 175.
Chénier, Marie Joseph de, 109.
Chevalier, Michel, 45.
Chicago Art Institute, 156.
Child, Lydia Maria, interprets Ole Bull's "Niagara," 193-195.
Chippewa (Chippeway, etc.), Can., in 1802, 168; in 1834, 287.
Chippewa (Chippeway) creek, 353.
Church, Frederic Edward, 143, 144.
Cincinnati Museum, 156.
"City of the Falls," project promoted by Burford's panorama, 153.
Civil War, one phase of its literature, 19; travel literature during, 64-70; effect on development of

INDEX.   429

the telegraph, 259; fasts and thanksgivings during, 264.
Clark, T. W., 212.
Clark, Willis Gaylord, 46.
Cleveland, Grover, *President,* A. W. Sangster's "Niagara" dedicated to him, 149; early residence in Buffalo, 242; associations with the old court house, 244; his law offices, 248; a Thanksgiving proclamation as governor of New York, 274.
Clinton, DeWitt ("Hibernicus"), 183, 310.
Clinton, *Gov.* George, portrait by Vanderlyn, 171; letter to, from Jos. Brant, 234.
Clinton, *Judge* George W., 205, 206.
Clinton, N. Y., 388.
Cobbett, Wm., 218, 219.
Cobden, Richard, 74.
Cockburn, *Lt.-Col.* —, 130.
Coffen, Stephen, 304, 305.
Cogniet, Léon, 155.
Coke, *Lieut.* E. T., 40, 132.
Cole, Thos., 137-141; journal of his Niagara visit, 139, 140; his point of view, 148.
Colton, C., 37.
Columbian Exposition, "Niagara" painted for, 145.
Columbian Magazine, 385, 392.
Combe, George, 48, 49.
Comettant, Oscar, 62.
Comstock, *Dr.* J. L., 179.
Conroy, Tom, Prof. Tyndall's guide at Niagara falls, 187.
Cooke, George, 204.
Cooper, Jas. Fenimore, 71; his historical fiction touching the Niagara, 77, 82.
Corcoran Gallery, Washington, 143, 144.
Cornell, Alonzo B., governor of New York, Thanksgiving proclamation, 274.
Cornell, Ezra, 259.
Cox, *Rev.* F. A., 46.
Coxe, Reginald C., 148.
Coyne, Jas. H., 14.
Craig, W. M., 126.
Crèvecoeur, Alexander St. John de, 346, 361.
Crèvecoeur, *Count* Robert de, 347.
Crèvecoeur, J. H. St. John de, 21; sketch of, 346-349; letter to his son about Niagara falls, 349-363.
Crowley, Mary C., 81.
Cruxio, *Rev.* Francisco, 14.
Curtis, G. T., 72.
Curtis, George Wm., 57, 71.

Dallion, *Rev.* Joseph de la Roche, 10.
Dalton, Wm., 32.
Daly, Frederic, 68.
Darby, Wm., 31.
Dardoize, —, 155.
Daubeny, *Dr.* Chas., 47.
Davies, *Capt.* Thos., 122, 123.
Davis, *Maj.* Henry, 130.
Day, David F., 205, 206.
Day, Samuel Phillips, 62.

Deal, Anna Izard, 17, 339.
"Death of Jane McCrea," painting by Vanderlyn, 172.
De Céloron's expedition of 1749, 176.
Deedes, Henry, 59.
De Haas, M. F. H., 146, 147.
De Lancey, *Lt.-Gov.* Jas., niece of, marries Ralph Izard, 340.
Denonville, Jacques René de Brisay, *Marquis de,* 81.
De Nouvel, Gabriel Edouard, *chevalier,* alleged builder of first Niagara fort, 298.
De Noyan, —, 175.
De Roos, *Hon. Lt.* Fitzgerald, 35, 132.
Deroy, —, artist, 134.
Delisle (Deslisle), Guillaume, his map, 321.
De Smet, *Rev.* Peter John, 168, 169.
Despard, John ("Despares"), 30.
Detroit, Mich., founding of, 81; in 1789, 233.
De Witt, Simeon, 164, 169.
Dickens, Charles, 50-53, 209.
Dinet, *Rev.* Jacques, 11.
Dixon, *Rev.* James, 54.
Doré, Gustav, 121.
Douglas, —, of the 65th regt., with Capt. Enys at Niagara, 1787, 366, 373, 374.
Doyle, *Gen. Sir* Hastings, Lt. Gov. of Nova Scotia, 65.
Dudley, *Hon.* Paul, 317, 318.
Dufferin, *Lady,* 64, 65.
Du Mond, F. V., 147.
Dummer, Ann, 222.
Dummer, *Lt.-Gov.* Richard, 222.
Duncan, John M., 31.
Dunlap, Wm., 83; founder, Nat'l Academy of Design, 84.
Dupressoir, —, artist, 134.
Durant, *Rev.* John, 20.
Dwight, *Dr.* Timothy, 25, 26; his fast-day sermons, 271.

Earthquake reported in Western New York, 190.
Eaton, Amos, 183, 204.
Ebelings, Christof Daniel, 21.
Edge, J., 130.
Edwards, C. R., 86.
"Eighteenth century visitors to Niagara, narratives of," 313-400.
Ellicott, Andrew, his drawing of Niagara Falls, 122; measures the falls, 176; describes them, 178; mentioned, 183, 184; his account of the falls, 384-385, 400.
Ellicott, Joseph, "Father of Buffalo," 176; surveys New Amsterdam, 241; his house, 243.
Ellsworth (Elsworth), Francis, a Loyalist at Niagara, 1785, 353; his plantation, 360 (map), 361, 362.
Encyclopaedia Brittanica, cited, 298.
Enys', *Capt.* —, narrative of his visit to Niagara in 1787, 363-378; speculation on recession of the falls, 375-378.
Engleheart, Gardner D., 60.

INDEX.

Erie Canal, romances of, 86; construction period, 257.
Erieechronons, 11.
European Magazine, 386.
Eutaw Springs, S. C., battle of, 218.
Evans, Estwick, 31.
Evans, Lewis, 204.
Everest, *Rev.* Robt., 59.
Evershed, Thos., 215.
Eyre, *Rev.* John, 41.

Fairchild, Herman Leroy, 188.
Fairholme, George, 180, 181, 184.
Farmer's Brother, 240.
Farrall, S. A., 37.
Featherstonhaugh, G. W., 184.
Fenian raid of 1866, 19.
Fenn, Harry, 147.
Ferguson, Wm., 59.
Fesch, Jos., *Cardinal*, 109.
Fidler, *Rev.* Isaac, 40.
Fields, Jas. T., 75.
Fillmore, Millard, 59; his former residence, 247; his offices, 248; as Vice-President, 249; aids Morse's telegraph project, 259; attitude towards a national thanksgiving, 264.
Fisher, *Capt.* —, Royal British Artillery, 125.
Fitzgerald, *Lord* Edward, his military career, 218, 219; visits Niagara, 219; letters to his mother, 220, 221; his Indian adoption, 221; his Niagara excursions, 227; visits site of Buffalo with Ann Powell and others, 229-231; at Detroit, 233; subsequent career and death, 235.
Fleming, *Dr.* Wm., 46.
Flint, Jas., 32.
Flint, Timothy, 75.
Flower, Roswell P., governor of New York, thanksgiving proclamation, 274.
Flynne, P. C., 145.
Forbes, Geo., 215.
Forster, John R., translator of Kalm's work on America, 324.
Forster, Wm., "Memoirs of," 33.
Forsyth, —, of Kingston, entertains Judge Powell's party, 1789, 226.
Fort Adams (Ft. Tompkins), 245.
Fort Brewerton ("Brewington"), 342, 346.
Fort Conti (Niagara), 298.
Fort Erie, 217; Ralph Izard at, 345; mentioned, 394.
Fort Frontenac (Kingston, Ont.), 81; wrongly located, 298.
Fort Herkimer ("Harkimer"), 341, 346.
Fort Johnson, 340.
Fort Niagara, 1; its importance in history of the region, 2, 3; in 1789, 217; early mail service, 256; Peter Kalm at, 325; sound of the falls heard there, 328; M. Bonnefons at, 335; Ralph Izard at, 342; its ruinous state in 1765, 345; its state in 1785, 363; in 1792, 391.

Fort Ontario, 342.
Fort Oswego, 342, 389.
Fort Pontchartrain, 345.
Fort Porter, memorial tablet at, 244; old magazine, 245.
Fort Schlosser (Scuiler, Sckuiler, Slosser, Slausser, Toronto), 217, 229, 309, 336, 337, 339, 342, 343, 349, 353; Stedman's house at, 350, 356, 360 (map), 361; in 1787, 363.
Fort Schuyler, 341, 387, 388.
Fort Stanwix, 341, 347.
Foster's Flats ("Niagara Glen"), 205.
"Four (The) Kings of Canada" quoted, 316, 317.
Fowler, John, 37.
Frankenstein, G. N., 147; his Niagara paintings and panorama, 154, 155.
Franklin, Benj., corresponds with H. St. J. de Crèvecoeur, 348; at Franklin college, 349.
Franklin Institute, Philadelphia, *Journal of*, 177.
Free Soil Convention of '48, held in Buffalo, 247.
Friend, Washington, 131.
Friends Settlement, founded by Jemima Wilkinson, 389.
"From Indian Runner to Telephone,' 253-260.
Frost, *Rev.* Barzillai, 294.
Fuller, Susan Margaret, 53, 208.
Fulton, Linda de K., 87.

Galinée, René de Bréhant de, 12.
Galt, John, 85, 303.
Ganastogué Sonontoua Outinaouatoua, 13.
Garbett, E. L., 188.
Gardiner, *Rev.* John, of Boston, 271.
Geddes, Jas., 184.
Geneva, N. Y., in 1802, 166; in 1792, 389.
Genlis, *Mme. de*, 235.
Gentlemen's (The) Magazine, 121.
Gilbert, G. K., 188.
Giles, *Rev.* Charles, 29.
Giles, *Rev.* John, of Newburyport, 272.
Gilman, Caroline, 46.
Glen Iris, 239.
Glenny, John C., buys house begun by Joseph Ellicott, 243.
Godley, John Robert, 50.
Goldsmith, Oliver, his account of Niagara falls, 293.
Golovin, Ivan, 59.
Gorham, Nathaniel, 254.
Gosman, *Rev.* John, *D. D.*, 161.
Gosman, Robert, corrects Parton regarding Vanderlyn, 161-163; writes narrative of Vanderlyn's visit to Niagara, 163-169.
Gosse, Philip Henry, 181.
Gosselman, Carl August, 36.
Goupil, publishing house of, 131, 148.
Grabau, A. W., 183, 185.
Granger, Erastus, Buffalo's first postmaster, 256, 257.
Grant, *Sir* Alexander, 222.

INDEX.

Grant, *Lt.* Allen, commands at Ft. Stanwix, 1765, 341.
Grant, Janet (*Mrs.* Wm. Dummer Powell), 222.
Gray, Asa, 205.
Greenwich, Conn., 266.
Greenwood, *Rev.* F. W. P., 40.
Greenwood, Thos., 68.
Griffin, Zachariah, his house the oldest in Buffalo, 241.
Guest, *Lady* Theodora, 68.
Gull island, 339.
Gunning, W. D., 188.
Gurney, Joseph John, 48.
Gzowski, *Col. Sir* Cassimir S., 65.

Hale, *Rev.* Edward Everett, 294.
Hall, *Capt.* Basil, 36, 128, 129, 209.
Hall, *Lieut.* Francis, 29, 30.
Hall, Jas., N. Y. State Geologist, 184, 186.
Hall, Nathan K., 248.
Hall & Mooney, 148.
Halleck, Fitz-Greene, 72.
"Hambleton," see "Hamilton, Robt."
Hamilton, *Capt.* —, 41.
Hamilton, J., 147.
Hamilton, Robt., of Queenston, Can., 166, 227, 349, 362; his views on recession of Niagara falls, 375.
Hamilton, —, of the 53d Regt., conducts Capt. Enys about Niagara falls, 363-368.
Hamilton, Ont., 295.
Hanoteau, H., 155.
Hardy, *Lady* Duffus, 67.
Harper's Weekly, 128.
Harris, Wm. Tell, 32.
Harrowgate, in Yorkshire, 374.
Hatton, Joseph, 68, 131.
Hawthorne, Nathaniel, 37, 38, 71, 209.
Head, *Sir* Francis Bond, 46.
Henkle, Leonard, 213, 214.
Hennepin, *Rev.* Louis, his "*Louisiane*," 4, 14, 315; other works, 15; his picture of Niagara falls, 116-118; "the Hennepin type," 118, 119; mentioned, 170, 291; illustration of his books, 295, 296; not the discoverer of Niagara falls, 299; his spelling of "Niagara," 299, 300; his first account of Niagara falls, 315, 316; mentioned, 317, 318, 319, 321; his veracity questioned by Peter Kalm, 327; mentioned, 328, 400.
"Hennepin's Point" (or "View"), 147, 308.
Henry, Alexander, 23.
Henry, *Dr.* Walter, 44.
"Henri Gaugain & Co.," 134.
Herriot, George, 25; as artist, 127.
Herkimer ("Harkimer"), Nicholas, 341.
Hervieu, A., 128.
"Hibernicus," *pseud.*, see Clinton, De Witt.
Hill, *Capt.* David, "*Karong hyontye*," Mohawk chief, 221, 222, 231; his dress described, 231, 232; mentioned, 235.
Hill, David B., governor of New York, Thanksgiving proclamation, 274.
Hill, J. Henry, 147.
Hingham, Mass., 277, 284.
"Historical Associations of Buffalo," 237-252.
Historical Building, Buffalo, paintings in, 148; mentioned, 5, 311.
"History that isn't so," 291-311.
Hitchcock, C. H., 185.
Hoby, *Rev.* J., 46.
Hoe, Robert, sale of his library, 4, 5.
Hoes, *Rev.* Roswell Randall, 163, 164.
Hole, *Rev.* S. Reynolds, 68.
Holland Land Co., surveys village of New Amsterdam, 241; the purchase, 254, 255.
Holloway, F., 148.
Holmes, Oliver Wendell, 292.
Homann (Homanno), J. B., of Nuremberg, 121.
"Horseshoe" fall, Niagara, first so designated by Charlevoix, 320.
Hottes, M., 150, 151.
Hough, F. B., 235.
Houston, *Mrs.* M. C., 55.
Howells, Wm. Dean, 71, 94, 195.
Howison, John, 30.
Howitt, E., 32.
Howitt, Mary, translator of Frederika Bremer's "Homes of the New World," 56.
Howland, Sarah, 17.
Hubbard, Elbert, 93.
Hudson, T. S., 67.
Hughes, *Gov.* Chas. Evans, features of his Thanksgiving proclamations, 261, 262, 275.
Hughes, Thomas, 63.
Humphry, —, with Capt. Enys at Niagara in 1787, 365-373.
Hunt, Wm. M., 145.
Hunter, *Col.* —, commanding at Ft. Niagara, 1789, 227.
Hunter, —, accompanies H. St. J. de Crèvecoeur to Niagara, 349, 358.
Huxley, Leonard, 186.
Huxley, Thos. Henry, 186.

"Indian ladders," at Niagara, used by Crèvecoeur, 1785, 356; in 1787, 372.
Indian legends, largely invented by whites, 88.
Indians swept upon Goat island, 330, 331; their rescue, 332.
Ingraham, Duncan, his journey to Niagara in 1792, 387-393.
Irving, *Sir* Henry, 68.
Irving, Washington, portrait by Vanderlyn, 170; visited by Harriet Martineau, 285.
Izard, Ralph, 17; sketch of, 339, 340; diary of his tour to Niagara, 340-346.

INDEX.

Jackson, Andrew, portrait by Vanderlyn, 171.
Jacottet, —, artist, 134.
James, Henry, 63, 64, 71, 209.
Jameson, *Mrs.* Anna Brownell Murphy, 47.
Jeffery, Louisa, companion of Harriet Martineau, 285.
Jemison, Mary, 239.
Jesuit Relations, meager data in them for Niagara region, 11, 14.
Johnson, Andrew, *President,* 265.
Johnson, Ebenezer, first mayor of Buffalo, 286, 289.
Johnson, *Sir* John, 391.
Johnson, *Sir* Wm., 17, 18, 21, 179; errors in his papers, 303-305, 339; entertains Ralph Izard, 340.
Johnson, —, relative of Sir John Johnson, 391.
Johnston, Jas. F. W., 55.
Johnstone, C. L., 68.
Joliet, Louis, 81.
Joly, —, artist, 134.
Joncaire, Louis Thomas de, *Sieur* de Chabert, 322, 323.
Joncaire, Philip Thomas de, *Sieur* de Chabert, ordered to escort Peter Kalm about Niagara Falls, 326.
Jones, *Capt.* —, commands at Ft. Schlosser, 1785, 352.
Joutel, Henri, 15, 309.

Kalm, Peter, 20, 121, 122; first naturalist to visit Niagara, 176; as botanist, 202, 203; his account of Niagara falls, 324-334; mentioned, 383, 400.
"*Karong hyontye,*" Mohawk name of Capt. David Hill, 221, 222.
Kayo, Oneida name of H. St. J. de Crèvecoeur, 347.
Kelug (? Kellogg), —, 319.
Kemble, Fanny, see "Butler, Frances Anne."
Kent, *Chancellor* James, 76.
Kent. Wm., 76.
Ketchum, Wm., his "History of Buffalo," 306.
Kibbe, Aug. S., 188.
King, Thos., police justice, 93.
Kingston, Wm. H. H., 58.
Kingston, N. Y., home of John Vanderlyn, 129, 162; pastorate of Dr. John Gosman at, 161; mentioned, 164, 170, 172, 173.
Kingston, Ont., 81, 226.
Kipling, Rudyard, 69.
Kirby, Wm., his "Annals of Niagara" cited, 306.
Kirkland, *Rev.* Saml., 393.
Kirkpatrick, John E., 75.
Knox, *Capt.* John, 17.
Kohl, J. G., 59.
Köllner, August, 131.
Kroupa, B., 68.

Laubinois, *M. de,* 175.
Lebron, —, artist, 141, 143.
La Bruyère, quoted, 57.
Lafayette, *Gen.,* 35.

La Harpe, Jean François de, 109.
La Hontan, Louis Armand Lom d'Arce, *baron de,* 15; his description of Niagara falls, 291-292, 295; mentioned, 315, 316, 317, 321, 322, 400.
"Laird of Mackintosh," see Tonnaleuka.
Lake Conti (Erie), 292.
Lake Ontario, alluded to in 1641, 11; in 1647, 12; in 1669, 12, 13, 80; in 1794, 21; in 1807, 27; in Cooper's fiction, 82; in Bartlett's drawings, 135; mentioned by Michaux, 203; by Lord Edward Fitzgerald, 220; by Ann Powell, 227, 232.
Lake St. Louys (Ontario), 11.
Lalemant, *Rev.* Jerome, 11, 299.
Lancaster, Pa., 348.
"Landing (The)," see Queenston, Can.
"Landing of Columbus," painting by Vanderlyn, 172.
Lane, Ezekiel, 218.
Langdon, Andrew, stage-driver in 1810, 257.
Langheim, F., 132.
La Potherie, M. de Bacqueville de, 16.
La Salle, René Robert Cavelier, *sieur de,* 10, 12; inadequacy of fiction dealing with him, 80, 81; his expedition of 1678, 116, 297; his trading-post "built in 1679," 298; not a chevalier, 298, 299; claim that he discovered Chautauqua lake, 305; Devil's Hole absurdity, 308.
La Salle, N. Y., 296, 297.
Laugel, Auguste, 62, 147.
Lavasseur, A., 35.
Leach, "Bobby," 293.
Le Beau, C., 79, 80.
"Le Cain" (Duquesne), 304.
Le Clerc, S., 120, 121.
Le Clercq, *Rev.* Christian le, 4, 11.
Lee, *Maj.-Gen.* Chas., 400.
Le Moyne, Charles, see "Longueuil, *Baron de.*"
Léry, Gaspard Chaussegros de, 3.
Lescarbot, Marc, 4; cited, 10, 16.
Lesdiguieres, *Duchesse de,* 320.
Letchworth, Wm. Pryor, memorial to, 423.
Lever, Chas., 82.
Lewis, F. C., engraver of Vanderlyn's "Niagara," 130.
Lewis, *Rev.* G., 54.
Lewis, *Gov.* Morgan, 306.
Lewis & Clarke exploring expedition, 308.
Liancourt, *Duc* de la Rochefoucault, 22, 400.
Lieber, Francis, 45.
Lincoln, Abraham, proclamations for fasts or thanksgivings, 264; the quality of his English, 265; his Thanksgiving proclamations of 1863 and 1864, 263, 265, 273.
Lion's den (The), on the Niagara, 375.

INDEX.

Little Falls, N. Y., sketched in 1802 by John Vanderlyn, 164.
Livingston, David, 125.
Livingston, Robt. R., 172.
Lombardo, Alberto, 67.
London *Art Journal*, 131.
Longueuil, *Baron de*, 20, 175, 318.
Lorne, *Marquis of*, 68.
Loti, Pierre, *pseud.*, 68.
Louis XIV., builder of Fort Niagara, 1.
Louis Philippe Joseph, *Duke of Orleans*, 235.
Lowell, Jas. Russell, 55, 294.
Lutaud, *Dr.* Auguste, 68.
Lyell, *Sir* Chas., 179, 183, 186.

McCauslin, *Dr.* Robt., 178, 179.
Mackay, Alexander, 54.
Maclay, Wm., 178, 179, 184.
Madan, H. G., 206.
Madison, Jas., portrait by Vanderlyn, 171; proclamations, 263; his policies opposed by New England, 269, 270; proclamation of Apr. 13, 1815, 272.
Magazine of American History, 347.
Maiook (Mayouk), fictitious Indian chief, 301, 302.
Maitland, *Sir* Perigrine, 34, 35.
Majoribanks, Alexander, 57.
"Mammoth Cave and the Prairies," panorama of, 153.
Manchester (Eng.), *Times*, 54.
Manlius, N. Y., 165.
Mante, Thomas, 17.
Marcou, Jules, 62.
Margry, Pierre, publication of documents cited, 16.
Marin, Paul, commands an expedition of 1753, 303.
"Marius at Carthage," painting by Vanderlyn, 163, 170.
"Mark Twain," *pseud.*, 71, 94.
Marquette, *Rev.* Jacques, 81.
Marryat, *Capt.* Frederick, 47, 48.
Marshall, Chas., 66.
Marshall, Orsamus H., entertains Prof. Huxley in Buffalo, 186; finds and publishes letter of H. St. J. de Crèvecoeur, 346, 347.
Marshall, W. G., 67.
Martineau, Harriet, her comment on "lawless Buffalo," 45, 208; "On the Niagara Frontier with," 277-290; her career, 277-279; describes the burning of Buffalo, 279-283; letter from Niagara Falls to Rev. Chas. Brooks, 284-289; letter to her mother, 289-290.
Mason, *Gen.* John T., 286.
Mason, Stevens Thompson, governor of Michigan, 286.
Massachusetts Bay Colony, 262.
Mass. Hist. Society *Collections*, 387.
Massachusetts Magazine, 384, 386.
Massasoit, 268.
Mateos, *Don* Juan A., 84.
Mather, Alonzo C., 215.
Matheson, *Rev.* Jas., 45.

Matthews, —, 33.
Maude, John, 23; as artist, 126.
Maverick, Peter, regarded as first American wood-engraver, 33, 128.
Maxwell, *Lt.-Col.* A. M., 49.
Mayhew, *Rev.* Jonathan, *D. D.*, 267.
McCarroll, Jas. ("*Scian Dubh*"), 93.
McKinley, Wm., *President*, house in Buffalo where he died, 248; error as to place of assassination, 311.
McLean, —, publisher, Haymarket, London, 130.
Medley, Julius George, 65.
Melish, John, 28, 29.
Mental (The) Elevator, Seneca periodical, 240.
Merigot, —, engraver of Vanderlyn's "Niagara," 130.
Merriam, Geo. S., 76.
Merwin, Samuel, 81.
Meyer, Hermann J., 137.
Michaux, André, 204.
Michaux, F. A., 203, 204.
Middaugh, Martin, 218.
Mignot, Louis R., 145.
Milbert, Jacques-Girard, 133, 134.
Milet, *Rev.* Pierre, 14.
Military (The) Road, Lake Ontario to Lake Erie, 256.
Moll, Herman, vignettes of Niagara Falls on his maps, 119.
Moniteur (Le), Paris journal, 25.
Monroe, Jas., *President U. S.*, 30; portrait by Vanderlyn, 171.
Montmorency (Montmorrency, *i. e.*, Luna) fall at Niagara, 371.
Montule, E., 30.
Moodie, *Mrs.* Susanna, 58.
Moore, George, 53.
Moore, Tom, 25, 191, 192; his life of Lord Edward Fitzgerald, 218, 221; mentions Gull island, 339.
Morandrier, *Mons.* —, 176, 328.
Morgan, Wm., his incarceration at Fort Niagara, 311.
Morley, John, his "Life of Cobden" quoted, 74, 75.
Morpeth, *Lord*, see "Carlisle, *Earl of*."
Morris, Robt., 254.
Morris, Thos., 166, 167, 169.
Morris, Wm., 66.
Morse, Samuel F. B., 259.
Munger, Gilbert, 149, 150.
Murray, *Hon.* Amelia M., 58.
Murray, *Hon.* Chas. A., 45.
Myers, P. Hamilton, 86.

Napoleon I., awards gold medal to painting by Vanderlyn, 170.
Nash, Willis, 66.
National Academy of Design, 146.
Navy Island, early engravings of, 127.
Neal, John, 42, 72.
Neuters, nation of aborigines, 11.
Neutral nation, see Neuters.
New Amsterdam, see Buffalo.
New York Academy of Design, 171.
New York City, Metropolitan Museum of Art, 156.

INDEX.

New York Rotunda, erected by John Vanderlyn, 171.
Newberry, J. S., 188.
Niagara, variants in spelling, 299, 300.
Niagara, Cyclorama of, see "Niagara panoramas."
Niagara panoramas, 151-156; Burford's, 152; Brewer's, 153, 154; Frankenstein's, 154; Cyclorama of Niagara in London, 155, 156; in Chicago, 156.
Niagara Falls, 5; described by Galinée, 12-13; fictitious account of discovery, 300-303.
Niagara Frontier Landmarks Association, 243, 244.
Niagara Glen ("Foster's Flats"), 205.
Niagara, Ont., 1.
Niagara-on-the-Lake, see Niagara, Ont.
Niagara region, "Early Literature of," 9-23; defined, 9; how settled, 18.
"Niagara (The) in Art," 113-158.
"Niagara (The) Region in Fiction," 77-96.
"Niagara (The) in Science," 175-216.
"Nineteenth Century visitors (to Niagara) who wrote books," 25-76.
Noah, *Maj.* M. M., 87.
Noble, *Rev.* Louis L., 137, 138.
Norris, Frank, 93.
Norris, *Capt.* Thos., 342.
Norumbega, 5.

Offenbach, Jacques, 66.
Ogden, *Rev.* John Cosens, 21, 400.
O'Hara, *Gen.* —, 218.
"O. Henry," *pseud.*, 93.
"Old Smoke," Seneca chief, 239.
"Oliver Optic," *pseud.*, 87.
"On the Niagara Frontier with Harriet Martineau," 277-290.
Oneida, N. Y., 388.
Oneida Hollow, N. Y., 165.
Oneida lake, 165, 342, 388; lake or river, 301.
"Ongiara catarractes" (Niagara falls), on Cruxio's map, 1660, 14; early spelling of "Niagara," *q. v.*, 299.
Onguiaahra (Niagara), 11, 299.
Onondaga falls, 342.
Ontario co., N. Y., in 1790, 260.
Ontario Historical Society, 14.
Orcutt, Wm. Dana, 80.
Oswegatchie ("Oswegachy," *i. e.*, Ogdensburg), 345.
Oswego river, 342.
Outaways (Ottaways, etc.), swept over Niagara, 322, 323.

Painter's Point, below Niagara falls, Canadian side, 371, 375.
Palacio, *Don* Vicente Riva, 84.
Pamela, daughter of Louis Philippe Joseph, marries Lord Edward Fitzgerald, 235.
Pan-American Exposition, 248.
Paris Exposition of 1867, Church's "Niagara" exhibited at, 144.

Parish, *Rev.* Elijah, of Newburyport, 271.
Park, Mungo, 383.
Parkman, Francis, 1, 17; at Niagara in 1845, 53.
Parton, Jas., his "Life and Times of Aaron Burr" quoted, 159-161; statements corrected, 161-163.
Patriot War, literature of, 19.
Patten, Edmund, 58.
"Paul Pry, Jr.," *pseud.*, 88.
Pavillon du Flores, part of the Louvre, 2.
Payne, A. H., 130.
Pennell, Jos., 147.
Pennsylvania Academy of Fine Arts, 172.
Pequots, annihilation of, 266.
Perry, *Com.* Oliver Hazard, as character in juvenile fiction, 85.
Pfeiffer, Ida Meyer, 61.
Pfister, *Lt.* —, contractor at Ft. Schlosser in 1765, 342.
Phelps, Oliver, 254.
"Phelps and Gorham Purchase," 254, 255.
Philadelphia *Medical and Physical Journal*, 393.
Philadelphia *Portfolio*, 204.
Philippoteaux, Paul, 155, 156.
Philip, Geo., reputed travels of, 307, 308.
Pidgeon, David, 67.
Pierie, *Lieut.* Wm., 122-124.
Piquet, *Abbé* François, his account of Niagara falls, 334.
Pitt, Wm., 219.
Pittsburg, Carnegie Institute, 156.
Plymouth, Mass., 301.
Pohlman, *Dr.* Julius, 184.
Point Abino, 298.
Pole, William, 210.
Pontiac ("Pondiach," etc.), at Ft. Oswego, 342.
Popple, Henry, 121.
Portage, N. Y., 205.
Porter, *Hon.* Augustus, his first bridge at Niagara Falls, 148.
Porter, *Gen.* Peter B., his Buffalo house, 242.
Pouchot, *Capt.* Francois, 17, 335.
Powell, Ann, her family, 222; her journal of visit to Niagara and site of Buffalo in 1789, 223-234.
Powell, John, of Boston, 222.
Powell, Wm. Dummer, 222.
Power, Tyrone, 41, 42, 128; quoted, 217.
Prentice, Archibald, 54.
Prescott, W. H., 141-143.
Preston, T. R., 47.
Prevost, J. B., 162.
Price, Joseph, alleged discoverer of Niagara falls, his adventures, 300-303.
Priest, Josiah, 307.
Priest, Wm., 182.
Prieto, Guillermo, 66.
Prince of Wales (Edward VII.), 60, 131.
Princess Louise, 131.

INDEX. 435

Prior's *"Universal Traveler,"* 128.
"Prospect Point" at Niagara Falls, 176.

Quai Voltaire, book-stalls of, 3.
Queen Victoria Park, 123, 124.
Queenston, Can. ("The Landing"), 182, 228, 287, 399.

R———, C. von, 34.
Rafinesque, Constantine, 205.
Ragueneau, *Rev.* Paul, cited, 12, 299.
Ramsay, *Sir* Andrew C., 186.
Randolph, John, portrait by Vanderlyn, 171.
Rankine, Wm. Birch, 215.
Rawdon, *Lord*, 218.
"Rawdon, Clark & Co.," 127.
Raumer, Frederick von, 53.
Red Jacket, Seneca chief, described by Audubon, 199; by Ann Powell, 232, 234, 235; his home, 239.
Red Jacket's widow, 41.
Reed, *Rev.* Andrew, 45.
Reid, Robt., 141.
Rhodesia. 125.
Richardson, *Maj.* John, 82.
Richardt, F., 130.
Richmond Hill, residence of Aaron Burr, 162.
Rivera y Rio, Jose, 87.
Robertson, Felix, 393.
Robertson, Wm. Parish, 57.
Rochefort, Henri, 65, 66.
Rogers, *Lt.* Jonathan, 342.
Rogers, *Maj.* Robt., 400.
Rome. N. Y., in 1802, 165.
Rondout, N. Y., Robt. Gosman's letter from, 161-163.
Roosevelt, Theodore, Buffalo house in which he took oath as President, 248; one of his proclamations as governor of New York, 272, 273, 274.
Rush, *Dr.* Benj., Andrew Ellicott's description of Niagara sent to, 384.
Russell, W. Howard, 62.
Ruysdaël, Jacob van, the "Niagara" he would have painted, 147.

Sabatier, —, artist, 134.
Sagard, Gabriel, 4, 11, 16.
Sagra, *Don* Ramon de la, 46.
St. James Hall, Buffalo, 75.
St. John de Crèvecoeur, see Crèvecoeur.
St. Louis City Art Museum, 156.
St. Mary's-on-the-Wye, Huron mission, 11.
St. Paul's Churchyard, London, bookshops of, 3.
Sangster, Amos W., 149.
Sanson, Joseph, 30.
Saunders, Wm., 66.
Saussaye, Dagneaux de la, 305.
Savery, William, 54.
Scajaquada creek, 238.
Schofield, Wis., 212.
Schoolcraft, Henry, on the building-place of the Griffon, 298.
Schultz, Christian, *Jr.*, 27, 28.

"Scián Dubh," *pseud.*, Jas. McCarroll, 93.
Scott, *Gen.* Winfield, headquarters at Williamsville, in War of 1812, 242.
Scotland, National Gallery of, 144.
Scott, *Gen.* Winfield, alleged headquarters in Buffalo, 311.
"Scuyler" ("Sckuiler"), see Fort Schlosser.
Sedgwick, Catherine Maria, 33, 72; visited at Stockbridge by Harriet Martineau, 285.
Sellars, Robt., 85.
Sellers, *Dr.* Coleman, 215.
Selwyn, *Dr.* Alfred Richard Cecil, of the Canadian geological survey, 363.
Seneca Mission, Buffalo, 240.
Seneca Mission Press, 240.
Seneca villages, in present site of Buffalo, 238, 239.
Senneville, *Capt. de*, 20, 175.
Severance, Frank H., his "Niagara and the Poets" cited, 78, 196.
Seward, Wm. H., Thanksgiving proclamation as governor, 262, 263.
Shaler, N. S., 188.
Sharan, Jas., 23; sketch of, 378, 379, 383; his Niagara narrative, 379-383.
Shawanees (Chanouanons), 305.
Sheriff, Patrick, 42.
Shulz, Adrien, 155.
Sidway, *Mrs.* Jonathan (Parnell St. John), 283.
Siemens, *Sir* Carl Wilhelm, 209-211.
Sigourney, *Mrs.* Lydia Huntley, 208.
Silliman, Augustus E., 50.
Silliman, Benjamin D., 50.
Simcoe, *Mrs.* John Graves, 128.
"Simcoe's ladder," 396.
Sinclair, *Rev.* John, 59.
Skinner, *Mrs.* Martha St. John, 283.
Smith, Goldwin, 74.
Smith, *Rev.* John, Salem, N. H., 270.
Smith, Mortimer L., 156.
Smith, *Col.* —, commands at Ft. Niagara, 1792, 391.
Smoke's creek, 239.
Society of Friends, 18.
"Some Thanksgiving Contrasts," 261-275.
Southesk, *Earl of*, 60.
Spencer, J. W., 185, 188.
Springfield (Mass.) *Republican*, 75.
Stamford, Ont., 34.
Stanley, H. A., 86.
Stansbury, P., 32.
Stedman, Edmund Clarence, 73, 74.
Stedman, Philip, his house at Niagara, 350, 352, 367, 368.
Steele, *Mrs.* Eliza A., 50.
Steele's Press, Buffalo, 148.
Stoddard, Wm. O., 81.
Stone, Wm. L., his life of Sir Wm. Johnson, 18.
Story, Joseph, Justice U. S. Supreme court, 35.
Stratemeyer, Edward, 87.
Stringer, Geo. Alfred, 79.

INDEX.

Stuart, Gilbert, instructs John Vanderlyn, 162.
Stuart, Jas., 36.
Sturge, Joseph, 49.
Sutcliff, Robt., 27.
Swartwout, *Gen.* John, 166.

Table Rock, fall of, 143.
Talbot, Edward Allen, 33.
Tallack, Wm., 59.
Taylor, Bayard, 61, 62, 71.
Taylor, F. B., 185.
Taylor, *Mrs.* Anna Edson, 293.
Taylor, T., 147.
Taylor, Zachary, portrait by Vanderlyn, 172.
Terrapin Point, Niagara Falls, 187.
Thackara & Vallance, 122.
Thanksgiving contrasts in American history, 261-275.
Thayer, Eugene M., 195, 196.
Thomas, *Rev.* Abel C., 57.
Thompson, S. P., "Life of Lord Kelvin," 216.
Thomson, E. W., 87.
Thomson, *Sir* Wm. *(Lord Kelvin)*, 215.
Thoreau, Henry David, 73.
Thornton, *Sir* Edward, British Minister at Washington, 65.
Thornton, *Maj.* John, 55.
Thouinville, siege of, 108.
Ticknor, George, 72, 192.
Tinling, *Lt.* —, of the 29th regt., opens a vista at Niagara, 371.
Tirpenne, —, artist, 134.
Tomlinson, Everett T., 87.
Tonawanda ("Tonawanta," etc.) swamp in 1802, 167.
Tonawondoe (Tonawanda) village, 399.
Tonnaleuka, Mingo prophet (fictitious), 307.
Tonnoraunto (Tonawanda), 390.
Tonty (Tonti), Henri de, 15, 309.
Toronto (Fort Schlosser), 336, 337.
Toronto (York Bay), 335.
Tounshend, F. French, 63.
Tourgee, *Hon.* Albion W., 86.
Train, Geo. Francis, 56.
Trollope, Anthony, 60, 61; comments on Niagara in art and letters, 158.
Trollope, *Mrs.* Frances, 39, 40, 209; British estimate of her book, 287.
Trouvé, *Mons.* —, 13.
Trowbridge, J. T., 86, 191.
Trumbull, Wm., 147.
Turrettini, *Col.* Theodore, 215.
Tyndall, John, 186, 187.
"Tyndall's Rock," 187.

Unonius, *Rev.* Gustav, 55.
Unwin, W. C., 215.
Upham, Warren, 184, 185, 188.
Utica, N. Y., visited by John Vanderlyn, 1802, 164.

Van Buren, Martin, entertains the Earl of Carlisle, 50; calls on Harriet Martineau, 286.

Vanderlyn, John, first American artist to paint Niagara falls, 129, 130; "Visit to Niagara Falls in 1802," 159-173; relations with Aaron Burr, 159-161; account of journey to Niagara, 164-169; his later life, 170-173; work characterized, 173.
Vanderlyn family, 162.
Van Rensselaer, *Mrs.* Schuyler, 68.
Vaudricourt, A., 132.
Veazie, Wm., 262.
Verplanck, Gulien C., 171.
Victoria Falls on the Zambesi, 125.
Vigne, Godfrey T., 40.
Villeneuve, —, artist, 134.
Vivian, H. Hussey, 66.
Vivian, W., 132.
Volney, Chas. F., 22, 23, 183, 310.
Voltaire, *"Charles Douze,"* 3.

Wadsworth, *Gen.* James, entertains E. S. Abdy at Geneseo, 41; entertains the Earl of Carlisle, 50.
Waldo, S. Putnam, 30.
Wall, —, painter, 127.
Wallis, T., 126.
War of 1812, service of Farmer's Brother, 241; Buffalo during, 241; sites of batteries in Buffalo, 244; of forts and battlefields, 245; soldiers of, buried in Delaware Park, 245, 246; postal rates during, 258.
Warburton, Eliot, 53.
Warner, Chas. Dudley, 71, 94-96.
Warner, H. H., 150.
Warner, Susan, 87.
Washington, Geo., 263; fictitious adventures of, 306, 307; corresponds with H. St. J. de Crèvecoeur, 348.
Waterton, Charles, 33, 34.
Waylen, *Rev.* Edward, 53.
Weld, Charles, 58.
Weld, Isaac, *Jr.*, as writer, 22; as artist, 125; mentioned, 400.
West, *Dr.* Chas. E., 190.
West Point, N. Y., 285.
Western Monthly Review, Cincinnati, 75.
White, *Dr.* Andrew D., his "Warfare of Science with Theology" quoted, 181, 182.
White, John, 59.
Whitestown, N. Y., 388.
Whitman, Walt, 66, 67.
Wied-Neuwied, *Prince* Maximilien, 119, 120, 134.
Wilcox, Ansley, his historic residence, 248.
Wilkeson, *Judge* Samuel, his grave, 246; his house, 246, 247.
Wilkeson, *Mrs.* Samuel (Sarah St. John), friend of Harriet Martineau, 279-283.
Wilkie, D., 46, 47.
Wilkinson, Jemima, 389.
William I., *Emperor of Germany*, commissions Gilbert Munger to paint Niagara Falls, 150.
Williamsburg, on the Genesee river, 389, 390.

INDEX.

Williamson, Chas., describes Niagara in 1799, 399-400.
Williamson, Peter, his American travels, 309, 310.
Williamsville, N. Y., Evans homestead at, 242.
Williamsville road, 241.
Williamsville stage, 250.
Wilmington, Henry, alleged discoverer of Niagara falls, 300-303.
Willis, N. P., 42, 71; interprets Ole Bull's "Niagara," 193.
Wilson, Alexander, 128; his Niagara visit, 196, 197; letter introducing F. A. Michaux, 203, 204.
Wilson, Thos., 59.
Wilson, Wm. R. A., 81.
Wilson, —, resident at Niagara Falls in 1806, 203, 204.
Winchel, Alexander, 188.
Winthrop, Theodore, 72.

Withrow, W. H., 85.
Wolfe, *Gen.* Jas., lines on his exploit, 311.
Wood, Joanna E., 86.
Woods, Nicholas Augustus, 60.
Woodcock, T. S., 141.
Woodward, R. S., 188.
Wooster, *Gen.* David, 21.
Worcester (Mass.) Art Museum, 156.
Wright, *Rev.* Asher, 240.
Wright, *Mrs.* Asher, 240.
Wright, Francis, 31.
Wright, G. Frederick, 185, 188.

Young, Julia Ditto, 87.
"*Youth's (The) Casket*," editor of, 87.

Zangwill, Israel, 87.
Zavala, *Don* Lorenzo de, 39.
Zincke, F. Barham, 62.

www.ingramcontent.com/pod-product-compliance
Lightning Source LLC
Chambersburg PA
CBHW051623230426
43669CB00013B/2155